ENTREPRENEURSHIP, INNOVATION, AND THE GROWTH MECHANISM OF THE FREE-ENTERPRISE ECONOMIES

EDITED BY

Eytan Sheshinski, Robert J. Strom, and William J. Baumol

PRINCETON UNIVERSITY PRESS PRINCETON AND OXFORD

Published by Princeton University Press, 41 William Street, Princeton, New Jersey 08540
In the United Kingdom: Princeton University Press, 3 Market Place, Woodstock, Oxfordshire OX20 1SY

Library of Congress Cataloging-in-Publication Data
Entrepreneurship, innovation, and the growth mechanism of the free-enterprise economies / Eytan Sheshinski, Robert J. Strom, and William J. Baumol (editors).
p. cm.
Includes bibliographical references and index.
ISBN-13: 978-0-691-12945-7 (cl : alk. paper)
ISBN-10: 0-691-12945-2 (cl : alk. paper)
1. Technological innovations—Congresses. 2. Entrepreneurship—Congresses.
3. Economic development—Congresses. I. Sheshinski, Eytan. II. Strom, Robert J.
III. Baumol, William J.

HC79.T4E59 2006
338—dc22

2006045696

British Library Cataloging-in-Publication Data is available

This book has been composed in Sabon

Printed on acid-free paper. ∞

pup.princeton.edu

Printed in the United States of America

10 9 8 7 6 5 4 3 2 1

ENTREPRENEURSHIP, INNOVATION, AND THE GROWTH MECHANISM OF THE FREE-ENTERPRISE ECONOMIES

Contents

Preface

THE CRITICAL OBSERVATION that must be made here is that it is Eytan Sheshinski who contributed the idea for this book and for the conference that underlies it. Not only that—in addition, he lured some of the key participants into acceptance of our invitation to join the enterprise. The rest was almost straightforward. Of course, we encountered some of the usual tribulations, speakers who found themselves forced to withdraw at the last minute, food arrangements that needed to be rearranged, and the like. But those were all to be expected.

The enterprise began one day when Eytan and I, out on a walk, found ourselves discussing my (then) recent book, *The Free-Market Innovation Machine: Analyzing the Growth Miracle of Capitalism.* Convinced that at least some of its materials are new and somewhat heterodox, he suggested that it would be interesting to elicit reactions and further ideas from leading minds in the arena. The rest of the enterprise followed.

Actually, the notion of some sort of conference on the general subject had come up somewhat earlier, in my first meeting with Bob Strom who, from his position at the Ewing Marion Kauffman Foundation, was pursuing ideas for enhanced research on entrepreneurship and the training of entrepreneurs. It soon became clear that the two conversations were complementary, and that Bob could be counted upon for advice, insights, and encouragement, as well as just support for our application to the Foundation.

It is for this reason that Eytan and Bob are listed as editors of this volume. But it must be confessed, that the term "editor" is more than a bit misleading. As a matter of fact, very little of the editing was carried out by us. The work was done primarily by the authors themselves, by Richard Isomaki, the very capable copyeditor provided by Princeton University Press, and, as always, by my permanent editor, research colleague, and advisor, Sue Anne Batey Blackman. The importance of her role struck me yet once again as I reread my own chapter in the book, when I recognized large sections of the material as having come from her computer rather than mine. As usual, I am incapable of fully delineating my debt to her here.

Then there were the organizers of the conference itself, no minor matter, recognizing that the participants had to be provided the wherewithal to eat and sleep and an appropriate venue for their discourse. Here, the complications compounded as the date for the meeting approached, but it was handled masterfully and capably by my other deeply appreciated associate, Janeece Roderick Lewis, and, at the final moments, in tandem with the very capable Glory Olson of the Kauffman Foundation.

I must also thank our two editors at the Princeton University Press, Peter Dougherty and Tim Sullivan, who, in addition to guidance of this volume, ensured that my earlier work in the general arena did not go unnoticed by the world. They energetically and effectively elicited the interest of the press, where my book and related matters received welcome attention beyond what I could readily have expected. I also appreciate the fine job done by Scott Gray and Lauren Lepow, our production editors at Princeton University Press, Shani Berezin, editorial assistant, and Shane Kelley, graphics artist.

Finally, and indeed heartfelt, are my thanks to the Kauffman Foundation and my associates there. Of course, we appreciate the funding they provided. But much more than that, they have given us ideas, stimulus, and friendship. The fact that this is not the only volume of which they and I are to be jointly responsible as editors or authors should be a clear indication that our association goes well beyond the usual relation between researchers and the foundations that support their work.

Will Baumol

ENTREPRENEURSHIP, INNOVATION, AND THE GROWTH MECHANISM OF THE FREE-ENTERPRISE ECONOMIES

Introduction

EYTAN SHESHINSKI AND ROBERT J. STROM

THE FREE-ENTERPRISE ECONOMIES, whatever their imperfections, have succeeded in one task to a degree that has not been approached by any alternate form of economic organization, now or in the past. This primary accomplishment is their unparalleled record of technological innovation, in putting innovations to practical use, in elimination of obsolete products and processes, and in the resulting spectacular economic growth. The consequence has been remarkable progress toward reduction of poverty within countries where the free market has been left to direct the economy. Understanding the sources of this accomplishment is of the utmost importance, most immediately for the many countries of the world that are still far behind in per capita income. But even the industrialized countries have not yet succeeded in conquering poverty, with all of its serious consequences for the health and welfare of the society as well as that of the individual.

The essays presented in this volume are designed to increase our understanding of the general subject of the contribution of the market to innovation and economic growth.[1] They take as their point of departure the recent book *The Free-Market Innovation Machine: Analyzing the Growth Miracle of Capitalism* (Princeton University Press, 2002) by William J. Baumol. That book focuses on the implicit partnership between independent entrepreneurs, who are the primary source of innovative breakthroughs in the marketplace, and high-tech corporations with their routinized research and development activities—whose primary and important accomplishment has been the steady improvement of the innovative products and processes contributed by independent entrepreneurs and the vast increase in the capacity and capability of those products and processes. The emphasis in this analysis is upon the critical role of the entrepreneur.

The essays in this volume are collectively a forum to analyze the growth in free-enterprise economies through the lens of Baumol's "free-market innovation machine." Each of the eight parts features a pair of chapters by leading scholars, who focus their discussion on the various themes developed in Baumol's book. Each pair of essays (except in part I) is preceded by an introduction and comments by a third scholar.

Part I: Introductory: The Macroeconomics and Microeconomics of Growth

Two chapters by Kenneth J. Arrow and by Robert M. Solow provide the backbone for the remainder of the volume. In his essay, "On Macroeconomic Models of Free-Market Innovation and Growth," Solow examines how aggregative growth theory models innovations and, accordingly, what can be said about macro conditions conducive to such processes. The creator of the "Solow Model"—the "workhorse" of neoclassical growth theory—argues that the approach to technical progress (TP) in models of aggregate growth, including those with "endogenous TP," is mechanical and simple-minded, perhaps because of a fixation on steady states that confines the analysis to particular ("labor augmenting") forms of TP.

Solow emphasizes the distinction between discrete, large-scale innovations (e.g., the combustion engine) and the more abundant small-scale, piecemeal innovations carried out internally with the aid of learning-by-doing or imitation. He speculates that a high-pressure (on capacity) economy with intensive innovative competition produces the best environment for increases in productivity. One hopes that empirical studies will shed light on this question.

Kenneth Arrow's chapter, "The Macro-context of the Microeconomics of Innovation," follows Joseph Schumpeter's distinction between invention and innovation, the latter being the (costly) processing of inventive ideas. Social systems, in particular markets and science (knowledge), influence both. The major relevant institution common in market economies is a regime of property rights implemented by a legal system of licensing and patents. Competition in innovations endangers incumbent monopolists' profits, thereby creating incentives for further innovation. This will lead, argues Arrow (following ideas promoted by Baumol), to an "optimal portfolio of innovations." For effective dissemination of knowledge, Arrow points out, externalities created by the mobility of labor engaged in research and development (R&D) are important. More generally, the educational system, based on incentives that are only partially financial, provides trained users of knowledge.

It is noteworthy that Arrow and Solow, two leading theorists of economic growth, conclude that economic models have not provided deep insight into the process of innovation. Rather, they hope that ad hoc case studies will eventually shed sufficient light to enable construction of a cohesive theory on the relative importance of markets and knowledge.

Part II: Institutional Bases for Capitalist Growth

In this part, introduced by Michael Weinstein, Douglass C. North brings a historical perspective to the Baumol "free-market innovation machine" in a chapter titled "Institutional Bases for Capitalist Growth." In considering the preconditions for capitalist society in both historical specifics and abstract concepts, North offers a valuable lens through which to view the issues this volume addresses. North, like Baumol, examines the underlying elements of a capitalist society. While Baumol looks at the realities of the individual players in capitalism, most importantly the interplay between the small independent entrepreneur-innovators and the large, established corporations, North focuses on a broad historical overview in the context of markets, transaction costs, and, most importantly, incentives. He explores the set of conditions that produced the free-market innovation machine and allowed it to create impressive growth in the West. North's view complements Baumol's work in his discussion of what kind of institutional structure will best accommodate such a machine. North asks what incentive structure will support the dynamic features of Baumol's model, and answers that it is institutions that serve as the incentives to produce these features.

The second chapter in this part, Barry Weingast's "Capitalism and Economic Liberty: The Political Foundations of Economic Growth," focuses on the political requirements for a market economy that stimulates innovation and growth effectively. Weingast writes that the economic literature does consider the role of government, but implies that in developing countries the main problem for markets is inefficient government intervention that creates monopolies, market restrictions, and inefficiency. The implication for the creation of markets is that the necessary policy entails dismantling of political controls on markets and laws creating new markets. But Weingast emphasizes that the protection of property and hence the development of a robust economy arises only with the control of arbitrary government. This requires the creation of a set of political institutions that constrain politics so that it serves the interests of citizens. The political system must be properly constructed so that it is capable of sustaining a thriving market economy rather than preying on it.

Weingast posits that the problem in the developing world is that it has neither a capitalist system nor a government capable of sustaining one. Governments in the developing world all too frequently use their policy means to expropriate the wealth of some of their citizens rather than to provide market-enhancing public goods. This type of governmental opportunism is incompatible with a thriving capitalist market system. Further, successful constitutions create focal solutions to central coordination dilemmas over citizens' rights. When citizens fail to agree about their rights, governments can take advantage of them by transgressing the rights of some citizens while retaining the political support of others. In contrast, constitutions that create focal solutions to citizen-coordination problems allow citizens to react in concert against potential transgressions, and thereby deter the government from abusing citizens' rights.

Weingast concludes that market reform without corresponding political reform under development or in transition is doomed to fail: Without creating political reform compatible with markets, the political system is likely to hobble or prey on nascent markets, hindering their development into a thriving capitalist system.

Part III: Innovation in Modern Corporations

The essays in this part, introduced by Ying Lowrey, narrow the focus to address the issue of innovation in the modern corporation. Taken together, the two essays shed new light on aspects of the "David-Goliath" partnership (between the independent entrepreneur-innovators and the large corporations) that is necessary for Baumol's free-market innovation machine to produce growth in capitalist economies.

In his chapter, "Endogenous Forces in Twentieth-Century America," Nathan Rosenberg argues that science and technology have become a great deal more endogenous in twentieth-century American capitalism as a result of both organizational changes and associated changes in economic incentives. With its emphasis on the endogeneity of technology and science in the twentieth century, this essay illuminates many aspects of Baumol's free-market innovation machine.

Rosenberg discusses some of the ways in which changes in the organization of research activities have contributed to growth, and he considers how and why both technology and science have been rendered a great deal more endogenous over the course of the past century. Like Baumol, Rosenberg looks to the key role of corporate research labs. Rosenberg credits the effective performance of the corporate research labs to a network of other institutions. These institutions include universities for their trained scientists, engineers, and graduate students who have continued to expand the frontiers of knowledge; federal government patronage, particularly in areas where it is clear that social returns will exceed private returns; and, finally, private philanthropic foundations, which were an especially important source of research support in the first half of the twentieth century. Rosenberg's discussion, informed by more than one hundred years of economic history, presents a compelling story of the way in which the forces of technology have come to shape the various realms of science.

"Interfirm Collaboration Networks: The Impact of Network Structure on Rates of Innovation," by Melissa A. Schilling and Corey Phelps, is grounded in the literature on interfirm and interorganizational networks that lead to the creation of knowledge and innovation. Schilling and Phelps examine the trade-off between creating bandwidth in the network through collaboration and cooperation versus creating greater reach by engaging a broader range of knowledge resources. They argue that small-world connectivity is a key to resolving the apparent trade-off, allowing bandwidth and reach to be achieved simultaneously. Utilizing data on alliance networks and patent output in a number of industries, they demonstrate how small-world properties may enhance the patent output of the network.

Part IV: The Continuing Role of Independent Innovators and Entrepreneurs

In this part, introduced by Sylvia Nasar, "The Small Entrepreneur," by Boyan Jovanovic and Peter L. Rousseau, focuses on new firms and their response, more elastic than that of incumbent enterprises, to new technology and evolving incentives. Jovanovic and Rousseau start with an examination of the data on initial public offering (IPO) activity, and then provide a number of models of the timing decision for the execution of an IPO. Finally, they deal with indicators of inventive activity, focusing on the contribution of firms that are small and young. Examining the evidence, the essay notes that firms often introduce their first innovation soon after founding, but it may take decades before they list on a stock exchange. Moreover, these delays vary in length in different time periods. It is suggested that part of the reason may be secrecy—IPO prospectuses reveal business plans, so delay of an IPO may occur for the same reason a firm may avoid patenting an idea, instead developing it in secret.

The authors provide a number of neoclassical models in which, at the initial public offering, the public pays for the firm exactly what it is worth. However, Jovanovic and Rousseau conjecture that more can be learned by starting from the alternative hypothesis of waves of irrational exuberance. If such irrationality is likely, before their IPO, firms may be waiting in the wings to take advantage of it. In addition to its theoretical analysis, the essay's analysis rests heavily on long data series and observations drawn from economic history. The data are used to show, for example, that overall the ages of the firms that are the market leaders vary considerably with time. The central conclusion is that, overall, firms that are small and young do better when there is faster technological change. Incumbents do well when it is "business as usual."

The second chapter in part IV is William J. Baumol's "Toward Analysis of Capitalism's Unparalleled Growth: Sources and Mechanism." Baumol starts by emphasizing the explosion in economic growth and innovation in the free-enterprise economies during the past two centuries, which far exceeds anything experienced under any other economic arrangements. He assigns primary roles to two groups: the independent inventors and entrepreneurs; and the large high-tech corporations. He cites suggestive evidence indicating that these two groups play very different and highly complementary roles in the processes of innovation and growth. The really revolutionary technological changes have been introduced preponderantly by independent inventors and then brought to market, often in relatively undeveloped form by the inventors' companion entrepreneurs. Sometimes the inventions have been sold or leased to large enterprises for further development, while in other cases success has enabled the initiating small firms to grow and join the large enterprises that specialize in cumulative incremental improvements.

The large firms account for what is by far the preponderant share of R&D spending, at least in the United States, and while the individual innovative contributions that emerge from their laboratories are generally not revolutionary, when taken together over more extended periods of time, the values they contribute are often enormous.

The initial Industrial Revolution is attributed to the appearance of an abundance of productive entrepreneurs, who were attracted to innovation and productive activity by what may be deemed historical accident that changed economic institutions so as to reduce rent-seeking opportunities and increased the amount and security of the reward to innovative activity. In contrast, the more routinized innovative activity of the larger firms arose from market pressures as those firms began to use innovation as their primary competitive weapon, thereby inaugurating an arms race in which no participant dares to relax its innovative efforts. These changes in incentives for large firms and small are a unique product of the free-enterprise economy and, Baumol suggests, go far to explain the unprecedented economic accomplishments of the past two centuries. They also constitute a useful model for the developing countries as well as for the developed countries that are seeking to retain their economic leadership.

Part V: Dissemination of Technology and the Patent System

This section of the volume, introduced by Edward N. Wolff, begins with "Patents, Licensing and Entrepreneurship: Effectuating Innovation in Multi-Invention Contexts," by Deepak Somaya and David J. Teece.

This chapter is virtually a manual on choice in the management of patents and the role of the entrepreneur in the process. It focuses on the particular opportunities and challenges afforded by multi-invention (systemic) innovation. It starts off from the observation that, from the perspective of the patent-owner, a patent may have special value in a multi-invention context that calls upon special bargaining and negotiating skills. But for the actual or potential infringers, patents they do not own may play the role of roadblocks. The essay explores the solutions to the problems and the choices available to these two parties, a matter apparently not previously explored in the literature. The focus is not on the many legal tactics and maneuvers afforded by patent law, but on the broader strategic role played by patents in establishing competitive advantage at the enterprise level.

In the many industries characterized by a large numbers of inventions that are typically combined to yield their end products, the analysis grows complex and calls for dealing with matters such as design of a special framework for understanding issues of innovation and organization. This is used, for example, to analyze the implications of the transaction costs associated with licensing. Thus, Somaya and Teece note that licensing is particularly attractive in markets where the transactions costs are low, as they tend to be in component markets. The authors point out that this is so because the patent is simply bundled with a tangible good, and no separate patent issues normally arise.

The authors discuss the valuation problems entailed in licensing and technology trading, the issue of patent "ambushing," in which the proprietor of a patent conceals its existence and lures rivals into unintentional infringement or other costly mistakes. Finally, having discussed the implications for the affected business firms, the chapter provides insights on the lessons for public policy. In sum, the chapter can be characterized as an illuminating manual on patent practice, strategy, and the pertinent policy issues.

In the second chapter in this part, Naomi R. Lamoreaux and Kenneth L. Sokoloff consider the innovation process in the United States in the nineteenth and twentieth centuries. Their essay, "The Market for Technology and the Organization of Invention in U.S. History," provides two important and related contributions. They first discuss the division of labor, within-firm or among economic units, that will best support innovation and growth. Then they provide a thorough review of the U.S. patent system.

On the division of labor, Lamoreaux and Sokoloff note that the latter half of the nineteenth century was characterized by an expansion of trade in new technological ideas. This was followed by a rise in within-firm research and development labs in the first half of the twentieth century, accompanied by a decrease in market exchange. The authors report a more recent decrease in in-house research and development, as firms began acquiring outside technology.

The authors conclude that the advantage of a within-firm division of labor is its reduction of asymmetric information problems that restrict the ability of inventors to sell their new technological ideas at arm's length. They also point out, however, that patent rights provide enough protection for inventors to engage in market exchange even if these rights are not fully enforced, and that contracting problems may reduce incentives for scientists and engineers to develop new technologies in-house.

As part of their analysis, Lamoreaux and Sokoloff provide a thorough discussion of the establishment of the modern U.S. patent system in 1836 and the economic consequences of this system. The authors' historical analysis of the patent system concludes with a discussion of the increase in the rate of both patenting and trading in patented technologies in recent years. Consistent with the thesis of the free-market innovation machine, Lamoreaux and Sokoloff suggest that there is a growing consensus that these changes may be indicative of a rise in the technological dynamism of the U.S economy.

Part VI: Innovation and Trade

In this part, introduced by Yochanan Shachmurove, Ralph E. Gomory and William J. Baumol pose some very interesting questions about the impact of technological change and innovation on the setting of world trade and the nature of goods traded. Entitled "Innovation and Its Effects on International Trade," their chapter considers the relevance of the standard textbook case for comparative advantage in a world in which natural advantages between countries play an increasingly insignificant role.

Based upon a standard linear Ricardo model of international trade, the authors attempt to determine the beneficiaries of trade in a world in which technology and innovation have changed the way global firms can bring together labor, capital, and knowledge. The authors conclude that often, although not always, a country is better off with a less developed trading partner. While only indirectly related to the central theme of this volume, this chapter calls into question some of the standard conclusions drawn from the comparative advantage model and offers an important perspective on issues of outsourcing and similar aspects of international trade.

The second chapter, "Innovation, Diffusion, and Trade," is by Jonathan Eaton and Samuel Kortum. They investigate what underlies patterns of research specialization, studying how technology dissemination affects the volume of innovation. They begin by noting that only a small group of countries allocate much in the way of resources to inventive activity. While the countries that invest heavily in research tend to be wealthy, not all wealthy economies do so; some depend heavily on imported research results. Moreover, the most innovative countries have continued to be so for more than half a century. The article goes on to consider the determinants of a country's research intensity, and the consequences of openness to trade and ease of dissemination of innovation.

The authors proceed to utilize a static Ricardian two-country model of technology, production, and trade. They consider the complicated case in which a disseminated innovation is used for the same commodity in both countries. In the case where technology is the same in both countries and diffusion can serve as a substitute for trade, trade ceases when similarities in efficiency in the countries eliminate the opportunities that would otherwise be offered by comparative advantage. The model is then expanded to incorporate dynamic elements and to take account of endogenous inventive activity.

The relatively simple Ricardian models yield the naturally corresponding results. If the differences between the productivity of research in the two countries exceed trade barriers, countries specialize in research in the pattern dictated by comparative advantage. But if differences in research productivity are below trade barriers, countries carry out their own research. Flows of knowledge replace flows of goods as the means by which countries benefit from one another's innovations.

The essay provides results that are at least suggestive for policy. In the simplest case with no technology transfer, countries carry out the same amount of research, unaffected by size and research productivity, but the more productive countries are wealthier. With dissemination possible, the relation between productivity and trade barriers determines the allocation of research activity. Intermediate levels of diffusion introduce results with complex patterns of research specialization, so that among the most active researchers are both very small and very large countries.

Part VII: Finance and Innovation in the Free-Market Economy

This part, introduced by Alan S. Blinder, includes chapters by Robert J. Shiller and Burton G. Malkiel.[2] Each of these contributions is based on both theory and direct experience. While Malkiel shows that efficient financial markets were responsive to and supportive of new technologies, Shiller highlights the yet unrealized promise of new innovative insurance markets.

Robert Shiller's discussion in "Radical Financial Innovation" predicts radical extensions of risk management, pooling, diversification, and hedging as practiced by insurance firms. In particular, these practices will include the pooling of worldwide risks. Shiller observes that income and consumption correlations within and across countries indicate imperfect risk sharing, and he argues that large welfare gains can be expected from additional insurance. He elaborates on many of the much-discussed behavioral difficulties of individuals in assessing risks and on the various inconsistencies in decision making, framing problems, and money illusion. He notes that there is reason for hope that these difficulties will be reduced as insurance becomes more extensive.

Shiller's description of innovations in home insurance is particularly interesting. To mitigate the moral hazard problem (for example, the disincentive for adequate protection of valuable property that results from the promise of restitution of the value of stolen property by insurance), he advocates the use of price indexes that cannot be distorted by any individual's actions. Country risks can be reduced by indexing payouts to gross domestic product. It should be pointed out that implementation of Shiller's proposals, with their systemwide implications, requires cooperation among firms, individuals, and countries.

In his chapter, "Finance and Innovation," Malkiel draws attention to the importance of financial markets in the "free-market innovation machine." Venture capital firms provide the necessary seed capital and managerial support. This is particularly evident in data that Malkiel presents on the biotech and information technology industries, but it applies to practically all the leading-edge firms. He shows that venture capital firms were successful in screening the more promising innovations and bringing these products to the market. Malkiel presents dramatic figures on the superiority of the United States over Europe in venture capital finance and in initial public offerings, leading to faster growth of these industries in the United States. He also points out the dark side of the abundance of investment outlets, which leads to overinvestment and market bubbles.

Part VIII: Toward Some Lessons

The final part of the book, introduced by Robert J. Strom, features chapters by Edmund S. Phelps and by Eytan Sheshinski. Taken as a pair, these chapters extend the concept of the free-market innovation machine to the critical issues of the performance of the continental western European economies and the economic welfare of developing economies.

The Phelps chapter, "The Economic Performance of Nations: Prosperity Depends on Dynamism, Dynamism on Institutions," argues that one can view the selection of economic institutions as a key factor in the economic policymaking that is necessary for innovation and growth. Contending that there is an important linkage between the degree of dynamism in a nation's economy, the development of particular economic institutions, and the nation's subsequent prosperity, he points to the failure of the continental western European countries to provide the ingredients necessary for the success of a free-market innovation machine. In his critique of policies that resulted in low employment and slow growth, Phelps argues that too much emphasis has been given to neoclassical policy instruments (e.g., tax rates, social contributions, and public expenditures) at the expense of more innovative thinking about policies that will support a well-performing economy. Corporatism specifically, he contends, has been harmful for both productivity and prosperity.

As described by Phelps, corporatism constricts the engine of Baumol's free-market innovation machine—the innovation that comes from the activity of independent entrepreneurs. In Baumol's model, corporatism restricts the actions of independent entrepreneurs in favor of a broader social framework for economic and business decisions, thus robbing the free-market innovation machine of the fuel it requires from those entrepreneurs to produce economic growth.

The chapter by Sheshinski, "Pharmaceutical Patenting in Developing Countries and R&D," examines the potential welfare dilemma inherent in exempting countries from pharmaceutical patents. Sheshinksi's compelling discussion analyzes the impact of both competitive and monopolistic pricing strategies on global welfare, the economic welfare of the developing country, and the incentives for the firm and industry to engage in research and development expenditures.

A Final Word

It is appropriate that the works in this volume take as their point of departure William Baumol's *Free-Market Innovation Machine.* Will Baumol, perhaps more than any other scholar in the last half century, has encouraged our thinking about and advanced our understanding of the role of entrepreneurship and innovation in the growth of capitalist societies. Beginning with his seminal article, from 1968, "Entrepreneurship in Economic Theory" (*American Economic Review* 58 (2): 64–71), Baumol introduced the entrepreneur as "at the same time one of the most intriguing and one of the most elusive characters that constitutes the subject of economic analysis." While the entrepreneur remains absent in much of the economics literature, Baumol continues to raise our awareness of the important place of the entrepreneur and innovator in a growing economy. For example, in his book *Entrepreneurship, Management, and the Structure of Payoffs* (MIT Press, 1993), he examined the allocation of the entrepreneur's contribution between productive and unproductive activities.

The thoughtful essays included in this volume follow closely from the content of *The Free-Market Innovation Machine*. Perhaps the best way to make the transition to these discussions is to reproduce part of a May 16, 2002, review of Baumol's book that appeared in *The Economist* magazine: "William Baumol has written a splendid new book. Building on the insights of Schumpeter and even of Marx, he argues that it is, above all, the ability to produce a continuous stream of successful innovations that makes capitalism the best economic system for generating economic growth."[3]

Notes

1. This volume includes papers presented at the conference "Entrepreneurship, Innovation, and the Growth Mechanism of the Free-Enterprise Economies," held November 6–8, 2003, at New York University. The conference was sponsored by the Ewing Marion Kauffman Foundation and New York University's C. V. Starr Center for Applied Economics.

2. At the 2003 conference in New York where the papers in this volume were originally presented, Robert C. Merton, Professor at the Harvard Business School and winner of the 1997 Nobel Prize in Economics, delivered a most illuminating paper on the subject of finance and innovation in the free-market economy. Unfortunately, because of other commitments, he was unable to contribute a chapter for this volume.

3. "The Growth Machine," *The Economist* magazine, May 16, 2002, available at http://www.economist.com.

Part I

INTRODUCTORY: THE MICROECONOMICS AND MACROECONOMICS OF GROWTH

Chapter 1

On Macroeconomic Models of Free-Market Innovation and Growth

ROBERT M. SOLOW

IN THE ORIGINAL PLAN for the conference at which the essays in this volume were presented, Ken Arrow was asked to talk about microeconomic models of innovation, and I about macroeconomic models. It might have been interesting if we two had been interchanged, so that Kenneth had talked about macroeconomic models and I about microeconomic models. But maybe there can be too much innovation. We will never know. There seem to be two possible lines of thought I could pursue under the general heading I was given.

> (a) How have the causes and consequences of innovation been treated in aggregative models of capitalist growth?
>
> (b) What sort of macroeconomic conditions seem to favor innovation and growth in a market economy?

If (a) were done right, if there were a really good theory of innovation embedded in growth models, the answer to (b) would no doubt follow. We are not so lucky, however. But question (b) can be pursued on its own in an ad hoc semi-informal way.

My impression is that the process of innovation is still treated rather mechanically in the new generation of "endogenous" growth models. Maybe that is the best one can hope for. The ambition to model free-market innovation has been there from the beginning of endogenous growth theory. Innovative activity has been treated as an only slightly atypical profit-seeking use of resources. The state of technology is represented as a one-dimensional level of total factor productivity. That is probably necessary in an aggregative model. Then there is some well-defined resource-using process that generates a known increase in TFP, with at most a little stationary stochastic jiggle.

There are attempts to model the intensity of competition as a determinant of innovative activity, though probably inadequately given the ambiguities and nonprobabilistic uncertainties that seem to be present. There are some self-consciously "Schumpeterian" models—though I am perhaps a minority of one in thinking that this is not entirely a compliment—complete with creative destruction and all that. Still, the air of clockwork is necessarily there, though it seems somehow self-contradictory in the context of innovation-driven growth. All these models seem to me to contain implausibilities.

It is remarkable how little joint research there has been between those who construct macroeconomic models with technical change, and those who study the inner workings of the "innovation machine" in industrial research groups and the history of particular innovations, large and small. That is explainable: the two groups have different talents and mind-sets. Model-builders have little patience with anecdotes and exceptions; and students of specific behavior-histories have little patience with the legitimate intellectual needs of model-builders. But of course that difference is exactly why it would be useful to combine both kinds of activity.

Not a lot of "behavioral economics" has found its way into growth theory; but detailed study tends to be all behavioral economics. No doubt some behavioral quirks get smoothed away over long enough periods of time by a Darwinian process. But this might be a place to get some serious, enduring behavioral regularities into aggregative model-building.

Part of the problem, I suspect, is the ubiquitous focus in growth theory—"endogenous" or not—on *the* steady-state growth rate as a theoretical object. This error may have been introduced by Roy Harrod, out of mathematical naïveté. There seems to be no way for this not to lead to excessively easy assumptions of linearity: in economic terms a casual willingness to postulate with very little basis that the level of X determines *the growth rate* of Y. Much more attention should be paid to this bad habit: these easy linearity postulates tend to distort the rest of the models in which they are embedded in ways that do not seem to capture the process of innovation and its uncertainties. This seems to be so even in self-consciously "Schumpeterian" models where one might expect to find more idiosyncrasy. This kind of linearity also leads to simple-minded "policy prescriptions."

More constructively, I think it might be helpful to model two kinds of innovation. One is more-or-less discrete large-scale innovation, presumably but not necessarily of a general-purpose kind: the internal combustion engine, the electric motor, the securitized mortgage, the computer, some altogether new way of cooking the books or otherwise stealing. These innovations lift the whole perceived horizon of productivity or market scope. But there is a lot of smaller-scale, piecemeal innovation needed to exploit the possibilities opened up by a major innovation: these can take the form of learning-by-doing, or learning-by-imitating. In any case, they certainly need not involve any identifiable research and development activities; they are often perceived and developed on the shop floor, by foremen and other production workers. They may be, but not necessarily, often tied to investment in new capital, and often occur upstream or downstream from the parent innovation. The analytical obsession with steady-state growth hinders the filling-in of a theory of this kind of limited, adaptive innovation.

An example of the influence of steady-state myopia: we know, from the mathematics, that only purely labor-augmenting exponential increase in TFP is compatible with steady-state exponential growth. A lot of first-class theoretical effort goes into inventing theories to show why technological progress should tend to be purely labor-augmenting. But there is no good empirical evidence in favor of labor-augmentation, and some evidence against it. Nor is it clear that capitalist growth tends to be exponential with only rare changes in the growth rate. Of course any fairly short segment of an accelerating time series can be approximated by an exponential. If log x is rising through time, then the linear approximation makes x exponential. But piecewise exponential curves are not exponential.

I have nothing against steady states. The problem is that insisting on them has led growth theorists to accept mechanisms for endogenous technological change that have no other merit than that they do the endogenous-growth-rate trick. Even that could be harmless, except that it leads in turn to simplistic policy preconceptions and the debasement of talk about "policies for growth." Can one model major innovations? I wonder. Surely they are not just a matter of serendipity: resources matter, and can be applied more intensively or less; necessity may be the legitimate mother of invention. The question is whether there is a systematic theory that somehow allows properly for the element of serendipity. The technician's instinct is to model discrete innovations as random arrivals in a Poisson process, maybe with an accompanying probability distribution describing the "magnitude" of the innovation that has just arrived. But that standard device is probably too mechanical to do justice to discrete innovations.

Here is another casual thought that might lead somewhere. Since we are talking about macro-models, it is worth remembering that one of the ways capital, labor, and resources are substituted for one another aggregatively is through substitution on the consumption side: shifting the weights of capital-intensive, labor-intensive, and resource-intensive goods in the aggregate consumption bundle. A theory of the bias of technological change has to take this into account; innovative activity can be stimulated by shifts in consumption patterns that affect the return to investment. Pure production-function reasoning at the aggregate level may miss an important part of the story.

Now let me turn to question (b) about the macroeconomic conditions that seem to be good for successful innovation. There is, of course, the old question about whether it is monopoly or competition that better fosters innovation. Presumably not either extreme. The arguments are well worn. There is plenty of evidence that exposure to competition from best practice is a very important stimulus to industrial performance. But of course "pure" competition will hardly provide the necessary rewards, so some element of market power may be favorable. It is possible that the mere time advantage accruing to the innovator may be adequate compensation for the resource costs and risks involved; but the lead time is itself an element of market power.

On the macro side, my earlier remarks suggest separating out two questions. (1) What macroeconomic circumstances favor major innovations? (2) What macroeconomic circumstances favor rapid exploitation and improvement of major innovations, including the making of the necessary capital investment? In both aspects, we should think about an economy open to trade and foreign direct investment.

To be more specific, is a high-pressure economy likely to produce more innovation than a low-pressure economy? (By "pressure" I mean the pressure of demand on capacity.) Low pressure implies the need for firms to "do something" to create and extend their markets; but low pressure is much less promising when it comes to motivating and financing the necessary investment. We are all familiar with the firm that cuts back on its R&D spending as soon as sales and profits weaken. High pressure implies a high return to new capacity, even higher if the new capacity involves improved product and more efficient production. High pressure also has the advantage of providing internal funds to finance the required investment. But then there is Alexander Field's surprising finding that the decade of the 1930s was a fertile period for growth of total factor productivity, and laid the groundwork for later success. Presumably whatever the 1930s created, it was not the in-fill type of innovation, because gross investment was at rock bottom during that interval.

Possibly the best circumstances are fairly high macroeconomic pressure accompanied by active competition, especially from abroad because that creates a need to rival innovations made elsewhere or in neighboring industries. It may be that for major innovations macroeconomic conditions are not a key factor. Relatively free trade certainly has the advantage that the possibility of increasing market share in world markets is a constant incentive for innovative activity.

One last point: it is too easy to lapse into the tacit presumption that "innovation" consists of new products and new technology only, whereas an important component is organizational innovation, the improved organization of functions and tasks. Unfortunately it may be too difficult to represent the rate of such innovations along a quantifiable scale, though the accompanying rise in productivity is the same as that from technological innovations. Different sorts of models may be needed. But that need not be an obstacle to a sort of natural history or ecology of innovation-friendly institutions in this broader sense. That might be a good compromise.

Chapter 2

The Macro-context of the Microeconomics of Innovation

KENNETH J. ARROW

1. General Orientation

The essays in this volume and much research in economic analysis are devoted to an attempt to understand and explain a remarkable phenomenon. Beginning around 1750 in England and spreading through most of the world, there has emerged an unprecedented upward trend in income per capita. When Malthus wrote in 1798, he was recapitulating the world as it broadly had been; there was indeed technological progress, but every increase in productive power enabled more people to live and thereby brought per capita income down again. As an analysis, there are few better examples in social science; as a forecast, it could hardly have been worse.

As William Baumol (2002) has so masterfully argued, the acceleration of innovation in the last quarter-millennium is the chief new phenomenon that calls for explanation (the demographic transition is also relevant but not the subject here). The economist's natural and fruitful response is to seek out the incentive structure that will induce innovation on the basis of market motivations. Baumol has illustrated richly the role of profit incentives in inducing innovation in the modern economy and the ways these incentives work themselves out.

The emphasis of Baumol and others on the microeconomic motives needs to be supplemented by understanding the macro-context. Even in the most standard realms of microeconomic analysis, the individual's behavior is motivated by his or her understanding of the macro-economy, a point given great emphasis recently by Frank Hahn (2003), under the intriguing sobriquet of "the macrofoundations of microeconomics."

Here, by the "macro-context," I don't have in mind what we usually term "macroeconomic phenomena," fluctuations in demand or monetary disturbances. It is not that these are unimportant for innovation, at least in the short run. It is certainly widely believed that the extraordinary rates of productivity growth during the 1950s and 1960s in Europe and the United States were due in part to an accumulation of knowledge that had not found productive use because of the Great Depression (as well as World War II). But I have in mind broader social phenomena, in particular, the scientific viewpoint and the growth of appropriate institutions and social relations, not merely those devoted to clearing obstacles to the supremacy of the market.

One aspect of the issues involved is the distinction between endogenous and exogenous theories of growth. More precisely, we are concerned with *intensive* growth (i.e., per capita or per worker, or per unit of aggregate input), not *extensive* (which might simply reflect population or labor force growth). That is, we are concerned with productivity changes. These may come from outside the economic system (e.g., as a by-product of scientific curiosity) or from inside.

Under the latter, there are several subheads. One is simply capital accumulation; total factor productivity might be constant, but labor productivity rises with capital accumulation. In this story, "innovation" is simply the emergence of new forms of production that embody increasing capital labor ratios. In the modern formulation, capital includes human capital. The so-called neoclassical revival has sought to show that this model fits international cross-section data (Mankiw, Romer, and Weil 1992); the spirit is that of Lucas (1988), but this point of view has little explanatory power with respect to changes over time, as has been understood since the first serious attempts to measure growth (Tinbergen 1942; Abramovitz 1956; Solow 1957). These early studies did not account for human capital, but careful studies show that including it does not change the general importance of increased total factor productivity, even with an inclusive definition of factors (Klenow and Rodríguez-Clare 1997).

A somewhat different endogenous theory is that of increasing returns to scale, already introduced by Adam Smith in his opening chapters (1776, book 1, chaps. 1–3). This aspect of Smith's work found no echo in his immediate followers (David Ricardo, J. S. Mill), but eventually it was codified as an explanation for growth by Allyn Young (1928). The post-1950 literature is filled with many variations on the increasing-returns hypothesis: straightforward economies of scale (Kaldor 1961), learning by doing (Arrow 1962a), and, most relevant here, the widely held hypothesis that the costs of innovation are independent of the size of the market, while the reward is proportional to it, so that innovations are induced by growth (extensive or intensive) and these in turn are a cause of growth (Romer 1986). For the currently most complete account, see Aghion and Howitt 1998.

Exogenous theories of growth, the models of Tinbergen (1942) and Solow (1956), have in many ways dominated empirical work, especially in time series studies. Innovation here takes the form of changes in total factor productivity, but the latter is not really analyzed, except for the simple hypothesis that it grows exponentially. One may restate this theory as the proposition that growth in knowledge (total factor productivity) is produced out of knowledge under constant returns. Since resources other than knowledge obviously enter into the innovation process and, in part at least, must be compensated for on the market, this theory is inadequate and certainly does not help in the formulation of innovation policy. But it does leave open the possibility that the creation of productive knowledge is partly explained by a system in which market incentives are not all-encompassing.

My own view is that both endogenous and exogenous elements are important in explaining innovation. Incentives certainly play a role, but so does the general state of scientific knowledge, which is not directly produced by profit-making entities. To give an example, pharmaceutical companies devote large efforts to developing new antiretroviral drugs and antidepressants but not to antimalarial drugs, obviously because the effective market (measured in purchasing power) for the former drugs is much greater than for the latter. But antiretroviral drugs could not have been developed without fundamental improvements in genetics and in analytic technology, improvements themselves financed from public funds and driven by the usual academic incentives of curiosity and the desire for fame. (For the contrasting view, see Dasgupta and David 1987.) An extreme case of the public orientation is the development of a new class of antimalarial drugs, the artemisinins, by a group of Chinese scientists, under public sponsorship; not only was no patent taken, but the original publication was anonymous, so that we cannot even say with Milton, "Fame is the spur . . . / That last infirmity of a noble mind" (see Arrow, Gelband, and Panosian 2004).

It is interesting to see that Joseph Schumpeter (1934; for a compact restatement of his views, see 1939, 84–109) has a somewhat similar dichotomy. He distinguishes between "inventions" and "innovations." An invention is an idea that might be used in production; an innovation is the process of turning an "invention" into an actual product. Schumpeter, of course, emphasizes the role of entrepreneurs, those who innovate. In Schumpeter's story, inventions are abundant, a free good. However, it takes resources and entrepreneurship, both scarce, to turn inventions into innovations.

Of course, treating inventions as a free good requires some assumptions about the invention-creating process. New inventions must be created at a sufficiently rapid rate if they are not to be a scarce factor. How is this achieved? Schumpeter does not dwell on this important matter, but there is certainly implicit a creative process, like science, that creates "inventions" and cannot be regarded as economically determined.

Thus, a number of social systems impact the process of innovation. We have already mentioned two, markets and science (or knowledge). As Baumol points out, the aspects of markets relevant to innovation are not those emphasized in standard economic theory when the efficiency of the price system is argued. Rather it is the role and meaning of property rights (particularly but not only intellectual property rights) that is of concern. Thus, the legal system is also part of the macro-environment that governs the innovative performance of an economy.

Finally, there is a social or cultural element that has proved very refractory to analysis but which is nevertheless real. Failure at innovation is not merely a matter of pecuniary loss; it is also, and in many cases more importantly, a matter of reputation. Is the failed entrepreneur regarded as having demonstrated permanent incompetence, or is he or she looked on as one who is willing to try new ideas and who will likely succeed eventually? Such expectations are self-fulfilling, and so many equilibria are possible. It is striking that the institution of venture capital, which one might say has shown its success in Silicon Valley, has proved so difficult to re-create elsewhere. I have nothng myself to add on this subject, but see Saxenian 1996 on the cultural differences between such similar places as Silicon Valley and Route 128 near Boston.

I will not explore all these points further but do wish to give some consideration to some of the broader elements that affect the process of innovation. I will assemble these remarks under two headings, the proximate factors in firm decision-making about innovation, and the knowledge environment of innovation.

2. Innovation as a Decision Problem of the Firm

Even if we confine ourselves to the internal decisions of the firm about innovation, there are many questions of context. Of course, the elementary starting-point is that innovation is the production of a form of knowledge, and knowledge is not a product like those standard on markets and in economic analysis. It can be used either for production or for transfer without being consumed. The cost of reproduction is generally much lower than the cost of production. Hence, an innovation, once acquired, can relatively easily be used by someone else, perhaps a competitor, so that appropriability of the benefits is weakened. The creation of intellectual property rights is an attempt to restrict this erosion of incentives with, of course, consequent implications for monopolization and blockage of future related innovations.

With this remark in mind, what specifically are the incentives to innovate? The firm may sell the product derived from the innovation, or it may sell the knowledge. In the first case, the gain is in the form of monopoly profits. In the second, it may take the form of licensing or of selling the firm. The last must be derived from monopoly profits for the buyer, and, of course, the license is an indirect way of deriving monopoly profits through agents. There are many intricate questions that arise here. For example, if we assume specialization, firms that are good at innovation are not necessarily good at producing or selling. If this mismatch results in licensing or sale of the firm, there is a bargaining situation, so that the incentive to innovate is correspondingly reduced. It is notorious that licensors generally receive far less of the total profits than licensees.

To the extent that information can indeed be kept from leaking (or being used), innovated goods are indeed likely to lead to imperfect competition. From the characteristics of knowledge, the cost is independent of the amount used (unlike more normal inputs), while the value in use depends on the output. We have then a classical case of increasing returns (for a formal proof of this obvious point, see Arrow 1998). Hence, if the postinnovation competition is with substitute products also derived by innovation, the competition will necessarily be imperfect and at least possibly give rise to the profits needed to motivate innovation. Note, though, that the incentives to innovate may bear little relation to the net social value; for example, the ease of developing substitute products may have led to overinvestment in innovation.

In addition to the role of postinnovation production competition, it is essential to consider the role of competition in innovation. Clearly, potential competition from other innovators is both a spur and a barrier. In the absence of competition, the incentives of an existing monopolist to innovate are weakened, since existing monopoly profits are eroded (see Arrow 1962b, 619–22). In the presence of potential competition, however, monopoly profits are endangered anyway, and the incumbent has an incentive to innovative. In the literature, much discussion is focused on the patent race. But the current discussions for the most part make assumptions that are out of line with general economic analysis. For example, it is usually assumed that each firm has a particular given approach, that its chances of success are independent of those of others, and that aggregate profits are split in case of simultaneous innovation. In fact, oligopoly theory argues that aggregate profits are reduced by competition; at one extreme (Bertrand), any competition reduces aggregate profits to zero. (In a paper in process, I make both the innovation process and the decision to enter endogenous and assume Bertrand competition. Then it turns out that the competitive decisions to engage in innovation can lead to an optimal innovation portfolio, thereby formalizing one of Baumol's emphases.)

There are other contextual elements in the firm's decisions to innovate that need still more study than they have received. A leading issue is the financing of innovation. Knowledge of the prospects for a potential innovation is surely asymmetric information; the responsible individual or group within the firm knows more than the management, and the management knows more than outside financers. Hence, there are issues of both inside and outside capital markets. But I will omit further discussion of this point.

3. The Knowledge Environment

The creation of knowledge that constitutes an innovation is in turn dependent on the acquisition and application of existing knowledge; information is an input into the production of information. This background knowledge and the ability to use it are the most important elements of the social context of individually motivated innovation.

Here we find that markets and, in fact, most forms of capitalist enterprise play only a partial role in explaining the knowledge input into innovation. I have already referred to the existence of licensing, which provides a market for innovations; I now emphasize its role as input rather than output of knowledge.

But licensing provides only a limited range of knowledge and may not be the basis for additional steps in innovation. Another market-based source of knowledge is mobility of research and development labor. The economics of this has been explored only to a limited extent. An individual working on research and development in one firm will acquire knowledge in the process and become more valuable to other firms. Even if trade secrets laws prevent carrying highly specific knowledge to the new employer, there will be more general knowledge embodied in the worker. The implications for wage determination are rather complex, particularly since the knowledge about what knowledge a mobile worker has is clearly distributed asymmetrically.

But we know from experience and many studies that knowledge is acquired in many other ways. One is simply general acquaintance, the tendency of those in the same industry to exchange information. Thus, we have the trade conventions, where new products are exhibited. More broadly, the very act of putting an innovated product on the market reveals information; it is an unavoidable part of the marketing process. But the social links among the members of the same trade are stronger than that. Informal exchanges are clearly valuable; they explain the agglomeration of economic activity (e.g., Silicon Valley), since it is valuable to be near others who are innovating and so get information early and in detail. (Incidentally, this proposition of economic geography is based on the generalization that propinquity reduces information costs, a fact that suggests that face-to-face communication still dominates more modern forms of telecommunication.)

Beyond this local interaction, there is the broader source of knowledge derived from education or the indirect contacts (e.g., books) based on it. At the national level, it is usually held that this form of human capital is a resource complementary to current technological knowledge. Thus, the role of the educational system in providing trained users of knowledge enters as still another contextual variable.

Finally (for our present purposes), knowledge is accumulated outside the economic sector, through the university and other research institutes, a point already noted.

L'envoi

In a somewhat hit-or-miss fashion, I have tried to lay out some of the broader contexts in which the profit-oriented innovation strategies of firms are located. I have mentioned for the most part those that influence profits and incentives but are nevertheless variables that are needed to explain the remarkable course of productivity gain in the last 250 years in some places. From the policy viewpoint, it raises questions about a purely laissez-faire attitude towards encouraging innovation and stresses the need for complementary positive policies. Needless to say, there is little that can be asserted with great definiteness; rather, I call attention to some of the items for a research agenda in this area.

References

Abramovitz, M. 1956. "Resource and Output Trends in the United States since 1870." *American Economic Review Papers and Proceedings* 46: 5–23.

Aghion, P., and P. Howitt. 1998. *Endogenous Growth Theory*. Cambridge: MIT Press.

Arrow, K. J. 1962a. "The Economic Implications of Learning by Doing." *Review of Economic Studies* 29: 155–73.

———. 1962b. "Economic Welfare and the Allocation of Resources for Invention." In *The Rate and Direction of Inventive Activity: Economic and Social Factors*. Princeton: Princeton University Press.

———. 1998. "Innovation and Increasing Returns to Scale." In *Increasing Returns and Economic Progress*, ed. K. J. Arrow, Y.-K. Ng, and X. Yang. Baskingstoke, UK: Macmillan; New York: St. Martin's Press.

Arrow, K. J., H. Gelband, and C. Panosian, eds. 2004. *Saving Lives, Buying Time: Economics of Malaria Drugs in an Age of Resistance*. Report of the

Institute of Medicine of the National Academies. Washington, D.C.: National Academies Press.
Baumol, W. J. 2002. *The Free-Market Innovation Machine.* Princeton: Princeton University Press.
Dasgupta, P., and P. David. 1987. "Information Disclosure and the Economics of Science and Technology." In *Arrow and the Ascent of Modern Economic Theory*, ed. G. Feiwel. London: Macmillan.
Hahn, F. 2003. "Macro Foundations of Micro-Economics." *Economic Theory* 21: 227–32.
Kaldor, N. 1961. "Capital Accumulation and Economic Growth." In *The Theory of Capital*, ed. F. A. Lutz and D. C. Hagues. New York: St. Martin's Press.
Klenow, P. J., and A. Rodríguez-Clare. 1997. "The Neoclassical Revival in Growth: Has It Gone Too Far?" In *NBER Macroeconomiucs Annual, 1997*, ed. B. Bernanke and J. Rotemberg. Cambridge: MIT Press.
Lucas, R. E. 1988. "On the Mechanics of Economic Development." *Journal of Monetary Economics* 22: 3–42.
Mankiw, N. G., D. Romer, and D. N. Weil. 1992. "A Contribution to the Empirics of Economic Growth." *Quarterly Journal of Economics* 107: 407–37.
Romer, P. 1986. "Increasing Returns and Long-Run Growth." *Journal of Political Economy* 94: 1002–37.
Saxenian, A. 1996. *Regional Advantage: Culture and Competition in Silicon Valley and Route 128.* Cambridge: Harvard University Press.
Schumpeter, J. 1934. *The Theory of Economic Development.* Trans. Redvers Opie. Cambridge: Harvard University Press.
———. 1939. *Business Cycles.* New York: McGraw-Hill.
Smith, A. 1776. *An Enquiry into the Nature and Causes of the Wealth of Nations.* London: Strahan and Cadell.
Solow, R. M. 1956. "A Contribution to the Theory of Economic Growth." *Quarterly Journal of Economics* 65: 65–94.
———. 1957. "Technical Change and the Aggregate Production Function." *Review of Economic Statistics* 39: 312–20.
Tinbergen, J. 1942. "Zur Theorie der langfristigen Wirtschaftsentwicklung." *Weltwirschaftsliche Archiv* 55: 511–49.
Young, A. A. 1928. "Increasing Returns and Economic Progress." *Economic Journal* 38: 527–42.

Part II

INSTITUTIONAL BASES FOR CAPITALIST GROWTH

Introduction and Comments

MICHAEL M. WEINSTEIN

DOUGLASS C. NORTH AND Barry R. Weingast address an intimidating question: what are the institutional foundations of capitalist-based economic growth? Their discussions return us to yesteryear, when great economic minds indulged readers in big thoughts, a quaint exercise called political economy. But most economists long ago turned away from the big-think questions of political economy. Its questions were vague; the answers formless. Economists turned instead to questions of shriveling dimension but to which they could provide elegantly precise answers. Professors North and Weingast turn the clock back, with predictably challenging but impressionistic results. Their musings yield no chiseled formal theorems or rigorous insights. But these chapters do provide an exciting direction for future research.

North starts, no surprise, at the (relative) beginning. He notes that the evolution of impersonal exchange, the hallmark of modern markets, requires institutional structures that run "counter to the innate genetic predispositions that millions of years of hunter/gatherer heritage had prepared humans for." He attributes the prosperity that the developed world has achieved over the past 10 centuries or so to institutional flexibility—a flexibility that allows economies to grope by trial and error for productive responses to unpredictable external forces. He says that economists and historians know what it takes to produce productive economics. He says that they also know the sources of productivity growth and the institutions that make markets work. But, North observes, we (collectively) know not where beliefs come from or how to create in real time the institutional foundations for growth.

North is surely correct when he cites what it is we don't know. I'm not so sure he's correct when he says what it is we do know.

He focuses on a central observation: a government strong enough to protect private property and to provide the other essentials of markets is also strong enough to victimize holders of private property. In the felicitous expression of Andrei Shleifer and Robert Vishny, strong governments threaten to replace the invisible hand with the grabbing hand. Professor North argues that the keys to a productive society lie in structured, institutionalized interactions that reward hard work and innovation—"that is exactly what institutions are—incentives."

But that generality leaves unclear what important facts it might help us understand. How, for example, does the association of growth with incentives help to explain why living standards in the United States and western Europe are comparable despite the fact that the Europeans, so the accusation often goes, stomp out many of the rewards that are deemed central to the operation of the U.S. economy? Perhaps the generalities that rule North's chapter don't work at the granular level of differences across continents.

North moves toward the specific when he asks what structures a society needs to produce the dynamic features of the capitalist systems recently described by William Baumol's writings on innovation. In recent writings, Baumol takes the reader on a fascinating tour of businesses that mostly abandon the strategy of competing on price—the basis of more than 100 years of modern economic analysis—to adopt instead the strategy of using innovation as the primary means of competition. To do that, oligopolistic companies respond to North's "ubiquitous uncertainty" by investing in each others' research operations—participating in joint ventures, the technological fruits from which the participating firms will share. Under such compacts, IBM will work with a competitor like Hitachi, as each promises to license future innovations to the other for a set fee. In a phrase I have previously used to describe Baumol's theses, capitalism hums, he shows, by making innovation institutionally humdrum.

North and Baumol each expose the fundamental mechanisms of capitalism. But North takes his snapshot of markets, transaction costs, and incentives from 20,000 miles above the earth. Baumol, by contrast, takes his from the trenches—drawn from the detailed records of firms for which he has consulted. We surely learned something new and refreshing from Baumol's trench warfare, as from North's abstractions about capitalism.

Barry Weingast rivets on constitutional perquisites of capitalist growth. Like North, he confronts the problem that a government strong enough to protect private property and provide other market essentials is also strong enough to prey on private property rights. He isolates what he regards as two fundamental problems.

First, there is the "rationality of fear." Citizens whose most basic rights are threatened by government will fight back—by violent, nonconstitutional means if necessary. To solve this problem, a constitution needs to "lower the stakes" of playing by constitutional rules by protecting what "citizens "hold most dear." If, for example, a constitution prevents elected officials from victimizing opponents, then losing an election becomes a tolerable option. Second, a constitution needs to provide for enforcement. The tricky part of enforcement is to create institutions that overcome the inherent difficulty that citizens have in coordinating their efforts to protect their basic rights. Coordination problems, Weingast points out, pave the way for the time-honored policy of "divide and conquer," by which governments victimize the property rights and liberties of a swath of citizens even as it panders to a set of other citizens, thereby locking in enough support to survive effective challenge. Citizens threatened by a rapacious government can keep governments in check only by coordinating resistance. Growth-compatible constitutions provide means for such coordination.

Weingast's point, which he tracks in seventeenth-century England and eighteenth-century United States, is that a prosperous capitalist system requires not only a powerful government but also the constraints that keep the state from trampling political and economic liberty. His two-problem analysis of constitutional order provides an interesting scheme for taking a fresh look at societies, past and present. Weingast concedes that his framework is incomplete. Yet it provides for a fruitful investigation of constitutional orders to examine the variety of mechanisms that they have tried in an effort to isolate those that work best under various conditions.

Toward that end, Weingast provides interesting commentaries on China and Mexico. China lacks a written constitution, relying instead on political rules that serve as an informal constitution. It lacks, then, the formal protection of private property that would appear essential for the growth of markets. But China's growth after 1978 has been phenomenal, a fact that Weingast explains by pointing to its informal rules. Mexico, by contrast, offers a formal constitution that, like the U.S. Constitution, builds in formal checks and balances among the separate branches of government, including an independent judiciary. In fact, however, Mexico provides weak protection of property rights. Its economy stagnates.

But this China-Mexican comparison flirts with tautology. We know China grows rapidly. So it must be that individuals have found ways to do what's in their productive self-interest. Weingast can march in after the fact, describing the observed institutions as growth enhancing. By contrast, we know Mexico stagnates. So historians can cite the institutions that exist as growth retarding. But suppose Weingast had been given rich anthropological detail about both countries circa 1978. Would he have made the right call about which institutions would work best to promote future growth?

As the China-Mexico comparison suggests, a mapping between constitutional structures and economic outcomes will be anything but tight. Indeed, an intriguing paper by Professor Dani Rodrik (2005) draws a related picture of governance, albeit in the context of international relations. Rodrik recognizes that markets evolve within specific cultural frameworks. But he's struck by the lack of one-to-one symmetry, the variety of market institutions spawned by any cultural context. Take China. It has, at least until recently, provided few legal protections to investors. That would not seem a feasible progrowth framework. But China has provided enough informal assurances to draw soaring amounts of capital from foreign investors. The combination works to promote spectacular rates of growth. Or take Europe, the United States, and Japan. They achieve comparable living standards despite seemingly very different systems of risks and rewards. Japan provides skimpy social insurance but generous protection from private-sector decisions, including lifetime jobs for a substantial number of workers. The United States provides, by comparison, more social insurance than does Japan but less protection from private-sector uncertainty.

There are, then, lots of feasible ways to structure market and nonmarket institutions. One neat marriage would map the constitutional imperatives outlined by Weingast to the institutional variations examined by Rodrik. If Rodrik is right, the mapping won't be simple—individuals find ingenious ways to accommodate institutional constraints, including constitutional imperatives, imposed by society. But perhaps, it will turn out that market and nonmarket institutions cannot be combined elastically. A searching scrutiny of past and present choices might reveal surprising, interesting patterns.

North and Weingast agree that for capitalism to work, political and economic systems must be inextricably intertwined. The obvious lesson—known to anyone working to reform the former Soviet Union—is that economic reform in the absence of political reform will not work. Another lesson is that there are complicated, surprising ways to structure political institutions so that markets can prosper. Private parties find creative ways to circumvent ravenous governments and other obstacles to enrichment. The challenge posed by these two chapters is to resurrect political economy for the purpose of discovering the essential political bases of growth. The old-style political economy was ditched because it failed to generate findings with anywhere near the precision of the calculus. North and Weingast urge a return to big think, with a research agenda that might, with all we have learned about doing theory in the social sciences, make tangible progress.

Reference

Rodrik, Dani. 2005. "Feasible Globalizations." In *Globalization: What's New*, ed. Michael M. Weinstein. New York: Columbia University Press.

Chapter 3

Institutional Bases for Capitalist Growth

DOUGLASS C. NORTH

CAPITALISM MAY BE THE engine of progress, but it becomes such an engine only under particular institutional conditions. Baumol describes the features of the free-market economy that make it 'fantastically productive' and the engine of progress as follows: "This book will emphasize three components of that explanation: the fierce competition among many of the economy's enterprises, seeking to come up with the better mousetrap or the better way to produce the old mousetrap: the resulting routinization of the innovation process that reduces the firm's dependence upon fortunate happenstance in the form of an appropriate invention that just happened to appear: and the competitive pressure to disseminate proprietary technology voluntarily—to make it available, for a suitable return of course, even to direct competitors" (2002, 20).

In this essay I shall both explore the very special historical conditions that produced such an engine in the West and further explore just why capitalism has failed to produce such results in much of the rest of the world; I will then specify the relationship between institutions and economic performance; I am then in a position to specify the necessary economic institutions; and then explore the unique conditions that produced the "free-market innovation machine." In conclusion I shall set this discussion in time to demonstrate the essential contribution that economic history can make to our understanding of economic performance.

Historical Conditions in the West

The rise of the West was the ascendancy of a relatively backward part of the world to world hegemony in the millennium after the tenth century. But it was more than that. It was part of a fundamental shift in the focus of institutional change from dealing with the uncertainties of the physical environment to dealing with the uncertainties of the increasingly complex human environment. The conquest of the physical environment with the growth of scientific knowledge entailed a far more complex human environment; a necessary prerequisite was a social, political, and economic structure of interdependence, ubiquitous externalities, and impersonal exchange. The Western world evolved gradually to provide the necessary structure to realize, very imperfectly, the potential of the application of this growing knowledge to solve problems of human scarcity. Adam Smith was correct that the wealth of nations was a result of specialization, division of labor, and the size of the market. But he could only dimly have envisioned the complex societies that would result. The shift from personal to impersonal exchange requires a political, economic, and social structure that runs counter to the innate genetic predispositions that millions of years of hunter/gatherer heritage had prepared humans for.[1] Realizing the potential of human well-being possible with this scientific knowledge entails a fundamental restructuring of societies. The necessary political and economic structure developed over centuries.[2] The essential conditions are the creation of an incentive structure that rewards productive activity and discourages antisocial behavior in the specific setting of impersonal markets, both political and economic. But the necessary institutional changes to create such an incentive framework must overcome the innate genetic predisposition that evolved with a hunter/gatherer environment.

The widening gap between rich and poor countries that we are observing in modern times is a reflection of our inability to reproduce the

TABLE 3.1
Per Capita Income, Selected Rich and Poor Countries, 2000

Rich Countries		Poor Countries	
Britannica		*Latin America*	
United Kingdom (7)	68.1	Bolivia (35)	8.2
Australia (9)	76.3	Chile (13)	29.2
Canada (14)	80.7	Uruguay (34)	28.9
Ireland (3)	76.4	Argentina (29)	32.9
Europe		*Africa*	
Switzerland (9)	79.2	Ethiopia (124)	2.0
Denmark (14)	80.1	Kenya (87)	3.7
Luxembourg (5)	137.5	Zimbabwe (146)	7.3
Asia		*Asia*	
Hong Kong (1)	78.3	Indonesia (114)	11.3
Japan (14)	72.8	China (114)	10.8
Singapore (2)	80.4	India (133)	7.5

Source: Penn World Tables; O'Driscoll, Holmes, and Kirkpatrick 2001.

Note: Figures are percentages of U.S. per capita income. The country's rank in the Index of Economic Freedom in 2001 is given in parentheses.

necessary conditions in countries with a heritage of personal exchange. Most of these countries are (at least nominally) capitalist but in no way reflect the "free market" that Baumol has in mind. Rather they exhibit an inability to restructure their political and economic frameworks to reap the benefits of the productive potential that we possess. Table 3.1 gives a capsule summary of the contrast.

While the figures exaggerate the difference for all the reasons we are familiar with in national income accounting, they are nevertheless startling; even more so because of the persistence of the difference. In figure 3.1 trends in per capita income as a percentage of U.S. per capita income not only show the persistence of the gap in Latin America, but in the case of Argentina show the decline of a country that in 1940 had the sixth highest income in the world. The reason is clear. We know the sources of productivity growth and we even know the essential institutions, political and economic, to produce the desired results. We have only a very imperfect understanding of how to get those conditions.

The Relationship between Institutions and Economic Performance

The key to economic performance is to structure human interaction to reward productive activity. It is institutions that are the incentive structure of societies, and therefore it is necessary to understand just "how they work" and why they work "imperfectly." We are some distance from having a complete theory of institutions that would explain their formation, just how they influence performance and the process of change, and their integration with neoclassical (price) theory. But we have made a good deal of progress, and the thriving development of ISNIE (International Society of the New Institutional Economics) promises substantial further improvement. Recent studies that have contributed to our understanding are those dealing with the movement from personal to impersonal exchange (Greif 1994; Milgrom, North, and Weingast 1990), the structure of property rights (Barzel 1997), and the interplay between the mind and the environment (Donald 1991; Hutchins 1995).

Institutions are composed of formal rules, informal constraints, and their enforcement characteristics. Formal rules are constitutions, laws, rules and regulations; informal constraints are made up of conventions, norms of behavior, and self-imposed constraints on conduct. Enforcement is either first person (self-imposed), second person (retaliation), or third person (ranging from peer pressure to governmental enforcement). Together they determine the way the game is played.

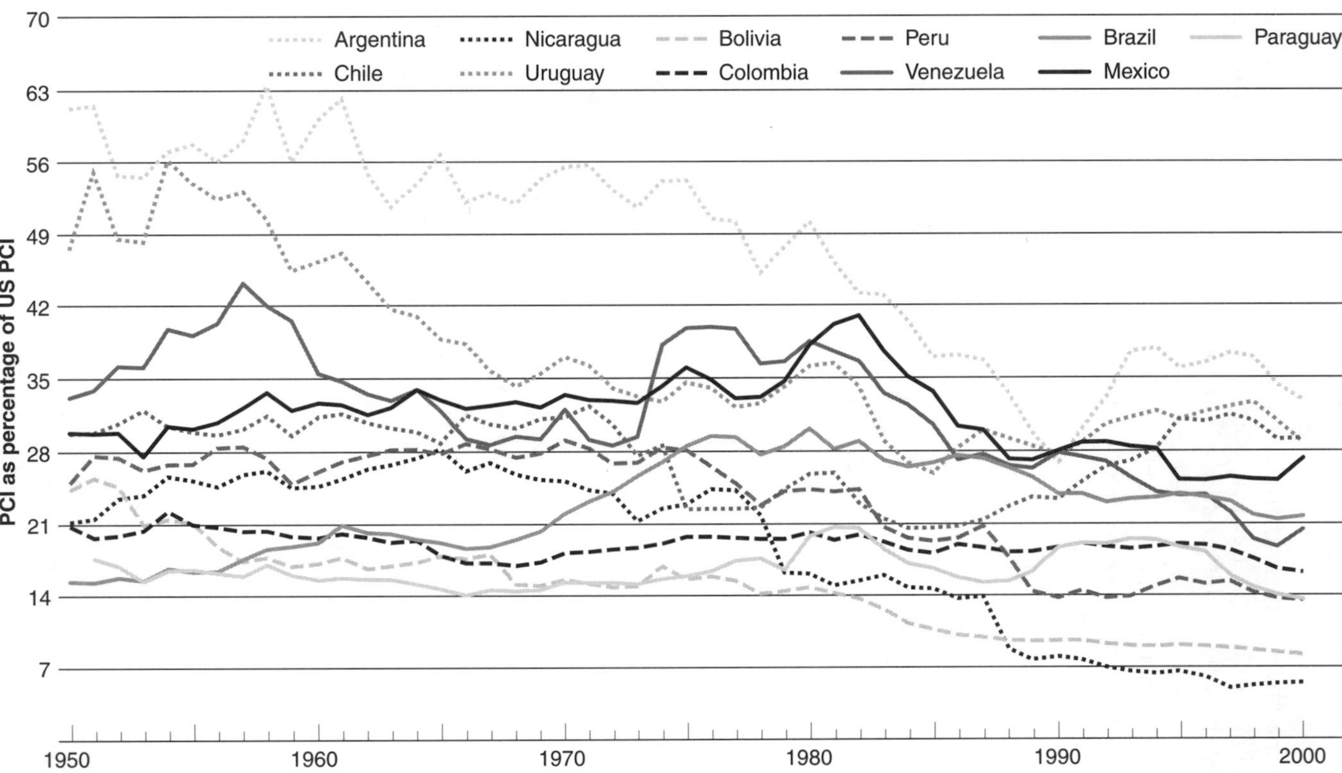

Figure 3.1. Trends in Per Capita Income Relative to the United States: Latin America, 1950–2000

Let me illustrate from professional team sports. Professional football (to illustrate) is played on the basis of formal rules, informal constraints (such as not deliberately injuring the quarterback of the opposing team), and umpires and referees to enforce both formal rules and informal norms. Enforcement is always imperfect, and accordingly it frequently pays to violate the rules or norms. Obviously the way the game is in fact played is a function of the degree of imperfection of enforcement, which is in turn a function of the strength of norms of behavior, the effectiveness of the umpires, and the severity of penalties for violation. But beyond that, the rules themselves were devised by interested parties, so that even the fundamental characteristics of the game can be understood only by examining the interests of the parties structuring it, as Barry Weingast will make clear in the next chapter.

In essence, understanding the performance of political/economic systems entails analysis of all the same issues, including the imperfect nature of enforcement. Formal economic rules are made by polities, and therefore we must be able to model polities as a first requirement. Ever since James Madison's insightful comments in Federalist 10 we have been aware of the fundamental dilemma of polities. If a polity is strong enough to enforce the rules of the game, it is strong enough to be employed by special interests to pursue their own objectives at the expense of the society as a whole. Creating a polity that is strong but "limited" is an essential condition. In the economy, it is competition that turns the interests of the individual producer into a social "good." But what kind of competition? It must be competition that gets the players to compete via price and quality rather than at some other margin like killing one's competitor (as a Russian banker cheerfully confided to me he had done in the 1990s) or some other socially undesirable behavior. Norms of behavior may constrain the players, but where do they come from and how strong are they? Indeed the last sentence gets to a fundamental issue. Where do the beliefs, norms, and institutions come from? Economics is a theory of choice, but what is the source of choices? This may be easy to answer when one goes to the supermarket, but it is vastly more complicated when one tries to account for the institutions in various societies. The incentive system implicit in neoclassical theory is dependent on a specific belief system. Widely different belief systems throughout history and in the present day produce different incentive systems and accordingly different choices when confronting the same source of uncertainty. It should not be necessary to belabor this point in the aftermath of the terrorist attacks of September 11, 2001. We have a way to go in cognitive science before we have a sufficient understanding of the operation of the mind and brain to provide definitive answers to the issues of consciousness that can produce on the one hand a Mozart or Einstein and on the other hand a Savonarola or Hitler. But such understanding is crucial to our survival in a world that can produce weapons that can destroy whole societies. The crucial issue to be confronted is not just the individual's belief but the existence of belief systems that will provide widespread support for violence and terrorism.

The institutions essential to a dynamic capitalism must create a polity that will in turn put in place and maintain economic rules of the game that will provide the incentive structure for continuous innovation, including a competitive structure to get the players to compete at socially productive margins. It requires a belief system that will provide the necessary incentives. More than that, with changes in technology, information costs, and relative prices, the essential political and economic entrepreneurs must adjust the institutions to continue to provide the appropriate incentives in the face of such alterations. An additional dilemma is that we are evolving political/economic/social structures that are radically different from and more complex than any in our past, and therefore the evolving human environment has no historical precedent from which to derive theoretical inspiration. The degree to which the decision makers understand the changes in this novel environment and act accordingly is problematic. And even if they do have an understanding, they may find that the necessary changes threaten their survival, as the self-destruction of the Soviet Union bears witness. The relative success of the United States and other developed economies has entailed a flexible institutional structure that encourages the kind of trial-and-error structure argued by Hayek as an essential prerequisite for survival in a world of ubiquitous uncertainty. Such adaptively efficient structures have evolved over a long time and depend on the development of strong informal norms that will constrain the players in the face of the ubiquitous drive of economic and political actors to engage in rent seeking and eventually produce the stagnation and inefficient societies that Mancur Olson (1982) thought were inevitable without periodic revolutions.

We tend to "get it wrong" when the accumulated experiences and beliefs derived from the past do not provide a correct guide to future decision making. The reason is twofold. (1) The set of mental models, categories, and classifications of the neural networks that have evolved in our belief system through which the new evidence gets filtered has no existing pattern that can correctly assess the new evidence. (2) In cases where conflicting beliefs have evolved, the dominant organizations and their entrepreneurs may view the necessary changes as threats to their survival. To the degree that the entrepreneurs of such organizations control decision making, they can thwart the necessary changes. The first of these factors stems from our not correctly comprehending what is happening to us; the second stems from an inability to make the necessary institutional changes.

The shift from personal to impersonal exchange has produced just such a stumbling block both historically and in the contemporary world. Personal exchange relies on reciprocity, repeat dealings, and the kind of informal norms that tend to evolve from strong relationships of reciprocity. Impersonal exchange requires the development of economic and political institutions that alter the payoffs in exchange to reward cooperative behavior even when the other party is a complete stranger. The creation of the necessary institutions requires a fundamental alteration in the structure of the economy and the polity that is frequently not in the feasible set given the historically derived beliefs and institutions of the players. The unique development of the Western world from the relative backwardness in the tenth century to world hegemony by the nineteenth century gives us a glimpse of the kind of long-run historical evolution that made such change possible. But we do not know how to create those conditions in the short run.

Necessary Economic Institutions

We can explore those conditions by examining the sources of the dramatic growth of transaction costs in the American economy over the past century, an increase that largely reflected the increasing complexity of the economy. Between 1870 and 1970 the transaction sector of the American economy increased from 25 percent to 45 percent of GNP, reflecting the dramatic alteration of an economy shifting focus from the uncertainties associated with the physical environment to the increasingly complex human environment (see Wallis and North 1986). The most dramatic part of the increase reflected growing specialization and division of labor with the growing size of the market. Multiplying the number of exchanges with growing specialization entailed an overall increase in transacting. The increase in transaction costs arose as a result of the costs of

1. measuring the multiple valuable dimensions of a good or service;
2. the protection of individual property rights;
3. the enforcement of agreements;
4. the integration of the dispersed knowledge of the society.

Let me elaborate on each:

1. Goods and services typically have multiple dimensions that have utility to the individual. To the degree that these individual dimensions can be measured,

we can define property rights more precisely and thereby increase the utility to the individual and reduce the overall costs of exchange.

2. The development of effective third-party enforcement with all that it entails in terms of institutions and organizations is always supplemented by resources the individual devotes to protecting his or her property.

3. Enforcement of agreements involves the cost of monitoring and metering exchanges to see that the terms of exchange are being lived up to and developing effective punishment for violations.

4. The greater the specialization and division of labor in a society, the more dispersed is knowledge in the society and the more resources must be devoted to integrating that dispersed knowledge.

Improving economic performance means lowering production and transaction costs, and the key is modifying institutions to accomplish this objective. This includes the development of a uniform system of weights and measures (and technological research to achieve better measurement), the creation of an effective judicial system and enforcement mechanisms, and the development of institutions and organizations to integrate the dispersed knowledge in a society as well as to monitor and meter agreements and adjudicate disputes. The overall consequence is a dramatic increase in the overall costs of transacting that is much more than offset by dramatic decreases in production costs.[3]

Conditions That Produced the Free-Market Innovation Machine

Baumol's description of the free-market innovation machine poses a distinct challenge. Just what kind of an institutional structure will support such a machine? He provides a number of clues, including a thoughtful discussion of productive activity in the thirteenth to fifteenth centuries, the trading of property rights to constituents for income, which was the initial source of representative government, and other factors leading to the rule of law (2002, chap. 5). Indeed he asserts in discussing the critical role of the entrepreneur, "How entrepreneurs act at a given time and place depends heavily on the prevailing 'rules of the game'—ie the reward structure in the economy" (61). His chapter on the historical evidence (chap. 14) tells a story full of "implicit" institutions in which it would appear that they are dependent variables in the story and therefore not worth independent attention. But such free-market institutions do not evolve automatically, as Baumol himself implies in the following passage: "The historical episodes that will be reviewed also underscore a critical point. The availability of human capital may be necessary but is surely not sufficient by itself to insure a firm connection between invention and economic growth. This requires, in addition, a set of powerful incentives, such as the free market provides to insure a continuous flow of inventions and their transformation through the innovation stage into a direct contribution to productivity and output growth" (246). And that is exactly what institutions are—incentives. Let me see if we can be more specific. Just what incentive structure will produce the dynamic features of Baumol's model?

Beyond the rule of law which he does specify (Baumol 2002, 68), "Capitalism requires markets in which the participants can have confidence in any agreement arrived at" (69). Such confidence comes from enforcement mechanisms that at low cost of transacting will assure that agreements are met. But personalized exchange runs counter to such a structure. One has only to witness the legal system in most Latin American countries to be acutely aware of this dilemma. It is not just that it is not a "level playing field" for all participants, but also that altering the judicial actors at the whim of political actors is a recurring phenomenon, as the history of Argentina (to take but one of many examples) abundantly illustrates (see, e.g., Alston 2003).

But beyond a set of property rights and enforcement mechanisms, much more is required to provide the essential underpinnings of Baumol's "machine." Baumol lists them as follows:

1. "Oligopolistic competition among large high-tech business firms with innovation as a prime competitive weapon ensuring continued innovative activity and, very plausibly, their growth."
2. "Routinization of these innovative activities, making them a regular and even ordinary component of the activities of the firm and thereby minimizing the uncertainty of the process."
3. "Productive entrepreneurship encouraged by incentives for entrepreneurs to devote themselves to productive innovation rather than to innovative rent seeking."
4. "The rule of law."
5. "Technology selling and trading, in other words, firms' voluntary pursuit of opportunities for profitable dissemination of innovations and rental of the right to use them, via licensing, even to direct competitors." (2002, 4, 5)

Moreover, a persistent oligopolistic structure in which the kind of collusion that Baumol considers essential is only possible with a particular antitrust policy, as he states (114–15). Both productive entrepreneurship, which must be encouraged by incentives, and the rule of law are essential requirements. But the truly innovative part of Baumol's argument stems from his disenchantment with the traditional building blocks of neoclassical theory. After acknowledging Solow's pioneering argument, he explores the subsequent development of the "new growth economics" and finds that literature not completely satisfactory. "The central point is that each of these models employs a production function that contains a growth component, but that none of them has any attribute uniquely related to free-enterprise economies rather than some other economic form. That is what makes these models ahistorical. Moreover, when they do take account of innovation, the mechanisms of the activity enter only implicitly. There is no equation or other relationship that attempts to describe, for example, the incentive structure that leads to determination of the magnitude of this activity" (2002, 265).

We are some distance from understanding the complex structure that underlies the Baumol engine of progress. David Mowery and Nathan Rosenberg in *Paths of Innovation* describe the changes as follows: "Changes in the structure of the U.S. intellectual property system in the early 20th century, as well as the treatment of intellectual property by the judiciary, thus enhanced firms' incentives to both internalize industrial research and to invest in the acquisition of technologies from external sources. Against the backdrop of tougher federal enforcement of antitrust statutes, judicial decisions affirming the use of patents to create or maintain positions of market power also created additional incentives to pursue in-house R&D. Stronger, more consistent intellectual property rights also improved the operation of a market for intellectual property, making it easier for firms to use their in-house research facilities to acquire technology" (1998, 19–20).

But there is more to the story than a changing judiciary and antitrust policy. The integration of the dispersed knowledge of the complex human environment that we have created takes more than a "well oiled" price system to produce the desired results. Integrating the dispersed knowledge requires a much more complex structure. Paul David describes the issues: "Nor has economics yet had much to say about what types of contractual arrangements, institutional forms, and organizational policies have proved to be especially conducive (or inimical) to the process of "knowledge transfer." "Until very recently most economists studying the inside of the 'black box' of private sector R&D have not thought it important to understand the variety of mechanisms responsible for the 'spillovers' that theoretical analysis holds would result in industrial innovators reaping private benefits from the work of publicly supported academic and governmental research organizations" (David 1991, 68). Indeed Baumol's argument would be strengthened by devoting specific attention to the necessary growth of transaction costs that must accompany and permit the innovation machine to operate.

Conclusion

Baumol is right on track when he criticizes the new growth economics for being ahistorical. Indeed his account is an enormous improvement over the purely theoretical, noninstitutional, nonhistorical accounts that pervade the growth literature.[4] The key to this overall explanation for the "innovation machine" is an incremental account through time of the evolution of the essential institutional/organizational complex that has produced these results in particular settings. This must be an analytical narrative through time that begins, in the case of American economic history, with the transfer of beliefs and institutions into colonial America and follows their development in the context of the resource-rich environment of the New World and the institutional changes that resulted from the turbulent social upheaval in the nineteenth century. It would include the growth of higher educational investment with the enactment of the Morrill Act of 1862 and the subsequent expansion of the competitive structure of universities in the United States (in contrast to Europe) that eventually led to their preeminent position in supporting and integrating knowledge and specifically providing the context for the innovations of the twentieth century (see Rosenberg 2000). It would of necessity integrate the story with the development of antitrust legislation and its evolution—and beyond that, integrate it with the rich historical context of twentieth-century political and economic events. For Europe and Japan and other developed economies, each would be a particular historical narrative but with common denominators of the essential institutions that underlie the innovation machine.[5] It is only thus that we can do justice to explaining Baumol's innovation machine. If economic history is to fulfill its promise of adding the dimension of time to economic (and political) analysis, the analytical historical narrative is the proper vehicle. A beginning has already been made with the works of Nathan Rosenberg and Paul David already cited. Joel Mokyr's *The Gifts of Athena* (2002), with its emphasis on the historical origins of the knowledge economy, is a further contribution. But we have a ways to go before we can properly provide the dimension of time to economic analysis, a necessary development if we are to enrich our understanding of economic performance.

Notes

1. There is a rich treasure trove of experimental research currently being undertaken to give us a better understanding of human behavior. An up-to-date summary can be found in McCabe 2003.

2. See the studies by Milgrom, North, and Weingast (1990), North and Weingast (1989), and Greif (1994) for description of the institutional changes that were an essential part of this transformation.

3. It is important to emphasize that not all transaction costs have been associated with productivity increases even in the past century of dramatic growth. Institutional changes that have gone in the other direction, such as the long-run consequences of the creation of the Interstate Commerce Commission for railroad productivity, are also a part of the story.

4. See, for example, the symposium on "new growth theory" in the *Journal of Economic Perspectives*, winter 1994.

5. It is important to stress that the key is to create the necessary incentive structure, not to slavishly imitate the institutions of the developed countries. China's accelerated development from the household responsibility system to the TVEs (town-village enterprises) and so on has created the essential incentive system with unique specific institutions.

References

Alston, L. 2003. "The Erosion of Rule of Law in Argentina, 1930–1947: An Explanation of Argentina's Economic Slide from the Top 10." Working paper, University of Illinois.

Barzel, Yoram. 1997. *Economic Analysis of Property Rights*. 2nd ed. Cambridge: Cambridge University Press.

Baumol, William. 2002. *The Free-Market Innovation Machine*. Princeton: Princeton University Press.

David, P. 1991. "Positive Feedback and Research Productivity in Science: Reopening Another Black Box." In *Economics of Technology*, ed. O. Grandstrand. Amsterdam: Elsevier Science.

Donald, Merlin. 1991. *The Origins of the Modern Mind*. Cambridge: Harvard University Press.

Greif, Avner. 1994. "On the Political Foundations of the Late Medieval Commercial Revolution: Genoa during the Twelfth and Thirteenth Centuries." *Journal of Economic History* 54: 271–87.

Hutchins, Edwin. 1995. *Cognition in the Wild*. Cambridge: MIT Press.

McCabe, Kevin. 2003. "Reciprocity and Social Order: What Do Experiments Tell Us about the Failure of Economic Growth." Working paper, Experimental Economics Laboratory, George Mason University.

Milgrom, Paul, Douglass C. North, and Barry R. Weingast. 1990. "The Role of Institutions in the Revival of Trade: The Law Merchant, Private Judges, and the Champagne Fairs." *Economics and Politics* 2 (1): 1–23.

Mokyr, Joel. 2002. *The Gifts of Athena*. Princeton: Princeton University Press.

Mowery, David C., and Nathan Rosenberg. 1998. *Paths of Innovation: Technological Change in 20th Century America*. Cambridge: Cambridge University Press.

North, Douglass C., and Barry R. Weingast. 1989. "Constitutions and Commitment: The Evolution of Institutions Governing Public Choice in Seventeenth Century England." *Journal of Economic History* 49: 803–32.

O'Driscoll, Gerald P., Jr., Kim R. Holmes, and Melanie Kirkpatrick. 2001. *2001 Index of Economic Freedom*. Washington, D.C.: Heritage Foundation and Dow Jones & Company, Inc.

Olson, Mancur. 1982. *The Rise and Decline of Nations*. New Haven: Yale University Press.

Rosenberg, Nathan. 2000. "American Universities as Endogenous Institutions." In *Schumpeter and the Endogeneity of Technology*. London: Routledge.

Wallis, J., and D. North. 1986. "Measuring the Transaction Sector in the American Economy, 1870 to 1970." In *Long Term Factors in American Economic Growth*, ed. S. Engerman and R. Gallman. Chicago: University of Chicago Press.

Chapter 4

Capitalism and Economic Liberty: The Political Foundations of Economic Growth

BARRY R. WEINGAST

1. Introduction

Adam Smith is the patron saint of economics. Ever since his *Wealth of Nations*, economists have emphasized markets as the source of economic success. Economists today emphasize the creation of markets as the central problem of development, encapsulated in the oft-used phrase, "Get prices right": developing countries should create the conditions for the market's hidden hand to work its magic, just as it has in the developed world. As Baumol (2002) shows, free markets are the engine of growth. In the economists' approach, the role of the government is to provide a set of market-enhancing public goods, such as defined property rights, enforceable contracts, a stable macroeconomy, and an appropriate distribution of income. According to this view, the principal problem with markets in developing countries is inefficient "government intervention" that creates monopolies, market restrictions, and inefficiency. The policy implication of this view focuses on creating markets, which requires both dismantling political controls on markets and establishing new laws creating new markets.

The patron saints of the new political economy of development are Thomas Hobbes, John Locke, and James Madison, whose classics, *Leviathan*, *The Second Treatise on Government*, and *The Federalist Papers*, emphasize the central importance of politics in economic success and failure. Politics is not only about providing market-enhancing public goods, but also about using the coercive power of government to take from some and give to others. In this world, politics is at the center of the problem of economic development. As Locke emphasized, the protection of property and hence the development of a robust economy arises only with the control of arbitrary government. The policy implication, according to Locke and Madison, is to create a set of political institutions that constrain politics so that it serves the interests of citizens—in their case, protecting property and creating a political environment that fostered markets. Indeed, I present below a short catalog of governmental opportunism and expropriation simply inconsistent with market development.

The thesis of this essay is that the problem of economic development requires building on both ideas. In particular, the political system must be properly constructed so that it is capable of sustaining a thriving market economy rather than preying on it.

To put these two disparate perspectives together, consider the *fundamental political dilemma of the economy* (Weingast 1995). The economists' prescription is for the government to define and protect property rights, enforce contracts, create a stable macro environment and provide for the appropriate distribution of income. The fundamental political dilemma observes that any government capable of these tasks is also capable of confiscating the wealth of all its citizens. The principal question then becomes, why do some governments do one and not the other?

Creating markets and capitalism is a necessary part of economic development. When a market-fostering government creates the appropriate institutional basis for markets, then capitalism can indeed be the engine of growth. But fostering growth requires that the condition of this statement also be met—that the government be market-fostering rather than market-preying. Economists have developed a rich theory about how to create markets, and the Washington consensus rightly rests on this.

Unfortunately for developing countries, the Washington consensus is not enough. Attempting to get prices right without simultaneously reforming politics has a fatal flaw: The economy remains vulnerable to arbitrary respecifications of rights and simple expropriation.

The purpose of this chapter is to discuss the role of politics and political institutions in creating the conditions for government to be market-enhancing rather than market-predating—or, to use Shleifer and Vishny's (1998) phrase, to foster the invisible hand rather than the grabbing hand. Economists have the second half of the puzzle correct—the need to create markets. The first part of the puzzle, however, is that the appropriate political institutions must be created that provide incentives for political officials to foster and preserve markets.

The central idea, then, is to create limited government, often discussed in the late seventeenth and eighteenth centuries as the problem of creating liberty.[1] To see how markets are lodged in a political framework capable of sustaining them, I present two problems facing constitutions and two principles suggesting how they are solved. The first problem is called the rationality of fear and suggests that when people feel what they hold most dear is threatened by the state, they are willing to support extra-constitutional action. This implies that all successful constitutions must short-circuit this process. The second problem is the fundamental citizen coordination problem, which rests on the observation that when citizens react in concert to a potential governmental transgression of their rights, they threaten the government's future. This threat, in turn, provides the government with the incentive to honor rather than transgress citizens' rights. Of course, the whole question then concerns how this coordination problem is solved. I argue that there are no natural solutions to this coordination problem, so that the most natural outcome is coordination failure. Successful constitutions must solve this problem by constructing focal solutions that help citizen coordinate and hence to police the government.

I apply this framework to the evolution of liberty in the modern world, first looking at seventeenth-century England and then the early United States. I also discuss the foundations of liberty in modern China. Finally, I show how the failure of these principles helps explain authoritarian regimes, examining the case of modern Mexico.

This chapter proceeds as follows. The next section presents a short and familiar catalog of governmental opportunism and abuse of economic liberty. The third section presents a theory of the polity, emphasizing two problems and two principles of constitutionalism. Sections 4 through 7 then apply the perspective to seventeenth-century England, the early United States, modern China, and modern Mexico respectively. My conclusions follow.

2. A Short Catalog of Abuses of Liberty and Their Economic Effects in Developing Countries

Locke, Hobbes, and Madison all studied the problem of "arbitrary" government, by which they meant governmental opportunism and expropriation. Montesquieu called such abuses a *grand coups d'autorité*. They were quite common in early modern Europe, though less so now in contemporary America. And yet, such behavior, most recently emphasized in Shleifer and Vishny (1998) as "the grabbing hand," remains prevalent in the developing world.

The problem with the possibility of expropriation is that the attending political risk is not only an additional cost of economic activity, but creates an insidious selection effect: the more successful a business, the more likely is expropriation. This obviously discourages investment. Indeed, a country cannot develop a thriving economy based on this weak political foundation. So developing countries have two sources of plagues: inefficient market intervention and expropriation.

Consider a short list of such behavior from the developing and socialist economies: Mass subscription bonds helped the Soviet Union finance industrialization in the 1930s and World War II. In the late Stalinist period, such subscriptions were used to finance deficits. When bond sales were terminated in 1957, interest and redemption were postponed 20 years. At the time, the average household held six to seven thousand rubles in bonds, approximately one-half its annual income (Holzman 1957, 476; see also Millar 1990, 115–18, 127), a significant expropriation of savings.

After independence, a great many of the sub-Saharan Africa nations raised taxes to extract the maximum revenue possible. Many of these countries have a comparative advantage in produce from trees: coffee, jute, palm oil, cocoa. As Bates (1981) shows, country after country forced farmers to sell their products to monopsonistic marketing boards at prices approximately one-third the world price. These tax rates were sufficiently high that farmers stopped tending the trees, letting them die, and planting corn, which could be consumed or sold on the black market without taxes. The net effect, of course, was a significant national decapitalization.

Kings in early modern Europe regularly sold monopolies, sometimes out from under existing businesses.

Examples in Latin America abound. For example, in the early 1980s, Mexico allowed Americans to open dollar-denominated bank accounts (apparently in part to evade paying American income tax on the income). In 1982, the government forced the American depositors to accept a "haircut" when it announced it would no longer allow these accounts and forced the conversion of dollars into pesos at the official rate of 35 pesos to one dollar, less than half the market rate of 75 pesos to the dollar. In September of that year, the government nationalized all the banks, expropriating nearly all their value from their owners.

Mexico also expropriated foreign oil companies in 1938, as did Venezuela over a period of years in the 1950s through 1960s.

In India and many states in sub-Saharan Africa, opening a new business requires so many permits, licenses, and permissions of various officials and offices that the bribes required to obtain them seem designed to extract the expected profits of any investment.

The Problem to Be Solved

This type of governmental opportunism represents the problem that must be solved. Thriving markets require that government act to provide market-enhancing public goods rather than to prey on markets.

3. The Political Institutions and Economic Liberty

In this section, I provide some insights into the nature of the constitution necessary to help embed a market within a political system that can sustain it.[2] This outline sketches the beginnings of a theory that remains incomplete and will thus be in many ways unsatisfactory.

In what follows, I define two problems faced by all constitutions, and two principles about how these problems are solved or mitigated. Most solutions to problems of political reform involve democracy. However, representative democracy is not a single system but a category of systems whose political and economic performance differs significantly. A nation can embed democracy within its constitution in different ways.

The benefits of democracy are so obvious that many people often ignore its costs. Indeed, democracy often involves significant risks. Elections empower winners to impose taxes, regulate business, take property, and jail people. These are all powers that can be abused, and even if not abused, can impose enormous harms.

This brings us to the first problem, which I call the "rationality of fear" (de Figueiredo and Weingast 1999; Weingast 2006). Consider something that a group of citizens holds dear—perhaps their assets or the freedom to practice their own religion. Call the value they put on these assets or practices the "stakes." Suppose that there is a risk that the government will threaten this asset or practice, say with probability p. The rationality of fear holds that for a given set of stakes, there exists a threshold probability, p^*, such that if $p > p^*$, the citizens are willing to support extra-constitutional action to protect themselves. The model holds that, the larger the stakes, the lower is p^*. Further, the model shows that for very high stakes, p^* can be quite small, much closer to 0 than to 1 (de Figueiredo and Weingast 1999).

This model has a wide range of applications. In 1973 in Chile, when landowners felt threatened by the socialist regime under President Salvador Allende, they supported a bloody coup to remove Allende and bring on a dictatorship more favorable to their interests. A variant on this scenario occurred during the Second Republic in Spain in 1936, when the incumbent Socialist regime threatened traditional pillars of Spanish society who supported Generalissimo Franco in the Civil War. Similarly, many southern slaveholders in the United States felt threatened by the election of President Abraham Lincoln and believed that they could not remain in the country, resulting in secession followed by Civil War.

The solution to this problem combines two principles. The first principle is the notion that all successful constitutions lower the stakes of politics. The reason builds on the rationality-of-fear problem. If citizens provide support for extra-constitutional action when what they hold dear is threatened, then constitutions that protect what they hold dear make them less likely to support extra-constitutional action. Put another way, this argument suggests a selection effect: those constitutions that protect what citizens hold dear are more likely to survive.

The mechanisms by which constitutions do this are twofold. First, they typically impose a range of familiar restrictions on governmental decision-making, such as the horizontal separation of powers; the vertical separation of powers, that is, federalism, with significant powers reserved for subnational governments; and a set of citizens rights that the government must abide by.

Second, the constitution must provide a mechanism by which these provisions are enforced. I argue that this involves the solution to a fundamental political coordination problem, to which I now turn.

One of the fundamental principles of policing a government is coordination.[3] To remain in office, political officials need sufficient support from their citizens, as the generals running Argentina learned in 1983 when they were forced to give up power.[4]

The requirement for sufficient political support, in turn, provides the foundation for the incentive system faced by officials. When citizens react in concert to violations of their rights by withdrawing their support, they threaten the future of government officials. This threat, in turn, provides leaders with an incentive to honor citizens' rights.

The conditional in this last statement, however, is central to understanding this aspect of liberty—the government honoring citizen rights. What determines when citizens have the ability to coordinate? I argue that this is one of the fundamental problems of liberty and, further, that citizens have no natural way of coordinating. The reason is that their situations, positions in the economy, and perspectives differ sufficiently that there is no natural focal solution to this coordination problem. Because there are too many different ways to specify rights, there are too many different ways to coordinate. Moreover, because different ways of specifying rights have significant distributional consequences, citizens are not likely to devise a means of coordinating on their rights.

This implies that the natural solution to this coordination problem is coordination failure: the government retains the support of some subset of citizens, respects their rights, but transgresses the rights of other citizens. A ruler will honor supporters' rights because they hold a credible threat to depose the ruler by withdrawing their support. This is the traditional "divide and conquer" strategy for maintaining power. Most governments that exist now and that have existed in the past are of this form.

Solving this coordination problem requires the construction of a focal solution, typically through a pact, which is an agreement among contending elites who compromise over the form of the political rules and citizens' rights.[5] Pacts are replete in the history of most countries with democracy. For Great Britain, the various problems of liberty in the seventeenth century were resolved in a pact during the Glorious Revolution of 1689; Magna Carta was another such pact. For the United States, the Articles of Confederation and the Constitution were major pacts, as were the various nineteenth-century compromises of 1820, 1833, 1850, and 1877. Many of the southern European democratizations in the mid–twentieth century (e.g., Greece and Spain) were brought in by pacts, as were many of the democratizations in Latin America (e.g., Colombia in the mid-1950s, El Salvador in the early 1990s).

The importance of pacts is that they create focal solutions to the citizens' coordination problem by distinguishing a particular way of coordinating around a specific set of procedures by which governments may act and around a set of citizen rights. Although the literature has long emphasized the importance of pacts, it fails to explain why some pacts work and others fail. The answer is that some pacts are self-enforcing (Weingast 1997, 2006).

To be self-enforcing, a pact must meet four conditions (Weingast 2006):

- First, as just noted, it must create structure-and-process focal solutions to the problem of governance and citizen rights.
- Second, it must make all parties to the pact better off.
- Third, it must create a simultaneous move by all parties to the pact.
- Fourth, each party to the pact must be willing to punish violations of the pact.

Each of these conditions is necessary for a pact to work. The structure and process is necessary to construct the focal solution to the citizens coordination problem. This refers to the processes of governmental decisionmaking and the rights of citizens. But why, per the fourth condition, would citizens defend a pact, especially if a potential violation would benefit them? The answer is given by the second condition. If all parties are better off under the pact, then a short-run violation may produce short-run benefits, but it also destroys the pact. And if all parties are better off under the pact, then violations make them worse off in the long run.

Consider the example of an independent judiciary. In 1937, at the height of popularity for President Franklin Roosevelt's New Deal—including the Constitution's specified requirements of two-thirds majorities in the Congress and three-quarters of the state legislatures—Roosevelt sought to break the power of the Supreme Court, which had declared critical features of the New Deal unconstitutional. This involved his famous "Court-packing plan," which sought to expand the Supreme Court, allowing

Roosevelt to create a pliant majority. Of course, this precedent would have also destroyed the independent nature of the Supreme Court.

Although the New Deal was immensely popular, at no time during consideration of the Court-packing plan did a majority support it.[6] In other words, sufficient numbers of New Deal supporters, despite potential benefits from extending the New Deal, opposed packing the Court as a means of achieving this goal.

This behavior contrasts with behavior of presidents in a range of countries around the world, including Latin America and Africa. For example, after being elected president in 1989, Carlos Menem sought to pack the Argentine Supreme Court, and met with little resistance (see Chavez 2004).

One additional aspect of democratic constitutions facilitates citizens' coordination and hence citizen policing of governmental respect for citizen rights. An important advantage of democracy is that it grants citizens a regular means of reacting to violations of their rights by the government: elections allow them to "throw the rascals out" by voting for the opposition. This not only gives the opposition the incentive to be ever vigilant of citizen rights, as Madison noted in the Federalist Papers, but it forces incumbents to decide whether to honor the election results or to set them aside. By virtue of this choice, they send a simultaneous, unambiguous, and common-knowledge signal to all citizens about whether they will honor the constitutional rules of election results (Fearon 2000). This focus makes it far easier for citizens to coordinate against the government, for though they may disagree about the efficacy of public policy and expanding powers of the government, most citizens agree that setting aside elections is a problem, to be supported only in desperate times.

Economic Implications of Limited Government

The two principles studied in this section have important implications for maintaining an economy. A thriving economy requires that asset holders, businesses, and consumers all believe that their rights are free from the arbitrary abuse of power by the government. The short catalog of arbitrary power in the previous section demonstrates that developing countries have failed to solve this problem. The struggles in the developed West indicate that these problems are not easy to solve.

The two principles discussed here provide insights into how nations do solve them. In the following sections, I study how these issues have been resolved to varying degrees in early modern Britain, the early United States, and modern China, and have failed to be resolved in a developing country like Mexico.

4. Emergence of Limited Government in Seventeenth-Century England

The bitter political struggles during seventeenth-century England led to a bloody Civil War at midcentury and the Glorious Revolution in 1689. The revolution put an end to many of the controversies and set the stage for two centuries of economic growth, including the Industrial Revolution and the rise of Great Britain to the status of dominant power in the world (North and Weingast 1989).

The struggles during this century, including their resolution in the Glorious Revolution, follow the principles developed above. For most of the century, the English were deeply divided over politics, economics, and religion. The agrarian constituency supported the Crown throughout much of the century, including the Civil War. The commercial constituency opposed the Crown.

The fiscal system, inherited from the Middle Ages, proved inadequate for the exigencies of the modern world. Put simply, the English Crown had too little fiscal resources to cover a growing range of expenses. To make ends meet following the expense of defeating the Spanish, Elizabeth I sold off 25 percent of the Crown lands, the principal source of state revenue. In the four decades following her death in 1603, the Stuart kings sold off the remaining lands. An inadequate fiscal system forced the Crown to look for additional sources of revenue, in turn leading to arbitrary use of power.

The dilemma of the seventeenth century was how to solve this problem: many landholders and commercial constituents believed that granting the center fiscal independence without greater constraints would allow too much mischief, so they were reluctant to agree to such a bargain. Similarly, throughout this century, the Stuart kings refused to accept bounds on their behavior as the price of greater fiscal resources. The result was something of a standoff, leading to considerable problems, as the Civil War demonstrates.

Citizens of the political nation were deeply divided on foundational matters, such as the rights of citizens. For example, those who became the Tories believed in the divine right of kings. Although kings could harm their citizens, citizens nonetheless had a duty to obey. Sir Robert Filmer's famous *Patriarcha* exemplifies this tradition.

In opposition to this group stood those who by century's end became known as the Whigs. Whigs were Lockean in their beliefs. Indeed, Locke was a Whig whose famous *Second Treatise on Government* was written as a revolutionary tract in the years prior to the Glorious Revolution, and published just after that event. Whigs believed that the Crown had a duty to honor citizen rights and that citizens had a corresponding duty to obey the Crown only so long as the Crown honored these rights. In the face of abuse of rights, Locke argued, citizens had a duty to react.

> It is an oversimplification to see the Whigs as the party of business and the Tories of seigneurial power. Some of the greatest aristocrats were resolute Whigs, and some of the keenest battles in the City of London were fought between rival groups of businessmen with Whig and Tory backing. But one can safely contrast emphasis on commerce as a point in the Whig profile, and emphasis on agriculture as a point in the Tory one. So, too, the Whigs tended to internationalism, to "Dutch finance" under William and "no peace without Spain" under Anne; while the Tory was inward-looking and protectionist. . . . The Whig favoured immigration, especially of refugee Protestants, the Tory deplored the admission of "useless and necessitous foreigners"; the Tory tended to peace, the Whig to war. (Carswell 1973, 40–41)

During the Stuart reign, Parliament was not a modern legislature with an everyday share in running the government. Indeed, the role of Parliament as a constraint on the Crown remained uncertain in important respects. Although additional taxes on land could only be granted by Parliament, the degree to which Parliament controlled other sources of taxation remained in doubt. For an extended period, the Stuarts sought to live without having to call Parliament. Whigs sought a greater role for Parliament, especially as a constraint on the Crown.

These political and ideological divisions implied a lack of consensus. By the principle of coordination above, this division implies that it was difficult to force the Crown to honor citizens' rights. The Crown protected the Tories, but abused the rights of the Whigs.

This setting might have been stable for a considerable time, were it not for two changes in the 1680s. First, Charles II died, replaced by his ambitious brother, James II, who sought to grab more power. This ambition led him to challenge his own supporters. Second, James II was openly Catholic, which offended a great many in the nation, including his own supporters.

In reaction to James II, many Tories joined the Whigs to create the Glorious Revolution. This revolution was first a coup, but not only so. It was also a critical constitutional revision through the form of a pact, negotiated among the contending parties in Parliament, passed as a law of Parliament, and signed by the new Crown, William and Mary.

The Glorious Revolution and the decade following abounded in constitutional changes. These revisions began with the Revolution Settlement. One of its principal components was the Bill of Rights, passed by Parliament in early 1689. It was composed of several parts, the first of which contained two lists. The first enumerated a set of violations of the rights of citizens by James II, and began:

> Whereas the late King James The Second, by the assistance of divers evil counsellors, judges, and ministers employed by him, did endeavour to subvert and extirpate the protestant religion, and the laws and liberties of this kingdom. (Quoted in Williams 1960, 26)

The list contained 12 items by which James had done so, including: "By assuming and exercising a power of dispensing with and suspending of laws, and the execution of laws, without consent of parliament"; levying money without parliamentary approval; "raising . . . a standing army within this kingdom in time of peace, without consent of parliament"; "By causing several good subjects, being protestants, to be disarmed, at the same time when papists were both armed and employed, contrary to law"; and "By violating the freedom of election of members to serve in parliament" (quoted in Williams 1960, 27). A second list, paralleling the first, provided for a set of limits on royal authority, making it clear that the powers abused by James II were beyond royal authority.

The significance of the Bill of Rights' enumerations lies in stating a set of relatively unambiguous principles defining boundaries on the Crown's behavior. Agreeing on these limits in advance and assuring that they became part of the constitution via the Bill of Rights provided an explicit mechanism for coordinating members of society. Although gray areas could never be fully eliminated, the Bill of Rights improved the ability of citizens to coordinate their judgments that a transgression had taken place and that a reaction was required. The fact that these limits were produced under time of relative consensus rather than by one group's forcing them on another made them credible as the focal point of national attention with respect to the king's future behavior. Thereafter, citizens could coordinate their reactions based on whether the Crown overstepped one of these boundaries, not on their separate, diverse judgments about whether one of the Crown's actions constituted a transgression. This narrowed considerably the ability of the Crown to exploit this diversity of opinion among the citizenry because it made the withdrawal of the minimal support the Crown enjoyed more likely. Put another way, the explicit agreement represented by the Bill of Rights improved the capacity of the community to penalize certain actions by the Crown, in turn making them less likely. Violating constitutional enumerations would come at the Crown's own peril.

In addition to an attempt to clarify and produce consensus about the limits on royal authority, parliamentarians initiated a series of institutional changes designed to promote their goals. The first and foremost concerned the Parliament itself. The Glorious Revolution ushered in the era of the

"King in Parliament." No longer would the Crown demand obedience by appealing to the divine right of kings. The new prescription was implemented in a series of steps that were designed to make Parliament a full participant in the decision making and management of the government.

When designing the new institutions in 1689, Parliament sought to prevent the Crown from living on its own by granting it much less revenue, thus requiring the Crown to appear regularly before Parliament in order to ensure adequate funds. This system attempted to foster cooperation between Crown and Parliament and to forestall attempts by the former to "end-run" the latter. Moreover, to make the principle explicit, these institutions proscribed any attempt by the Crown to rule without Parliament by calling for frequent elections.[7]

One of the beneficial effects of the new arrangements resulted from the creation of multiple "veto" centers over policy (Ekelund and Tollison 1981; North and Weingast 1989). Policy required approval not only of the Crown, but of Parliament. Because each had its own interests and constituents, the three veto centers, Crown, Lords, and Commons, had different preferences over policies. Several consequences followed. First, any attempt to change the status quo had to gain the support of a larger segment of society than before. Second, those represented in Parliament could more readily block undesirable policy initiatives of the Crown.

In relatively short order, this system evolved into one in which Parliament gained considerable power over the policies of the government. In money matters, the Crown had the power to propose and Parliament the right to accept or reject (Campion 1958; Reid 1966).

The success of the pact satisfies the four conditions noted above. First, it created new procedures and rights for governmental decision-making, especially the role of the Crown in Parliament. Second, it made nearly everyone party to the pact better off. Third, it was a simultaneous move to the new system. And fourth, all parties had incentives to defend the pact, since failing to do would destroy it and, by condition 2, make them worse off.

The main implication of this analysis is that the struggle to create a modern government required not only the creation of a government with more powers—the power to run a modern state and advance that state's interest in a hostile world—but also the creation of political and economic liberty that constrained the powers of the Crown.

As evidence in favor of the enormous change brought by this revolution, North and I show the striking change in government debt (North and Weingast 1989, drawing on Dickson 1967). Prior to the revolution, the English Crown could hardly raise £50,000 in the London market, and total government debt was on the order of £2 million, or about 5 percent of estimated GDP. The reason for this credit constraint was simple—too little constrained the Crown to repay its debt, and frequently in this century, it chose not to do so.

The new institution granted the government the ability to make credible commitments, including to debtors. As a consequence, debt was far more secure and thus available. In the eight years following the Glorious Revolution, debt rose to £16.7 million or about 40 percent of GDP (in pursuit of a war with France). Consistent with my argument in this section, the financial evidence suggests a remarkable change in reliability of the Crown.

5. The Political Foundations of Liberty and the Economy in Post-independence United States

The United States emerged from the Revolutionary War as a confederation of sovereign states. The constitution, the Articles of Confederation, deliberately kept the national government weak, for example, lacking its own authority to levy taxes to pay for those public goods it was charged with providing. The Articles were an unstable political equilibrium in the sense they could not last for any length of time.

In modern language, the Articles of Confederation created a series of common-pool problems for the states, causing the failure to provide a range of critical national public goods. Three public-goods failures were critical—the inability to provide for national security, a common market, and a common stable currency (Kaplanoff 1991; Middlekauff 1982). In each case, common-pool incentives led states to behave in ways deleterious to the nation. For defense, several states simply failed to honor their tax requisitions and pay their fair share. Several states erected trade barriers, plaguing the common market, and others exported their costs of budget deficits through inflating their currencies.

To the Federalists, the remedy was obvious: strengthen the national government (Kaplanoff 1991; Morgan 1977, chap. 9). The Anti-Federalists blocked these attempts (Middlekauff 1982, chap. 23), not because they denied the problems but because they feared the solutions (Rakove 1996, chap. 6). Granting the national government more power would in principle grant it the means to solve these problems. But more power also granted that government the potential ability to destroy citizens' liberty in the same way that the British had. The Federalists advanced this type of proposal on three occasions, failing each time.

In terms of the model above, the Anti-Federalists had a point: they argued that the new powers would not be self-enforcing in the sense that political officials would have incentives solely to use them in the manner prescribed by the Federalists.

The genius of the Federalists at Philadelphia was to devise a new pact toward solving the problems under the Articles: embed the appropriate range of new powers in a system of constraints that would limit the ability of the national government to abuse its authority.

First, the new Constitution created a set of new procedures for making public decisions, including the separation-of-powers system that sought to check "ambition with ambition" by creating multiple veto points (Madison, Federalist 46). This system turned out to be highly constraining for the new nation. For example, consider the commerce powers, perhaps the most important clause underpinning national economic intervention in the modern era. Despite being granted this power, the federal government failed to use it in a major way for 100 years, in part because of the set of mutual vetoes inherent in the separation-of-powers system.

Second, the national government created a strong system of federalism, granting only enumerated powers to the national government and reserving residual authority for the states. The new powers explicitly focused on the national public goods underprovided by the Articles. Federalism greatly limited the stakes of national powers by reserving for the states important powers over which the nation was deeply divided, such as slavery. Importantly, nearly all issues of property rights and business regulation were reserved for the states.

Third, in combination with the Bill of Rights, the Constitution created a series of substantive rights that the national government was prescribed to observe, including the takings clause requiring just compensation for the taking of property and the contract clause prohibiting the national government from abrogating private contracts.

But what made these rules self-enforcing? Here, too, the above theory helps us understand the nature of the national consensus that emerged to support the rules. As Rakove (1996) and Wood (1992) observe, it is wrong to think that this consensus was in place at the time of ratification. The reason is that many Federalists sought to expand the powers of the federal government beyond those enumerated. Confirming fears articulated by the Anti-Federalists during ratification, Alexander Hamilton sought to use the Constitution's necessary and proper clause (granting the national government all powers necessary to pursuing its delegated powers) to expand national power. Moreover, the Federalists sought to deal with growing opposition through the Alien and Sedition Acts (1798), allowing them among other things to jail opposition newspaper editors. The situation was sufficiently desperate that both Madison and Jefferson thought the Constitution had failed. In their Kentucky and Virginia Resolutions, they urged states to take the authority to interpret the Constitution to themselves, including what national laws were in fact constitutional. Had these measures been put into effect, the Constitution would have failed.

Yet the Constitution did not fail, in part because a sufficient number of Federalist voters agreed with Jefferson that the Federalists' use of powers was illegitimate, switching allegiance and booting out President John Adams in the election of 1800. This not only allowed Jefferson to become president, but created a new majority party in the nation.

Per the second principle noted above, the withdrawal of citizen support from the government is critical for maintaining the rules. Indeed, the Federalists considered setting aside the election if they lost in 1800, but decided against the attempt, in part because they didn't believe they would have the popular support to survive in power (see Freeman 2001; Sisson 1974). With Jefferson taking power in 1801, the Jeffersonians (including many former Anti-Federalists who opposed the Constitution) joined the remaining Federalists in supporting the Constitution.

As is widely agreed, the Constitution set the stage for the striking path of economic growth, ultimately transforming the United States from a tiny economy on the periphery of the Atlantic economy to the richest nation in the world (see, e.g., North, Summerhill, and Weingast 2000; and Wright 2003). The common market allowed a huge area of relatively unregulated markets, producing by 1815 a remarkable system of specialization and exchange across regions (North 1961).

In short, the creation of political liberty helped underpin the remarkable economic success of the United States.

6. Establishing Limited Government in Reform (Communist) China

As a socialist country with a history of excessive arbitrary government (notably, the "Great Leap Forward" and the "Cultural Revolution"), Communist China faced a significant problem in the late 1970s of creating limited government to help underpin economic reform.[8] Along one dimension of political reform, China has failed to make any progress, notably diluting its monopoly hold over power at the national level. The Chinese Communist Party remains unequivocally in control. As Tiananmen Square graphically illustrates, expression of demands for democratization will be crushed.

And yet it is wrong to think that China has undertaken no political reform. China's strategy has been very different from that recommended in the West. Rather than political reform and democratization at the national level—the path in much of eastern Europe and Russia—it has pursued devolution of power, namely, federalism (Montinola, Qian, and Weingast 1995).

In brief, political reform in China reflects both principles articulated above. Consider principle 1, that all successful constitutions limit the stakes of politics. Although China has no official, written constitution, it has established a set of new working political rules that form its informal constitution. In particular, China has established limits on the national government by granting a wide range of powers to its provinces and lower levels of governments (Oi 1992; Shirk 1993). These governments collected all taxes; they now have control over the property rights, contractual, and regulatory features of their local economies. And the reform provinces have created a competitive environment for their firms. It is widely agreed that township-village enterprises (TVEs) are the engine of local economic growth in China. Because townships and villages are the lowest levels of government in China and themselves face a hard budget constraint, so too do the TVEs they create. With limited sources of revenue, this means that the TVEs they create must be able to float on their own bottom, that is, to make a profit. In the economic downturn following Tiananmen Square, several million TVEs failed.

The political incentive that underpins this behavior during the high reform period (1982–93) were the fiscal incentive contracts negotiated between the national government and the provinces. Under this system, each province signed a multiyear agreement with the center whereby it would collect all locally generated taxes and send an agreed amount to the center. The typical form of these agreements was a sharing agreement up to some fixed level (say, 50-50), and then a much higher marginal retention rate for all taxes collected above this level. Jin, Qian, and Weingast (2005) calculate that the average marginal retention rate across all provinces during this period was 89 percent. Thus, at the margin, the typical province was able to retain 89 percent of all tax revenue.

These fiscal incentives, we believe, helped foster economic reform, as local governments and their officials had strong incentives to foster local economic prosperity as a means of expanding local budgets and power, developing financial independence from the center, and, also, personal prosperity.

The new political rules in reform China also reflect the logic of the second principle, namely, coordination to support the rules. The best example is given by the brief reactionary period following the suppression of the demonstrators at Tiananmen Square in 1989. This was the height of the ascendency of the antireform group. At the time, the premier, Li Peng, attempted to undo the fiscal decentralization providing provinces with financial independence from the center. Two previous waves of fiscal reform under Mao both ended with similar fiscal recentralizations unilaterally imposed by the center. Yet this attempt failed because, at a dramatic moment, the governor of Guandong Province, the most successful of the reform provinces, refused, and most other governors lined up behind him (see Montinola, Qian, and Weingast 1995; Shirk 1993, 194–195).

7. The Failure to Create Limited Government in Mexico

As in the United States, the Mexican constitution creates a presidential separation-of-powers system with an independent judiciary. It also specifies a federal system reserving considerable powers for the states. The similarity ends there, however, as the Mexican constitution has failed to prove self-enforcing over most of the twentieth century, particularly during the era of one-party dominance by the Revolutionary Party (PRI) from 1930 through the late 1990s.

The problem with the government honoring citizen rights in most developing countries is twofold. First, these countries typically fail to resolve the rationality-of-fear problem through the creation of limited government. Especially in authoritarian regimes, if the government falls, it is hard to predict what will happen. In particular, the stakes are very high for incumbent officials and their constituents, who could lose everything if they lost power. Indeed, giving up power can be quite dangerous for these groups' welfare. Second, per principle 2, these countries lack the consensus necessary to support and defend constitutional provisions.

The failure of both principles in Mexico, as is common in the developing world, implies that the government faces relatively few constraints. The high stakes of power imply that the government is driven to use all the instruments at its disposal to further this goal: coercion, political structure, the economy, and public policy generally.

To understand both the political structure of Mexico and how the state has structured the economy, consider the PRI's incentives. Through its monopoly on state power, the PRI has sought to control both politics and economics to maintain its power, explaining how it structured both state and economy in Mexico (Weingast 2003; see also Diaz, Magaloni, and Weingast 2006). The critical observation is that, to remain in power, political officials in developing countries typically do not need to win elections (and even if there are elections, they are not parallel with those in the developed West because of the risk that they will be canceled or their results set aside). Instead, officials must generate political support through their policy choices.

A central insight into understanding how such governments operate is that they create political dependence. The idea is that they seek to create a reward-and-punishment scheme so that the difference is sufficiently large to induce citizens to support them despite their predilections to support the opposition. This logic—the need to create sufficient dependence among voters, interest groups, and politicians—explains how the PRI designed both the state and its relationship to the economy in Mexico.

First, consider federalism. Centralized federalism, including policy and budgetary authority held by the central government rather than the states or local governments, implies central control over the dispersion of both budgets and policy benefits. States and localities that failed to support the PRI in elections were punished by withholding budgets and desired policies (see Diaz, Magaloni, and Weingast 2006). This contrasts with meaningful federalism in which states and localities command substantial resources of their own: under these circumstances, even if the central government punished a state for supporting the opposition, that state would have its own resources with which to meet local needs. Centralized federalism, in contrast, denies states and localities this option, thus tying voters to the PRI.

Second, consider the economy. Massive market intervention creates control, privilege, and dependence. Here too the political value of intervention is that it creates policy benefits to be lost if agents fail to support the PRI. This helps tie interest groups to the PRI, for defection to the opposition risks losing policy benefits that, in a controlled economy, often mean the difference between handsome profits and failing.

Finally, consider politicians. Maintaining the political cartel requires that political officials stay within the PRI umbrella rather than defecting and contesting power through competition. I have already suggested that centralized federalism denies politicians a major route for political independence—using the independent subnational offices to build a constituency base independent of the PRI. Here the rules prohibiting all officials from being reelected are critical.

In short, the structure of the state and economy in Mexico served the ends of the hegemonic PRI, helping to maintain it in power. Centralized control of the state and economy allowed the PRI to maintain the support of most elements of society: citizens qua voters were forced to support the regime at the polls; interest groups forced to maintain allegiance to the party rather than the opposition; and politicians forced to remain within the cartel umbrella rather than defecting to create real political competition. Democracy in this system was more a process of political control than of citizen choice.

The need to create political dependence implies considerable goal distortion. Policy choices are not aimed to provide market-enhancing public goods. Massive economic intervention therefore comes at a considerable cost in most developing countries—in Mexico's case, crippling the economy so that it has experienced little growth in per capita income between 1980 and the present. Moreover, the lack of constitutional restrictions on the government implies that property rights remain insecure. Banks, for example, have been expropriated on numerous occasions (see Haber, Razo, and Maurer 2003; Maurer and Haber, forthcoming).

In short, the absence of liberty not only grants governments in developing countries a freer hand to manipulate the political and economic structure of their societies, it makes it dangerous to give up power. This danger motivates the government to stifle forms of opposition, including alternative power centers. Economic freedom is often dangerous in this context because it may yield an opposition not dependent on the center and thus potential competition for power.

8. Conclusions

Creating a thriving capitalist system requires the simultaneous creation of a political system capable of sustaining it. The political and economic systems are inextricably intertwined. They cannot be separated, and trying to create markets apart from politics is foolhardy.

The problem in the developing world is that it has neither a capitalist system nor a government capable of sustaining one. The absence of limited government—that is, a government capable of honoring citizen rights—implies that governments in the developing world all too frequently use their policy means to expropriate the wealth of some of their citizens rather than to provide market-enhancing public goods. The threat of this type of governmental opportunism—the grabbing hand, in Shleifer and Vishny's (1998) language—is incompatible with a thriving capitalist market system.

Many of the great early modern philosophers, including Hobbes, Locke, and Madison, saw that solving the problem of an arbitrary and opportunist government was at the heart of creating political and economic liberty. Locke and Madison, for example, both believed that protecting property rights and the economy was a central task of limited government. In his *Second Treatise*, Locke outlined his solution to the problem, a separation-of-powers system combined with citizens rights and a citizenry willing to act against a government that failed to honor those rights. Madison in the Federalist Papers went considerably further in outlining the logic of how limited government must work, by "pitting ambition against ambition," by creating federalism that reserved sufficient powers to the states such that the national government not only remained limited, but would have to contend with a set of states with their own armies (the state militias) far larger than the federal government's. Both writers emphasized the importance of limited government as important not only for liberty, but for the economy.

In this chapter, I proposed two principles of successful constitutions, both focusing on the creation of limited government. The first principle is that all successful constitutions limit the stakes of power. This is necessary for several reasons. First, when citizens feel that what they hold most dear—whether assets or practicing their own beliefs—is threatened, they are willing to resort to extra-constitutional action to protect themselves. Landowners supporting the Chilean coup in 1973, deposing a legitimately elected democratic government, is an example. Constitutions that fail to create limited government are simply less likely to survive. Second, limiting the stakes lowers the costs to governmental officials and their constituents of giving up power when they lose elections. This means that they are far less motivated to use all the means at their disposal—including political intervention in markets—to remain in power. Third, limiting the stakes in a capitalist economy requires protecting markets.

The second principle is that successful constitutions create focal solutions to the central coordination dilemmas about citizens' rights. When citizens fail to agree about their rights, governments can take advantage of them by transgressing the rights of some citizens while retaining the political support of others. In contrast, constitutions that create focal solutions to the citizen-coordination game allow citizens to react in concert against potential transgressions, thus deterring the government from doing so.

These principles show why emphasizing market reform without corresponding political reform in the developing or transition context is doomed to fail: without creating political reform compatible with markets, the political system is likely to hobble or prey on the nascent markets, hindering their development into a thriving capitalist system.

I showed how this principle helped explain important features of the British constitution—such as embodying in 1689 the Lockean ideal that kings must honor citizens' rights or risk being deposed—and the U.S. Constitution, including a national government of limited powers. In contrast, central features of the Mexican constitution have been ignored, and it provides inadequate limits on government to protect property rights.

Notes

The author thanks Douglass North for helpful conversations.

1. In the second half of the twentieth century, political philosophers expanded the notion of liberty to cover a wider range of goals, though I will not be concerned with these notions.

2. This section primarily draws on Weingast 2006, but also on Weingast 1995, 1997.

3. The discussion of the fundamental coordination problem is based on Weingast 1997, which provides a game-theoretic interpretation of that problem.

4. Ames 1987 and Haggard and Kaufman 1995, among others, provide statistical support for this proposition. According to V. O. Key (1961, 3), "[E]ven in the least democratic regime opinion may influence the direction or tempo of

substantive policy. Although a government may be erected on tyranny, to endure it needs the ungrudging support of substantial numbers of its people."

5. A large literature exists on pacts, including Burton, Gunther, and Higley 1992; Diamond 1999; Karl 1986; O'Donnell and Schmitter 1986; and Weingast 1997.

6. Data from opinion polls suggest that at no time during the controversy did a majority of the country favor this plan (Epstein et al. 1994, table 8-26).

7. Specifically, they put in place legal constraints about the calling of Parliament, including a clause in the Bill of Rights and the triennial legislation of 1694.

8. This section is based on Montinola, Qian, and Weingast 1995; and Jin, Qian, and Weingast 2005.

References

Ames, Barry. 1987. *Political Survival: Politicians and Public Policy in Latin America*. Berkeley and Los Angeles: University of California Press.

Bates, Robert H. 1981. *Markets and States in Tropical Africa: The Political Basis of Agricultural Policies*. Berkeley: University of California Press.

Baumol, William. 2002. *The Free-Market Innovation Machine*. Princeton: Princeton University Press.

Burton, Michael, Richard Gunther, and John Higley. 1992. "Introduction: Elite Transformations and Democratic Regimes." In *Elites and Democratic Consolidation in Latin America and Southern Europe*, ed. John Higley and Richard Gunther. Cambridge: Cambridge University Press.

Campion, Lord. 1958. *Introduction to the Procedure of the House of Commons*. 3rd ed. London: Macmillan.

Carswell, John. 1973. *From Revolution to Revolution: England, 1688–1776*. New York: Scribner.

Chavez, Rebecca Bill. 2004. *The Rule of Law in Nascent Democracies: Judicial Politics in Argentina*. Stanford, Calif: Stanford University Press.

de Figueiredo, Rui, and Barry R. Weingast. 1999. "Rationality of Fear: Political Opportunism and Ethnic Conflict." In *Civil Wars, Insecurity, and Intervention*, ed. Barbara F. Walter and Jack Snyder. New York: Columbia University Press.

Diaz, Alberto, Beatriz Magaloni, and Barry R. Weingast. 2006. "Democratization and the Economy in Mexico: Equilibrium (PRI) Hegemony and its Demise." Working paper, Hoover Institution, Stanford University.

Diamond, Larry. 1999. *Developing Democracy: Toward Consolidation*. Baltimore: Johns Hopkins University Press.

Dickson, P.G.M. 1967. *The Financial Revolution in England: A Study in the Development of Public Credit, 1688–1756*. New York: St. Martin's Press.

Ekelund, Robert B., and Robert D. Tollison. 1981. *Mercantilism as a Rent-Seeking Society: Economic Regulation in Historical Perspective*. College Station: Texas A&M University Press.

Epstein, Lee, et al. 1994. *The Supreme Court Compendium: Data, Decisions, and Developments*. Washington, D.C.: Congressional Quarterly Press.

Fearon, James. 2000. "Why Use Elections to Allocate Power?" Working paper, Stanford University.

Freeman, Joanne B. 2001. *Affairs of Honor: National Politics in the New Republic*. New Haven: Yale University Press.

Haber, Stephen, Armando Razo, and Noel Maurer. 2003. *The Politics of Property Rights: Political Instability, Credible Commitments, and Economic Growth in Mexico, 1876–1929*. New York: Cambridge University Press.

Haggard, Stephan, and Robert R. Kaufman. 1995. *The Political Economy of Democratic Transitions*. Princeton: Princeton University Press.

Higley, John, and Richard Gunther. 1992. *Elites and Democratic Consolidation in Latin America and Southern Europe*. New York: Cambridge University Press.

Holzman, Franklyn D. 1957. "The Soviet Bond Hoax." *Problems of Communism* 6 (September–October): 47–49.

Jin, Hehui, Yingyi Qian, and Barry R. Weingast. 2005. "Regional Decentralization and Fiscal Incentives: Federalism, Chinese Style." *Journal of Public Economics* 89: 1719–42.

Kaplanoff, Mark D. 1991. "Confederation: Movement for a Stronger Union." In *The Blackwell Encyclopedia of the American Revolution*, ed. Jack P. Greene and J. R. Pole. Cambridge, Mass.: Basil Blackwell.

Karl, Terry Lynn. 1986. "Petroleum and Political Pacts: The Transition to Democracy in Venezuela." In *Transitions from Authoritarian Rule: Latin America*, ed. Guillermo O'Donnell, Philippe C. Schmitter, and Laurence Whitehead. Baltimore: Johns Hopkins University Press.

Key, V. O., Jr. 1961. *Public Opinion and American Democracy*. New York: Knopf.

Maurer, Noel, and Stephen Haber. Forthcoming. "Related Lending: Manifest Looting or Good Governance? Evidence from Mexican Economic History." In *Growth, Institutions, and Crises: Latin America from a Historic Perspective*, ed. Sebastian Edwards. Chicago: University of Chicago Press.

Middlekauff, Robert. 1982. *The Glorious Cause: The American Revolution, 1763–1789*. New York: Oxford University Press.

Millar, James R. 1990. *The Soviet Economic Experiment*. Ed. Susan J. Linz. Urbana: University of Illinois Press.

Montinola, Gabriella, Yingyi Qian, and Barry R. Weingast. 1995. "Federalism, Chinese Style: The Political Basis for Economic Success in China." *World Politics* 48 (October): 50–81.

Morgan, Edmund S. 1977. *The Birth of the Republic: 1763–89*. Rev. ed. Chicago: University of Chicago Press.

North, Douglass C. 1961. *The Economic Growth of the United States, 1790–1860*. New York: Norton.

North, Douglass C., William Summerhill, and Barry R. Weingast. 2000. "Order, Disorder, and Economic Change: Latin America vs. North America." In *Governing for Prosperity*, ed. Bruce Bueno de Mesquita and Hilton Root. New Haven: Yale University Press.

North, Douglass C., and Barry R. Weingast. 1989. "Constitutions and Commitment: The Evolution of Institutions Governing Public Choice in 17th Century England." *Journal of Economic History* 49 (December): 803–32.

O'Donnell, Guillermo, and Philippe C. Schmitter. 1986. *Transitions from Authoritarian Rule: Tentative Conclusions about Uncertain Democracies.* Baltimore: Johns Hopkins University Press.

Oi, Jean. 1992. "Fiscal Reform and the Economic Foundations of Local State Corporatism in China." *World Politics* 45 (October): 99–126.

Przeworski, Adam. 1991. *Democracy and the Market.* New York: Cambridge University Press.

———. 2001. "Democracy as an Equilibrium." Working paper, New York University.

Rakove, Jack. 1996. *Original Meanings: Politics and Ideas in the Making of the Constitution.* New York: Knopf.

Rakove, Jack, Andrew Rutten, and Barry R. Weingast. 2001. "Ideas, Interests, and Credible Commitments in the American Revolution." Working paper, Hoover Institution, Stanford University.

Reid, Gordon. 1966. *The Politics of Financial Control* London: Hutchinson University Library.

Shirk, Susan L. *The Political Logic of Economic Reform in China.* Berkeley and Los Angeles: University of California Press, 1993.

Shleifer, Andrei, and Robert W. Vishny. 1998. *The Grabbing Hand: Government Pathologies and Their Cures.* Cambridge: Harvard University Press.

Sisson, Daniel. 1974. *The American Revolution of 1800.* New York: Knopf.

Weingast, Barry R. 1995. "The Economic Role of Political Institutions: Market-Preserving Federalism and Economic Development." *Journal of Law, Economics, and Organization* 11 (Spring): 1–31.

———. 1997. "The Political Foundations of Democracy and the Rule of Law." *American Political Science Review* 91 (June): 245–63.

———. 2003. "The Performance and Stability of Federalism, Mexican Style: An Institutionalist Perspective." Working paper, Hoover Institution, Stanford University.

———. 2006. "Self-Enforcing Constitutions: With an Application to Democratic Stability in America's First Century" Working paper, Hoover Institution, Stanford University.

Williams, E. Neville. 1960. *The Eighteenth-Century Constitution: 1688–1815.* Cambridge: Cambridge University Press.

Wood, Gordon. 1992. *Radicalism of the American Revolution.* New York: Knopf.

Wright, Gavin. 2003. "The Role of Nationhood in the Economic Development of the United States." In *Nation, State and the Economy in History*, ed. Alice Teichova and Herbert Matis. New York: Cambridge University Press.

Part III

INNOVATION IN MODERN CORPORATIONS

Introduction and Comments

YING LOWREY

MY GROWING PASSION FOR economic research on entrepreneurship has been nurtured by studying the works of William Baumol, who is internationally recognized as an "entrepreneurial economist."[1] In this brief introduction, I would like to review and discuss some important issues Baumol addressed in his 2002 book, *The Free-Market Innovation Machine: Analyzing the Growth Miracle of Capitalism*. Those discussion points are also briefly related to the essays by Nathan Rosenberg and by Melissa Schilling and Corey Phelps that follow in this volume. These authors have been engaged in extensive research on corporate entrepreneurship.

Baumol finds "innovation" to be "a primary source of the capitalist growth miracle" (2002, 12). He says, "It can be argued that virtually all of the economic growth that has occurred since the eighteenth century is ultimately attributable to innovation" (13). According to him, only under the capitalistic free-market condition innovations are routinized. The mechanism that makes innovation a routine accounts for the extraordinarily superior growth of free-market economies (15–16).

Being an entrepreneurial economist, Baumol would never overlook the important role of (productive) entrepreneurship in economic growth. Baumol uses the word *entrepreneur* as "the independent innovator" in "the Schumpeterian sense to mean the bold and imaginative deviator from established business patterns and practices, who constantly seeks the opportunity to introduce new products and new procedures, to invade new markets, and to create new organizational forms." Those entrepreneurs engage in the "nonroutine innovation" that "does not emerge from established firms as part of their regular planning of competitive strategy" (2002, 56–57).

In line with Baumol's definition of the entrepreneur, I wish to argue three points: first, capitalism as an economic growth machine is a consequence of long-term social innovation that incessantly invents and adapts better ways to enable an economy to grow and people to prosper. Second, free competition and free enterprise that lead to prevalence of business ownership are vital in ensuring long-term economic growth. Third, it is the *entrepreneur* who carries out the process of adaptation and use of inventions that underlie the mechanism of the economic growth machine and make it more workable and more reliable. For all these reasons, the role of the entrepreneur deserves much more attention among economists.[2]

Rome Was Not Built in a Day

The growth machine did not appear fully developed or overnight. It evolved over long periods and was preceded by important contributions to economic growth and social development. An economy's routinization of innovation that is a critical component of the engine of economic growth does include technological innovation, but even more important, it entails social innovation. Social innovation includes creation of the constitution and institutions that were invented and evolved to protect the individual's political rights and economic interests and to create economic incentives, thereby stimulating long-term economic development.

Perhaps the first constitution in human history was drafted around 500 B.C. in Athens, and was one of the first and most influential of such social inventions—it has underlain "the system of Government for every modern society on earth" (Geokas and Papathanasis 2000). The influence of the Roman legal system going back as early as 450 B.C.E. is still with us today.[3] Another relevant illustration is the period of long-lasting economic development and growth in China's history during the Tang Dynasty, between 618 and 907, following a series of great social innovations brought about by its first emperor, Li Shimin, Tang Taizong. Before the Tang dynasty, the imperial examination system (or civil service examinations) was already used to open a door of opportunity for all commoners. This gave people the chance to become officials on the strength of their talents, and only the most talented were allowed to participate in the administration of the empire. This system was adopted and revised by Tang Taizong. Along with other systems included in the Tang Code, the examination system, which had proven to provide strong economic incentive for allocation of resources to education, was copied and is still used by many Asian countries including Japan, Singapore, and Korea. It is difficult to dispute the role of this examination system in those countries' economic miracles.[4]

Such social innovation will undoubtedly continue to play an important role in demolishing obsolete systems, and in creating institutions that will serve long-term economic growth, even in nations with strong constitutions and workable institutions. The most innovative and effective assistance that we can provide to many other nations that "have not yet shared in the growth benefits proffered by the market, and whose relative poverty seems actually to be increasing" (Baumol 2002, 2) is the transfer and dissemination of social inventions.

Ever since the end of the "Cold War," not only many former centrally controlled economies such as China and Russia, but also many Western nations such as England, Germany, and the Netherlands, have come to the U.S. Small Business Administration (SBA) to study the structure and know-how of this government agency in fostering small business and entrepreneurship. Social innovations possess characteristics of public goods that can be provided to additional users at zero marginal cost on a nonexclusive basis. The transfer and dissemination of social innovations is free of charge, and thereby encourages prospective users to take advantage of its spillovers. No one charges a patent fee for copying China's imperial examination systems. Similarly, there is no charge for adopting the small business loan programs, backed by the U.S. government, that have provided capital accesses to millions of business startups.[5] In 2003 alone, there were 838 visitors from 108 nations to the SBA headquarters. The SBA's Office of International Visitors provided seminars at the requests of those guests. The most popular topics of those seminars have been the SBA programs themselves and the management of those programs.

The Foundation of the Growth Machine

My second point is that the innovation machine must be built on a foundation of free competition and free enterprise symbolized by the prevalence of small business. "Only through full and free competition can free markets, free entry into business, and opportunities for the expression and growth of personal initiative and individual judgment be assured."[6] In other words, only through widespread participation in business activities can creativity be fully harnessed, massive technological and social innovations carried out, and new inventions quickly disseminated and adapted on a large scale, generating another sort of multiplier effect upon the national product.

The absence of extensive participation in business activities can sometimes undermine critical technological breakthroughs, and even undermine affluent societies. A colorful example is an ancient Chinese seismograph—an ornamental vessel of cast bronze, which registered earthquakes by means of a sensitive system of bronze balls dropped from the hinged mouths of nine carved metal dragons (representing nine different directions) that faced outward in a circle, to be caught by open-mouthed frogs stationed below, whenever the ground shook. The seismograph was invented during the first century A.D. in Luoyang, the capital of the Eastern Han Dynasty, with a population of 500,000.

Zhang Heng created his seismograph in an imperial observatory, where he also proposed the hypothesis that the earth was spherical. Luoyang also had an academy that was attended by 30,000 students; and a granary for times when food relief was needed.[7] Nevertheless, except for the value of the seismograph as a showy ornament that was possessed only by the emperor and displayed in the emperor's palace, the absence of a large body of business enterprises resulted in underutilization and then disappearance of this great invention.

The Soviet Union was first to send a satellite, *Sputnik*, into space in 1957. However, that country's prevention of widespread business ownership destroyed the incentive for utilization of this and other innovations for nonmilitary purposes, thereby inhibiting economic growth and exacerbating poverty. In contrast, the pro-business approach of East Asia had permitted the economic growth miracles of the Asian "Tigers" between the 1960s and 1990s. China's recent experience confirms this relationship. Between 1990 and 2000, the number of Chinese private enterprises achieved an average annual growth rate of 32.8 percent.[8] At the same time economic growth in China has persisted at an average annual rate exceeding 8 percent.[9]

My own studies have confirmed a positive correlation between the prevalence of business ownership and economic well-being in America (Lowery 2004). Business survey data for 50 states along with macroeconomic data were used to explain the large variations in economic well-being across America. The initial regression results show that raising business density (firm number per 1,000 persons) by 1 percent increases average household income by 2.3 percent and government tax revenue by 1.7 percent. An increase in the share of women- and minority-owned business in total state businesses seems to have an even stronger positive effect on the economic well-being variables such as gross state product per capita and home ownership.

The Entrepreneurs and Their Disappearance from Microtheory

After several decades of persistent effort, culminating in his 2002 book on the free-market innovation machine, William Baumol helped to restimulate entrepreneurial research. He has even credited the individual "productive entrepreneurs" with bringing "the free-enterprise economy into existence" (Baumol 2002, 71). However, he also points out that though the "place of entrepreneurs in the process of growth is well recognized and widely accepted," "their general absence from the theoretical [economics] literature is noteworthy" (57). Some others even make the more radical claim that there is no theory of the entrepreneur in economics

(Casson 1982). Surely an increased effort devoted to elimination of this critical gap can help to make the dismal science much less dismal.

Rosenberg's and Schilling and Phelps' Contribution to Study of Entrepreneurship

Two valuable contributions on entrepreneurship, innovation, and growth are the essays by Nathan Rosenberg and by Melissa Schilling and Corey Phelps that follow.

Rosenberg's primary research activities have dealt with the economics of technological change. He has examined the diversity of forces generating technological change across industrial boundaries, as well as the mutual influence of scientific research and technological innovation. He has authored a number of invaluable books in this arena, including *Schumpeter and the Endogeneity of Technology* (2000); *Paths of Innovation* (1998; coauthored with David C. Mowery); *The Emergence of Economic Ideas* (1994); *The American System of Manufactures* (1969; editor); *Perspectives on Technology* (1976); *Inside the Black Box* (1982); *Exploring the Black Box* (1994); *Technology and the Pursuit of Economic Growth* (1989; coauthored with David C. Mowery) and *How the West Grew Rich* (1986; coauthored with L. E. Birdzell Jr.)

Rosenberg takes as axiomatic the increasing importance of the role of technology and science in the economic life of advanced industrial economies. He believes that "this increasingly important role has been a direct consequence of organizational changes, along with associated changes in economic incentives, that have made technology and science much more responsive to the changing economic needs of expanding capitalist economics." Rosenberg argues that science and technology became "a great deal more endogenous in the course of the twentieth century," and that there is a high degree of endogeneity in the behavior of institutions such as universities and corporate labs. This increasing endogeneity means, according to Rosenberg, that "the manner in which new knowledge is produced, and then transformed into new goods and services of commercial value, became much more directly connected to decision-making processes on the part of maximizing agents, that is, business decision-makers who were responding to signals, and opportunities, transmitted by normal market forces."

Here, Schumpeter's routinization of innovation and Rosenberg's endogenous forces simultaneously describe an important side of capitalism's economic growth machine. Rosenberg examines historically how engineering disciplines and new products have shaped science and, particularly, how corporate research labs "determined the extent to which the activities of the scientific community could be made to be responsive to the needs of the larger economy."

But those corporate research labs rely upon a network of other institutions such as universities and government patronage and philanthropic foundations. That brings us to the contribution of Melissa Schilling and Corey Phelps and their work on communication in networks.

Schilling and Phelps' research focuses on technological innovation and knowledge creation. They have studied how firms fight battles over technology standards, and how they utilize strategies of collaboration, protection, and timing of entry. They also study how product designs and organizational structures migrate toward or away from increasing modularity. Their most recent work focuses on knowledge creation, including how variation (rather than specialization) can accelerate the learning curve, and how the structure of the knowledge networks affects their overall capacity for knowledge creation.

Schilling and Phelps' chapter addresses interfirm collaboration networks. They adapt recent advances in graph theory and hypothesize that the structure of interfirm networks can influence firms' capacity for knowledge creation and thereby affect their innovation. They test this hypothesis using panel data on interfirm alliance networks and patenting output in 10 technology-intensive industries. The results support their observation that the combination of clustering and research is associated with significantly higher patenting output. Schilling and Phelps' research constitutes yet another step toward the creation of a fruitful formal body of theory dealing with the role and structure of innovation and organization for entrepreneurial activity.

Notes

The statements, findings, conclusions, and recommendations found in this paper are those of the author and do not necessarily reflect the views of the Office of Advocacy, the Small Business Administration, or the United States government.

1. Eliasson and Henrekson (2004) briefly review William Baumol's contribution to the economics of entrepreneurship and economic growth.

2. I have carried out preliminary research attempting to construct a theoretical model of the entrepreneur. See Lowrey 2003 and 2006.

3. The Twelve Tables. See "Roman Legal System" at http://www.dl.ket.org/latin1/mores/law/legalsystem.htm.

4. http://www.travelchinaguide.com/intro/history/tang.htm.

5. Many disadvantaged groups including veterans, women, and minorities have benefited from the program and become business owners.

6. Small Business Act, Public Law 85-536.

7. "Ancient China's Technology." Available at http://www.east_west_dialogue.tripod.com.

8. See DIHK-ACFIC Partnership Project, available at http://www.acfic.com.cn/dihtpage.

9. http://www.iwep.org.cn/wec/2003_5-6/hu_an_gang.pdf.

References

Baumol, William J. 2002. *The Free-Market Innovation Machine: Analyzing the Growth Miracle of Capitalism*. Princeton: Princeton University Press.

Casson, Mark. 1982. *The Entrepreneur: An Economic Theory*. Totowa, N.J.: Barnes and Noble.

Eliasson, Gunnar, and Magnus Henrekson. 2004. "William J. Baumol: An Entrepreneurial Economist on the Economics of Entrepreneurship," *Small Business Economics* 23, 1 (August): 1–7.

Geokas, M. C., and A. T. Papathanasis. 2000. "The Greek-Americans, Smithereens in the Wind?" Available at http://demokritos.org/ANEMO-2.htm.

Lowery, Ying. 2003. "The Entrepreneur and Entrepreneurship: An Neoclassical Approach." Office of Advocacy Working Paper, U.S. Small Business Administration, http://www.sba.gov/advo/stats/wkp03yl.pdf.

———. 2004. "Business Density and Economic Well-Being in the 50 U.S. States: An Empirical Examination." Presentation at the Chinese Economist Society Beijing Symposium.

———. 2006. "An Examination of Entrepreneurial Effort." American Economic Association Annual Meetings, http://www.aeaweb.org/annual_mtg_papers/2006papers.html.

Chapter 5

Endogenous Forces in Twentieth-Century America

NATHAN ROSENBERG

Introduction

My purpose in this essay is to argue that both technology and science have been rendered a great deal more endogenous in the course of the twentieth century. I am not merely saying that technology and science have come to play roles of increasing importance in the economic life of advanced industrial economies, which I take as axiomatic. Rather, I am suggesting that this increasingly important role has been a direct consequence of organizational changes, along with associated changes in economic incentives, that have made technology and science much more responsive to the changing economic needs of expanding capitalist economies. I will develop my case primarily by drawing upon the American experience, where, I believe, these forces have been carried the farthest.

Obviously, there are degrees of endogeneity. No human generation has ever started out from scratch. Each one necessarily builds upon an institutional and intellectual inheritance derived from preceding generations, and, in this sense, history does indeed matter (but how could it be otherwise?). Present-day research activities add, each year, only a relatively small amount to the total stock of useful knowledge that has been inherited from the past, and that inheritance powerfully influences the directions in which current research can move. Isaac Newton was explicitly acknowledging the importance of this inheritance when he stated, of his own remarkable intellectual accomplishments: "If I have seen further it is by standing on the shoulders of giants." Newton stood firmly, of course, on the shoulders of one particular giant, Johannes Kepler, and his theory that all planets move in an elliptical orbit around the sun, a theory that made possible a much more precise calculation of planetary orbits. The general point that I want to start with is simply that today's research is powerfully shaped by yesterday's research findings.

It should be candidly admitted at the outset that I am somewhat skeptical of the possibility of constructing rigorous theoretical models of technological innovation—that is, models from which we can derive general principles that will, in turn, be useful for forecasting purposes. I do, however, believe that there is a great deal of valuable knowledge concerning the innovation process that can be derived from historical and empirical research, even though the highly contingent nature of innovations, along with their multiple sources, will not allow us to forecast the eventual outcome of research and development activities.

Having said this, I believe that the resurgence of interest in a theory of endogenous technological change during the 1990s, largely triggered by Romer's 1990 paper in the *Journal of Political Economy*, was a valuable step forward. I am not alone in believing that the attempt to develop a theory of economic growth, without some discussion of the role of technological change and its economic determinants, is very much akin to playing Moby Dick without the whale. Romer's 1990 paper has provided a powerful push in what I regard as the "right" direction. For those with an interest in economic history, this new focus of interest is especially welcome because, as I would like to suggest, an excellent way to understand the determinants of technological change is to study aspects of its history.

At the same time, my own position is distinctly more radical than Romer's, in the special sense that he has shown how *technology* can be modeled as an endogenous variable while the growth of knowledge remains exogenous. I will argue that the realm of *science* became far more endogenous in the course of the twentieth century. And, of course, Romer's work occupies the realm of theory, whereas my work will be in the realm of history, including much recent history.

Some disclaimers are in order. There is no "penumbra of approbation" around my use of the term *endogeneity*. I am simply calling attention to certain forces that were unleashed during the twentieth century. I take no particular joy in documenting the growing influence of technological changes and associated market forces upon the enormous expansion of scientific knowledge in the twentieth century. Moreover, it should go without saying that I strongly deplore any weakening of financial support for "blue-sky" research, that is, research that is not based upon any calculation of short-term benefits.

I believe that the growth of endogeneity has led to the production of much excellent science, but that does not mean that I am advocating an indefinite expansion of the reliance upon market forces in directing the scientific enterprise; nor that I would be unconcerned over a decline in the share of support allocated to blue-sky research. I have no doubt that both society and science itself would be vastly impoverished under such circumstances. Increasing reliance upon market forces would lead to serious neglect (or at least substantial underfunding) of many fields of research—particle physics, astronomy, cosmology—even though, ironically, an industrial lab (Bell Labs) was responsible for what was perhaps the single most important breakthrough in the realm of cosmology in the twentieth century (see below). There are major areas of scientific research that are likely to remain unaffected by industrial priorities. Indeed, the neglect of support for blue-sky research might well result, in the long run, in the failure to uncover the scientific basis for entirely new industries.

I propose, therefore, to discuss the growth of useful knowledge, and some of the ways in which certain changes in the organization of research activities have shaped that growth. More specifically, what I want to do is to suggest that both technology *and science* have been rendered a great deal more endogenous in the course of the twentieth century, and I want to ask how and why that has happened. However, the most ambitious and novel thrust of this chapter lies in my claims concerning the growing endogeneity of science. I will argue that, *from the perspective of the endogeneity of science*, market forces have influenced that endogeneity very considerably through the intermediating roles exercised by technological forces. My focus will be on the American experience, where, I believe, the growth of endogenous forces has been most powerful. *Why* that has been the case is a subject that still warrants much more scholarly attention.

I will suggest that, in the course of the twentieth century, the manner in which new knowledge is produced, and then transformed into new goods and services of commercial value, became much more directly connected to decision-making processes on the part of maximizing agents, that is, business decision-makers who were responding to signals, and opportunities, transmitted by normal market forces. This is precisely what I mean by "endogenous."[1]

I am also well aware that the treatment that follows pays no attention to the consideration of intellectual property rights, especially as they currently pertain to university patenting activities. This is a very big issue that deserves far more attention than can be given here.[2]

Corporate Research Labs

The proposition that technological and scientific changes have become increasingly endogenous in the course of the twentieth century must necessarily begin with an examination that focuses on a key organizational innovation: the industrial research laboratory. And, of course, Baumol's "free market innovation machine" has relied heavily upon the contributions of industrial labs. It was these corporate labs that determined the extent to which the activities of the scientific community could be made to be responsive to the needs of the larger economy. But such labs have never been able to stand alone. They have always depended for their effective performance upon a network of other institutions. These included, in particular, universities, which had two major roles to play: (1) they trained scientists and engineers, many of whom would eventually take up employment in corporate labs where their training might make essential contributions to innovative activities; and also (2) graduate students at American universities participated in various kinds of research that would push out the frontiers of useful knowledge. It is important to add here that the United States has been almost unique among OECD countries in the extent to which it concentrated scientific research in its universities.[3]

The network of other institutions would also include extensive federal government patronage, in the post–World War II years, supporting research in areas where it was anticipated that the social returns were likely to be substantially higher than the private returns. Private philanthropic foundations were also particularly significant sources of research support, especially in the first half of the twentieth century—the Rockefeller, Guggenheim, and Carnegie foundations. In the prewar period as well, universities often relied on financial support from local industry for carrying out certain classes of research. This was especially true of state universities, where it was essential to provide evidence of assistance to local industry in order to justify the imposition of taxes upon the citizens of each state. This situation was transformed after World War II, when the federal government became the dominant patron of scientific research. In that period, contract research for local industries did not decline in real dollar terms, although it declined drastically as a share of total support for university-based research.

In the high-tech sectors of the economy, corporate research workers devoted considerable attention to monitoring the research activities that were being conducted within the university community. But it needs to be emphasized that, in order for industrial firms to exploit recent university research findings, it was essential to have some substantial in-house research capabilities of their own. These capabilities are essential in evaluating the findings and the possible implications of university research. In advanced industrial societies that have been simply flooded by an enlarged flow of information, not only from universities, but from professional journals on library shelves or electronically via Internet search engines, the exploitation of this vast flow of information requires an internal competence that, typically, only in-house scientists can provide. Indeed, America's commercial successes in high-tech markets over the past 50 years have owed a great deal to these internal competences in private industry. Industrial scientists have played a critical role in the transfer of potentially useful knowledge generated by university research, not only because of their scientific sophistication, but also because they have had a deep awareness of their firms' commercial priorities and technological capabilities (see Rosenberg 1990; Mowery and Rosenberg 1998).

It is also important that the research activities of the industrial labs should not be judged, as they often are by academics, by the usual academic criteria. The industrial lab is essentially an institutional innovation (the origins of which go back to the German organic chemicals industry of the late nineteenth century) in which the research agenda is largely shaped by short-term needs, but also, in many notable cases, by the longer-term strategies of industrial firms. The role of industrial scientists and engineers is to improve the performance (especially the reliability) of the firms' products and to reduce their costs, as well as to invent entirely new technologies. Thus, the critical achievement of the growth of the American industrial lab in the course of the twentieth century was to subject science, more and more, to commercial criteria. In so doing, it has rendered science, more and more, an endogenous activity, whose directions were increasingly shaped by economic forces and concentrated on the achievement of economic goals. Science has become gradually incorporated, over the past century, into a crucial part of the growth system that has propelled industrial societies along their long-term growth trajectories.

When seen from this perspective, what is regarded today as corporate R&D spending is, for the most part, spending on products that have been around for many years, and in some cases even for several decades, as a result of past economic activities. This has been confirmed by a variety of sources. Several surveys in the post–World War II years (such as those of McGraw-Hill) have asked the appropriate corporate decision-makers to estimate how much of their R&D budgets were devoted to (1) improving products that already existed, as compared to (2) the invention of new products. The fairly consistent response was that approximately 80 percent of R&D expenditures was devoted to improving old products, and only 20 percent to the invention of new ones. Similarly, aggregate annual R&D data for the America economy as a whole, as reported by the NSF over the last few decades, have broken down into one-third devoted to scientific research, and two-thirds to development activities. Development, it seems fair to say, is primarily focused upon the modification, the improvement, and the redesign of preexisting products rather than the design of entirely new ones. Thus, the huge growth in corporate R&D activities over the course of the twentieth century has undoubtedly raised the share of national expenditures that can be classified as endogenous.

It is wrong, then, to think of R&D expenditures as if they were resources that were primarily committed to the search for major breakthrough innovations of the Schumpeterian type. Rather, their main goal, as already suggested, has been to improve the performance and to reduce the cost of old technologies. A moment's reflection suggests that this should not be surprising. The transistor, which has so dominated technological change in electronics in the postwar years, is now well over 50 years old (I will return to transistors shortly). The automobile has been around for over 100 years, if one dates it from the earliest working models in late-nineteenth-century Germany and France, and the airplane has just recently celebrated its centenary. Yet transportation equipment is the largest sector of the American economy when sectors are ranked by company-financed R&D. These two "old" transportation forms, cars and airplanes, continue to absorb the great bulk of such transportation sector R&D.

Consider electricity. The generation of electricity for commercial purposes in the United States is usually dated from the year 1882, when the Pearl Street Station, on the lower end of the island of Manhattan, began to deliver electricity to customers. This event set the stage for more than a century of R&D involving, for the most part, individually small improvements in the modification of boiler design, the introduction of alloys of higher performance, pulverization of the coal, and a steady rise in operating pressures and temperatures, over many decades. Although only specialists would be able to identify more than a few of the innumerable improvements, the amount of coal required to generate a kilowatt-hour of electricity declined by almost an order of magnitude between 1910 and the 1960s. The cumulative effects of individually small improvements, carried out over a sufficiently long period of time on what is now called a general purpose technology, have transformed the world economy. And of course, as is suggested by the very term *general purpose technology*, the powerful effect of a cumulation of individually small improvements requires, as a precondition, an earlier invention of much larger scope (Bresnahan and Trajtenberg 1995).

Finally, consider the telephone, which has been around for well over 100 years, but its performance has recently been enhanced by facsimile transmission, electronic mail, voice mail, cellular phones, conference calls, and, far from least, by toll-free numbers (800). One may respond that some of these "enhancements" really deserve to be regarded as the invention of major new products in their own right, rather than a "mere improvement" upon an old invention. I would certainly not be inclined to argue with such a labeling, but I would insist that the "old" product, the standard telephone, constituted the technological platform on which the more recent products were built. That is to say, what we are observing over the course of time is in fact a cumulative process in which successful earlier investments in inventive activities have created economic opportunities and incentives that have generated many years of further investments in product improvement and product innovation. These investments, which now dominate the R&D budgets of the high-tech corporate world, are thus clearly endogenous. There are, in other words, significant intertemporal externalities.[4]

How Engineering Disciplines Have Shaped Science

I would like now to call attention to what has been another major force for advancing the endogeneity of science in the course of the twentieth century. The development of engineering disciplines in the past century has exercised a powerful effect in the industrial world on the incentive to undertake research of a scientific nature. And here, it should be recalled that, in recent years, private industry has accounted for a large and rising fraction of the U.S. economy's scientific research, the R of R&D. Moreover, even if we focus exclusively on the narrow category of basic research alone, the National Science Foundation (2000) reports that, in the year 2000, more than 30 percent of basic research in the United States was financed by industrial firms. There is, at the very least, a strong presumption that privately financed basic research would not be undertaken by private profit-making firms in the absence of some potential financial payoff.

It is common to characterize engineering disciplines as being essentially applied science. This is a misleading characterization. A more careful unwinding of the intertwining of science and technology suggests that the willingness of profit-seeking firms to devote money to scientific research is very much influenced by the prospect of converting such research findings into finished, marketable products. The actual conduct of scientific research may not be undertaken with specific objectives in mind, but rather with an increased confidence that, whatever the specific research findings, an enlarged engineering capability will substantially increase the likelihood of using these findings to bring improved or new products to the marketplace.

From this perspective, there is a serious sense in which the economist may argue that the science of chemistry should be thought of as an application of chemical engineering! Alternatively put, the growing sophistication of engineering disciplines has had the result of strengthening the endogeneity of science. I do not want this point to be made to sound too paradoxical. I mean to suggest that the willingness of private industry to commit financial resources to long-term scientific research is vastly strengthened by the progress of the appropriate engineering disciplines. Such progress raises the confidence of corporate decision-makers that the findings of basic research may eventually be converted to profitable uses. The discipline of chemical engineering, for example, deals with the design of chemical process plants, a designing activity that cannot be deduced from the principles of chemistry or from the laboratory experiments that have produced new chemical entities. The skills of the chemical engineer draw upon mechanical engineering, mathematics, and even economics, in addition to a knowledge of the basic principles of chemistry. Similarly, the design of a new generation of aircraft requires extensive information of the aeronautical engineer, which is often quite remote from theoretical aeronautical dynamics.[5]

Consider the scientific discipline of polymer chemistry. In the United States at least, polymer chemistry is a field that has long been dominated by the industrial research community. The fundamental research contributions to polymer chemistry of Wallace Carothers at du Pont, beginning in 1927, owed a great deal to the increasing maturity of chemical engineering in the preceding decade or so, an engineering discipline to which du Pont had made important contributions.[6] Carothers's research findings led directly to the discovery of nylon, the first of the synthetic fibers that came to constitute an entirely new subsector of the chemical industry after the Second World War. But it is doubtful that du Pont would have committed itself to Carothers's costly, fundamental researches in polymer chemistry, in the first place, had it not been for the considerable progress that took place in the discipline of chemical engineering in the decade or so preceding 1927. Thus, progress at the technological level (in this case chemical engineering) increasingly strengthened the willingness to spend money on science, which I see as a growth in the endogeneity of science (Rosenberg 1998).

How New Products Have Shaped Science

The next related observation with respect to the growing endogeneity of scientific research goes beyond the role played by engineering disciplines in strengthening the private incentives to perform scientific research. The argument here is that the development of some specific new *product* that is perceived to have great commercial potential may provide, and often *has* provided, a powerful stimulus to scientific research. This proposition is surprising only if one is already committed to a rigid, linear view of the innovation process, one in which causality is always expected to run from *prior* scientific research to "downstream" product design and engineering development. There is in fact, however, a straightforward endogenous explanation. A major technological breakthrough typically provides a strong signal that a new set of profitable opportunities has been opened up in some precisely identified industrial location. Consequently, it is understood that scientific research that can lead to further improvements in that new technology may turn out to be highly profitable.

Thus, the introduction of new technologies has often generated strong positive feedbacks in the appropriate scientific community. The problems encountered by sophisticated industrial technologies, and the anomalous observations and unexpected difficulties that they have encountered, have served as powerful stimuli to much fruitful scientific research in the academic community as well as the industrial research laboratory. In these ways the responsiveness of scientific research to economic needs and technological opportunities has been powerfully reinforced.

This was dramatically demonstrated in the case of the advent of the transistor, which was announced at Bell Labs in the summer of 1948. Within a decade of that event, solid-state physics, which had previously attracted the attention of only a small number of researchers and was not even taught at the vast majority of American universities (MIT, Princeton, and Caltech were leaders) had been transformed into the largest subdiscipline of physics. The number of basic publications in semiconductor physics rose from less than 25 per annum before 1948 to over 600 per annum by the mid-1950s (Herring 1957). It was the development of the transistor that changed that situation by dramatically upgrading the potential financial payoff to research in the solid state. J. A. Morton, who headed the fundamental development group that was formed at Bell Labs after the invention of the transistor, reported that it was extremely difficult to hire people with a knowledge of solid-state physics in the late 1940s (see Morton 1971). Moreover, it is important to emphasize that the rapid mobilization of intellectual resources to perform research in the solid state occurred in the university community, as well as in private industry, immediately *after* the announcement of the momentous findings of Shockley and his research colleagues at Bell Labs (Braun and MacDonald 1978).

The chronology of the events referred to is essential to my argument. Transistor technology was not the eventual consequence of a huge prior buildup of resources devoted to solid-state physics, although it was of course also true that some of the twentieth century's most creative physicists had been devoting their considerable intellectual energies to the subject in the interwar years. Rather, it was the initial breakthrough of the transistor, as a functioning piece of hardware, that set into motion a vast subsequent commitment of financial support for scientific research.

Thus, the difficulties that Shockley encountered with the operation of the early point-contact transistors led him into a systematic search for a deeper explanation of their behavior in terms of the underlying quantum physics of semiconductors. This search not only led eventually to a vastly superior amplifying device, the junction transistor; it also contributed to a much more profound understanding of the science of semiconductors. Indeed, Shockley's famous and highly influential book, *Electrons and Holes in Semiconductors*, drew heavily upon this research, and the book was the direct outgrowth of an in-house course that Shockley had taught for Bell Labs' personnel. Moreover, Shockley even found it necessary to run a six-day course at Bell Labs in June 1952 for professors from some 30 universities as part of an attempt to encourage the establishment of university courses in transistor physics.

Clearly, the main flow of scientific knowledge during this critical period was from industry to university, and not the other way around. Indeed, for a considerable period of time, Stanford and the University of California at Berkeley had to employ scientists from local industry to teach courses in solid-state physics/electronics. And of course, more recently, Jack Kilby was awarded the Nobel Prize in Physics in the year 2000 for his fundamental researches in the development of the integrated circuit—an invention that provided the basic platform for modern information technology. Kilby's research was carried out, not at a major research university, but at an industrial firm—Texas Instruments.

A similar sequence can be seen in the commitment of funds to research in the physics of surface phenomena, after problems with the reliability of early transistors pointed in that direction. More recently, and to compress a much more complex chain of events, the development of laser technology suggested the feasibility of using optical fibers for communications technologies and data processing. This possibility naturally pointed to the field of optics, where advances in scientific knowledge could now be expected to have potentially high economic payoffs. As a result, optics as a field of scientific research experienced a great resurgence in the 1960s and after. It was converted by changed expectations, based upon recent and prospective technological innovations, into a burgeoning field of research (see National Research Council 1986, 55–56; Bromberg 1991, esp. chap. 4). Additionally, lasers have become one of the most powerful of scientific instruments. They have been essential to research programs that have led to the award of several Nobel prizes in chemistry and physics. Moreover, different kinds of lasers gave rise to different categories of fundamental research. As Harvey Brooks has noted: "While the solid-state laser gave a new lease of life to the study of insulators and of the optical properties of solids, the gas laser resuscitated the moribund subject of atomic spectroscopy and gas-discharge physics" (1968, 399).

I draw the conclusion from this examination that, under modern industrial conditions, technology has come to shape science in the most powerful of ways: by playing a major role in determining the research agenda of science as well as the volume of resources devoted to specific research fields. One could examine these relationships in much finer detail by showing how, throughout the high-tech sectors of the economy, shifts in the technological needs of industry have brought with them associated shifts in emphasis in scientific research. When, for example, the semiconductor industry moved from a reliance upon discrete circuits (transistors) to integrated circuits, there was also a shift from mechanical to chemical methods of fabrication. When Fairchild Semiconductors began to fabricate integrated circuits, they did so by employing new methods of chemical etching that printed the transistors on the silicon wafers and also laid down the tracks between them. This chemical technique did away with much expensive wiring, and also produced integrated circuits that operated at much higher speeds. At the same time, the increased reliance upon chemical methods brought with it an increased attention to the relevant subfields of chemistry—in this case surface chemistry.

I cite the experience of changing methods of wafer design and fabrication to indicate one of the wide variety of ways in which the changing needs and priorities of industry have provided the basis for new priorities in scientific research. The world of transistors gave rise to numerous new fields of scientific research. Transistors, for example, could not be efficient unless the materials employed were of extremely high purity in order to carefully control the nature and concentration of deliberately implanted impurities. The properties of electronic materials thus quickly became a high priority in the new discipline of materials science. But it is essential to emphasize that these new priorities exercised their influence, not only upon the world of industrial research, but upon the conduct of research within the university community as well (see, e.g., Bever 1988).

Serendipity

There is a further source of causation running from technology to sciences that calls for special attention, even though it overlaps with some of the categories that have already been discussed, that is, serendipity. It is, of course, to be expected that well-trained minds are likely to turn up unexpected findings in many places. As Pasteur expressed it in the mid-nineteenth century: "Where observation is concerned, chance favors only the prepared mind." By way of contrast, consider Thomas Edison, by universal consent a brilliant inventor, but someone whose field of vision was intensely focused on observations that had immediate practical relevance. In 1883 he observed the flow of electricity across a gap, inside a vacuum, from a hot filament to a metal wire. Since he saw no practical application and had no formal scientific training, he merely described the phenomenon in his notebook and went on to other matters of more direct potential utility in his effort to enhance the performance of the electric light bulb.

Edison was, of course, observing a flow of electrons, and the observation has since even come to be referred to, strangely, as the "Edison effect"—named after the man who had *failed* to discover it. Had he been a curious (and patient) scientist, less preoccupied with matters of short-run utility, Edison might later have shared a Nobel Prize with Owen Richardson, who analyzed the behavior of electrons when heated in a vacuum, or conceivably even with J. J. Thomson for the initial discovery of the electron itself. Edison's "prepared mind," however, was prepared only for observations that were likely to have some practical relevance in the short run. However, in view of Edison's extensive contributions to the world of technology, it would be uncharitable in the extreme to criticize Edison for his failure to contribute to fundamental science as well.

A distinctive feature of the twentieth century in dynamic capitalist economies was the vastly increased numbers of scientifically "prepared minds" in both the universities and private industry. The pursuit of the possible implications of unexpected observations became the basis, on many occasions, for fundamental breakthroughs that occurred serendipitously when appropriately "prepared minds" were available to pursue the implications of the unexpected. Surely the most spectacular, and happiest, instance of serendipity in the twentieth century was achieved by Alexander Fleming, the Hunterian professor at the Royal College of Surgeons in London. Fleming's brilliant conjecture, in 1928, was that the unexpected bactericidal effect that he had observed in the cultures in his petri dish had been caused by a common bread mold on his slides. Fleming published this finding in 1929, but no substantial progress was made in producing a marketable product until more than a decade later, when the exigencies of wartime led to a joint Anglo-American "crash" program to accelerate the production of the antibiotic (Elder 1970).

It is at least a plausible speculation that, had Fleming made his marvelous discovery while working in a pharmaceutical lab, penicillin would have become available, in large quantities, far more swiftly than was in fact the case.[7] In the context of this chapter, it is also worth pointing out a little-known historical fact, that the technology to produce the antibiotic in bulk was achieved not, as would ordinarily have been expected, by the pharmaceutical chemist, but by chemical engineers. It was the chemical engineers who demonstrated how a technique called "aerobic submerged fermentation," which became the dominant production technology, could be applied to the large-volume production of this complex product (Elder 1970).

The growth of organized industrial labs in twentieth-century America vastly enlarged the number of trained scientists in the industrial world who encountered strange phenomena that were most unlikely to occur, or to be observed, except in some highly specialized industrial context. In this sense, the huge increase in new high-tech products, along with dense concentrations of well-trained scientific specialists in industry, increased the likelihood of serendipitous discoveries.

Consider the realm of telephone transmissions. Back at the end of the 1920s, after transatlantic radiotelephone service had been established, the quality of the service was discovered to be poor due to a great deal of interfering static. Bell Labs asked a young man, Karl Jansky, to determine the source of the noise so that it might be eliminated or at least reduced. He was given a rotatable antenna to work with. Jansky published a paper in 1932 in which he reported that he had found three sources of noise: local thunderstorms, more distant thunderstorms, and a third source that he described as "a steady hiss static, the origin of which is not known." It was this "star noise," as Jansky labeled it, that marked the birth of the entirely new science of radio astronomy.

Jansky's experience underlines why the frequent attempt to distinguish between basic research and applied research is extremely difficult to carry out in practice. Fundamental scientific breakthroughs have often occurred while dealing with very applied, practical problems, problems relating to the performance of new technologies in an industrial context.

But the distinction breaks down in another way as well. It is essential to distinguish between the personal motives of the individual researchers and the motives of the decision makers in the firm that employs them. Many scientists in private industry might honestly assert that they are attempting to advance the frontiers of basic scientific knowledge, without any concern over possible applications. At the same time, the motivation of the research managers, who make the decisions whether or not to finance research in some basic field of science, may be strongly driven by expectations of eventual useful findings.

This certainly appears to have been the case in the early 1960s when Bell Labs decided to support research in astrophysics because of its potential relationship to the whole range of problems and possibilities in the realm of microwave transmission, and especially in the use of communication satellites for such purposes. It had become apparent that, at very high frequencies, annoying sources of interference in transmission were encountered.

This source of signal loss was a matter of continuing concern in Bell Labs' development of the new technology of satellite communications. It was out of such practical concerns that Bell Labs decided to employ two astrophysicists, Arno Penzias and Robert Wilson. Penzias and Wilson would undoubtedly have been indignant if anyone had suggested that they were doing anything other than basic research. They first observed the cosmic background radiation, which is now taken as confirmation of the "big bang" theory of the formation of the universe, while they were attempting to identify and measure the various sources of disturbance in their antenna and in the atmosphere. Although Penzias and Wilson did not know it at the time, the character of the background radiation that they discovered was just what had been postulated earlier by cosmologists at Princeton who had devised the big bang theory. Penzias and Wilson shared a Nobel Prize in Physics for this finding. Their findings were as basic as basic science can get, and it is in no way diminished by observing that the firm that had employed them did so because the decision makers at Bell Labs hoped to improve the quality of satellite transmission.

The parallelism between the fundamental discoveries of Jansky and Penzias and Wilson is, of course, very striking. In both episodes, the Bell Labs researchers stumbled upon scientific discoveries of the greatest magnitude while they were involved in projects that were motivated by the desire of Bell Labs to improve the quality of telephone transmission. In the case of Penzias and Wilson, they were conducting their research with a remarkably sensitive horn antenna that had been constructed for the earlier Echo and Telstar satellite projects. Wilson later stated that he was originally attracted to work at Bell Labs because working there would provide access to a horn antenna that was one of the most sensitive of such antennas in existence (Penzias and Wilson 1979, 13).

I have called attention to two episodes at Bell Labs in which industrial researchers discovered natural phenomena of immense scientific significance while the firm that employed them did so in the hope that they would solve problems connected with improving the performance of a new communications technology. In one sense, it is fair to say that important scientific findings by profit-making firms are sometimes achieved unintentionally—they have discovered things that they were not looking for, which I take to be the generic meaning of Horace Walpole's mid-eighteenth-century neologism, serendipity. Such breakthroughs in the private sector are difficult to understand if one insists on drawing sharp distinctions between basic and applied research on the basis of the motivations of those performing the research. I find it irresistible here to invoke, once again, the shade of the great Pasteur: "There are no such things as applied sciences, only applications of science."[8]

In fact, I would go much further: when basic research in industry is isolated from the other activities of the firm, whether organizationally or geographically, it is likely to become sterile and unproductive. Much of the history of basic research in American industry suggests that it is likely to be most effective when it is highly interactive with the work, and the concerns, of applied scientists and engineers within the firm. This is because the high-technology industries have continually thrown up problems, difficulties, and unexpected observations that were most unlikely to occur outside of specific high-technology contexts.

The sheer growth in the number of trained scientists in industrial labs, along with the growth of new, highly complex, specialized products that appeared in the course of the twentieth century, powerfully increased the likelihood of serendipitous findings. High-tech industries provide certain unique vantage points for the conduct of basic research, but, in order for scientists to exploit the potential of the industrial environment, it is necessary to create opportunities and incentives for interactions with other components of the firm. Bell Labs before divestiture (1984) is probably the best example of a place where the institutional environment was most hospitable for basic research. I do not suggest that Bell Labs was, in any respect, a representative industrial lab. Far from it. AT&T was, after all, a regulated monopoly that could readily recoup its huge expenditures on research. But, perhaps even more important, it came to occupy a location on the industrial spectrum where, as it turned out, technological improvements required a deeper, scientific exploration of certain specific portions of the natural world that had not been previously studied.

Instrumentation

Of course, my examination of the endogeneity of science has, so far, been no more than a very modest and partial sketch. Entire categories of the influence of technology upon science have been completely ignored here, such as the massive impact of new instrumentation, that is, technologies of observation, experimentation, and measurement. Indeed, scientific instruments may be usefully regarded as the capital goods of the research industry. Much of this instrumentation, in turn, has had its origins in the university world and, to underline the extent of the intertwining of technology and science in recent years, some of the most powerful of those instruments, such as nuclear magnetic resonance, had their origins in fundamental research that was originally undertaken in order to acquire some highly specific pieces of scientific knowledge. In the case of NMR, two university scientists, Felix Bloch at Stanford and E. M. Purcell at Harvard, shared the Nobel Prize in Physics in 1952 for research leading to a deeper understanding of the magnetic properties of atomic nuclei that, in turn, provided the basis for powerful instrumentation, especially in chemistry, for determining the structure of certain molecules, and medical diagnostic technologies (see Rosenberg 1997; and also Kruytbosch 1997).

Clearly, instrumentation and techniques have moved from one scientific discipline to another in ways that have been full of consequences for the progress of science. In fact, it can be argued that an understanding of the progress of individual disciplines is generally unattainable in the absence of an examination of how different areas of science have influenced one another through technology transfer. This understanding is frequently tied directly to the development, the timing, and the mode of transfer of scientific instruments among disciplines. This flow of disciplinary "exports" appears to have been particularly heavy from physics to chemistry, as well as from both physics and chemistry to biology, to clinical medicine, and, ultimately, to the delivery of health care. There has also been a less substantial flow from chemistry to physics and, in recent years, from applied physics and electrical engineering to health care.

The transistor revolution was a direct outgrowth of the expansion of solid-state physics, but the successful completion of that revolution was, in turn, heavily dependent upon further developments in chemistry and metallurgy, which made available materials of a sufficiently high degree of purity and crystallinity. Finally, physics has spawned subspecialties that are, inherently, interdisciplinary: for example, biophysics, astrophysics, and materials science.

One further point, however, is implicit in what has already just been said. The availability of new or improved instrumentation or experimental techniques in one academic discipline has often been the source of interdisciplinary collaboration. In some critical cases, "collaboration" has involved the migration of highly trained scientists from one field to another. Such was the case of physicists from the Cavendish Laboratory at Cambridge University who played a decisive role in the emergence of molecular biology. This emergence had depended heavily upon scientists, trained in the skills of physicists at Cavendish, who transferred the indispensable but, apparently, maddeningly difficult tool of x-ray crystallography into the very different realm of biology. Molecular biology was the product of interdisciplinary research in the special sense that scientists trained in one discipline crossed traditional scientific boundary lines and brought the intellectual tools, concepts, and observational methods into the service of an entirely new field.[9]

The German physicist Max von Laue discovered the phenomenon of x-ray diffraction in 1912. Its applications were, in the early years, employed by William Bragg and Lawrence Bragg, primarily in the field of solid-state physics. The Braggs, father and son, were joint recipients of the Nobel Prize in Physics in 1915. The main center of the methodology of x-ray diffraction was, for many years, the Cavendish Laboratory, presided over by Lawrence Bragg. Numerous scientists went there in order to learn how to exploit the technique, including Max Perutz (at the time a chemist), James Watson, Francis Crick, John Kendrew, all later to receive Nobel Prizes in physiology or medicine. The transfer of skills in x-ray diffraction was facilitated by the highly unusual step of the establishment of a Medical Research Council unit at the Cavendish, headed by Perutz but under the general direction of the physicist William Bragg (Crick 1988, 23). To infer the three-dimensional structure of very-large-molecule proteins through the technique of x-ray crystallography, which offered only two-dimensional photographs of highly complex molecules, provided much of the basis for the new discipline of molecular biology.

It is important to observe that the two separate communities—academic scientists (including medical school clinicians) and commercial instrument makers—interacted with and influenced one another in ways that were truly symbiotic. Precisely because these two communities marched to the tunes of very different drummers, each was ultimately responsible for innovative improvements that could not have been achieved by the other, had the other been acting alone (see Gelijns and Rosenberg 1999). It should be added that the applications of physics research have usually moved more readily across disciplinary boundary lines in industry than they have in the academic world. Profit-making firms are not particularly concerned with where those boundary lines have been drawn in the academic world; they tend to search for solutions to problems regardless of where those solutions may be found (National Research Council 1986).

Thus, the technological realm has not only played a major role in setting the research agenda for science, as I have argued. Technology has also provided new and immensely more powerful research tools than existed in earlier centuries, as is obvious by mere reference to electron microscopy in the study of the micro-universe, to the Hubble telescope in the study of the macro-universe, and to the laser, which has become the most powerful research instrument throughout the realm of the science of chemistry, as well as a major contributor elsewhere.

Finally, since this manuscript is being written within easy walking distance of the Stanford Linear Accelerator, it seems appropriate to close with the following observation. In the realm of modern physics it appears that the rate of scientific progress has been largely determined by the availability of improved experimental technologies. In the succinct formulation of Wolfgang Panofsky, the first director of SLAC: "Physics is generally paced by technology and not by the physical laws. We always seem to ask more questions than we have tools to answer." Exactly.

It seems fair to conclude that the ways in which technological forces have come to shape the various realms of science deserve far more attention than they have so far received.

Notes

I am grateful for valuable comments on an earlier draft by Ken Arrow, Sidney Drell, David Mowery, Richard Nelson, and Douglass North.

1. I have also argued, elsewhere, that there is a high degree of endogeneity, in this sense, in the behavior of decision makers (including faculty) at American universities—considerably more than one finds in other OECD countries. See Rosenberg 2000, 2003.

2. For a thoughtful and balanced appraisal of the issues, see Mowery et al. 2001. For a broad-gauged, trenchant examination, see Nelson 2003.

3. For some perceptive comments on this organizational feature in the United States, see Kennedy 1986.

4. I understand that Romer is seeking to capture a similar process when he states that a new blueprint today spills over to lower the cost of future blueprints.

5. For extensive evidence from aeronautical history, see the book by Walter Vincenti, *What Engineers Know and How They Know It* (1990), from which I have learned very much.

6. See Rosenberg 1998; and the excellent, comprehensive volume by Hounshell and Smith (1988).

7. For a contrary view, see Bernal 1971, 926–27.

8. For a radically different approach toward the definitions of the separate realms of science and technology, see Dasgupta and David 1994.

9. For extensive detail, see the magisterial yet highly accessible volume by Horace Judson (1979) on the early history of molecular biology.

References

Bernal, J. D. 1971. *Science in History.* Vol. 3. Cambridge: MIT Press.

Bever, Michael. 1988. Metallurgy and Materials Science and Engineering at MIT: 1865–1988. Cambridge: MIT Press.

Braun, Ernest, and Stuart MacDonald. 1978. *Revolution in Miniature*. New York: Cambridge University Press.

Bresnahan, T., and M. Trajtenberg. 1995. "General Purpose Technologies: Engines of Growth?" *Journal of Econometrics* 65 (1): 83–108.

Bromberg, Joan Lisa. 1991. *The Laser in America, 1950–70*. Cambridge: MIT Press.

Brooks, Harvey. 1968. "Physics and the Polity." *Science* 160: 396–400.

Crick, Francis. 1988. *What Mad Pursuit: A Personal View of Scientific Discovery.* New York: Basic Books.

Dasgupta, Partha, and Paul David. 1994. "Toward a New Economics of Science." *Research Policy* 23: 487–521.

Elder, Albert Lawrence, ed. 1970. *The History of Penicillin Production*. New York: American Institute of Chemical Engineers.

Gelijns, Annetine, and Nathan Rosenberg. 1999. "Diagnostic Devices: An Analysis of Comparative Advantages." In *Sources of Industrial Leadership: Studies of Seven Industries*, ed. David C. Mowery and Richard Nelson. New York: Cambridge University Press.

Herring, Conyers. 1957. "The Significance of the Transistor Discovery for Physics." Paper presented at a Bell Labs symposium on the Nobel Prize.

Hounshell, David, and John Smith. 1988. *Science and Corporate Strategy: Du Pont R&D, 1902–1980*. New York: Cambridge University Press.

Judson, Horace. 1979. *The Eighth Day of Creation*. New York: Simon and Schuster.

Kennedy, Donald. 1986. "Basic Research in the Universities: How Much Utility?" In *The Positive Sum Strategy: Harnessing Technology for Economic Growth*, ed. Ralph Landau and Nathan Rosenberg. Washington, D.C.: National Academy Press.

Kruytbosch, Carlos. 1997. "The Role of Instrumentation in Advancing the Frontiers of Science." In *Equipping Science for the 21st Century*, ed. John Irvine with Ben Martin, Dorothy Griffiths, and Roel Gathier. Lyme, N.H.: Edward Elgar.

Morton, J. A. 1971. *Organizing for Innovation*. New York: McGraw-Hill.

Mowery, David C., Richard Nelson, Bhaven Sampat, and Arvids Ziedonis. 2001."The Growth of Patenting and Licensing by U.S. Universities: An Assessment of the Effects of the Bayh-Dole Act of 1980." *Research Policy* 30: 99–119.

Mowery, David C., and Nathan Rosenberg. 1998. *Paths of Innovation: Technological Change in 20th Century America*. New York: Cambridge University Press.

National Research Council, Panel on Scientific Interfaces and Technological Applications. 1986. *Scientific Interfaces and Technological Applications*. Washington, D.C.: National Academy Press.

National Science Foundation. 2000. *Science & Technology Indicators, 2000*. Washington, D.C.: National Science Board.

Nelson, Richard. 2003. "The Market Economy and the Scientific Commons." LEM Paper Series 2003/24.

Penzias, Arno A., and Robert C. Wilson. 1979. "The Light of Creation—an Interview with Arno A. Penzias and Robert C. Wilson." Interview by Steven Aaronson. *Bell Laboratories Record*, January, 12–18.

Romer, Paul. 1990. "Endogenous Technological Change." *Journal of Political Economy* 98: S71–S102.

Rosenberg, Nathan. 1990. "Why Do Firms Do Basic Research?" *Research Policy* 19: 165–74.

———. 1997. "The Economic Impact of Scientific Instrumentation Developed in Academic Laboratories." In *Equipping Science for the 21st Century*, ed. John Irvine with Ben Martin, Dorothy Griffiths, and Roel Gathier. Lyme, N.H.: Edward Elgar.

———. 1998. "Technological Change in Chemicals: The Role of University-Industry Relations." In *Chemicals and Long-Term Economic Growth*, ed. Ashish Arora, Ralph Landau, and Nathan Rosenberg. New York: John Wiley.

———. 2000. "America's Universities as Endogenous Institutions." In *Schumpeter and the Endogeneity of Technology: Some American Perspectives*. New York: Routledge.

———. 2003. "America's Entrepreneurial Universities." In *The Emergence of Entrepreneurship Policy*, ed. David Hart. New York: Cambridge University Press.

Vincenti, Walter. 1990. *What Engineers Know and How They Know It*. Baltimore: Johns Hopkins University Press.

Chapter 6

Interfirm Collaboration Networks: The Impact of Network Structure on Rates of Innovation

MELISSA A. SCHILLING AND COREY PHELPS

INTERFIRM NETWORKS HAVE BEEN shown to be important engines of knowledge creation and innovation (Ahuja 2000; Allen 1977; Freeman 1991). Interorganizational relationships enable firms to pool, exchange, and jointly create information and other resources (Kogut 1991; Powell, Koput, and Smith-Doerr 1996; Saxenian 1990; Vonortas 1997). By providing member firms access to a wider range of resources than individual firms possess, interfirm networks enable firms to achieve much more than they could individually (Liebeskind 1996; Rosenkopf and Almedia 2003).

As firms forge and maintain collaborative relationships with each other, they weave a network of paths that enable them to access, disseminate, and combine information. The specific pattern that such relationships exhibit represents the structure of the network. The structure of an interfirm network influences the rate and extent of information diffusion through the network, including the types of information to which firms have access and how readily they may access it (Rogers 1995; Valente 1995; Yamaguchi 1994, 2002). By influencing the rate and extent at which firms can access new information or recombine information in new ways, the structure of the interfirm network influences the knowledge creation and utilization by the firms in the network (Kogut 2000; Monge and Contractor 2003; Powell, Koput, and Smith-Doerr 1996).

While research has long recognized the importance of alliance networks in firm innovation (see Freeman 1991 for a review), nearly all of this work has treated the network concept as a metaphor, rather than a construct with measurable properties. Only recently have researchers begun to assess the formal structural properties of alliance networks and their impact on firm innovation and knowledge acquisition (e.g., Ahuja 2000; Baum, Calabrese, and Silverman 2000; Smith-Doerr et al. 1999; Soh 2003). Most of this emerging body of research has focused on a firm's position within its immediate network neighborhood rather than the structure of the overall network. For example, studies have examined a firm's centrality (Smith-Doerr et al. 1999), number of alliances (Ahuja 2000; Deeds and Hill 1996; Rothaermel 2001; Shan, Walker, and Kogut 1994), and the structure of its local network (Ahuja 2000; Baum, Calabrese, and Silverman 2000). To our knowledge, there has been no empirical test of the impact of global network structure on the innovation of member firms. This raises the following questions: Does the global structure of the interfirm network influence the rate of knowledge creation in the network? If so, what structural properties are more likely to enhance innovation?

To address these questions, we apply recent advances in graph theory to interfirm networks. A fundamental insight from "small-world" network research is that a high degree of clustering and short average path lengths can coexist in a sparse network. That is, even if a network has relatively few links and many of those links are redundant (as when a firm's partners are also partners of one another), the network can still have a remarkably short path length to a wide range of firms. This finding has very important implications for information diffusion. The dense connectivity of clusters creates *bandwidth* in a network, enabling large amounts of information to be diffused rapidly, while short path lengths to a wide range of firms provides *reach* in the network, ensuring that diverse information sources can be tapped. In a network with small-world connectivity, there is almost no trade-off between bandwidth and reach—both can be achieved simultaneously, even in a very sparse network. We argue that small-world properties in interfirm networks will significantly enhance their creative output irrespective of other varying differences. We test this hypothesis using longitudinal data on interfirm alliance networks in 10 technology-intensive industries.

This research offers several important contributions to understanding knowledge creation in interfirm networks, as well as knowledge networks and knowledge creation in general. First, we provide a theoretical argument showing that the structural properties of interfirm networks will significantly influence their innovative output. Other things being equal, structure matters, and small-world structures have marked advantages for knowledge creation. Second, we demonstrate the robustness of the theory in explaining patent output at the interfirm network level. To our knowledge, no other study has attempted to assess the structural properties of industry-level interfirm network structures on the collective innovation of network members. Third, whereas recent studies have demonstrated the existence of small-world network structures and their possible causes (Barabasi 2002; Baum, Shipilov, and Rowley 2003; Watts 1999a), relatively little research has examined the *consequences* of small-world structures in an industrial setting.

We begin by describing recent work on small-world networks and demonstrate its implications for diffusion and search within an interfirm knowledge network. From this we derive a hypothesis about how the structure of interfirm knowledge networks influences their innovative output. We test this hypothesis using panel data on interfirm alliance networks in 10 technology-intensive industries.

Small-World Networks

Before discussing small-world networks, it is necessary to briefly explain some basic network concepts. A network is any set of *nodes* (individuals, firms, computers, etc.) that are connected in some way (familial relationships, contracts, data transmission lines, etc.). A *link* is a path that connects two nodes directly. The *length of the path* connecting two nodes A and B is the number of intermediate links that must be traversed in reaching A from B, so that the minimum possible length of a path is unity. A network is *sparse* if a small proportion of its nodes are linked directly. It is *clustered* if it consists of a number of subsets of nodes within which the nodes are profusely linked, resulting in multiple redundant paths between them.[1] A network is *decentralized* if there is no one node (or small set of nodes) that is directly connected to a large portion of the other nodes.[2]

A *small-world network* is one in which the average length of all the paths in the network is small (close to unity), despite being sparse, clustered, and decentralized. Often there are many paths that can be used to reach one node from another, but one (or more) of these paths is the shortest. This shortest distance is the minimum number of links that must be traversed in order for information, electricity, a contagion, or the like to travel from one node to the other. If no path exists between a pair of nodes, the path length is said to be infinite. The average of all such minimum paths in a network is a measure of the network's overall degree of connectivity or "closeness" of nodes in the network.[3] If a network is sparse, clustered, and decentralized, one might expect that the network would have a very long average path length or that there would be disconnected clusters of nodes that are unreachable (leading to an infinite path length). Surprisingly, however, many real-world networks that are sparse, clustered, and decentralized exhibit remarkably short path lengths. This has aroused intense interest in the ways in which such structures emerge, and how they affect various outcomes.

Small-world analysis has its roots in work by mathematical graph theorists (e.g., Erdos and Renyi 1959; Solomonoff and Rapoport 1951), but research specifically on the small-world phenomenon did not commence until the 1960s, when de Sola Pool and Kochen (1978) estimated both the average number of acquaintances that people possess and the probability of two randomly selected members of a society being linked by a chain of no more than two acquaintances. At about the same time, psychologist Stanley Milgram was conducting an innovative empirical test of the small-world hypothesis (1967).

Milgram addressed a number of letters to a friend in Boston who was a stockbroker. He then distributed these letters to a random selection of people in Nebraska. He instructed the individuals to pass the letters to the addressee by sending them to a person they knew on a first-name basis who seemed in some way closer (socially, geographically, etc.) to the stockbroker. This person would then do the same, until the letters reached their final destination. Many of the letters did eventually reach the stockbroker, and Milgram found that on average the letters had passed through about six individuals en route. Milgram had demonstrated that the world was indeed small, and this finding was dubbed "six degrees of separation" (Guare 1990).

If links in social networks were formed randomly, we would expect short average path lengths even in sparse networks (Bollobas 1985): if every person has z acquaintances, and every acquaintance also has z acquaintances, the number of people an individual can reach multiplies very quickly with the number of acquaintances they have and the number of steps taken. The number of degrees of separation increases only logarithmically with the size of the network, causing the average path length to be very small even for very large networks. Similarly, if a single (or a few) central node were connected to every other node in the network, it would again be expected that every pair of nodes would be connected by a relatively short path length through this central vertex. Finally, if the number of links relative to the number of nodes were large, we would expect very short path lengths. As the number of links per node approaches the number of nodes in the network (i.e., maximum density), it becomes possible for every node to be directly connected (i.e., path length unity) to every other node.

However, social networks are not random. Instead, they are highly clustered, with many local areas exhibiting significant redundancy in links. Furthermore, social networks are (with some exceptions) decentralized, and extremely sparse. No single individual is connected to all the others, and the maximum number of acquaintances of any individual in the network is a tiny fraction of the entire population (Watts 1999b). Intuitively, such clustered networks should require a long path to connect individual nodes in different clusters with one another because of the sparseness of connections between clusters, making the finding that path lengths can be short in social networks quite surprising. In their influential 1998 article, Watts and Strogatz demonstrated how this could occur: as a few random or long-spanning connections are added to a highly clustered network, the average path length drops much more quickly than the clustering coefficient.[4] Thus in the range between highly clustered (locally ordered) networks and random networks, there is an interval in which high clustering and short path lengths can coexist (see fig. 6.1).

To understand this more clearly, consider two extreme cases. The first is a network that consists of numerous highly clustered cliques that are connected to each other with only one link. Such a network is both highly clustered and extremely sparse. Watts (1999b) refers to such a network as a "connected caveman graph" and argues that it is an appropriate benchmark for a large, clustered graph (see fig. 6.2, panel a). The contrasting case is a random graph, which exhibits minimal clustering and represents a good approximation to a network with minimal average path length

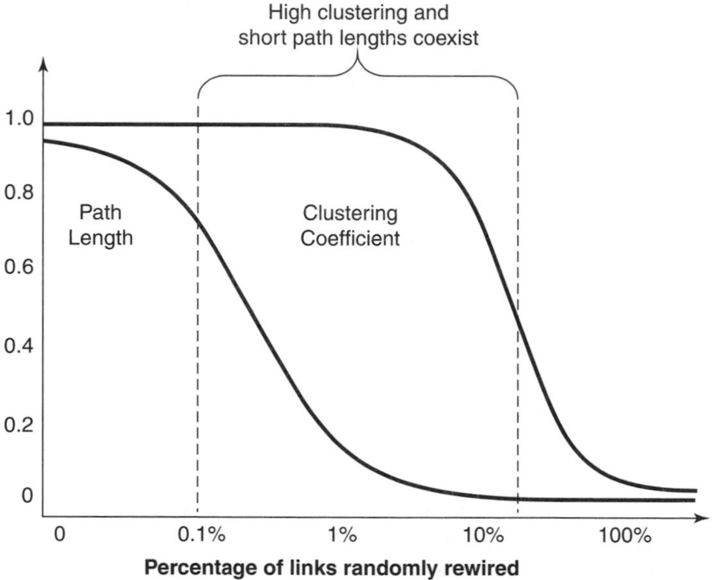

Figure 6.1. Path Length versus Clustering Coefficient as Links are Randomly Rewired[1]

[1]The graph depicts the values of the path length and clustering coefficient, normalized by the path length and clustering for a regular lattice (no rewired links). A logarithmic horizontal scale is used to resolve the rapid drop in path length corresponding to the onset of the small-world phenomenon. During the drop, the clustering coefficient remains almost constant.

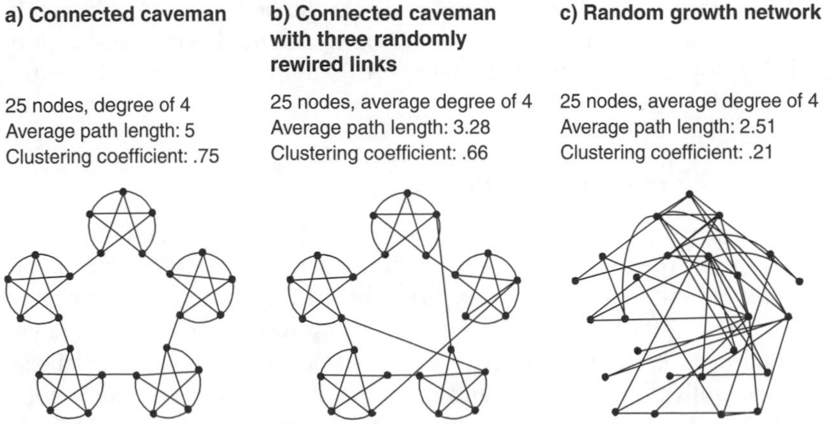

a) Connected caveman

25 nodes, degree of 4
Average path length: 5
Clustering coefficient: .75

b) Connected caveman with three randomly rewired links

25 nodes, average degree of 4
Average path length: 3.28
Clustering coefficient: .66

c) Random growth network

25 nodes, average degree of 4
Average path length: 2.51
Clustering coefficient: .21

Figure 6.2. Connectivity Properties of "Connected Caveman" and Random Networks

(see fig. 6.2, panel c). Consistent with the preceding intuitive description, the connected caveman network has a very large average path length when compared with the random graph.

However, highly clustered and globally sparse networks need not be large worlds. Watts and Strogatz (1998) demonstrate that by randomly "rewiring" a very small percentage of links in the highly clustered graph, the network exhibits the small-world properties of high clustering and short average path length. Because nodes that are initially widely separated in the network are as likely to become connected as those that are near neighbors, the network contracts as ties within clusters are replaced with ties that span them (Kogut and Walker 2001; Watts 1999b). In figure 6.2, replacing three of the links in panel a with randomly generated links decreases the path length 34 percent, from 5 to 3.28, while its clustering coefficient decreases by only 12 percent, from .75 to .66 (see fig. 6.1, panel b).

The structural properties of small-world networks have significant implications for network dynamics. Watts (1999a) demonstrates how the topology of a small-world network affects the degree to which a contagion (e.g., information, fashion, disease) is disseminated throughout the network and the rate at which this diffusion occurs. Watts's simulation results demonstrate that a contagion can spread completely and far more rapidly in a small-world network than in a large world and nearly as fast as in a random network. Yamaguchi (1994) obtained similar results in his examination of the rate of information diffusion in a variety of network structures. Wilhite (2001) extends this work to an industrial setting by using a simulation to explore the impact of small-world properties on bilateral trade networks. Wilhite shows that small-world properties in a bilateral trade network enable agents to find goods at the best price quickly, resulting in an economy that reaches a Pareto optimal equilibrium more rapidly, and with lower search and negotiation costs than those incurred in alternative trade network structures.

Small Worlds in Interfirm Networks

Interfirm networks also display sparsity, decentralization, and clustering. First, interfirm networks tend to be extremely sparse because forging and maintaining connections between firms has a cost in terms of time and effort, and connections that are not reinforced over time diminish (Cummings 1991). When firms forge relationships with other organizations (or individuals) to share and exchange information and knowledge, they face a variety of search, monitoring, and enforcement costs (Joskow 1987; Williamson 1985). Firms face search costs in finding alliance partners that fit well with the firm's objectives. Monitoring and managing of alliances is also complex and costly, causing the firm's effectiveness at managing its alliances to decline with the number of alliances to which it is committed (Cummings 1991; Shan 1990). Thus, because of the cost constraints in forging and maintaining links, interfirm knowledge networks tend to have far fewer links than if all pairs of firms were directly connected. Second, interfirm networks tend to be decentralized. While interfirm networks do tend to have "hub" firms that have very large numbers of connections, most interfirm networks have several "hubs" rather than a single dominant firm that directly connects to all the other firms in the network (Baum, Shipilov, and Rowley 2003; Gulati and Gargiulo 1999).

Finally, interfirm knowledge networks tend to be highly clustered (i.e., some groups of firms have more links connecting them to each other than to the other firms in the network). There are several mechanisms leading to clustering in interfirm knowledge networks, but two of the most common are linking based on similarity or complementarity (Doz and Hamel 1997; Saxenian 1994; Venkatraman and Lee 2004). Firms tend to interact more intensely or frequently with other firms with which they share some type of proximity or similarity (e.g., geographic, technological) (Baum, Shipilov, and Rowley 2003; Rogers 1995; Saxenian 1994; Schutjens and Stam 2003), leading to strong clustering. Proximity, similarity, and the resultant clustering enhance firms' ability and willingness to exchange information and knowledge. First, firms may be unable to transfer knowledge that is complex or tacit without frequent interaction and a shared dialect (Szulanski 1996; Zander and Kogut 1995). Thus proximity and similarity directly affect firms' ability to exchange knowledge. Second, a thicket of redundant ties among a group of firms (as when a firm's partners are themselves also allied) helps to create trust and reciprocity norms that may make firms more willing to share knowledge (Bourdieu 1986; Coleman 1988; Granovetter 1992; Kreps 1990; Portes 1998; Uzzi 1997).

Small-World Connectivity and Knowledge Creation

Knowledge creation occurs when new information is integrated within the network, or when existing information within the network is recombined in new ways. A long line of research has emphasized the latter method, suggesting that the creation of new knowledge is most often the result of novel recombinations of known elements of knowledge, problems, or solutions (Fleming 2001; Gilfillan 1935; Nelson and Winter 1982; Schumpeter 1934; Usher 1954) or the reconfiguration of the ways in which knowledge elements are linked (Henderson and Clark 1990). The structure of the network through which search and diffusion takes place is integral to this recombination process. Integrating the small-world network ideas outlined earlier with existing sociological research on network structure indicates that interfirm networks with small-world network properties have significant advantages relative to other global network structures in enabling knowledge creation.

The dense connectivity of clusters enables information that is introduced into the cluster to reach many firms in the cluster quickly. Shared dialects and norms permit richer information, and greater amounts of information, to be exchanged and integrated more readily, thus accelerating the rate of knowledge creation in the network from a given amount of new information (Szulanski 1996; Uzzi 1997; Zander and Kogut 1995). Furthermore, new information that is integrated within a dense cluster may be more fully utilized since it will have multiple points of access and influence.

Much of the information and knowledge shared within a cluster will eventually become homogenous and redundant (Burt 1992; DeMarzo, Vayanos, and Zwiebel 2003; Granovetter 1973): the dense links provide many redundant paths to the same actors and thus the same sources of information and knowledge. This limits knowledge creation. However, given the different initial conditions and causes for formation of each cluster, clusters of firms will tend to be highly heterogeneous across a network with respect to the knowledge they possess and produce. The diversity of knowledge distributed in different clusters across the network provides the requisite variety for recombination and indicates the importance of shortcuts between clusters. Global networks that contain bridges between clusters provide firms *within* clusters access to diverse information while simultaneously contracting the path length of the network. As described previously, the diffusion of information and knowledge occurs more rapidly and with more integrity in networks with a short average path length than in networks with longer paths (Watts 1999a, 1999b). Consequently, in networks with a high degree of clustering and short average path lengths (i.e., small worlds), firms can benefit from the diverse knowledge located in different clusters throughout the network while preserving the benefits of their membership in clusters.

Since forging of alliances is costly and constrained, there appears to be a trade-off between forming dense clusters to facilitate rapid exchange and integration of knowledge, versus forging links to a wider range of firms to tap more diverse knowledge. Small-world network properties help to resolve this trade-off by enabling both dense clustering and wide reach to coexist, even in a sparse and decentralized network. By forging links that provide bridges between clusters, interfirm networks can retain a high degree of clustering, while achieving a short path length to diverse knowledge sources (Hansen 2002; Hargadon 1998). The combination of clustering and short average path lengths enables a wide range of information to be exchanged and integrated rapidly, leading to greater knowledge creation. This leads to the following hypothesis:

Hypothesis 1: *Interfirm knowledge networks that combine both a high degree of clustering and short average path lengths exhibit significantly more knowledge creation than networks that do not exhibit these characteristics.*

Methods

We tested hypothesis *1* using data on alliance networks and patent production in 10 high-tech manufacturing industries: Aerospace Equipment (SICs: 3721, 3724, 3728, 3761, 3764, 3769); Automotive Bodies and Parts (3711, 3713, 3714); Chemicals (281-, 282-, 285-, 286-, 287-, 288-, 289-); Computer and Office Equipment (3571, 3572, 3575, 3577); Household Audiovisual Equipment (3651); Medical Equipment (3841, 3842, 3843, 3844, 3845); Petroleum Refining and Products (2911, 2951, 2952, 2992, 2999); Pharmaceuticals (2833, 2834, 2835, 2836); Semiconductors (3674), and Telecommunications Equipment (3661). These industries have been designated as high tech in numerous Bureau of Labor Statistics studies (e.g., Hadlock, Hecker, and Gannon 1991; Hecker 1999; Luker and Lyons 1997). To be considered high tech, the industry's employment in both research and development and other technology-oriented occupations must be at least twice the average for all industries in the Occupational Employment Statistics Survey. From the list of high-tech manufacturing industries, we then eliminated industries that make very little use of alliances (e.g., special-industry machinery (355), electrical industrial apparatus (362), search and navigation equipment (381), and photographic equipment and supplies (386)).

This resulting sample of industries provides an excellent basis for the current study for three reasons. First, the creation of knowledge is fundamental to the pursuit of competitive advantage in high-technology industries (Teece, Pisano, and Shuen 1997). Second, each of these industries makes active use of alliances in pursuit of their innovation activities (Vonortas 1997). Third, because we use patent data for our dependent variable, it is important to select industries that use patents. There is evidence that these industries actively patent their intellectual property (Levin et al. 1987).

Alliance Networks

Though many forms of interfirm relationships (e.g., board interlocks, participation in technical committees, etc.) may influence information diffusion, we chose to measure the network structure created by publicly reported strategic alliances for several reasons. First, there is a rich history of research on the importance of strategic alliances as a mechanism for knowledge sharing among firms (Freeman 1991; Gulati 1998; Hamel 1991; Smith-Doerr et al. 1999). Second, alliances are used by a wide range of firms (including both public and private firms) in a wide range of industries, and they are used for the exchange and joint creation of a wide range of information, including highly technical information. In contrast, board interlocks are only relevant for publicly held firms, and are unlikely to be utilized for the exchange of substantive technical data. Technical committees do enable exchange and creation of highly technical information, but are much more likely to be used in industries in which compatibility standards are important (e.g., computers, telecommunication) than in other industries. Furthermore, recent research has shown that participation in technical committees facilitates future alliance formation among participants. Therefore, technical committee participation can be seen as a "pre-alliance network" (Rosenkopf, Metiu, and George 2001). To the extent that this is true, measurement of the alliance network should capture the network structure of technical committee relationships formed in prior periods.

Determining the boundaries of interfirm networks is not a trivial task (Marsden 1990). Prior research in social networks has provided three procedural indicators for empirical establishment of network boundaries: attributes of actors that rely on membership criteria, such as membership in an industry; types of relations between actors, such as participation in strategic alliances; and participation in a set of common events (Laumann, Marsden, and Prensky 1983; Marsden 1990). Following these precedents, we employed two rules to guide our construction of the 10 industry networks analyzed in this study. First, each alliance included at least one participant that was a member of the target industry (indicated by its primary four-digit SIC). Second, to be included in the target industry network, each alliance had to operate in that industry, as indicated by its primary SIC of activity.[5] These rules help to ensure that the industry networks entail alliance activity focused on the designated industry. Because an industry member's partners can come from both within or beyond its industry, there is some overlap between the alliance networks. Notably, some well-known firms such as IBM, Hewlett Packard, AT&T, and General Motors appear as partners in multiple alliance networks. We included alliance partners from beyond the target industry because excluding them would eliminate our ability to observe many of the indirect relationships between industry members, thus biasing our measures of network connectivity. Recent alliance network research has employed similar network construction criteria (Rowley, Behrens, and Krackhardt 2000).

Alliance data were gathered using Thomson's SDC Platinum database. The SDC data have been used in a number of empirical studies on strategic alliances (e.g., Anand and Khanna 2000; Schilling and Steensma 2001; Sampson 2004). For each industry, the alliances collected were those announced between 1990 and 1997. Separate alliance networks were created for each industry according to their U.S. SIC code. Both public and private firms are included. We chose to use data on only U.S. firms because the SDC data on alliances are much more complete for U.S. firms than for non-U.S. firms (Phelps 2003). Furthermore, to avoid overlooking relationships between parent firms and their subsidiaries and to reduce the complexity of reconciling company names, all alliance announcements were aggregated up to the parent corporation level.

The resulting data set includes data on 3,517 alliance announcements, broken down as follows: Aerospace Equipment (64); Automotive Bodies and Parts (94), Chemicals (263), Computer and Office Equipment (595), Household Audiovisual Equipment (40), Medical Equipment (273), Petroleum Refining and Products (39), Pharmaceuticals (1253), Semiconductors (440), and Telecommunications Equipment (456). Many of the alliance announcements included more than two participating firms, so the number of dyadic alliance pairs is much higher than the numbers reported above. Since any type of alliance may provide a path for knowledge diffusion, and because prior studies indicate that the breadth of an alliance's true activity is often much greater than what is formally reported (Powell, Koput, and Smith-Doerr 1996), we include all alliance types in our analysis. However, it is also reasonable to assume that an alliance formed specifically for the purpose of joint research and development or technology exchange might have more impact on innovation than, for example, a supply agreement or marketing alliance. We explore this possibility by including a measure of the proportion of alliances that are flagged in the SDC database as research and development, cross-technology transfer, or licensing agreements.

Alliance relationships typically last for more than a year, but alliance termination dates are rarely reported. This required us to make an assumption about how long the alliances last. We took a conservative approach and assumed that alliance relationships would last for three years, consistent with recent empirical work on the average duration of alliances (Phelps 2003). Other research has taken a similar approach, using windows ranging from one year to five years (e.g., Bae and Gargiulo 2003; Gulati and Gargiulo 1999; Stuart 2000). We created alliance networks based on three-year windows (i.e., 1990–92, 1991–93, and so on, through 1995–97), resulting in six snapshots of the network structure for each industry, for a total of 60 alliance network snapshots. Each network snapshot was constructed as a binary adjacency matrix. A binary adjacency matrix is a square matrix with nodes (e.g., firms) as rows and columns. The entries in the adjacency matrix x_{ij} indicate which pairs of nodes are adjacent (i.e., have a relationship). In a binary matrix, a value of 1 indicates the presence of a relationship between nodes i and j, while a 0 indicates no relationship. Since our concern here is whether a path exists from one firm to another rather than the effect of multiplex relationships, multiple alliance announcements between the same pair of firms in any time window are treated as only one link. Alliance relationships are considered to be bidirectional, resulting in an undirected graph (Newman, Strogatz, and Watts 2000). Ucinet 6.23, a leading social network analysis software package, was used to obtain measures for each of these networks, as described below (Borgatti, Everett, and Freeman 2002).

Independent Variables

Clustering Coefficient. To capture the bandwidth created by clustering in the network, we used the weighted overall clustering coefficient measure (Borgatti, Everett, and Freeman 2002; Watts 1999a). The clustering coefficient for any node is the percentage of its immediate neighbors that are also connected to each other (known as triad closure in work on social networks). The weighted overall clustering coefficient of the network is the average clustering coefficient for all nodes that have two or more neighbors. While the density measure (defined under control variables) captures the global density (or sparsity) of the entire network, the clustering coefficient captures localized pockets of dense connectivity.

A network can be quite sparse globally, and still have a high clustering coefficient (high local density).

Reach. To capture the average reach of the network, we use a measure of average distance-weighted reach (Borgatti, Everett, and Freeman 2002). This is a compound measure that takes into account both the number of nodes that can be reached by any path from a given node, and the path length it takes to reach them. A firm's distance weighted reach is the sum of the reciprocal distances to every firm that is reachable from a given firm, i.e., $\Sigma_j \, 1/d_{ij}$, where d_{ij} is defined as the minimum distance (geodesic), d, from a focal firm i to partner j, where $i \neq j$. A network's *average distance-weighted reach* is this measure averaged across all firms in the network, $(\Sigma_n \Sigma_j \, 1/d_{ij})/n$, where n is the number of firms in the network. Other things being equal, a very large connected network with a very short average path length (e.g., a completely connected network where there are many firms and every firm is directly connected to every other firm, or a star graph where there are many firms and every firm is connected to the same central "hub" firm) will have the greatest average distance-weighted reach. Longer path lengths, smaller network size, or disconnects that fragment the network into multiple components all decrease average distance-weighted reach.

Reach × Clustering. Small-world connectivity enables high levels of reach and clustering to exist simultaneously. To capture this, we include as an interaction term the cross-product of reach and clustering. This measure is large when both reach and clustering are large, small when both reach and clustering are small, and takes on intermediate values when one variable is large and the other small.

Control Variables

Nodes. We control for the overall size of the network with the variable *nodes*. This variable refers to the total number of firms that constitute the network in a given time window and industry. This measure includes both firms with the designated primary SIC codes of the industry and their alters, which may be either from within the designated industry or from other industries.

Density. We control for the overall density of the network with the variable *density*. This variable measures the ratio of how many links exist in the network to how many potential links there could be if all possible pairs of nodes were directly connected. Density is the inverse of sparsity: the greater the ratio of existing links to the number of potential links in the network, the more dense (and less sparse) the network is, and vice versa.

R&D Intensity. Since R&D investment is a major input to technological innovation (Griliches 1990), we control for differences in R&D

intensity (R&D expenditures/sales) across the industries. These data are based on R&D expenditures and sales of publicly held firms in each industry as obtained from Compustat, and are calculated for the last year of each time period (the same year as the end of the alliance network snapshot). Since our alliance networks include both public and private firms, it would have been preferable to create R&D intensity measures based on both public and private firms in the industry; however, information on R&D expenditures for privately held firms is rarely available. We assume here that R&D intensity for the publicly held firms is a good proxy for R&D intensity of the industry.

Proportion of Alliances for R&D, Cross-Technology Transfer, or Licensing. While all types of alliances are conduits for information about technologies, market opportunities, manufacturing processes, and so on, alliances that are established for the purpose of conducting joint R&D activities, cross-technology transfer, or licensing agreements may be more directly related to rates of patented innovation. To examine this possibility, we include a measure of the percentage of alliance agreements in each network that were established explicitly for the purpose of joint research and development, cross-technology transfer, or licensing.

Dependent Variable: Patent Intensity

One way that knowledge creation is manifest is in the form of inventions (Schmookler 1966). As such, inventions provide an indicator of an organization's knowledge creation activities. Patents provide a measure of novel invention that is externally validated through the patent examination process (Griliches 1990). Patent counts have also been shown to be closely related to new product introductions and invention counts (Comanor and Scherer 1969; Basberg 1987). Indeed, Trajtenberg (1987) concludes that patents are perhaps the most valid and robust indicators of knowledge creation. Use of patent output to measure innovation can be challenged on the ground that the propensity to patent may vary with firm size or industry sector—a potential source of bias (Bound et al. 1984; Levin et al. 1987). However, since the factors that influence propensity to patent are likely to be stable within industry sectors (Griliches 1990), we control for this possible source of unobserved heterogeneity by controlling for industry.

In the current research we do not consider the allocation of the knowledge benefits of the network structure among the firms in the network—we argue only that the structure should affect collective knowledge creation by influencing the accessibility, utilization, and diversity of available information. We thus measure the collective innovation output of the firms in the network. This approach is consistent with the wide range of economic studies that aggregate firm-level data to the industry or national levels to examine aggregate outcomes such as gross domestic product, total factor productivity, or employment. For each network year, patent data were collected for every firm in the network whose primary SIC code matched the industry, consistent with the way we formed the alliance networks. We do not include the patenting output of extra-industry partners since these partners are likely to have their own networks of alliances that influence their patenting output. We used the Delphion database to collect yearly patent counts for each of the firms, aggregating subsidiary patents up to the parent level. We then aggregated the patent counts for all firms in each alliance network for each year, and divided the total number of patents in an industry network by the number of firms in the network to form a measure of patent intensity. While only patents that were ultimately granted were counted, patents were counted in the year of application. Since it can take varying amounts of time for patents to be granted, using the date of application more precisely captures the time of knowledge creation (Griliches 1990). Yearly patent counts were created for the time range 1993 to 2000 inclusive, enabling us to assess different lag specifications between alliance network structure and patent output.

Model Specification

Because we have observations on the same 10 industries over six discrete time periods, we pooled the data and estimated our model using panel regression techniques. Because the data do not suffer from attrition or other sources of missing data, the panel is balanced and consists of 60 observations. A panel design offers several advantages that are of particular importance to this study. First, pooling cross-sectional and time-series data improves estimation efficiency by increasing available degrees of freedom. Second, panel data allow us to control explicitly for unobserved heterogeneity (the possibility that estimated results are attributable to omitted variables), thereby minimizing the possibility of biased parameter estimates and spurious results (Greene 1997). Finally, by measuring a given set of units (i.e., industries) over time as they change status on some variables of interest, before-and-after effects can be observed within and across units. As a result, panel data and their related estimation techniques allow researchers to infer more confidently the causal relationships among dynamic phenomena (Hsiao 1986).

The dependent variable in this study, industry patent intensity, is a continuous measure that is suitable for estimation using linear regression methods. Following prior research that investigates the relationship between interfirm alliances and innovation (e.g., Ahuja 2000; Sampson 2004; Stuart 2000), we employ alternative lags of our independent variables relative to our dependent variable. Specifically, we estimate three models: the first using a one-year lag, the second using a two-year lag, and the third using a three-year lag. We do so to explore the robustness of our findings across alternative specifications.

Two statistical issues complicate estimation. First, the longitudinal design of this study adds the possibility of serial correlation in the residuals, which violates the independence of errors assumption of ordinary least squares. Autocorrelation of this nature can result in inefficient parameter estimates and biased standard errors (Kennedy 1998). Second, unobserved heterogeneity, a form of specification error (Heckman 1981), may be present. There may be unmeasured (or unmeasurable) differences among observationally equivalent industries that affect their patenting intensity. Failure to account for these differences can result in biased results.

Given the continuous nature of the dependent variable, the pooled cross-section time-series design, and the two estimation issues just described, we employed both fixed and random effects linear regression methods to estimate our models. We carried out both using a two-factor design in which both observational units (cross sections) and time periods were controlled for, using dummy variables (fixed effects) or individual error components (random effects). While statisticians differ in their recommendation of fixed versus random effects specifications in terms of whether the panel represents a census of the population of interest or a random sample (see Kennedy 1998), there is a more concrete criterion by which to judge which specification is appropriate. The random effects specification assumes that unmodeled, or purified, errors are uncorrelated with the regressors. To assess whether or not this assumption was violated in our data, thus indicating which specification to use, we used a Hausman (1978) test to check for significant contemporaneous correlation between errors and regressors. We also checked for the presence of first-order serial autocorrelation and corrected for it when necessary.[6] We discuss which specifications were used and why in the results section, which follows. Finally, we employ White's (1980) robust variance-covariance matrix to correct calculated standard errors for heteroscedasticity. All models were estimated using Limdep 8.0.

Results

A summary of the network statistics and patent counts for each industry is provided in table 6.1. As shown in the table, there is substantial variation in the number of firms among the industries that participate in alliances. This is largely due to differences in industry size. The average number of alliances for firms in each industry exhibits much less variation.[7] The next

TABLE 6.1
Network Statistics and Patent Counts for Industry Networks, Averages over 1992–2000

Industry	Average Number of Firms from Industry in Alliances[a]	Average Number of Alliances per Firm	Average Network Size (*nodes*)[b]	Clustering Coefficient			Average Path Length			Average Distance-Weighted Reach	Average Number of Patents per Firm per Year
				Actual	Random Graph	Actual/Random	Actual[c]	Random Graph[d]	Actual/Random		
Aerospace	9	3.05	28	0.4	0.11	3.67	6.25	2.99	2.09	4.83	134.22
Automotive	15.67	3.43	53.2	0.47	0.06	7.29	10.23	3.22	3.17	5.51	47.04
Chemicals	45.17	2.97	199.8	0.36	0.01	24.22	55.51	4.87	11.41	3.9	27.08
Computers and Office Equipment	79.67	4.48	347	0.24	0.01	18.59	18.93	3.90	4.85	20.64	49.88
Household Audio-visual Equipment	9	1.5	28.3	0.13	0.05	2.45	13.91	8.24	1.69	2.04	2.74
Medical Equipment	66.17	1.66	172.33	0.06	0.01	6.23	59.67	10.16	5.87	2.90	5.81
Petroleum Refining and Products	5.3	2.65	24.83	0.22	0.11	2.06	10.63	3.30	3.23	2.33	19.58
Pharmaceuticals	218.33	2.54	510	0.09	0.00	18.07	11.39	6.69	1.70	46.32	7.46
Semiconductors	58.67	3.51	204	0.13	0.02	7.56	11.16	4.24	2.63	19.65	39.31
Telecommunication Equipment	44.83	6.53	266.33	0.21	0.02	8.56	11.4	2.98	3.83	23.78	28.08

[a] This number includes only those firms with the designated primary SICs; it does not include alters in the network that are not in those SICs.
[b] Includes all U.S. firms in network, including both those with the designated primary SICs and their alters irrespective of SIC.
[c] Since the networks are not fully connected, the average path length is calculated using a harmonic mean technique (see Newman 2000).
[d] This is the expected diameter of a random graph, or the length of the largest geodesic (i.e., shortest path between two nodes), which is the upper limit of the average path length of a random graph (Newman 2000).

column provides the average network size (number of nodes) of each network. This number includes firms from the industry and their partners, some of which are not in the target industry.

The next set of columns refers to the clustering coefficients of the alliance networks. First, the actual clustering coefficient of the networks (averaged across the time periods) is provided, followed by the clustering coefficient that would be expected of a random graph of similar size and degree, and the ratio of these two coefficients. Notably, each of the industry networks exhibits significantly more clustering than would be expected in a random graph of the same size and degree. The chemicals, computers and office equipment, and pharmaceutical industries have particularly high degrees of clustering. In the next set of columns, the actual path length of the alliance networks (averaged across time windows) is provided, with the upper limit of the expected average path length (the diameter) of a random graph of the same size and degree. The following column provides the ratio of the actual path length to the random graph path length. Comparing the clustering ratio to the path length ratio reveals that for some of the industries, the clustering coefficient is much greater than that of a random graph, but the path length is remarkably close to that of a random graph—these industries are small worlds. In particular, the pharmaceutical and computer and office equipment industries manifest significant small-world properties: for each of them, the ratio of the actual clustering coefficient to the random graph clustering coefficient is several times the size of the ratio of the actual path length to the random graph path length.

In the remainder of the analyses we will emphasize average distance-weighted reach (or simply *reach*) rather than average path length. This measure captures both how many firms can be reached by any path from any particular firm, and the average path length between them and thus is more congruent with our arguments about the role of both diversity of information and its rate of transmission. Given the variation in the number of nodes in the networks and in the average path lengths, it is not surprising that there is substantial variation in the average reach of the networks. The column showing the results for this measure indicates that firms in some industries can reach many others via a short path, while others can reach relatively few. The table also indicates that there is substantial variation in the patenting output of firms in different industries.

Table 6.2 provides the descriptive statistics and correlations for the variables. The means for density (.03) and clustering (.27) indicated that on average the networks are extremely sparse and quite clustered. Notably, clustering was negatively correlated with the reach of the network, consistent with previous work that has argued that there is typically a trade-off between formation of close, redundant connections in an interfirm network and ability to reach a wide range of knowledge

TABLE 6.2
Descriptive Statistics and Correlations

	Mean	SD	1	2	3	4	5	6	7	8	9
1. Nodes	171.09	154.40									
2. Density	.03	.03	−.699**								
3. R&D Intensity	.07	.03	.638**	−.370**							
4. R&D Alliances	.68	.17	.546**	−.524**	.676**						
5. Clustering	.27	.23	−.357**	.412**	−.248*	−.421**					
6. Reach	12.33	14.13	.887**	−.460**	.725**	.465**	−.304*				
7. Clustering × Reach	2.32	1.95	.565**	−.198	.426**	.204	.269*	.663**			
8. Patent Intensity 1-Yr Lag	31.95	26.29	−.023	.183	−.036	−.070	.300*	−.071	.325**		
9. Patent Intensity 2-Yr Lag	33.12	26.90	.011	.185	−.016	−.046	.282*	−.022	.372**	.975**	
10. Patent Intensity 3-Yr Lag	32.48	26.85	.028	.193	−.006	−.050	.253*	.019	.374**	.898**	.964**

** Correlation is significant at the 0.01 level (2-tailed).
* Correlation is significant at the 0.05 level (2-tailed).

resources via a short path. There is also, not surprisingly, a significant positive correlation between the number of firms participating in alliances (nodes) and the average reach of the network, suggesting that in general, when more firms participate in alliances in a network, the more firms each will be able to reach via a short path. R&D Intensity is significantly and positively correlated with the number of firms participating in alliances (Nodes) and with reach, but is significantly and negatively correlated with clustering. More interestingly, both patent intensity measures indicate a significant, positive correlation with the Clustering Coefficient, and the Reach × Clustering variable. There is no significant correlation between R&D Intensity and any of the patent intensity measures.

Table 6.3 reports the panel regression results for the three dependent variables (Patent Intensity$_{t+1}$, Patent Intensity$_{t+2}$, Patent Intensity$_{t+3}$). We estimated both two-factor fixed and random effects GLS models that corrected for first-order autocorrelation (AR1). Separate results are provided for three dependent variables. Models 1, 2, and 3 report the results using a one-year lag between the alliance network variables and patenting output (Patent Intensity$_{t+1}$). Models 4, 5, and 6 report the results using a two-year lag between the alliance network variables and patenting output (Patent Intensity$_{t+2}$). Models 7, 8, and 9 report the results using a three-year lag between the alliance network variables and patenting output (Patent Intensity$_{t+3}$). For each dependent variable, the first model (1, 4, and 7) includes the constant and control variables only, the second model adds the direct effects of clustering and reach (models 2, 5, and 8), and the third model adds the interaction term, Reach × Clustering (models 3, 6, and 9). This model specification controls for industry effects without generating coefficients for them. Time period effects were also estimated, but their coefficients are not reported to conserve space.

Since Hausman tests for some models indicated a random effects specification was appropriate and in others indicated that a fixed effects specification was appropriate, we have provided both sets of results. Our hypothesis receives strong support across the models, particularly those with a one-year or two-year lag. In most of the models, the control variables were not statistically significant. Density achieves significance in a few of the models, suggesting that there may be a positive relationship between overall density of the network and its patenting intensity. The models also indicate that clustering does not have a significant main effect on patenting intensity. Reach has a significant negative relationship with patenting intensity in both the fixed and random effects models with a one-year lag. It also has a significant negative coefficient in the random effects model with a two-year lag. These results suggest that by itself, reach may decrease patenting intensity, consistent with arguments about the trade-offs of focusing primarily on forging nonredundant

TABLE 6.3
Two-Factor Fixed and Random Effects (with group dummies and period effects)

	Patent Intensity$_{t+1}$			Patent Intensity$_{t+2}$			Patent Intensity$_{t+3}$		
	1	2	3	4	5	6	7	8	9
Fixed effects									
Constant	**50.98****	**48.64****	**50.42****	**46.60****	**43.63****	**45.20****	**36.63****	**35.61***	**36.31***
Nodes	−.06	−.03	−.01	−.04	−.04	−.03	−.02	−.04	−.03
Density	102.96	74.28	−5.22	**183.40***	153.83	84.12	114.12	107.25	75.81
R&D Intensity	−159.92	−155.06	−130.48	−159.17	−151.67	−130.13	5.67	8.92	18.64
R&D Alliances	−.21	.83	−3.02	.17	3.77	.40	−5.70	−3.32	−4.85
Clustering		4.50	−10.44		5.40	−7.70		1.72	−4.19
Reach		−.37	**−.85***		−.04	−.46		.20	.01
Clustering × Reach			**3.37***			**2.96****			1.33
Hausman	3.13	15.89*	28.22**	6.87	18.13**	27.84**	23.68**	21.44**	32.89**
	(Random)	(Fixed)	(Fixed)	(Random)	(Fixed)	(Fixed)	(Fixed)	(Fixed)	(Fixed)
Adj. R^2	.92	.92	.93	.96	.96	.96	.95	.95	.95
Random effects									
Constant	**29.05****	**20.51****	**27.79****	**26.39****	**19.73***	**26.26****	**18.54***	**21.73***	**25.26****
Nodes	−.01	.04	.04	.01	−.02	.03	**.50***	**.01***	−.01
Density	86.95	51.59	−16.13	160.37*	125.34	43.56	**268.05****	**203.51****	**192.50***
R&D Intensity	34.16	−12.31	18.04	−72.39	−71.91	−56.06	−149.17	−81.73	−110.56
R&D Alliances	6.82	12.65	4.06	9.90	16.94*	10.36	13.43	9.67	7.41
Clustering		11.11	−10.11		8.92	−10.26		1.25	−11.84
Reach		−.54	**−1.13****		−.18	**−.76****		.27	−.01
Clustering X Reach			**4.74****			**4.31****			**2.71***

$^*p < .05$, $^{**}p < .01$ (two-tailed tests for all variables using White's (1980) robust standard error).

alliances. Five of the six models, however, indicate that when reach is combined with clustering, this combination significantly and positively increases patent intensity. This supports hypothesis 1's prediction that the combination of reach and clustering would significantly enhance knowledge creation. Fixed effects models 3 (one-year lag) and 6 (two-year lag) both show significant positive coefficients for the Clustering × Reach variable (3.37, $p < .05$, and 2.96, $p < .01$ respectively). The Clustering × Reach variable for model 9 (three-year lag) is positive, but did not achieve statistical significance. The random effects models yield similar, and slightly stronger results. The full random effects models for all three lag specifications (3, 6, and 9) indicate significant positive coefficients for the Clustering × Reach variable (4.74, $p < .01$, 4.31, $p < .01$ and 2.71, $p < .05$ respectively). The results overall suggest that when clustering is low, high reach is associated with lower patent intensity. When reach is low, high clustering has no significant effect on patent intensity. However, when both clustering and reach are high, consistent with a small-world network, patent intensity is significantly increased.

These results are consistent with the arguments made earlier: bandwidth without reach may enable firms to exchange information easily, but much of this information is redundant. On the other hand, reach without bandwidth may enable the network to access a wide range of information, but this information is not shared or exchanged easily or quickly. The combination of bandwidth and reach enables a wide range of information to be shared and exchanged effectively and efficiently, significantly enhancing knowledge creation.

Discussion

We began by describing small-world networks and discussing their implications for diffusion and search. We argued that two structural properties in particular, clustering and path length, play crucial roles in network diffusion and search. Clustering enables a globally sparse network to achieve high bandwidth through locally dense pockets of closely connected firms. Short path lengths increase the reach of the network by bringing the information resources of more firms within relatively close range. It is typically assumed that there is a trade-off between bandwidth and reach: alliances that create redundant paths within a clique of partners yield bandwidth but forfeit reach, while alliances that create nonredundant paths to new firms create reach but forfeit bandwidth. However, integration of the knowledge network perspective with work on small-world networks reveals this need not be so. Small-world networks have both high clustering and short path lengths, achieving great reach while forfeiting little bandwidth. We thus argued that small world network properties would significantly enhance the knowledge creation of an interfirm network. We tested this argument using data on alliance networks and patenting output for 10 industries, and the results offered strong support for our argument: the combination of clustering and reach was associated with significantly higher patenting output. The results appear to be stro77nger for models employing a one- or two-year lag rather than a three-year lag, suggesting firms may reap the bulk of the innovation benefits of their alliance network structure within one or two years.

One of the key implications of this work is that free-market policies that enable firms to collaborate on innovation may result in benefits that extend well beyond the firms directly involved in a particular collaborative relationship. The larger network that emerges among a group of firms as a result of their alliances can facilitate greater information diffusion across the entire network, resulting in greater prospective innovation by all firms connected to the network. While large firms play a disproportionate role in the network's connectivity by creating "hubs" in the network, this does not necessarily mean that large firms control the flow of information to ensure that it benefits them primarily. First, while it might make sense for firms to try to restrict the flow of proprietary knowledge about particular technologies, much of the information that flows through a network would not be considered proprietary by most firms in the network. A wide range of information is likely to be exchanged in any kind of extended contact between two or more firms: information about new opportunities, new potential suppliers, new potential competitors, problems in search of solutions, solutions in search of problems, promising new processes, failed processes, and more. Given the nature of the recombinant search process and the crucial role of unexpected combinations between different kinds of knowledge (Schilling 2005), it would be nearly impossible for firms to predict what information could prove ultimately to be valuable to others in the network and prevent its diffusion. Furthermore, while "hub" firms should have an advantage in receiving knowledge that flows through the network because of their central positions, it would be difficult for them to prevent this knowledge from being diffused to other regions of the network via redundant paths.

The results of this study are also relevant for the economics literature on knowledge spillovers. Knowledge spillovers represent an externality in which the knowledge produced by one firm can be appropriated, at little cost, by other firms (Jaffe 1986). Spillovers are made possible by the public good nature of knowledge, which prevents it from being completely appropriated by the inventing firm (Arrow 1962). This reasoning suggests that the R&D efforts of a collection of firms serve as a pool of external knowledge for a focal firm, which may allow it to innovate at much less cost than otherwise possible (Griliches 1979). Thus, knowledge spillovers may serve as a positive externality that enhances the aggregate innovativeness of all firms (Jaffe 1989). Empirical evidence indicates that spillovers are important in explaining innovation and productivity growth (Griliches 1992). However, spillovers are not equally accessible to, or appropriable by, all firms. Prior research has shown that spillovers tend to be spatially bounded: their effect is more pronounced for firms conducting research in similar technological domains (Jaffe 1986, 1989) and geographic locations (Feldman 1999). Our results add to this literature as they suggest that interfirm networks are an impor-tant mechanism of knowledge spillovers. Our findings indicate that collaborative interfirm relationships can act as channels for knowledge spillovers and that the specific pattern these relationships exhibit can have important consequences for the aggregate innovativeness of networked firms. Specifically, interfirm network structures that combine a high degree of clustering with short average path length seem to enhance the spillover process and yield higher innovation rates.

This research has a number of additional contributions. First, whereas previous research on interfirm alliances has examined the impact of alliances on firm-level innovation, our study is the first that we know of to compare the alliance network structure across multiple industries, and examine its impact on network-level innovation. Similarly, whereas a few recent studies have demonstrated that some individual industries (e.g., banking) exhibit small-world connectivity properties (Baum, Shipilov, and Rowley 2003; Kogut and Walker 2001), to our knowledge this is the first study that has compared the small-world properties of multiple industry networks over time. More important, we link these network properties with knowledge diffusion and search, and demonstrate that small-world connectivity properties in interfirm networks can significantly enhance knowledge creation. Finally, this research speaks to the debate over whether innovation is enhanced by network density or efficiency: both local density and global efficiency can exist simultaneously, and it is this combination that enhances innovation.

These findings have important implications for ways in which interfirm networks may be deliberately structured to enhance knowledge creation. While no single actor may be able to control an entire industry network, there are some that can influence the structure of interfirm networks to take advantage of small-world properties. Government agencies involved in industrial policy can exert influence over the collaborative activities of industry members to foster greater innovation and competitiveness. For example, the European Union's EUREKA (European Research Coordinating Agency) R&D program plays a large role in organizing the collaborative R&D activities among European companies. MITI performs a similar function in Japan. Research consortia also play a powerful role in structuring relationships among consortia members. All of these organizations are in an excellent position to influence actively the structure of their respective collaborative networks. This suggests that these organizations could benefit from employment of network analytic tools and analyzing interfirm networks from a global network perspective.

The results of this study also have interesting public policy implications. The social welfare consequences of technical collaboration and their implications for antitrust policy have been the subject of much debate by economists (Baumol 2001; Brodley 1990; Jorde and Teece 1990; Katz and Ordover 1990). While one view stresses the efficiency gains that may be derived from technical collaboration in the form of enhanced diffusion, production, and adoption of innovations, the other perspective emphasizes the potential for collusive behavior in downstream product-markets. Consequently, proponents of the former view advocate substantial tolerance of technical collaboration by antitrust authorities (e.g., Jorde and Teece 1990), whereas supporters of the latter discourage such leniency (e.g., Brodley 1990). The debate is largely unresolved because of the limited empirical evidence on the topic. Nevertheless, in recent years U.S. antitrust enforcement has increasingly focused on innovation issues and has attempted to weigh the efficiency benefits from collaboration against their potential for monopolistic behavior (Kovacic and Shapiro 2000).

Our findings have important contributions to make to this policy debate. The analytic focus of this discussion has been the collaborative relationship and the firms participating in it. Researchers and regulators have ignored the potential influence on innovation of the *indirect* collaborative ties that connect firms to one another. The results of this study show that the network of such indirect ties can enhance innovation, independent of the effect of direct ties. As such, our findings provide empirical support for a lenient antitrust policy regarding interfirm technical collaboration. Furthermore, the results suggest that antitrust regulators should consider the influence of networks in assessing the potential welfare-enhancing effects of interfirm collaboration.

A promising topic for future research is the role of individual firms in the network. We have focused here on the global productivity of interfirm knowledge networks, and have not examined the implications of this model for individual firms in the network. Integration of these ideas with work on the consequences for particular firms in interfirm networks seems a valuable area for future research. For instance, how do small-world connectivity properties differentially benefit particular firms in an alliance network? Can a particular firm take advantage of small-world connectivity properties to create or leverage knowledge-brokering opportunities? Our results offer the prospect of illumination in this area of inquiry, as well as in the dynamics of knowledge creation at other levels of analysis.

Notes

The authors are grateful for the suggestions of William Baumol, Joel Baum, Lori Rosenkopf, Dan Levinthal, Anne Marie Knott, Joe Porac, Juan Alcacer, Mark Newman, Laszlo Barabasi, Bill McKelvey, Bill Greene and Duncan Watts.

1. For each node, its clustering coefficient is calculated as the proportion of its direct neighbors (other nodes to which it is directly linked) that are themselves also directly linked to each other. In a friendship network, this corresponds to a ratio of an individual's friends who are also friends with each other. If a node is connected to two other nodes and those nodes are also connected to each other (forming a triangle of connections), this is known as "triad closure." Thus clustering is often portrayed as the number of triangles (closed triads in a network) divided by the number of *potential* triangles (connected triples of nodes). The clustering coefficient of the overall network is the average of this measure across all nodes in the network.

2. There are several measures of centralization or decentralization. A common measure is the overall network degree of centrality as given by the following: For a given binary network with vertices $v_1, \ldots, v_n$ and maximum degree of centrality c_{max}, the network degree of centralization measure is $\Sigma(c_{max}-c(v_i))$ divided by the maximum value possible, where $c(v_i)$ is the degree centrality of vertex v_i (Borgatti, Everett, and Freeman, 2002).

3. Path lengths can easily be calculated for simple chains, but for networks that are more complex, path lengths are typically obtained algorithmically by a computer. On the methods employed by such algorithms see Watts 2002.

4. The clustering coefficient is measured as the percentage of a node's immediate neighbors that are also connected to each other, averaged across all nodes in the network.

5. The SDC alliance data provides the primary (four-digit) SIC code of activity of each alliance.

6. Doing so removes our ability to control for systematic period effects.

7. There is, however, substantial variation in the number of alliances per firm *within* each industry. Every industry demonstrated scale-free properties to some degree, meaning that the frequency of alliances per firm follows a power law distribution. That is, a small number of firms participated in very many alliances, while a large number of firms participated in very few alliances. The power law distributions of degree for the industries had exponents of 1.322 (aerospace), 1.493 (automotive), 1.940 (chemicals), 1.562 (computers and office equipment), 3.030 (household audiovisual equipment), 2.289 (medical equipment), 2.443 (petroleum refining and products), 1.737 (pharmaceuticals), 1.540 (semiconductors), and 1.676 (telecommunications equipment).

References

Ahuja, G. 2000. "Collaboration Networks, Structural Holes, and Innovation: A Longitudinal Study." *Administrative Science Quarterly* 45: 425–55.

Ahuja, G., and C. M. Lampert. 2001. "Entrepreneurship in the Large Corporation: A Longitudinal Study of How Established Firms Create Breakthrough Inventions." *Strategic Management Journal* 22: 521–43.

Allen, T. J. 1977. *Managing the Flow of Technology: Technology Transfer and the Dissemination of Technological Information within the R&D Organization*. Cambridge: MIT Press.

Anand, B. N., and T. Khanna. 2000. "Do Firms Learn to Create Value? The Case of Alliances." *Strategic Management Journal* 21: 295–315.

Arrow, K. 1962. "Economic Welfare and the Allocation of Resources for Inventions." In *The Rate and Direction of Innovative Activity*, ed. R. Nelson. Princeton: Princeton University Press.

Bae, J., and M. Gargiulo. 2003. "Local Action and Efficient Alliance Strategies in the Telecommunications Industry." INSEAD Working Paper #2003/20/0B.

Barabasi, A. L. 2002. *Linked: The New Science of Networks*. New York: Perseus.

Basberg, B. L. 1987. "Patents and the Measurement of Technological Change: A Survey of the Literature. *Research Policy* 16: 131–41.

Baum, J.A.C., T. Calabrese, and B. S. Silverman. 2000. "Don't Go It Alone: Alliance Network Composition and Startups' Performance in Canadian Biotechnology." *Strategic Management Journal* 21: 267–94.

Baum, J.A.C., A. Shipilov, and T. Rowley. 2003. "Where Do Small Worlds Come From?" *Industrial and Corporate Change* 12 (March): 597–725.

Baumol, W. J. 2001. "When Is Inter-firm Coordination Beneficial? The Case of Innovation." *International Journal of Industrial Organization* 19: 727–37.

Beckman, C., and P. Haunschild. 2002. "Network Learning: The Effects of Partner's Heterogeneity of Experience on Corporate Acquisitions." *Administrative Science Quarterly* 47: 92–124.

Bollobas, B. 1985. *Random Graphs*. London: Academic Press.

Borgatti, S. P., M. G. Everett, and L. C. Freeman. 2002. "Ucinet for Windows: Software for Social Network Analysis." Analytic Technologies.

Bound, J., C. Cummins, Z. Griliches, B. H. Hall, and A. Jaffe. 1984. "Who Does R&D and Who Patents?" In *R&D Patents, and Productivity*, ed. Z. Griliches. Chicago: University of Chicago Press for the National Bureau of Economic Research.

Bourdieu, P. 1986. "The Forms of Capital." In *Handbook of Theory and Research for the Sociology of Education*, ed. J. G. Richardson. Westport, Conn.: Greenwood Press.

Brodley, J. F. 1990. "Antitrust Law and Innovation Cooperation." *Journal of Economic Perspectives* 4 (3): 97–112.

Burt, R. S. 1992. *Structural Holes*. Cambridge: Harvard University Press.

Coleman, J. S. 1988. "Social Capital in the Creation of Human Capital." *American Journal of Sociology* 94 (supplement): S95–S120.

Comanor, W. S., and F. M. Scherer. 1969. "Patent Statistics as a Measure of Technical Change." *Journal of Political Economy* 77: 392–98.

Cummings, T. 1991. "Innovation through Alliances: Archimedes' Hall of Mirrors." *European Management Journal* 9: 284–87.

De Sola Pool, I., and M. Kochen. 1978. "Contacts and Influence." *Social Networks* 1: 5–51.

Deeds, D. L., and C.W.L. Hill. 1996. "Strategic Alliances and the Rate of New Product Development: An Empirical Study of Entrepreneurial Firms." *Journal of Business Venturing* 11: 41–55.

DeMarzo, P. M., D. Vayanos, and J. Zwiebel. 2003. "Persuasion Bias, Social Influence, and Unidimensional Opinions." *Quarterly Journal of Economics* 118: 909–68.

Doz, Y., and G. Hamel. 1997. "The Use of Alliances in Implementing Technology Strategies." In *Managing Strategic Innovation and Change*, ed. M. L. Tushman and P. Anderson. Oxford: Oxford University Press.

Erdos, P., and A. Renyi. 1959. "On Random Graphs." *Pulicationes Mathematicae* 6: 290–97.

Feldman, M. P. 1999. "The New Economics of Innovation, Spillovers, and Agglomeration: A Review of Empirical Studies." *Economics of Innovation and New Technology* 8: 5–25.

Fleming, L. 2001. "Recombinant Uncertainty in Technological Search." *Management Science* 47: 117–32.

Freeman, C. 1991. "Networks of Innovators: A Synthesis of Research Issues." *Research Policy* 20: 499–514.

Granovetter, M. 1973. "The Strength of Weak Ties." *American Journal of Sociology* 78: 1360–80.

———. 1992. "Problems of Explanation in Economic Sociology." In *Networks and Organizations: Structure, Form, and Action*, ed. N. Nohria and R. Eccles. Boston: Harvard Business School Press.

Grant, R. M. 1996. "Prospering in Dynamically-Competitive Environments: Organizational Capability as Knowledge Integration." *Organization Science* 7: 375–86.

Greene, W. H. 1997. *Econometric Analysis*. 3rd ed. Upper Saddle River, N.J.: Prentice Hall.

Griliches, Z. 1979. "Issues in Assessing the Contribution of Research and Development to Productivity Growth." *Bell Journal of Economics* 10: 92–116.

———. 1990. "Patent Statistics as Economic Indicators: A Survey." *Journal of Economics Literature* 28: 1661–1707.

———. 1992. "The Search for R&D Spillovers." *Scandinavian Journal of Economics* 94 (suppl.): 29–47.

Guare, J. 1990. *Six Degrees of Separation: A Play*. New York: Vintage.

Gulati, R. 1998. "Alliances and Networks." *Strategic Management Journal* 19: 293–317.

Gulati, R., and M. Gargiulo. 1999. "Where Do Interorganizational Networks Come From?" *American Journal of Sociology* 104: 1439–93.

Hadlock, P., D. Hecker, and J. Gannon. 1991. "High Technology Employment: Another View." *Monthly Labor Review*, July, 26–30.

Hamel, G. 1991. "Competition for Competence and Inter-partner Learning within International Strategic Alliances." *Strategic Management Journal* 12 (summer special issue): 83–103.

Hansen, M. T. 1999. "The Search-Transfer Problem: The Role of Weak Ties in Sharing Knowledge across Organization Subunits." *Administrative Science Quarterly* 44: 82–111.

———. 2002. "Knowledge Networks: Explaining Effective Knowledge Sharing in Multiunit Companies." *Organization Science* 13: 232–50.

Hargadon, A. B. 1998. "Firms as Knowledge Brokers: Lessons in Pursuing Continuous Innovation." *California Management Review* 40 (3): 209–27.

Hausman, J. 1978. "Specification Tests in Econometrics." *Econometrica* 46: 1251–71.

Hecker, D. 1999. "High Technology Employment: A Broader View." *Monthly Labor Review*, June, 18–28.

Heckman, J. 1981. "Heterogeneity and State Dependence." In *Studies of Labour Markets*, ed. S. Rosen. Chicago: University of Chicago Press for the National Bureau of Economic Research.

Hsiao, C. 1986. *Analysis of Panel Data*. New York: Cambridge University Press.

Jaffe, A. 1986. "Technological Opportunity and Spillovers of R&D: Evidence from Firms' Patents, Profits, and Market Value." *American Economic Review* 76: 984–1001.

———. 1989. "Characterizing the 'Technological Position' of Firms, with Application to Quantifying Technological Opportunity and Research Spillovers." *Research Policy* 18: 87–97.

Jorde, T. M., and D. J. Teece. 1990. "Innovation and Cooperation: Implications for Competition and Antitrust." *Journal of Economic Perspectives* 4 (3): 75–96.

Joskow, P. L. 1987. "Contract Duration and Relationship-Specific Investments: Empirical Evidence from Coal Markets." *American Economic Review* 77: 168–85.

Katila, R., and G. Ahuja. 2002. "Something Old, Something New: A Longitudinal Study of Search Behavior and New Product Introduction." *Academy of Management Journal* 45: 1183–94.

Katz, M. L., and J. A. Ordover 1990. "R&D Cooperation and Competition." In *Brookings Papers on Microeconomics*. Washington, D.C.: Brookings Institute.

Kennedy, P. 1998. *A Guide to Econometrics*. Cambridge: MIT Press.

Kogut, B. 1991. "Joint Ventures and the Option to Expand and Acquire." *Management Science* 37: 19–34.

———. 2000. "The Network as Knowledge: Generative Rules and the Emergence of Structure." *Strategic Management Journal* 21: 405–25.

Kogut, B., and G. Walker. 2001. "The Small World of Germany and the Durability of National Networks." *American Sociological Review* 66: 317–35.

Kogut, B., and U. Zander. 1996. "What Firms Do? Coordination, Identity, and Learning." *Organization Science* 7: 502–18.

Kovacic, W. E., and C. Shapiro. 2000. "Antitrust Policy: A Century of Economic and Legal Thinking." *Journal of Economic Perspectives* 14 (1): 43–60.

Kreps, D. 1990. "Corporate Culture and Economic Theory." In *Perspectives on Positive Political Economy*, ed. J. Alt and K. Shepsie. New York: Cambridge University Press.

Lane, P. J., and M. Lubatkin. 1998. "Relative Absorptive Capacity and Interorganizational Learning." *Strategic Management Journal* 19: 461–77.

Laumann, E. O, P. V. Marsden, and D. Prensky. 1983. "The Boundary Specification Problem in Network Analysis." In *Applied Network Analysis*, ed. R. S. Burt and M. J. Minor. Beverly Hills: Sage.

Levin, R., A. Klevorick, R. Nelson, and S. Winter. 1987. "Appropriating the Returns from Industrial Research and Development." *Brookings Papers on Economic Activity, Microeconomics* 3: 783–820.

Levinthal, D., and J. G. March. 1981. "A Model of Adaptive Organizational Search." *Journal of Economic Behavior and Organization* 2: 307–33.

Liebeskind, J. P. 1996. "Knowledge, Strategy, and the Theory of the Firm." *Strategic Management Journal* 17: 93–108.

Luker, W., Jr., and D. Lyons. 1997. "Employment Shifts in High-Technology Industries, 1988–96." *Monthly Labor Review*, June, 12–25.

March, J. G. 1991. "Exploration and Exploitation in Organizational Learning." *Organization Science* 2: 71–87.

Marsden, P. 1990. "Network Data and Measurement." *Annual Review of Sociology* 16: 435–63.

Mezias, S. J., and M. A. Glynn. 1993. "The Three Faces of Corporate Renewal: Institution, Revolution, and Evolution." *Strategic Management Journal* 14: 77–101.

Milgram, S. 1967. "The Small World Problem." *Psychology Today* 2: 60–67.

Monge, P. R., and N. S. Contractor. 2003. *Theories of Communication Networks*. New York: Oxford University Press.

Newman, M.E.J. 2000. "Models of the Small World." *Journal of Statistical Physics* 101: 819–41.

Newman, M.E.J., S. H. Strogatz, and D. J. Watts. 2000. "Random Graphs with Arbitrary Degree Distribution and Their Applications." Working paper, Santa Fe Institute.

Phelps, C. 2003. "Technological Exploration: The Role of Technical Diversity and Social Capital in Alliance Networks." Ph.D. diss., New York University.

Portes, A. 1998. "Social Capital: Its Origins and Applications in Modern Sociology." *Annual Review of Sociology* 24: 1–24.

Powell, W. W., K. W. Koput, and L. Smith-Doerr. 1996. "Interorganizational Collaboration and the Locus of Innovation: Networks of Learning in Biotechnology." *Administrative Science Quarterly* 41: 116–45.

Rogers, E. 1995. *Diffusion of Innovation*. 4th ed. New York: Free Press.

Rosenkopf, L., and P. Almeida. 2003. "Overcoming Local Search through Alliances and Mobility." *Management Science* 49: 751–66.

Rosenkopf, L., A. Metiu, and V. P. George. 2001. "From the Bottom Up? Technical Committee Activity and Alliance Formation." *Administrative Science Quarterly* 46: 748–75.

Rothaermel, F. T. 2001. "Complementary Assets, Strategic Alliances, and the Incumbent's Advantage: An Empirical Study of Industry and Firm Effects in the Biopharmaceutical Industry." *Research Policy* 30: 1235–51.

Rowley, T., D. Behrens, and D. Krackhardt. 2000. "Redundant Governance Structures: An Analysis of Structural and Relational Embeddedness in the Steel and Semiconductor Industries." *Strategic Management Journal* 21: 369–86.

Sampson, R. 2004. "The Cost of Misaligned Governance in R&D Alliances." *Journal of Law, Economics, and Organization* 20: 484–526.

Saxenian, A. 1990. "Regional Networks and the Resurgence of Silicon Valley." *California Management Review* 33 (1): 89–112.

———. 1994. *Regional Advantage: Culture and Competition in Silicon Valley and Route 128*. Cambridge: Harvard University Press.

Schilling, M. A. 2005. A small-world network model of cognitive insight. *Creativity Research Journal,* 17(2&3): 131–154.

Schilling, M. A., and K. Steensma. 2001. "The Use of Modular Organizational Forms: An Industry-Level Analysis." *Academy of Management Journal* 44: 1149–69.

Schmookler, J. 1966. *Invention and Economic Growth*. Cambridge: Harvard University Press.

Schumpeter, J. A. 1934. *The Theory of Economic Development*. Cambridge: Harvard University Press.

Schutjens, V., and E. Stam. 2003. "The Evolution of Young Firm Networks: A Longitudinal Perspective." *Small Business Economics* 21 (2): 115–34.

Shan, W. 1990. "An Empirical Analysis of Organizational Strategies by Entrepreneurial High-Technology." *Strategic Management Journal* 11: 129–39.

Shan, W., G. Walker, and B. Kogut. 1994. "Interfirm Cooperation and Startup Innovation in the Biotechnology Industry." *Strategic Management Journal* 15: 387–94.

Smith-Doerr, L., J. Owen-Smith, K. W. Koput, and W. W. Powell. 1999. "Networks and Knowledge Production: Collaboration and Patenting in Biotechnology." In *Corporate Social Capital*, ed. R. Leenders and S. Gabbay. Norwell, Mass.: Kluwer Academic Publishers.

Soh, P. 2003. "The Role of Networking Alliances in Information Acquisition and Its Implications for New Product Performance." *Journal of Business Venturing* 18: 727–57.

Solomonoff, R., and A. Rapoport. 1951. "Connectivity of Random Nets." *Bulletin of Mathematical Biophysics* 13: 107–17.

Spencer, J. W. 2003. "Global Gatekeeping, Representation, and Network Structure: A Longitudinal Analysis of Regional and Global Knowledge-Diffusion Networks." *Journal of International Business Studies* 34: 428–42.

Stuart, T. E. 2000. "Interorganizational Alliances and the Performance of Firms: A Study of Growth and Innovation Rates in a High Technology Industry." *Strategic Management Journal* 21: 791–812.

Szulanski, G. 1996. "Exploring Internal Stickiness: Impediments to the Transfer of Best Practice within the Firm." *Strategic Management Journal* 17(winter special issue): 27–43.

Teece, D., G. Pisano, and A. Shuen. 1997. "Dynamic Capabilities and Strategic Management." *Strategic Management Journal* 18: 509–33.

Trajtenberg, M. 1987. "Patents, Citations, and Innovations: Tracing the Links." National Bureau of Economic Research Working Paper No. 2457.

Usher, A. 1954. *A History of Mechanical Inventions*. Cambridge: Harvard University Press.

Uzzi, B. 1997. "Social Structure and Competition in Interfirm Networks: The Paradox of Embeddedness." *Administrative Science Quarterly* 42: 35–67.

Valente, T. 1995. *Network Models of the Diffusion of Innovations*. Cresskill, N.J.: Hampton Press.

Venkatraman, N., and C. Lee. 2004. "Network Evolution and Preferential Attachment: A Conceptual Model and Empirical Test in the U.S. Video Game Sector." Working paper, Boston University.

Vonortas, N. S. 1997. "Research Joint Ventures in the US." *Research Policy* 26: 577–95.

Watts, D. J. 1999a. *Small Worlds: The Dynamics between Order and Randomness*. Princeton: Princeton University Press.

———. 1999b. "Networks, Dynamics, and the Small-World Phenomenon." *American Journal of Sociology* 105: 493–528.

———. 2002. *Six Degrees: The Science of a Connected Age*. New York: Norton.

Watts, D. J., and S. Strogatz. 1998. "Collective Dynamics of 'Small-World' Networks." *Nature* 393: 440–42.

White, H. 1980. "A Heteroskedasticity-Consistent Covariance Matrix Estimator and a Direct Test for Heteroskedasticity." *Econometrica* 48: 817–38.

Wilhite, A. 2001. "Bilateral Trade and 'Small-World' Networks." *Computational Economics*, 18(1): 49–64.

Williamson, O. E. 1985. *The Economic Institutions of Capitalism*. New York: Free Press.

Yamaguchi, K. 1994. "The Flow of Information through Social Networks: Diagonal-Free Measures of Inefficiency and the Structural Determinants of Inefficiency." *Social Networks* 16: 57–86.

———. 2002. "The Structural and Behavioral Characteristics of the Smallest-World Phenomenon: Minimum Distance Networks." *Social Networks* 24: 161–82.

Zander, U., and B. Kogut. 1995. "Knowledge and the Speed of the Transfer and Imitation of Organizational Capabilities: An Empirical TEST." *Organization Science* 6: 76–92.

Part IV

THE CONTINUING ROLE OF INDEPENDENT INNOVATORS AND ENTREPRENEURS

Introduction and Comments

SYLVIA NASAR

IN *CAPITALISM, SOCIALISM AND DEMOCRACY*, written around 1940 when faith in free enterprise was dwindling fast, Joseph Schumpeter made the following observation: If the United States' economy were to grow as fast in the half century after 1928 as in the half century before, GDP would be 2.7 times higher in 1978 than in 1928. He wasn't predicting, just trying to impress his readers with capitalism's awesome pre-Depression record. Had he been extrapolating, he would have missed by a mile, however. When 1978 rolled around—by which time another world war, an arms race with the Soviet Union, the Arab oil embargo, and half a dozen recessions had become part of the record—GDP was actually *five* times higher than in 1928.

An eyewitness to the collapse of the Austro-Hungarian Empire after World War I, Schumpeter was far too sophisticated to believe that economic success alone could guarantee a society's survival. But he refused to agree with John Maynard Keynes that capitalism was innately failure-prone. Whatever its shortcomings—financial crises, depressions, social strife—it was capitalism's *nature* to deliver the goods, Schumpeter insisted. "The capitalist engine is first and last an engine of mass production," he scribbled breezily at a time when production had barely recovered from the 1929 crash. Thanks to that engine, he wrote in an oft-quoted passage, modern working girls could afford stockings that were once too costly for any women except queens.

Schumpeter was captivated by capitalism's compulsive creativity. "Capitalism is by nature a form or method of economic change and, not only never is, but never can be stationary," observed this intensely ambitious, workaholic, peripatetic man. The drive to create was fueled by competition, but of the technological rather than the price kind. In retail trade, for example, Schumpeter wrote that "the competition that matters arises not from additional shops of the same type, but from the department store, the chain store, the mail-order house and the supermarket." Competitive pressures forced—no, inspired—entrepreneurs to substitute new ideas, products, processes, organizations for old, he argued. Waves of "industrial revolutions" and "avalanches of consumer goods" were the result. Far from being aberrations, such upheavals were the norm. That's why Schumpeter called economic growth "creative destruction."

Having argued that capitalism is an ingenious social contrivance for harnessing creative genius, Schumpeter promptly predicted the system's demise: He replied to his own rhetorical question, "Can Capitalism survive?" with "No. I don't think it can." By then he was haunted by thoughts of death and fears that he himself had become little more than an anachronism. "A new economics" was needed, he wrote in his diary, but he did not feel up to creating it. "I do not carry weight." At Harvard, his ideas were increasingly regarded as quaint, just like his courtly manner and flowery speech, and for several decades after his death in 1950, the subject of economic growth hardly came up except among experts who worked in what had become an obscure subspecialty.

But a little over half a century later, economists are as obsessed by the "new economics" of growth as the great man could have wished. Like evolution in the mid–nineteenth century or the structure of DNA in the mid–twentieth, economic growth has become a scientific holy grail. The dramatic revolutions in living standards from one generation to the next, first in the United States and Europe, then in Japan, the Pacific Rim, China, and India, made it "hard to think about anything else," as Robert Lucas at the University of Chicago once said. A new generation of inventors and independent entrepreneurs has lent fresh credence to the notion that creativity might, after all, be the key to capitalism's multiplicative powers.

For twenty-first-century economics, the equivalent of natural selection or the double helix could well turn out to be a theory that explains how the "ingenious mechanism"—capitalism—stimulates creativity. William Baumol, long one of the most innovative thinkers in economics and an expert on the economics of innovation, outlines a first draft of such a theory in chapter 8 of this volume, "Toward Analysis of Capitalism's Unparalleled Growth: Sources and Mechanism." Baumol is less concerned with explaining individual creativity than explaining why innovation flourishes in some societies and flags in others. He adopts Schumpeter's "invaluable distinction" between innovation and pure invention and reminds readers that it is the former that leads to higher productivity and living standards. Consider Steve Jobs, whom *Fortune* recently described as neither "a programmer or a designer or an engineer or an MBA," but a "shrewd business strategist." Steve Jobs may be no Leonardo da Vinci, who seems to have thought of everything from submarines to flying machines at one time or another, yet Jobs has probably contributed much more than the iconic Renaissance man to society's *material* well-being. Similarly, historians agree that Victorian England was no more inventive than medieval China. The difference is that the railroad and lightbulb eventually touched the lives of every single English citizen, while the clock, umbrella, and other products of Chinese ingenuity were treated as novelties for the amusement of the emperor and his court.

Professor Baumol assumes that raw entrepreneurial talent is spread around more or less equally. What distinguishes a static from a dynamic society is not the amount of the raw resource, but what *fraction* of that talent gets channeled into marketable ideas as opposed to, say, military, administrative, or religious pursuits. In imperial Rome, the only professions that were prestigious and lucrative were those of general, landowner, or banker. In America, whose business is business, the merchant and manufacturer so despised in Rome have always been socially acceptable.

Thus, in Baumol's theory, incentives matter hugely. If he is right, the pace of innovation and economic growth should vary more with the social status of entrepreneurs, enforcement of patents, and capital gains tax rates than, for example, with the total number of scientists or engineers or the national savings rate. A bit of anecdotal evidence in support of the thesis: After the NASDAQ collapsed in 2000, fewer bright young men and women were eager to become entrepreneurs and more looked to traditional professions; MBA enrollments slumped while those in law schools surged.

Part of the reason Schumpeter was gloomy about capitalism's future was that he was convinced that the entrepreneur himself had become outmoded. No doubt, the feeling that opportunities for extraordinary individuals were shrinking reflected Schumpeter's midlife crisis and his slide into depression. But he was hardly alone at that time in equating the growing dominance of the giant corporation with a decline in technological dynamism. In the most innovative part of his chapter, Baumol shows how, and in what surprising ways, Schumpeter's fears proved to be unfounded. Rather than becoming extinct, it turns out that the independent entrepreneur has become a niche player. His specialty? The big breakthroughs that involve radical departures and result in whole new technologies that never existed before.

But they no longer dominate innovation the way they did in the nineteenth century. Baumol calls independent entrepreneurs Davids. Who then are the Goliaths? The P&Gs, Wal-Marts, and other behemoths of the business world who, as a group, spend two-thirds of the R&D dollars in the United States each year. Baumol's thesis is that those large corporations have been forced—by competition—to take over the least glamorous but comparably powerful part of the entrepreneurial function. This is the task of making the constant, incremental, cumulative improvements that bit by bit transformed, say, Orville and Wilbur Wright's airplane into an Airbus A380, John von Neumann's MANIAC into an IBM ThinkPad, and Ford's Model T into a BMW X3. "Each partner constitutes an indispensable part of the story," Professor Baumol writes. "The rise and continued contribution of the individual entrepreneurs may be a historical accident, but the continued efforts of the corporation are self-generating and self-enforcing."

The first chapter in this part provides dramatic support for Baumol's David-and-Goliath thesis. "The Small Entrepreneur," by Boyan Jovanovic and Peter L. Rousseau, experts in both finance and technological change, is an example of truly innovative empirical research. Jovanovic and Rousseau have collected an enormous number of individual company histories as well as detailed data on patents, incorporations, initial public offerings, and stock exchange listings—all spanning more than a century. This extraordinary data set gives them the means for examining the relationship between the age of companies and the pace of innovation. Among Jovanovic and Rousseau's conclusions: Compelling evidence of two golden ages of entrepreneurship, one at the beginning and one at the end of the twentieth century. The 1950s, 1960s, and 1970s, were, by contrast, relatively quiet and dominated, just as Schumpeter intuited, by corporate giants. The authors remain agnostic about whether the economic booms before World War I and in the 1990s stimulated innovation because they were good times to bring new ideas to market, or innovations produced the booms, but leave no doubt that the independents are still playing a key role.

If you find the relative contributions of independent entrepreneurs versus corporate giants intriguing, go and see *The Aviator* by director Martin Scorsese. Its hero is Howard Hughes, the Texas billionaire, movie mogul, aircraft designer, founder of TWA, and quintessential American entrepreneur. Hughes, played by Leonardo DiCaprio, is from Texas, completely crazy, and a visionary who "saw the future." He hangs out with engineers, tests his own planes, and designs new ones on stray scraps of paper. His nemesis, naturally, is a slick, sinister corporate bigwig, Juan Trippe, the CEO of Pan American. You have only to glimpse Alec Baldwin's tight-fitting double-breasted suits and fat Havanas to know that here is a money-hungry schemer who doesn't design or fly planes. He just buys them. Senators too.

As it turns out, Hollywood was engaging in a bit of creative role reversal. In *They Made America*, a wonderful new history of American inventors and innovators, Sir Harold Evans shows that Hughes actually "saw the future," especially the dominance of the jet, less clearly, and far later, than Trippe. Hughes was a real innovator in aircraft design, no question. But Trippe was the man who shaped commercial aviation. What made the man in the corner suite more of an innovator than the one in the cockpit? Ironically, especially in light of Hughes's obsessive-compulsive disorder, the answer Sir Evans gives is this: single-minded focus. For example, while Trippe was spending every waking minute snapping up hotels at every single potential Pan Am destination, Hughes was entertaining himself by buying RKO Studios, making movies, and dating Katherine Hepburn.

Oh well. You can't do it all. In the end, even Schumpeter, whose youthful ambitions included being Number One in five disparate pursuits—love, horsemanship, economics, politics, and art—couldn't.

Chapter 7

The Small Entrepreneur

BOYAN JOVANOVIC AND PETER L. ROUSSEAU

1. Introduction

In this chapter on the small entrepreneur we argue that

1. new capital (ideas and productive capacity brought in by new firms) responds more elastically than does old capital (capital in the hands of incumbent firms) to incentives, especially to new technology, and
2. that this fact is as true now as it ever has been. It was less true in the middle of the twentieth century than it was at either end of it.

The chapter is organized in three parts: First, a discussion of initial public offering (IPO) activity; second, a collection of simple models of the decision of when to IPO; and third, a discussion of some other indicators of invention, focusing on the contribution of small and young firms.

2. IPO Activity and Investment

IPOs perform two main functions:

1. They transfer ownership of the firm, usually to a more dispersed group of owners, and
2. They raise money to implement the firm's business plans.

Not all IPOs are for small firms, but an IPO wave tends to reflect a rise in the importance of smaller and younger firms. We begin the story with a striking fact about age: IPO-ing firms are not always young.

2.1 The Age of the Firm at its IPO

Figure 7.1 shows Hodrick-Prescott (HP) filtered average waiting times from founding, first product or process innovation, and incorporation to exchange listing based upon individual company histories and our extension of the stock files distributed by University of Chicago's Center

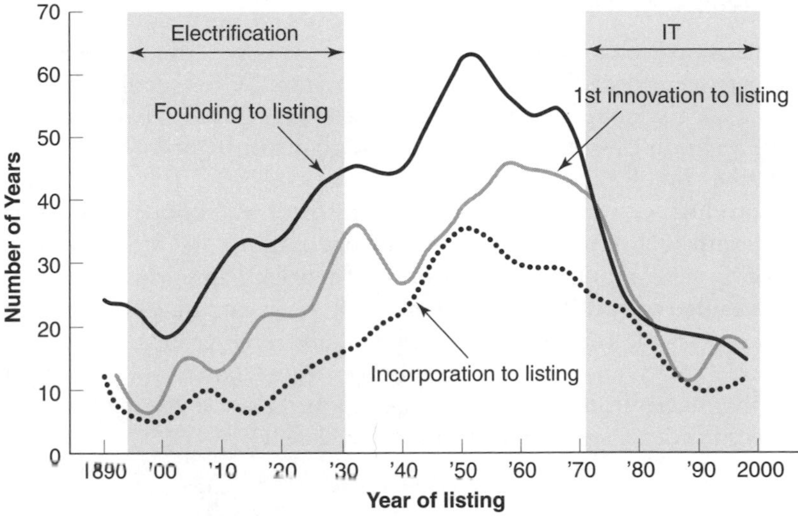

Figure 7.1. Waiting Times to IPO

for Research in Securities Prices (CRSP) from its 1925 starting date back through 1885.[1] The vertical distance between the solid and dotted lines shows that firms often have their first innovation soon after founding, but that it then takes years, even decades, to list on a stock exchange. Why delay longer at some times than others?

1. Secrecy motive: IPO prospectuses reveal business plans. The same arguments can be invoked for why a firm may not patent an idea but, rather, will develop it in secret.
2. Foregone earnings motive: By not raising the money needed to implement its plans, the firm gives up profits. Several models in this class are described in the next section.
3. Economies of scale in IPO activity and start-up activity: Examples are the thick search-market externalities of Diamond (1982), the pecuniary externalities of Shleifer (1986), or the informational scale economies of Veldcamp (2006). These could explain some IPO waves.

We now illustrate these arguments by naming some of the companies that entered the stock market at various dates. We also associate each firm with a particular technology because we suspect that the explanation has something to do with the technologies that the new firms brought in with them.

2.2. *Technology and Today's Giants*

The flagship technologies of the most recent wave, the computer and Internet, were brought into the market primarily by small and young firms. Can the same be said for e.g., electricity? Table 7.1 offers a look at the technologies that some of today's giants brought into the market when they first listed on an organized stock exchange. The table lists the first product or process innovation for some well-known companies, along with their dates of founding, incorporation, and stock exchange listing. It also includes the share of total market capitalization that can be attributed to each firm's common stock at the end of 2000. The firms appearing in the table separate into roughly three groups: those based upon electricity and internal combustion, those based upon chemicals and pharmaceuticals, and those based upon the computer and Internet. Let us consider a few of the entries more closely:

- *Electricity/internal combustion engine*: Two of the largest companies in the United States today are General Electric (GE) and AT&T. Founded in 1878, GE now accounts for 3.1 percent of total stock market value, and had already established a share of over 2 percent by 1910. AT&T, founded in 1885, contributed 4.6 percent to total market value by 1928, and more than 8.5 percent at the time of its forced breakup in 1984. Both were early entrants of the electricity era. GE came to life with the invention of the incandescent lightbulb by Thomas Edison in 1880, while AT&T established a long-distance telephone line from New York to Chicago in 1892 to make use of Bell's 1876 invention of the telephone. Both technologies represented quantum leaps in the modernization of industry and communications, and would come to improve greatly the quality of household life. Both firms listed on the New York Stock Exchange (NYSE) about 15 years after founding. General Motors (GM) was an early entrant to the automobile industry, listing on the NYSE in 1917—nine years after its founding. By 1931 it accounted for more than 4 percent of stock market value, and its share would hover between 4 and 6.5 percent until 1965, when it began to decline gradually to its current share of only 0.2 percent. These examples suggest that many of the leading entrants of the turn of the twentieth century created lasting market value. Further, the ideas that sparked their emergence were brought to market relatively quickly.
- *Chemicals/pharmaceuticals*: Procter and Gamble, Bristol-Myers-Squibb, and Pfizer are now all leaders in their respective industries, but took much longer to list on the NYSE than the electrification-era firms. In fact, both Pfizer and P&G were established before 1850, and thus predate all of them. Despite P&G's early start and creation of the Ivory soap brand in 1879, it was not until 1932 that the company took its place among the largest U.S. firms by exploiting advances in radio transmission to sponsor

the first "soap opera." Pfizer's defining moment came when it developed a process for mass-producing the breakthrough drug penicillin during the Second World War, and the good reputation that the firm earned at that time later helped it to become the main producer of the Salk and Sabin polio vaccines. In Pfizer's case, like that of P&G, the company's management and culture had been in place for some time when a new technology (in Pfizer's case, antibiotics) presented a great opportunity.

- *Computer/IT*: Firms at the core of the recent information technology (IT) revolution, such as Intel, Microsoft, and Amazon, came to market shortly after founding. Intel listed in 1972, only four years after starting up, and now accounts for 1.3 percent of total stock market value. Microsoft took 11 years to go public. Conceived in an Albuquerque hotel room by Bill Gates in 1975, the company, with its new disk operating system (MS-DOS), was perhaps ahead of its time, but later joined the ranks of today's corporate giants with the proliferation of the personal computer. In 1998, Microsoft accounted for more than 2.5 percent of the stock market, but this share fell to 1.5 percent over the next two years in the midst of antitrust action. Amazon caught the Internet wave from the outset to become the world's first online bookstore, going public in 1997—only three years after its founding. As the complexities of integrating goods distribution with an Internet front-end came into sharper focus over the ensuing years, however, and as competition among Internet retailers continued to grow, Amazon's market capitalization by 2001 had been cut in half to less than 0.1 percent of total stock market value.

These firms, as well as the others listed in table 7.1, brought new technologies into the stock market and accounted for nearly 16 percent of its value at the close of 2000. The firms themselves also seem to have entered the stock market sooner during the electricity and computer/Internet revolutions, at opposite ends of the twentieth century, than firms based on midcentury technologies.

2.3. *The Q-Elasticity of Capital in New versus Old Firms*

The regressions in table 7.2 show the apparently huge elasticity of supply of new capital relative to old capital. Here y refers to the real investment of IPO-ing firms and x to the real investment rate of stock-market incumbents. We measure x as the sum of total changes in the year-end gross capital stocks among incumbents in the Compustat database divided by the sum of their net capital stocks. We denote this measure of x by x_{real}. It is thus a value-weighted average of X/K. For y, we use the

TABLE 7.1
Key Dates in Selected Company Histories

Company Name	Founding Date	1 st Major Product or Process Innovation	Incorporation Date	IPO Date	% of Stock Market in 2000
General Electric	1878	1880	1892	1892	3.10
AT&T	1885	1892	1885	1901	0.42
Detroit Edison	1886	1904	1903	1909	0.04
General Motors	1908	1912	1908	1917	0.19
Coca-Cola	1886	1893	1919	1919	0.99
Pacific Gas &. Electric	1879	1879	1905	1919	0.05
Burroughs/Unisys	1886	1886	1886	1924	0.03
Caterpillar	1869	1904	1925	1929	0.11
Kimberly-Clark	1872	1914	1880	1929	0.25
Procter & Gamble	1837	1879	1890	1929	0.67
Bristol-Myers Squibb	1887	1903	1887	1933	0.94
Boeing	1916	1917	1916	1934	0.38
Pfizer	1849	1944	1900	1944	1.90
Merck	1891	1944	1934	1946	1.41
Disney	1923	1929	1940	1957	0.39
Hewlett Packard	1938	1938	1947	1961	0.41

Time Warner	1922	1942	1922	1964	0.41
McDonald's	1948	1955	1965	1966	0.29
Intel	1968	1971	1969	1972	1.32
Compaq	1982	1982	1982	1983	0.17
Micron	1978	1982	1978	1984	0.13
Microsoft	1975	1980	1981	1986	1.51
America Online	1985	1988	1985	1992	0.53
Amazon	1994	1995	1994	1997	0.04
eBay	1995	1995	1996	1998	0.06

Source: Data from *Hoover's Online*, Kelley (1954), and company websites.

The first major products or innovations for the firms listed in the table are GE 1880, Edison patents incandescent lightbulb; AT&T 1892, completes phone line from New York to Chicago; DTE 1904, increases Detroit's electric capacity sixfold with new facilities; GM 1912, electric self-starter; Coca-Cola 1893, patents soft-drink formula; PG&E 1879, first electric utility; Burroughs/Unisys 1886, first adding machine; CAT 1904, gas-driven tractor; Kimberly-Clark 1914, celu-cotton, a cotton substitute used in WWI; P&G 1879, Ivory soap; Bristol-Myers Squibb 1903, Sal Hepatica, a laxative mineral salt; Boeing 1917, designs Model C seaplane; Pfizer 1944, deep tank fermentation to mass produce penicillin; Merck 1944, cortisone (first steroid); Disney 1929, cartoon with soundtrack; HP 1938, audio oscillator; Time-Warner 1942, *Casablanca;* McDonald's 1955, fast food franchising begins; Intel 1971, 4004 microprocessor (8088 microprocessor in 1978); Micrsoft 1980, develops DOS; Compaq 1982, portable IBM-compatible computer; Micron 1982, computer "eye" camera; AOL 1988, "PC-Link"; Amazon 1995, first online bookstore; eBay 1995, first online auction house.

TABLE 7.2
Regressions of the Average Investment of New Listings (Y_{real}) and Incumbents (X_{real}) on Q^*, 1955–2001

	Dependent Variable			
	$\ln(Y_{real})$	$\ln(Y_{real})$	$\ln(X_{real})$	$\ln(X_{real})$
$\ln(Q^*-1)$	0.668 (4.87)	0.637 (4.63)	0.042 (0.76)	0.044 (0.77)
r_t		−0.063 (−1.37)		0.004 (0.19)
Trend	0.021 (3.38)	0.025 (3.67)	−0.006 (−2.37)	−0.006 (−2.19)
Constant	3.827 (20.80)	3.871 (20.94)	−1.857 (−25.15)	−1.859 (−24.51)
R^2	.441	.466	.138	.139
N	44	44	44	44

Note: t-statistics are in parentheses.

average year-end real net capital stock of firms that entered the CRSP database in each year.[2] We denote this measure by y_{real}. This method assumes that the firm accumulates all of its initial capital at the time of IPO.[3] The regressions in table 7.2 show that Q-theory, in other words, looks very good when applied to entrants, but the low response of incumbents remains a puzzle. We include r_t—the real rate on commercial paper—and it has little effect on the coefficients.

But is y_{real} really new capital or backlogged old capital in the form of stored, privately held ideas, as in Shleifer (1986)? Suppose that some firms hoard their ideas until Q is high and then release them, while others release them right away. This would mean that when Q is high, the average age of the released ideas would be highest. No such relation emerges, for example, in the 1990s IPO-ing companies that were very young, yet Q was at an all-time high.

Table 7.3 shows that the number of IPOs does not respond much, if at all, to Q. We build a series for the number of IPOs from 1927 to 2001 using Ritter 2003, table 5, p. 6, for 1975–2001 and then joining this to the number of new listings on the CRSP database from 1927 to 74.[4] The coefficient on $Q^* - 1$ is not statistically significant for 1955–2001 in the first column, and the coefficient on Q as measured by *Mcap/GDP* is not significant for the 1927–2001 period either. In all cases, however, the sign is negative, and is even statistically significant in the second column for 1955–2001.

TABLE 7.3
Regressions of the Number of IPOs (n) on $Q^* - 1$ and MCAP/GDP.

	Dependent Variable: n		
	1955–2001	1955–2001	1927–2001
$\ln(Q^*-1)$	−0.164 (−1.09)		
ln(MCAP/GDP)		−0.519 (−3.53)	−0.314 (−1.48)
r_t	0.211 (4.12)	0.185 (4.03)	0.103 (3.67)
Trend	0.111 (15.02)	0.114 (17.20)	0.083 (16.58)
Constant	0.507 (2.59)	0.053 (0.24)	−0.990 (−3.35)
R^2	.905	.925	.835
N	45	45	72

Note: t-statistics are in parentheses.

3. Some Models of IPOs Based on the Foregone-Earnings Motive

Let t denote the waiting time until IPO. Suppose that while it waits, the firm's potential output is

$$y = f(t).$$

We assume that

$$f' > 0, \; f'' < 0.$$

In this formulation the firm starts receiving y only *after* implementing the project (which is unreasonable in many instances—e.g., Goldman Sachs, McDonald's, etc.). At that point the project stops improving, that is, there is no learning by doing. This is therefore a learning *or* doing model. Moreover, there are no direct costs. It makes sense if

1. funds are a constraint for private companies,
2. IPOs can deliver the funds for a significant expansion, and
3. upon the initial expansion, the firm is irrevocably defined and "fossilized" as in the "putty clay" vision of investment.

In that case the IPO decision is much like the decision of how long to remain in school,[5] or how much time to spend perfecting an idea before taking out a patent on it.

3.1. Decision Problem

Suppose the firm lives forever and has the property rights to its project. It must just decide when to implement it. There are no direct costs, only implicit "foregone-earnings" costs. Therefore its problem is like that of optimally cutting down a tree

$$\max_T V(T),$$

where

$$V(T) = e^{-rT}\frac{1}{r}f(T).$$

The first-order condition (FOC) is

$$\frac{dV}{dT} = -e^{-rT}f(T) + e^{-rT}\frac{1}{r}f'(T) = 0. \tag{1}$$

Now the derivative of the first term is zero by (1) and so the second-order condition (SOC) is

$$\frac{d^2V}{dT^2} = -e^{-rT}f'(T) + e^{-rT}\frac{1}{r}f''(T) < 0. \tag{2}$$

Therefore, concavity of f is sufficient for (2) to hold.

Then (1) implies

$$f(T) = \frac{1}{r}f'(T), \tag{3}$$

that is,

$$\frac{f'}{f} = r.$$

The left-hand side (LHS) of (3) is the foregone-earnings costs of waiting another period. The right-hand side (RHS) is the gain from waiting. Since this gain is received in every subsequent (production) period, it is treated as an annual perpetuity, and hence the r in the denominator.

Do better ideas wait longer or less? It depends on how we put quality into f. Let z denote quality.

3.2. *Example 1: Hicks-Neutral Quality*

Suppose that

$$f(t, z) = zF(t).$$

Then z drops out of the formula $\frac{f'}{f} = r$, and does not affect the timing of the IPO.

3.3. *Example 2: Additive Quality*

Suppose that

$$f(t, z) = F(t) + z.$$

Then the formula $\frac{f'}{f} = r$ says

$$\frac{F'(t)}{F(t) + z} = r$$

and high-z firms come in earlier because z affects foregone earnings, but not the rate of improvement.

3.4. *Example 3: Direct Costs*

Suppose costs are the same for all regardless of quality, and suppose quality is Hicks-neutral. Let c be the direct cost incurred only during the waiting period (e.g., a research cost). Then

$$V(T) = e^{-rT}\frac{1}{r}zf(T) - \int_0^T e^{-rt}c\,dt$$

$$= e^{-rT}\frac{1}{r}zf(T) - \frac{c}{r}(1 - e^{-rT}),$$

and the FOC is

$$zf(T) + c = \frac{1}{r}zf'(T), \tag{4}$$

or

$$\frac{f'}{f + \frac{c}{z}} = r.$$

Now more productive firms do wait longer because for them the direct costs are a smaller deterrent to waiting.

The above were all neoclassical models in which, at IPO, the public pays for the firm exactly what it is worth. One needs to look at the alternative hypothesis of waves of irrational exuberance. Perhaps IPO-ing firms wait in the wings in order to take advantage of such exuberance. If so, the beneficiaries are neither the IPO-ing firms nor the participating venture capitalists themselves: Data from Ritter (2002, 2003) show that (while being times of high IPO volume) high-Q periods are, in fact, times of more severe underpricing of firms going public. In other words, models in which a naive shareholder buys overpriced firms will not explain the time-series correlation between the volume of IPOs and Tobin's Q. Perhaps it is only investment bankers who benefit from such exuberance.

4. Indicators of Invention

4.1. *Patents and Trademarks*

Other indicators of invention—by small and large firms—are general indexes of patents and trademarks. One measure typically used to summarize the climate for invention is patenting activity. Figure 7.2 shows patents per capita for the history of the United States.[6] Patents rise only very slowly until 1853, but then take a sharp upward turn. This growth may have as much to do with increased awareness of the patenting process and its potential benefits to entrepreneurs as with a greater tendency to

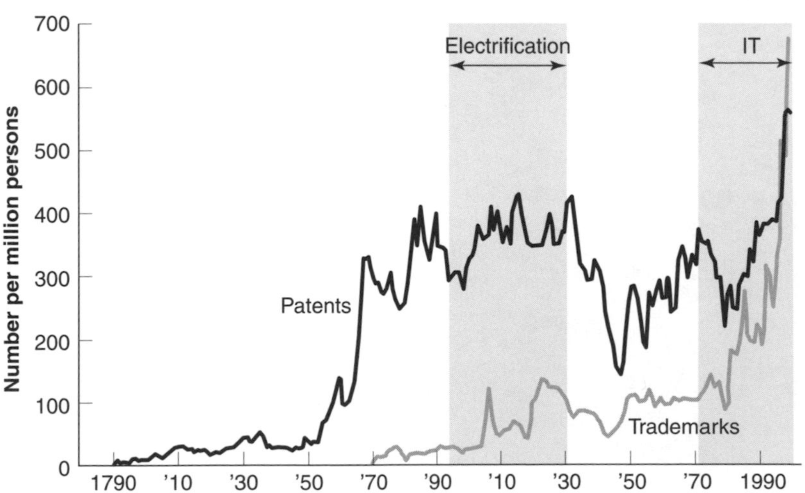

Figure 7.2. Patents and Trademarks

invent, but it is safe to say that citizens had embraced the system by the 1870s. Patents level off but remain high between 1890 and 1930, but then fall off quickly in the 1930s and 1940s. They begin to rise again after 1950, but after a regression in the 1970s, do not surpass their 1930 level until the latter half of the 1990's.

The U-shaped pattern of patenting across the twentieth century is more striking when one considers the shaded areas in figure 7.2, which correspond to the periods generally associated with the spread of two general purpose technologies (GPTs)—electricity and information technology (IT). If new ideas are more easily carried to market by innovators in periods of rapid technological change, and these innovators operate smaller-than-average-sized firms prior to the innovation, we might expect to see the small entrepreneur gaining ground over larger ones after a GPT arrives.

Trademarks do not have as strong a U-shaped pattern as patents since 1890, but the pattern does still emerge after detrending. Of course, trademarks may simply imply new brand names rather than actual new products. If new firms tend to enter the market based on an idea, while incumbents are mostly responsible for new brands, we would not expect the U-shaped pattern of trademarks to be as strong as that of patents.

4.2. *The Relative Price of Technology-Specific Capital*

Another index is the price of a commodity. When there is competition, innovation drives down the quality-adjusted price of that good and relative prices of technology-specific capital. Figure 7.3 aims to look at the

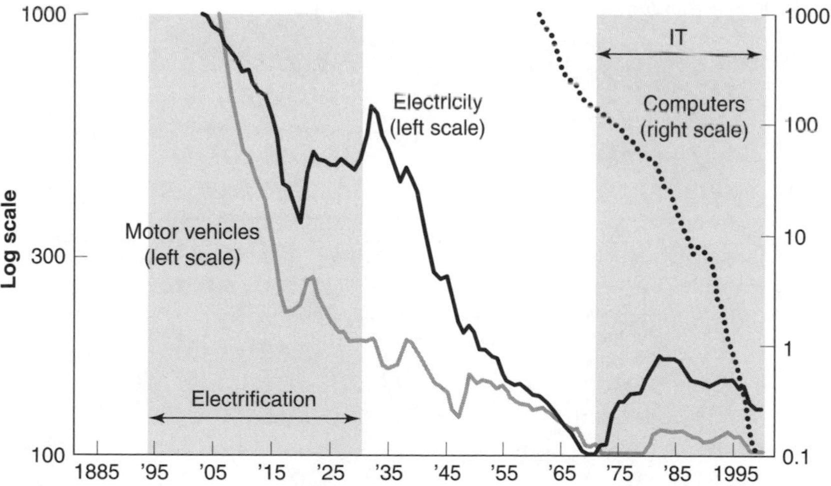

Figure 7.3. Prices Indexes for Products of Two Technological Revolutions

components of the aggregate capital stock; specifically, the components tied to the two GPTs. Because deflators for electrically powered capital are not available in the first half of the twentieth century, figure 7.3 compares the declines in relative prices associated with three GPTs—electricity, internal combustion, and computers—once again relative to the consumption price index.[7] The use of the left-hand scale for electricity and motor vehicles and the right-hand scale for computers underscores the extraordinary decline in computer prices since 1960 compared to the earlier technologies. While the electricity and the automobile indexes fall by a factor of 10, the computer index falls by a factor of 10,000.

4.3. Age of the Stock-Market Leaders

Neither figure 7.2 nor figure 7.3 deals with data that would distinguish the small vs large firm, or the young firm from the old firm. For the latter distinction, figure 7.4 shows that, overall, the age of the leaders is anything *but* steady. It sometimes rises faster than the 45-degree line, indicating that the age of the leaders is rising faster than the passage of time.

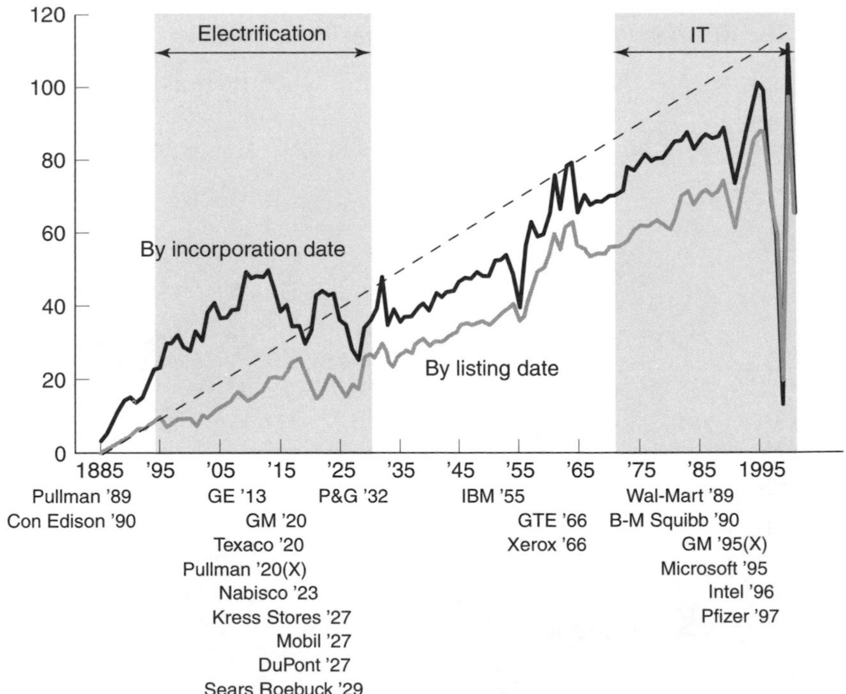

Figure 7.4. Age of the Leaders Accounting for 5 Percent of Stock-Market Value

At other times it is flat or falling, indicating replacement. Both figures show, however, that during the electricity and the IT eras, the lines are flat or falling, so that replacement was then high.

Specifically, figure 7.4 plots the value-weighted average age of the largest firms whose market values sum to 5 percent of GDP. "Age" is from incorporation and from exchange listing. We label some important entries and exits from this group (with exits denoted by "X"). Based upon years from incorporation, the leading firms were being replaced by *older* firms over the first 30 years of our sample, because the solid line is then steeper than the 45-degree line. In the two decades after the Great Depression the leaders held their relative positions as the 45-degree slope of the average age lines shows. The leaders got younger in the 1990s, and their average ages now lie well below the 45-degree line. The shakeout of 1999–2001 comes from Microsoft's huge rise in 1999, when it was worth more than 5 percent of GDP on its own, and its rapid decline in 2000, which transferred the full 5 percent share to GE. The two firms split the 5 percent share in 2001. The slopes of regression lines in figure 7.4 (estimated with constant and time trend) are 0.62 for years since incorporation and 0.67 for years since exchange listing.

4.4. *Small-Cap Firms versus Large-Cap Firms*

Young firms are smaller. If "creative destruction" does indeed mean that old firms give way to young firms, then we should see signs of it in figure 7.5, which depicts the relative appreciation of the *total* market value of small

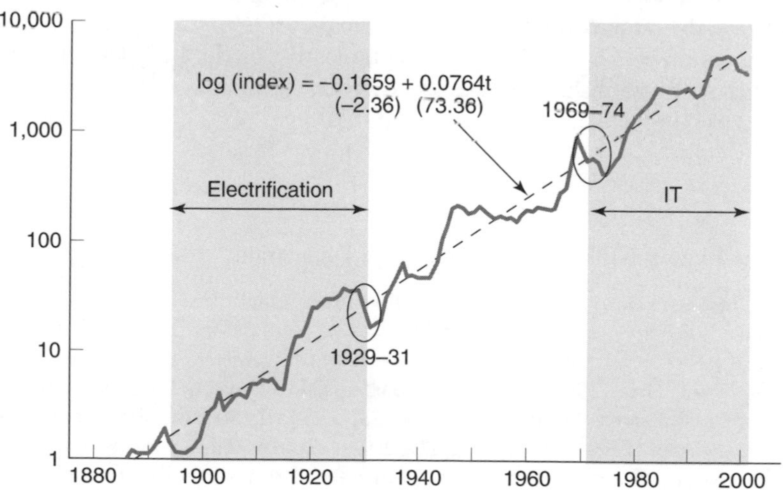

Figure 7.5. Relative Capital Appreciations of Small versus Large Firms

versus large firms since 1885.[8] We define "small" firms as those in the lowest quintile of CRSP, and "large" firms as those in the upper quintile. The figure shows that small firms outperform large ones in the long run and that the growth premium is about 7.5 percent per year. But the two technological epochs do not show a faster rise than the other epochs, and this is puzzling. The IT era shows, in particular, that the large firms regrouped after 1983. Surprisingly, recessions do not seem to hurt the long-term prospects of small firms: The relative index rises in 10 of the 23 NBER recessions.

The two periods that we wish to focus on are 1929–31 and the early 1970s. In both periods, the small-cap firms lost out relative to the large-cap firms. The first period comes at the end of the electrification era, and the relative decline of small-cap firms is what one would have expected. But the early 1970s come at the beginning of a new GPT, and small-cap firms should have outperformed the large-cap firms during that time. Yet the opposite happened. It is only after 1974 that the small-cap firms start to perform better.

5. Conclusion

Figures 7.4 and 7.5 measure the performance of small, young firms relative to large, old firms. As did the facts in figure 7.1, these results show that small, young firms do better when there is faster technological change. Incumbents do well when it is "business as usual." Because the data are not available, we have not said much about the independent inventor, the small family business, and so on. One would expect, however, that the contrast between the large corporation and the smaller IPO-ing firms or the smaller members of NYSE and NASDAQ is indicative of the broader differences between the established producer and the startup newcomer.

Notes

The authors thank the National Science Foundation for financial help.

1. Listing years after 1925 are those for which firms enter CRSP. For 1885–1924, they are years in which prices first appear in the NYSE listings of *The Annalist, Bradstreet's*, the *Commercial and Financial Chronicle*, or the *New York Times*. The 6,238 incorporation dates used to construct figure 7.1 are from *Moody's Industrial Manual* (1920, 1928, 1955, 1980), Standard and Poor's *Stock Market Encyclopedia* (1981, 1988, 2000), and various editions of Standard and Poor's *Stock Reports*. The 3,827 foundings are from Dun and Bradstreet's *Million Dollar Directory* (2000), Moody's, Kelley (1954), and individual company websites. The 482 first innovations were obtained by

reading company histories in *Hoover's Online* (2000) and company websites. We linearly interpolate the series between missing points before applying the HP filter to the time series in the figure.

2. The gross and net capital stocks are Compustat data items 7 and 8 respectively. An IPO is dated by the year that a firm enters the CRSP database, but we include its net capital stock (from Compustat) in our series for y_{real} only if the firm joins Compustat in the same year. We do this because the firm coverage of Compustat expanded as balance sheet data became available for particular firms, and this does not necessarily correspond to the year of IPO. Since CRSP includes all firms listed on the NYSE, the AMEX after 1962, and NASDAQ after 1972, the correspondence between entry year and IPO is reliable for all years other than 1962 and 1972, when existing AMEX and NASDAQ firms entered CRSP en masse. The 1962 and 1972 values are for this reason interpolated, and are excluded from the regression analysis. We also exclude American Depository Receipts (ADRs), which are indirect listings of large foreign firms through U.S. banks. Since most ADRs either were listed previously in other countries or from countries where a formal IPO was not possible, their inclusion would distort our analysis of the factors that influence the listing behavior of U.S. firms.

3. Moskowitz and Vissing-Jorgensen (2002) report this figure at closer to 30 percent.

4. We obtain similar results using the number of new listings on CRSP for the entire 1927–2001 period instead of the Ritter-CRSP figures. The two series have a correlation coefficient of 0.96.

5. Then t is the number of periods spent in school, and we can think of

$$f(t) = wh(t),$$

where $h(t)$ is the number of efficiency units of human capital created in school, and w is the wage per efficiency unit of that capital.

6. We use the total number of "utility" (i.e., invention) patents from the U.S. Patent and Trademark Office for 1963–2000, and from the U.S. Bureau of the Census (1975, series W-96, pp. 957–59) for 1790–1962. The number of registered trademarks is from the U.S. Bureau of the Census (1975, series W-107, p. 959) for 1870–1969, and from various issues of the *Statistical Abstract of the United States* for later years. Population figures, which are for the total resident population and measured at mid-year, are from U.S. Bureau of the Census (1975, series A-7, p. 8) for 1790–1970, and from the U.S. Bureau of Economic Analysis (2002) thereafter.

7. To construct a quality-adjusted price index, we join the "final" price index for computer systems from Gordon (1990, table 6.10, col. 5, p. 226) for 1960–78 with the pooled index developed for desktop and mobile personal computers of Berndt, Dulberger, and Rappaport (2000, table 2, col. 1, p. 22) for 1979–99. Since Gordon's index includes mainframe computers, minicomputers, and PCs while the Berndt et al. index includes only PCs, the two segments used to build our price measure are themselves not directly comparable, but a joining of them should still reflect quality-adjusted price trends in the computer industry reasonably well. We set the index to 1,000 in the first year of the sample (i.e., 1960).

Electricity prices are averages of all electric energy services in cents per kilowatt hour from U.S. Bureau of the Census (1975, series S119, p. 827) for 1903, 1907,

1917, 1922, and 1926–70, and from the *Statistical Abstract of the United States* for 1971–89. We interpolate under a constant growth assumption between the missing years in the early part of the sample. For 1990–2000, prices are U.S. city averages (June figures) from the Bureau of Labor Statistics (http:www.bls.gov). We then set the index to equal 1,000 in the first year of the sample (i.e., 1903).

Motor vehicle prices for 1913–40 are annual averages of monthly wholesale prices of passenger vehicles from the National Bureau of Economic Research (Macrohistory Database, series m04180a for 1913–27, series m04180b for 1928–40, http://www.nber.org). From 1941 to 1947, they are wholesale prices of motor vehicles and equipment from *Historical Statistics* (series E38, p. 199), and from 1948 to 2000 they are producer prices of motor vehicles from the Bureau of Labor Statistics (http://www.bls.gov). To approximate prices from 1901 to 1913, we extrapolate assuming constant growth and the average annual growth rate observed from 1913 to 1924. We then join the various components to form an overall price index, and set it to equal 1,000 in the first year of the sample (i.e., 1901).

8. Being a total value index, this differs from the relative stock price index that is plotted in Figure 8 of Hobijn and Jovanovic (2001). For the post-1925 period for which they overlap, the qualitative behavior of the two series is essentially the same.

References

Berndt, E. R., E. R. Dulberger, and N. J. Rappaport. 2000. "Price and Quality of Desktop and Mobile Personal Computers: A Quarter Century of History." Manuscript.

Bradstreet Co. 1885–1925, various issues, Bradstreet's. New York: Bradstreet Co.

Commercial and Financial Chronicle, 1885–1925, various issues.

Diamond, P. 1982. "Aggregate Demand Management in Search Equilibrium." *Journal of Political Economy* 90: 881–94.

Dun and Bradstreet, Inc. 2003. *D&B Million Dollar Directory*. Bethlehem, PA.: Dun and Bradstreet Inc.

Gordon, R. J. 1990. *The Measurement of Durable Goods Prices*. Chicago: University of Chicago Press.

Hobijn, B., and B. Jovanovic. 2001. "The IT Revolution and the Stock Market: Evidence." *American Economic Review* 91: 1203–20.

Hoover's Inc. 2000. *Hoover's Online: The Business Network*. Austin, Tex.: Hoover's Inc.

Jovanovic, B., and P. L. Rousseau. 2001. "Why Wait? A Century of Life before IPO." *American Economic Review (Papers and Proceedings)* 91: 336–41.

Kelley, E. M. 1954. *The Business Founding Date Directory*. Scarsdale, N.Y.: Morgan and Morgan.

Moody's Investors Service. 1920, 1929, 1931, 1941, 1951, 1956, 1961. *Moody's Industrial Manual*. New York: Moody's Investors Service.

Moscowitz, T. J., and A. Vissing-Jorgensen. 2002. "The Returns to Entrepreneurial Invesment: A Private Equity Premium Puzzle?" *American Economic Review* 92: 745–78.

National Bureau of Economic Research. 2000. *Macrohistory Database*. Cambridge, Mass.: National Bureau of Economic Research.

New York Times Co. 1913–25. *The Annalist: A Magazine of Finance, Commerce, and Economics*. New York: New York Times Co.

Ritter, J. R. 2002. "Some Factoids about the 2002 IPO Market." Manuscript, University of Florida.

———. 2003. "Long-run Returns on IPOs from 1970–2002." Manuscript, University of Florida.

Shleifer, A. 1986. "Implementation Cycles." *Journal of Political Economy* 94: 1163–90.

Standard and Poor's Corporation. 1973–2000. *Stock Reports*. New York: Standard and Poor's Corporation.

———. 1981, 1988, 2000. *Stock Market Encyclopedia*. New York: Standard and Poor's Corporation.

———. 2002. *Compustat Database*. New York: Standard and Poor's Corporation.

United States Bureau of the Census, Department of Commerce. 1975. *Historical Statistics of the United States, Colonial Times to 1970*. Washington, D.C.: Government Printing Office.

———. 1970–2000. *Statistical Abstract of the United States*. Washington, D.C.: Government Printing Office.

United States Bureau of Economic Analysis. 2002. *Survey of Current Business*. Washington, D.C.: Government Printing Office.

University of Chicago Center for Research on Securities Prices. 2002. *CRSP Database*. Chicago: CRSP.

Veldkamp, L. 2006. "Media Frenzies in Markets for Financial Innovation." *American Economic Review* 96: 577–601.

Chapter 8

Toward Analysis of Capitalism's Unparalleled Growth: Sources and Mechanism

WILLIAM J. BAUMOL

> Nordhaus brackets the growth of real wages over the past century as somewhere between a 20-fold and a 100-fold increase. Alan Greenspan . . . has suggested adjustments of the statistics that lead to an estimate of a thirty-fold increase of material wealth over the past century. (DeLong 2001)

IT IS, OF COURSE, WIDELY recognized that the economic performance of the free-market economies is impressive, but few, other than the three economists cited in the epigraph, and in addition, Marx, Engels and Schumpeter, seem to have recognized just how near incomprehensible that performance has been. Indeed, it can be maintained that there is no economic event, development, or other phenomenon that comes remotely close to it in importance for the standard of living, or as an ambition for the economy that would have been so unambiguously rejected as an unachievable fantasy by those who lived before its inception. Both the sheer magnitude of the outpouring of products that has been achieved and the fabulous character of its flood of inventions would generally have been considered beyond belief.

But though no economic phenomenon comes close as a sensational development, even more unnoticed is the mysterious absence of any serious theoretical literature that seeks to explain systematically to what this unparalleled record of accomplishment can be attributed. This statement should not be misunderstood. A number of outstanding economic historians have contributed invaluable work that is highly pertinent to this topic. One need only mention the writings of David Landes, Joel Mokyr, Douglass North, Nathan Rosenberg (I list them alphabetically), among others, to see how much light has been shed on the subject. Much important work has also been contributed on the theory of innovation, including that by William Nordhaus, Karl Shell, Philippe Aghion, and Peter Howitt, among many others. And then there are the illuminating general writings by learned contributors such as Richard Nelson and Frederick Scherer. But, so far as I have been able to find, only two pieces of economic literature deal directly with the issue—why is this economic system's growth so different from that of any other economic system? On this question, I have encountered only four oft-quoted pages in *The Manifesto of the Communist Party*, and six pages in Schumpeter's *Capitalism, Socialism and Democracy*. Like the dog that did not bark, there must be something significant that underlies the mysterious absence of such discussion in the literature.

It is my purpose neither to deplore this huge gap in the literature nor to seek to explain it. Rather, the goal of this chapter, like that of my 2002 book, is to take a first step toward analysis of the capitalist growth phenomenon itself. That is, it is my hope that this essay will contribute toward the launching of a literature worthy of the phenomenon, one that, by analyzing the sources of the free market's sensational success, can also suggest to struggling economies what promising steps they can undertake.

1. On Warts and Blemishes of Capitalism

It is helpful at the outset to avoid one misunderstanding about the position taken by this chapter. While it will describe in superlatives the accomplishments of the capitalist economy in terms of unprecedented growth and innovation, it is not to be misunderstood as a piece of procapitalist propaganda. Elsewhere I have, in various places, written about the shortcomings of what the unconstrained free-market economy can yield (see, e.g., Baumol and Blackman 1991). Even with repeated efforts at restraint and redirection by governmental rules and regulations, its problems have evidently by no means been overcome. In the United States, for example, inequality of income and wealth is substantial and has been mounting rapidly. Though perhaps less severe than they used to be, recessions, unemployment, and intervals of inflation continue to recur. Despite the wealth of the community as a whole, poverty has not been wiped out. Resources continue to be depleted and wasted. The environment continues to suffer a variety of insults, some of them constituting severe threats to the well-being of society.

My claim on behalf of capitalism is only that there are two arenas in which its accomplishments and capacity for further contribution are not remotely approximated by any other form of economy, ancient or recent: Those are the intertwined arenas of productivity and innovation. That this is no bias toward capitalism is attested by the even more enthusiastic expressions of approbation by those well-known right-wingers, Karl Marx and Friedrich Engels:

> The Bourgeoisie [i.e., capitalism] cannot exist without constantly revolutionizing the instruments of production. . . . Conservation of the old modes of production in unaltered form was, on the contrary, the first condition of existence for all earlier industrial classes. . . . The bourgeoisie, during its rule of scarce one hundred years, has created more massive and more colossal productive forces than have all preceding generations together. . . . It has accomplished wonders far surpassing Egyptian pyramids, Roman aqueducts and Gothic cathedrals. . . . Subjugation of nature's forces to man, machinery, application of chemistry to industry and agriculture, . . . clearing of whole continents for cultivation . . . what earlier generation had even a presentiment that such productive forces slumbered. . .? (Marx and Engels, *The Communist Manifesto*, 1847; ordering slightly modified)

2. Toward Grasp of the Astonishing Growth Achievements

My next objective is to impart some sense of the incredible magnitude of the free market's accomplishment in growth and innovation. But despite the evidence that will be offered next, I must concede that despite years of study of the subject its dimensions still elude me. I am aware that per capita income in the United States is estimated to have increased something like eight-fold in the past century (and that some informed observers consider this a great underestimate, as noted in this chapter's epigraph). But what does that mean? I simply do not understand what my family's life would be if my income now were that of an average American, and then, suddenly, seven out of eight (real) dollars were removed from me. But let me, nevertheless, try to convey something of the flavor of what has happened. There are two companion stories here, the "wave of gadgets" with which we have been provided and the sheer increase in purchasing power at our disposal.

The innovations that are taken to have launched the Industrial Revolution were mostly producers' goods—machinery that led to an explosion of productivity in the textile industries. The wealthy consumer had available some half dozen items that were unknown to ancient Romans (and they lacked a number of things the Romans possessed)—notably hunting guns, clocks and watches, generally not very accurate, windowpanes, and paper with printing on it. No sounds had ever been recorded, no one had traveled on land faster than on horseback, messages delivered from the Old World to the New required weeks and even months, so that the Battle of New Orleans could be fought after the peace treaty had been signed. We know the sound of Caruso's voice, and I have even heard Johannes Brahms speak, but we will probably never experience the reputedly gorgeous voice of the castrato Farinelli or the voice of George Washington.[1] Yet today the appearance of new gadgets for the consumer has reached a crescendo that shows no signs of slowing. The constant appearance of novel, generally unanticipated, objects and new models that are ever more powerful, more reliable, easier to use, and cheaper than their predecessors has become so commonplace that our children and grandchildren simply take them for granted.

Earlier eras were characterized by miserable living conditions even for the wealthy and powerful, up until the middle or even the end of the eighteenth century. Not that their wealth failed to give them ostentatious clothing, exotic foods, and armies of servants. But the problem for them was that little of the technology of human comfort had yet been invented. Two examples will illustrate my point. One is a description of the 1732 journey of the pregnant Wilhelmina, favorite sister of Frederick the Great, between Berlin and Bayreuth:

> Ten strenuous, abnormally frigid days were spent upon roads, bad enough in summer, now deep with snow. On the second day the carriage in which Wilhelmina was riding turned over. She was buried under an avalanche of luggage. . . . Everyone expected a miscarriage and wanted Wilhelmina to rest in bed for several days. . . . Mountains appeared after Leibzig had been passed. . . . Wilhelmina was frightened by the steepness of the roads and preferred to get out and walk to being whacked about as the carriage jolted from boulder to boulder. (Wright 1965, 142)

A second illustration of the standards of discomfort for the rich and powerful before the Industrial Revolution is the oft-cited report by the Princess Palatine, German sister-in-law of Louis XIV, that in the winter of 1695 in the Hall of Mirrors at Versailles, at the king's table, the wine froze in the glasses! (Braudel 1979, 299). I should add that throughout the nineteenth century, in much of the United States, it was expected that every winter the ink would freeze in the inkwells of the home.

Statistics and other pieces of evidence tell a story consistent with such anecdotes. Using genealogical records, Fogel estimates that between 1550 and 1700 the life expectancy at birth of members of the British nobility, male and female, was virtually the same as that of the population as a whole, at about 34 years (Fogel 1986). Indeed, the average longevity for the general male and female population slightly exceeded that for members of the peerage for a substantial part of this period. Soon after that, however, things began to change. The life expectancy of peers leaped upward and ahead of the rest of the British population. Early in the eighteenth century, indoor heating was revolutionized by inventions such as the Franklin stove. At the beginning of the nineteenth, railroads were born, and through these and other advances the upper classes in Victorian society soon enjoyed historically unprecedented levels of comfort.

But after that point the less affluent began to catch up. As Nathan Rosenberg and L. E. Birdzell Jr. note, "Western economic growth . . . benefited the life-style of the very rich much less than it benefited the life-style of the less well-off. . . . The very rich were as well-housed, clothed and adorned in 1885 as in 1985. . . . In fact, the innovations of positive value to the rich are the relatively few advances in medical care, air conditioning, and improvements in transportation and preservation of food" (1986, 26–27). In contrast, the lower classes still had very far to go. I need merely recall that regular famines, at least once per decade on average, with starvation widespread, had begun to disappear only in the eighteenth century. Still, famines continued occasionally well into the nineteenth, and not only in Ireland. Thus, in relatively wealthy Belgium, "During the great crisis of 1846, the newspapers would tell daily of cases of death from starvation. . . . At Wynghene, cases became so frequent that the local policeman was given the job of calling at all houses each day to see if the inhabitants were still alive" (de Meeüs 1962, 305).

The description of the horrors of the existence of the lower-income classes at that time can go on and on, but the point is clear. It is they who had the furthest to go. And improve their circumstances they did. There is no better way to demonstrate these advances than to report some figures on how much the purchasing power of an "average worker's" hour of labor has increased over the course of the twentieth century. The Federal Reserve Bank of Dallas reports that "earning our daily bread" literally takes less than one-third the time it did early in this century. In 1919 the average worker labored 13 minutes in order to earn enough to buy a pound of bread, compared to just 4 minutes in 1997. The work time required to buy a three-pound chicken in 1919—more than $2^1/_2$ hours—had fallen to just 14 minutes in 1997. In 1910, 345 hours of work time bought a kitchen range and 553 hours of work time bought a clothes washer; those numbers had dropped to 22 hours and 26 hours by 1997. There are many other eye-opening comparisons. The purchase of a calculating device in 1916 required 494 hours of labor time but only 46 minutes in 1996; a 1954 color television required 562 hours of work but 23 hours in 1997; and the purchase of a 1908 Model T automobile necessitated 4,696 hours of labor as against 1,365 hours for a 1997 Ford Taurus (Federal Reserve Bank of Dallas 1997, 5–17).

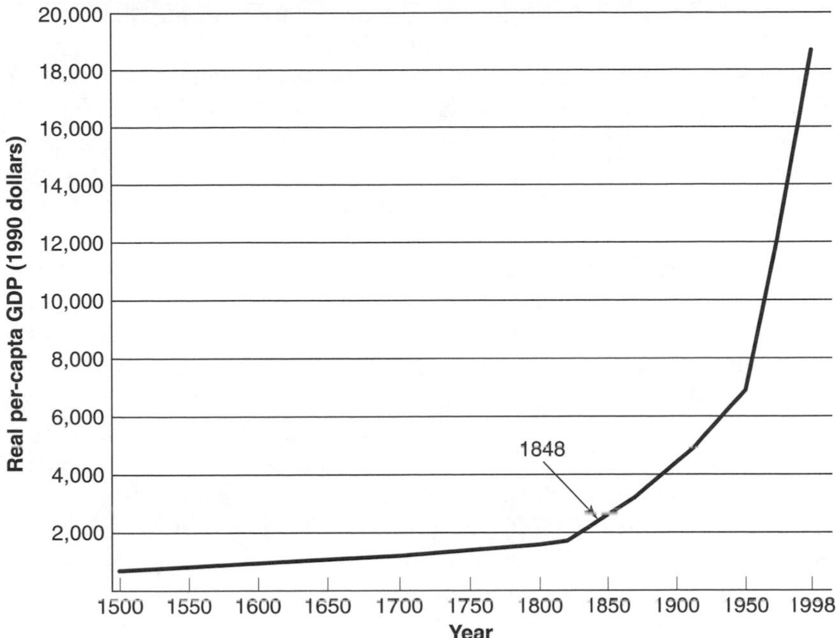

Figure 8.1. Real Per Capita GDP in the United Kingdom, 1500–1998

The story can be summed up with a graph of per capita GDP using Angus Maddison's (2001) estimates of UK GDP for five centuries (Fig. 8.1). It is clear that the pattern depicted is at least approximately exponential, with the slope of the graph growing ever steeper. Moreover, in such longer periods as are considered in the graph, there are no downturns. The effects of depressions and recessions are simply too insignificant, relative to the growth path, even to be noticed. Finally, it is worth pausing to note the position of the graph in 1848 (arrow). That is the year the preceding quotation from Marx and Engels made its appearance. Yet we see that at that date capitalist growth had hardly begun to take off. What foresight those authors displayed in their comments on the productive accomplishments of the free-market economy!

3. Innovation Rather Than Invention as the Unique Free-Market Accomplishment

As one schoolboy is reported to have summarized the matter, the Industrial Revolution that presumably began in the second half of the eighteenth century and took off in the middle of the nineteenth was constituted by a "wave of gadgets." This is surely no mischaracterization. It was invention that made possible the ways of living that previously had not been imagined and that permitted the explosion of output and the growth in productivity that brought general living standards in at least a few countries to unprecedented heights. Other contributory developments are frequently cited, notably the accumulation of human capital associated with expanding education and the sheer volume of investment that provided expanding capacity of plant and equipment. But it is not difficult to argue that without the invention and utilization of new productive techniques, neither the accumulation of physical capital nor the spread of education could have gone very far. The fact is that both of these are expensive propositions and the relatively impoverished economies that preceded the Industrial Revolution simply lacked the resources necessary to permit any material expansion of plant or education. Indeed, even in the first half of the nineteenth century the investment in a factory was minuscule by today's standards, and illiteracy was the norm. In short, without the inventions that permitted the rise in productivity that in turn began the outpouring of wealth, neither universal education nor the giant firm would appear to have been possible.

If this argument is valid, then the search for explanation of the capitalist growth miracle must focus on its unprecedented outpouring of innovation, and to that we will presently turn. But first I must emphasize my use of the word *innovation*, rather than *invention*, intending thereby to recall Schumpeter's invaluable distinction. He uses the latter term to mean more or less what it usually denotes—the creation of new products or processes or at least the ideas that underlie them. But the term *innovation* is employed to refer to all of the extended process of which invention is only the initial step. It includes development of the invention's design to the point at which it is ready for practical use, the introduction of the novel item to the market, and its subsequent adoption and utilization by the economy. The distinction is critical here because it can be taken to underlie the difference between the accomplishments of the capitalist economy and those of any and all of its predecessors, including those with a remarkable record of invention.

For invention is obviously nothing new. The accomplishments of Arab civilization and of medieval China immediately come to mind. In China were invented, as is well known, printing, paper, playing cards, the spinning wheel, an elaborate water clock, the umbrella, and, of course, gunpowder, to name but a sample. However, despite China's talent for the creation of novel technology, its performance in adoption and utilization of these inventions was modest at best. Rather, more than one invention was diverted to amusement rather than productive use,[2] and others, like the wondrous water clock, were soon totally forgotten. Even in the

Soviet Union, with its cadre of very capable scientists and engineers, there is evidence of a respectable record of accomplishment in the arena of invention, but a remarkably poor record of utilization of these inventions except in military activity. It is easy to propose plausible explanations for these cases (see, e.g., Baumol 2002, chaps. 4 and 14), but that is not the point here. I need only observe that the economic institutions in both medieval China and the Soviet Union not merely failed to offer incentives for innovative activity, but actually provided strong motivation leading to its determined avoidance. In short, while the free market's record of invention is noteworthy, it is its performance in innovation that is unique.

4. Two Phases and Four Sources of Free-Market Growth

There are four obvious sources of the free market's innovations. Many are contributed by universities and by government research agencies. There are, clearly, the products of individual inventor-engineers, who are the stuff of literature and legend. Finally, there are the outputs of industrial laboratories in giant corporations. Here I will say little about the first two of these. Their contributions are well recognized, and the incentives they provide for inventive activity are not directly intertwined with the free-market mechanism. Not that capitalism is irrelevant even for these—the market economy's elevation of the inventor's prestige, and the political pressures for funding of research that are engendered by the market's economic needs, surely have helped to stimulate both academic and government research activity. Moreover, as has already been suggested, the abundance that capitalism creates provides the resources needed for the expansion of educational institutions. It is equally clear that wealth is needed to fund the costly research and innovative activities of government and academia, so that only in an economy of abundance can such activities be carried out on any substantial scale.

But in contrast to university and governmental innovative enterprise, which are not inherently market-driven activities, those of the private entrepreneur and the giant corporations clearly are directly embedded in the workings of the market. And here is where the remainder of my discussion will focus.

First, a chronological observation is appropriate. It is only in the second half of the nineteenth century that the industrial laboratory made its appearance. It reportedly first occurred in the chemical industry in Germany. Competition ensured that the example would soon be followed by others. Once this had spread, as will be argued presently, the entire character of the innovation process underwent a major transformation. That is, inventive activity was not merely transferred from one set of players to another, from the independent entrepreneur to the large business firm, but the process itself was also significantly modified.

Until this development occurred, invention was the near exclusive domain of the independent inventor and his entrepreneur associate (though in a number of cases both roles were played by the same individual). The era of invention by unaffiliated individuals emerged at roughly the same time as the inception of modern capitalism, and there is reason to conclude that this was no coincidence. It was not primarily because either of these was an indispensable requisite of the other, but because both were driven by the same historical developments.

5. On Capitalism and the Entrepreneur

There is plausible reason to argue that the rise of productive entrepreneurship in England in the period leading up to and including the Industrial Revolution is in good part attributable to institutional developments that evolved throughout the later Middle Ages and reached their culmination under Charles I and Cromwell. These were the establishment of the rule of law and, with it, the protection of property against arbitrary expropriation and the enforceability of contracts. The engine of this change was the monarch's perpetual shortage of funds. The aggressive warfare that constituted his prime occupational obligation meant that he and his rivals had no option but continually to raise the financial ante in their endeavor to avoid military inferiority to the other. In seeking to induce his powerful barons to grant him these indispensable resources, the king was forced to make concessions that led cumulatively to the adoption of the rule of law.

It is clear that these developments stimulated the growth of the market economy and, indeed, that without them such an economy, if it could have arisen, would have been a feeble and truncated version of what had actually emerged.

At the same time, these institutional innovations surely also underlay the explosion of *productive* entrepreneurship. Entrepreneurship of a more general sort is no eighteenth-century innovation. As far as one can judge from recorded history, there have always been imaginative, inventive, and risk-taking individuals who followed the most promising avenue currently available in pursuit of wealth, power, and prestige. But the methods they used for the purpose were very different from those that became the norm in the capitalist era. The routes taken by those entrepreneurs varied, sometimes entailing military careers in which they served their kings or sometimes rivaled their sovereigns in aggressive enterprise, with chaos the usual result. Sometimes entrepreneurship found its outlet in climbing of the bureaucratic ladder or that of the church hierarchy. Nor has such variation in the forms taken by entrepreneurship disappeared in modern times. Who would deny that a high official in a dictatorial government or a godfather in a mafioso organization can be enterprising?

What is most noteworthy here is that the forms of exercise of entrepreneurial talent that have just been described rarely lead to increases in productivity of the economy or to technical innovation in arenas other than the military. In societies where expropriation of property accumulated by commercial and productive activity is a constant threat, and where, in addition, wealth accumulated by these means is disgraceful rather than prestigious, the absence of entrepreneurship in productive activities should elicit no surprise. It is the rule of law, and the consequent success of ever more inventors and entrepreneurs, with even kings finding it appropriate to invest in commerce, that the modern productive entrepreneurs and their productive innovations emerged and assumed a significant role in the economy. The entrepreneurs had arguably always been present, but it was the protection of contracts and property that enabled modern capitalism to emerge and that reallocated the input of entrepreneurship preponderantly into productive channels.

6. Revolutionary Breakthroughs: A Small-Firm Specialty

I will argue next that R&D in the large business organization is inherently conservative, and that these firms tend to avoid the risks of the unknown that the revolutionary breakthrough entails. The breakthroughs, rather, are left most often to the small or newly founded enterprises, guided by their enterprising entrepreneurs.

Though there is no knife's-edge boundary between inventions that can be considered revolutionary breakthroughs and those that are "merely" cumulative incremental improvements, there are some inventions that clearly fall into the former category. The electric light, alternating electric current, the internal combustion engine, and a host of other advances must surely be deemed revolutionary, while successive models of washing machines and refrigerators—with each new model a bit longer-lasting, a bit less susceptible to breakdown, and a bit easier to use—arguably constitute a sequence of incremental improvements.

The degree of asymmetry in the apportionment of these specialized activities, heterodox and incremental invention, between large and small firms is striking. The U.S. Small Business Administration has prepared a listing of breakthrough innovations of the twentieth century for which small firms are responsible, and its menu of inventions literally spans the range from A to Z, from the airplane to the zipper. Included are air conditioning, the cotton picker, the electronic spreadsheet, FM radio, the helicopter, the integrated circuit, the instant camera, prestressed concrete, quick-frozen food, the vacuum tube, and the photocopier, among a host of others, many of enormous significance for our economy.

Two recent studies,[3] also sponsored by the U.S. Small Business Administration (CHI Research 2003, 2004) provide more systematic evidence to similar effect. These reports examine technical change through patenting, and the role of "small firms" (defined as "businesses with fewer than 500 employees"). The first of these studies finds that "small firm patents are twice as likely than large firm patents to be among the 1 percent of most cited patents." Among other conclusions, in the words of its authors, this study reports that "Small firms represent one-third of the most prolific patenting companies that have 15 or more U.S. patents. . . . Small firms are more effective in producing high-value innovations—the citation index for small firm patents averaged 1.53 compared to 1.19 for large firms. . . . A small firm patent is at least twice as likely to be found among the top 1 percent of highest-impact patents as a patent from a large firm" (2003, 3).

Moreover, the more recent study found that "The technological influence of small firms is increasing. The percentage of highly innovative US firms (those with more than 15 US patents in the last five years) that are defined as small firms increased from 33% in the 2000 database to 40% in the 2002 database." In addition, "Small companies represent 65% of the new companies in the list of most highly innovative companies in 2002" (2004, ii).

One is, then, led to conclude that most of the revolutionary new ideas of the past two centuries have been, and are likely to continue to be, provided more heavily by independent innovators who, essentially, operate small business enterprises. Evidently, the small entrepreneurial firms have come close to monopolizing the portion of R&D activity that is engaged in the search for revolutionary breakthroughs.

That would seem to leave very little scope for invention by the large enterprise, which, as we will see, accounts for a very large and growing share of R&D investment. Given the apparently critical and continuing innovative role of the entrepreneur and the small firm, little would appear to be left for the large enterprise to do. That, as we will see next, however, is a very misleading conclusion.

7. The Large Enterprise, Innovation, and Growth

Private real investment in R&D is rising sharply. Figure 8.2, which provides the U.S. data for the bulk of the half century since World War II, indicates that it, too, is following something like an exponential path

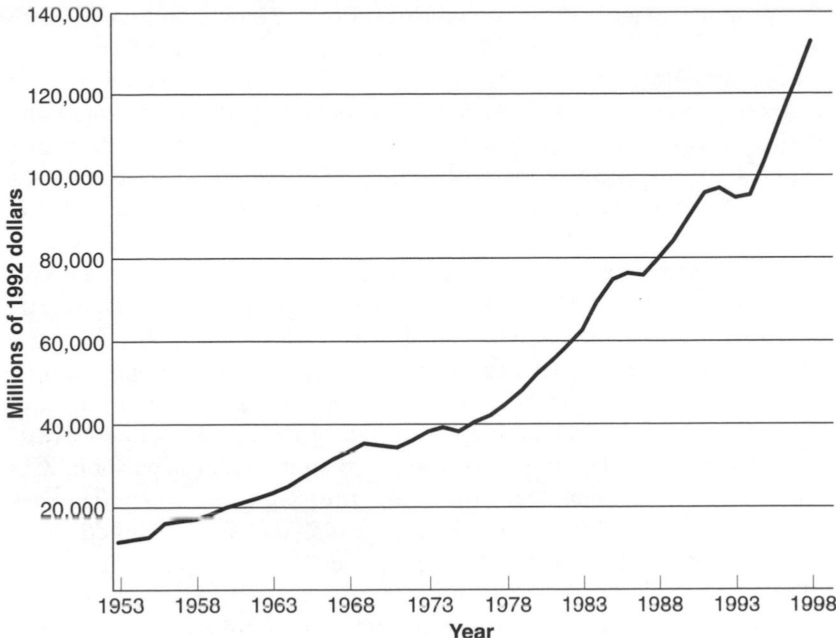

Figure 8.2. Real U.S. Private R&D Expenditures, 1953–1998

and, perhaps even more surprising, that it exhibits no significant declines in periods of recession (National Science Board 2000).

Increasingly, at least in the United States, the funding for innovation has been supplied by large oligopolistic enterprises, rather than by independent inventors or small, newly founded entrepreneurial firms. Today some 70 percent of R&D expenditure in the United States is carried out by private business. Most of this growing outlay is provided by the larger firms. According to data gathered by the National Science Foundation (National Science Board 2000), in 2000, 46 percent of total U.S. industrial R&D funds were spent by 167 companies with 25,000 or more employees; 60 percent of these funds were spent by 366 companies with at least 10,000 employees, and 80 percent was spent by 1,990 firms of 1,000 or more employees. At the other end of the spectrum, about 15 percent of total U.S. industrial R&D funds were spent by 32,000 companies with fewer than 500 employees each.

There can be little doubt that this performance can be ascribed primarily to competition. It can hardly have escaped the notice of the earlier entrepreneurs that possession of a superior innovative product or process confers a substantial competitive advantage upon its possessor. This made invention into a very valuable product and Naomi Lamoreux and her colleagues (see her chapter coauthored with Kenneth Sokoloff in this volume) have provided fascinating descriptions of markets in inventions and patents, already arising in the 1830s and becoming widespread in the decade after the Civil War. But given their importance for the competitive position and even the survival of the firm, it was surely predictable that the larger enterprises would seek to break their dependence on the fortuitous availability of inventions made by independent inventors and offered for sale or lease to these established companies. Rather, these larger firms could be expected to launch their own internal inventive activities in an effort to minimize the risks entailed in dependence on others—on the unpredictable cadre of independent inventors.

This development is particularly evident in the rivalry among oligopolistic firms—those large firms in markets dominated by a small number of sellers. Particularly in the high-tech sectors of the economy, these enterprises increasingly rely upon *innovation* as their main battle weapon, with which they protect themselves from competitors and with which they seek to beat out those competitors. And much of this inventive activity is carried out within the firm.

The evidence shows that there is a rather sharp differentiation between the contributions to the economy's innovation that are provided by entrepreneurs and those that are offered by established businesses and their large internal research and development laboratories. In their effort to contain the risks inherent in the innovation process, large business firms have tended to follow relatively routine goals. They have been slanted toward incremental improvements rather than revolutionary breakthroughs. User friendliness, increased reliability, marginal additions to application, expansions of capacity, flexibility in design—these and many other types of improvement have come out of the industrial R&D facilities, with impressive consistency, year after year, and often preannounced and preadvertised. The directions taken by their R&D are often bureaucratically determined by management, which also sets the budget and the number of employees and their qualification standards. The spirit of corporate R&D activity is eloquently described by Ad Huijser, executive vice president and chief technology officer of one such giant firm, Royal Phillips Electronics:

> In established businesses, innovation is mostly shaped through small, incremental steps of additional features to augment basic functionalities. With short product lifecycles, time to recoup R&D investments is limited. . . . Success is relatively predictable through the execution of well-defined innovation processes and in-depth knowledge of their markets in the respective business units. (Huijser 2003)

These routinized innovative activities may appear to be trivial in their results and secondary in their contribution. Nevertheless, taken in aggregate, they have accomplished a great deal. Though their individual outputs have usually been less dramatic and less spectacular, if one takes their incremental contributions together and sums their achievements, it becomes clear that their accomplishment has been very substantial. An example is the airplane. The comfort, speed, and reliability of the modern passenger aircraft and the complexity and power of the military flying machines evidently, by contrast, make the Wright brothers' revolutionary device into a historical curiosity. The modern flying machine's automatic piloting and communication, location, and computing equipment were surely undreamed of in the years following the first flights. And most of the sophistication, speed, and reliability of today's aviation equipment is probably attributable to the combined incremental additions made by routine research activities in corporate facilities.

There are other, even more startling examples of the magnitude of the innovative contributions of the large companies, whose incremental advances can compound to results of enormous magnitude. Thus, it is reported of the Intel Corporation, the leading manufacturer of successive generations of computer chips and transistors, that over the period 1971–2003, the "clock speed" of Intel's microprocessor chips—that is, the number of instructions each chip can carry out per second—has increased by some *3 million percent*, reaching about 3 billion computations per second today (Markoff 2003). During the period 1968–2003, the number of transistors embedded in a single chip has expanded more than *10 million percent*, and the number of transistors that can be purchased for a dollar has grown by *five billion percent*. Added up, these advances surely contribute enormously more computing capacity than was provided by the original revolutionary breakthrough of the invention of the electronic computer. Of course, that initial invention was an indispensable necessity for all of the later improvements. But it is only the combined work of the two together that made possible the powerful and inexpensive apparatus that serves us so effectively today. Other careful observers have extended such examples and have concluded that incremental and routinized innovation activities have been responsible for a very respectable share of the contribution of innovation to economic growth in the twentieth century.

8. Technical Preparation of Corporate Researchers and Independent Entrepreneurs

There is another noteworthy distinction between the innovative activities of the independent entrepreneurs and those of the giant corporation: an apparently marked difference in the formal educational attainment of their personnel.[4] Unsystematic observation of a number of major firms with substantial R&D activities indicates that these enterprises generally employ at least some, and often a profusion of, persons with advanced technical training and higher academic degrees. In contrast, a preliminary sample of successful entrepreneurs and independent inventors indicates that they frequently have had only a basic education and that though at least some of them have consulted closely with more extensively trained advisors, the core ideas were contributed by the sparsely educated entrepreneurs and inventors themselves.

We know that many of the legendary inventors, including the Wright brothers and Thomas Edison, had no more that an elementary education, and often little of that. In contrast, corporate employment of individuals with advanced education is substantial. I cite only one striking example:

> P&G has a world class, global research and development organization, with over 7,500 scientists working in 22 research centers in 12 countries around the world. This includes 1250 Ph.D. scientists. For perspective, this is larger than the combined science faculties at Harvard, Stanford and MIT.
>
> P&G holds more than 24,000 active patents worldwide, and on average, receives about 3,800 more patents per year. (Procter & Gamble 2003)

This difference in the levels of education suggests a hypothesis that may prove of some value in the design of educational policy. It seems to suggest that the educational approaches that are most effective in providing mastery of the already extant body of intellectual materials actually tend to handicap a student's ability to "think outside the box" and thus discourage unorthodox ideas and breakthrough approaches and results. This does not mean that the education that produces the skilled engineer and the capable director of a corporate laboratory is in any sense inferior or undesirable. On the contrary, given the importance and value of the complex incremental improvements, the highly demanding training best suited to the discovery and design of such improvements must not be undervalued. Rather, one must just recognize that such training may entail the sort of trade-off in terms of foreclosure of heterodox thinking that has just been suggested.

Yet it is arguable that such formal education of the sort that focuses on received approaches and knowledge is becoming increasingly indispensable. As time passes, the cumulative character of technological information makes it increasingly complex, and this imposes an ever more severe handicap upon relatively unaided intuition. Even ill-educated entrepreneurs, Bill Gates being apparently a prime example, cannot usually get along without at least some limited knowledge of physics, chemistry, computer technology, or some other body of analysis and information. This complicates to some degree the implied hypothesis about the ideal education of the innovative entrepreneur.

That hypothesis must apparently be modified to assert that while overrigorous education is an impediment to exercise of the imagination, the entrepreneur's prime professional instrument, nevertheless the minimum educational attainment characteristically needed for the task is growing. No carpenter such as John Harrison, who solved the longitude problem, no mere bicycle repairmen such as the Wright brothers, can any longer hope to contribute, for example, today's mind-boggling medical breakthroughs. An illustration is (the already extant and workable) equipment that makes it possible for surgery to be carried out by computer-guided robots, with immediate and automatic restocking (without reordering or human intervention) of surgical equipment and medication, and remote surgery in which the operating surgeon (who operates the computer) may be thousands of miles from the patient during the procedure (as has, reportedly, already been done with success) (American Philosophical Society 2003).

9. Dissemination of Invention and Rapid Termination of the Obsolete

I turn, finally, to another feature of the innovation process under the free-market regimes that has, arguably, contributed critically to their growth: the speed with which use of improved products and production techniques becomes widespread. There is a well-recognized problem here. One of the attributes of an effective economic arrangement for the encouragement of beneficial technological change is the innovator's opportunity for financial gain derived from the temporary acquisition of what appears to be monopoly power through the improved product or process in his possession. However, encouragement of growth also requires rapid *dissemination* of any improved techniques and products and their widespread adoption by others beside the innovator. These two desiderata would, however, seem to be in conflict. After all, rapidity and ease of dissemination can threaten the innovator's market power and reward. I will argue next that, while the free market has hardly eliminated this conflict, it has nevertheless ameliorated the problem to a considerable degree.

As is to be expected, many business firms do guard their proprietary technology and strive with the aid of patents, secrecy, and other means to prevent other firms, notably rivals, from using the new products and processes. This is unfortunate for economic progress because it means that consumers who purchase from other firms are forced to accept obsolete features in the items they buy.[5] Moreover, two firms that deny one another access to their proprietary improvements in the firms' common product may evidently both be able to survive, marketing their somewhat differentiated outputs, each of which is rendered inferior in terms of what is currently possible technologically by the obsolete features that it is forced to provide.

Happily, however, that is hardly the norm. On the contrary, voluntary licensing of access to proprietary technology is widespread in the economy. Many firms derive substantial incomes from the sale of such licenses. The logic is straightforward. Suppose firm A invents a new widget and expects to make a net profit of x dollars per widget of the new type that it produces. Then if rival firm B offers firm A a license fee of y dollars ($y > x$) for each unit of the new widget it is able to sell, then A obviously can be better off letting B do so, even if every widget sold by B means one less sale for A.

Of course, B will generally be able to afford so high a fee only if it is a more efficient *producer* of widgets than A, even though it may be an inferior inventor. In this way the price mechanism will not only encourage licensing, but will, as usual, elicit efficient specialization: inventive activity will be undertaken primarily by the more effective inventor, while production of the resulting products will be undertaken predominantly by the more efficient producer. This sort of unreciprocated licensing does take place in practice, but it seems most frequently to entail the sale of licenses by large firms that are in a position to undertake extensive R&D activity, the licensees being smaller enterprises that cannot afford to carry out such activity and do not possess personnel qualified to do so.

There are a number of other incentives for such profitable and voluntary exchanges in the free market. For example, the most straightforward reason, and the one that seems most frequently offered by businesspersons, is the very high cost of R&D activity. By entering into some sort of sharing consortium, this burden can obviously be divided and reduced for each participant. Given the public-good attribute of the resulting information, it is far less expensive (per user) to provide such information to several firms than only to supply it to one. Another reason is reduction of risk. In any given year, a single firm's R&D division may fail to come up with any significant contributions. The fear by management of firm A that this will happen to it in a year when its rival, B, manages a significant breakthrough is a fear that is replicated in firm B. Since, as already emphasized, product and process improvement are a matter of life and death in the high-tech industries characterized by vigorous oligopolistic competition, technology-sharing agreements serve as effective insurance policies, protecting each participant from such catastrophes.

A further, and less obvious, reason for voluntary dissemination also entails trading of technology, but it is undertaken because it protects the firm from entry. To see how this works, consider, for example, an industry with 10 firms of identical size, each with an R&D division with staffing and funding similar to those of the others. Each firm in such a consortium will then have available to it not only the discoveries of its own R&D establishment, but those of 9 other firms in addition. Now suppose an eleventh firm wants to enter the market, but is not invited to join the technology-sharing consortium. Having only the products of its own R&D division at its disposal, while the other firms each obtain the outputs of 10 R&D establishments, the entrant can clearly find itself at a severe competitive disadvantage.

Such technology-exchange arrangements can be shown to stimulate innovative effort (provided that anticompetitive conspiracy is absent). For, like the other forms of compensated licensing, it helps to internalize the externalities generated by the innovative efforts of each firm. Indeed, if as happens in practice, in such an exchange each firm undertakes compensation equalization payments to any other member of the consortium if the latter's innovations are of a market value significantly superior to its own, then the firm has a direct incentive to come to the contract-bargaining table with a menu of valuable innovations to offer. It can also be shown that the formation of such a consortium tends to be welfare-enhancing (Baumol 2002, chap. 7).

There is at least one more reason for voluntary technology sharing that is highly significant and appears to be growing in importance—the problem of "patent thickets" and the widespread patent pools that have been formed to deal with the thicket problem. A complex piece of equipment, such as a computer, characteristically is made up of many components each of which is covered by patents, and the patents pertinent for such an item are usually owned by a number of different firms,[6] many of them direct competitors in the final-product market. This puts many of these firms in a legal position that can enable each to bring the manufacturing process of the others to a halt. The most effective way to prevent the catastrophic consequences this threatens for each of them is the formation of a patent pool in which each allows use of its patents by the other members of the pool, and even by outsiders (as a step to avoid intervention by the antimonopoly authorities), all on preset compensation terms. There are many such pools in the United States, with widely varying membership rules, license fee arrangements, and other differences that are not germane here.

The main point, evidently, is that the market mechanism itself has introduced powerful incentives for rapid dissemination of novel products and processes and has done so without creating a major disincentive for investment in the innovation process. That is surely no minor accomplishment and no minor contribution to technical progress and growth.

10. Concluding Comment

In the end, there seems to be little mystery about what underlies the market economy's unprecedented growth performance. Much of what has been said here seems almost self-evident, even though it has not often been said explicitly before. The most powerful components of the mechanism are constituted by a combination of the profit motive, confidence that one can keep what one earns, and the competitive pressures that play themselves out using innovation as a principal weapon. Together, these forces leave little option to the firms most directly concerned, which are driven forcibly to invest up to industry standards in R&D, to put their new technology to use, to bring their new products to market, to seek to acquire the right to use others' intellectual property, and to make their own available to others on terms as lucrative as possible. In contrast, these pressures have not only been absent from other economic regimes; but more than that, these regimes have been characterized by powerful institutions that impeded, delayed, and indeed sabotaged utilization and dissemination of productive inventions. If this is correct, it identifies the general directions that should be taken in economies where policymakers have ambitions focused on economic prosperity and growth.

Notes

1. The following paragraphs are taken, with some modification, from my Brookings Institution paper (2000).
2. This persisted into a much more recent era. Westerners, bringing mechanical clocks as gifts to the emperors, found that time-keeping accuracy elicited little appreciation, but marching or dancing figures run by the clockwork were highly valued.
3. Quoting the release describing the study, "A total of 1,071 firms with 15 or more patents issued between 1996 and 2000 were examined. A total of 193,976 patents were analyzed. CHI [the firm that carried out the study] created a database of these firms and their patents. This list excluded foreign-owned firms, universities, government laboratories, and nonprofit institutions" (2). The 2004 study expanded the sample to 1,270 firms and dealt with the period 1995–99, and a total of 1777,899 patents.
4. This section refers to research currently being carried out by Melissa Schilling, Edward Wolff, and the present author under the sponsorship of the Ewing Marion Kauffman Foundation.

5. It is, however, not always recognized that patents are not designed to *prevent* the spread of information about novel technology. On the contrary, patent holders are required to make full information on their inventions public so that others can profit from the ideas even if they cannot replicate the patented products themselves without the patent holder's permission.

6. E.g., Peter N. Detkin, vice president and assistant general counsel at Intel Corporation (the world's largest semiconductor company), estimates that there were more than 90,000 patents generally related to microprocessors held by more than 10,000 parties in 2002 (Federal Trade Commission 2002, 667).

References

American Philosophical Society. 2003. Richard M. Satava, "Biomedical, Ethical, and Moral Issues Being Forced by Advanced Medical Technologies." *Proceedings of the American Philosophical Society* 147 (3).

Baumol, William J. 1993. *Entrepreneurship, Management and the Structure of Payoffs*. Cambridge: MIT Press.

———. 2000. "Rapid Economic Growth, Equitable Income Distribution, and the Optimal Range of Innovation Spillovers." In *Economic Events, Ideas, and Policies*, ed. George L. Perry and James Tobin. Washington, D.C.: Brookings Institution Press.

———. 2002. *The Free-Market Innovation Machine: Analyzing the Growth Miracle of Capitalism*. Princeton: Princeton University Press.

Baumol, William J., with Sue Anne Batey Blackman. 1991. *Perfect Markets and Easy Virtue: Business Ethics and the Invisible Hand*. Cambridge, MA and Oxford: Blackwell Publishers.

Braudel, Fernand. 1979. *Civilization and Capitalism, 15th to 18th Century*. Vol. 1. New York: Harper and Row.

DeLong, Bradford. 2001. "The Economic History of the Twentieth Century—Slouching toward Utopia?" www.j-bradford-delong.net. Accessed September 2001.

De Meeüs, Adrien. 1962. *History of the Belgians*. New York: Frederick A. Praeger.

Federal Reserve Bank of Dallas. 1997. *Time Well Spent: The Declining Real Cost of Living in America, 1997 Annual Report*. Dallas.

Federal Trade Commission. 2002. "Statement of Peter N. Detkin." Session on "Business Perspectives on Patents: Hardware and Semiconductors." FTC Hearings on "Competition and Intellectual Property Law and Policy in a Knowledge-Based Economy," February 28, p. 667. Available at http://www.ftc.gov/opp/intellect.

Fogel, Robert W. 1986. "Nutrition and the Decline of Mortality since 1700: Some Preliminary Findings." In *Long-Term Factors in American Economic Growth*, ed. S. L. Engerman and R. E. Gallman. Chicago: University of Chicago Press.

Huijser, Ad. 2003. Presentation at the EFACT conference, Tilburg, the Netherlands, September.

Maddison, Angus. 2001. *The World Economy: A Millennial Perspective.* Paris: Organization for Economic Cooperation and Development.

Markoff, John. 2003. "Technology; Is There Life after Silicon Valley's Fast Lane?" *New York Times,* Business/Financial Desk, sec. C, April 9, 1.

National Science Board. 2000. *Science and Engineering Indicators, 2000.* Washington, D.C.: Government Printing Office.

Nelson, Richard R. 1996. *The Sources of Economic Growth.* Cambridge: Harvard University Press.

Nordhaus, William D. 1969. *Invention, Growth and Welfare.* Cambridge: MIT Press.

———. 1997. "Do Real-Output and Real-Wage Measures Capture Reality? The History of Lighting Suggests Not." In *The Economics of New Goods,* ed. Timothy Bresnahan and Robert J. Gordon. Chicago: University of Chicago Press.

Procter & Gamble. 2003. Website, accessed January 14. http://www.pg.com/about_pg/science_tech/research_development/our_commitment.jhtm.

Rosenberg, Nathan, and L. E Birdzell Jr. 1986. *How the West Grew Rich: The Economic Transformation of the Industrial World.* New York: Basic Books.

Scherer, F. M. 1965. "Firm Size, Market Structure, Opportunity, and the Output of Patented Inventions." *American Economic Review* 59: 1097–1125.

U.S. Bureau of the Census. 1975. *Historical Statistics of the United States, Colonial Times to 1970.* Part 1. Washington, D.C.: Government Printing Office.

———. 1997. *Statistical Abstract of the United States, 1997.* 117th ed. Washington, D.C.: Government Printing Office.

U.S. Small Business Administration. 2003. "Small Serial Innovators: The Small Firm Contribution to Technical Change." CHI Research, Inc. for SBA Office of Advocacy, Contract No. SBAHQ-01-C-0149, February 27.

———. 2004. "Small Firms and Technology: Acquisitions, Inventor Movement, and Technology Transfer." CHI Research, Inc. for SBA Office of Advocacy, Contract No. SBAHQ-02-M-0491, January.

Wright, Constance. 1965. *A Royal Affinity: The Story of Frederick the Great and His Sister, Wilhelmina of Bayreuth.* London: Frederick Muller.

Part V

DISSEMINATION OF TECHNOLOGY AND THE PATENT SYSTEM

Introduction and Comments

EDWARD N. WOLFF

I AM PLEASED TO REPORT ON two excellent chapters to follow in this part of the volume. Both concern the role of the patent system and licensing arrangements in promoting innovation. The second essay, "The Market for Technology and the Organization of Invention in U.S. History," by Naomi R. Lamoreaux and Kenneth L. Sokoloff, is a fascinating historical study of the licensing of inventions in the United States. The authors note that large benefits can accrue to inventive persons from a division of labor that allows them to specialize in inventive activity and allows others to concentrate on the commercialization of these inventions. The division of labor can occur within a firm, as when, for example, a firm sets up a separate R&D laboratory, or "it can develop across economic units and be coordinated by the market."

The advantage of a within-firm division of labor is that "problems of asymmetric information severely limit inventors' ability to sell new technological ideas at arm's length." On the other hand, the existence of a patent system may provide enough protection to inventors to enable them to attempt to sell their new technology. Moreover, there are contract problems with motivating scientists and engineers to develop new technology in-house.

It is impossible to tell a priori which system is superior. Rather, it is more likely that the relative incidence of in-house invention versus market exchange will depend on external factors such as the nature of the technology (for example, whether it is easy to patent or not), its cost (particularly in terms of the capital needed to develop the new technology), and the development of financial institutions (such as the availability of venture capital). In fact, Lamoreaux and Sokoloff show that the market for new technology has expanded and contracted over the last two centuries. During the latter part of the nineteenth century, trade in new ideas expanded. During the first half of the twentieth century, in-house R&D laboratories grew very rapidly, and there was a corresponding decline in the extent of market exchange for patented inventions. However, over the last half of the twentieth century, in-house R&D has been reduced, and the market for new ideas has once again expanded.

The essay discusses the first two of these phases (a few concluding remarks are made regarding the current phase).

The authors argue that in the mid-1800s, inventors had two ways to exploit their new creations: (1) by starting their own businesses or (2) by transferring the rights to others to commercialize the inventions. The development of the U.S. patent system offered a level of protection that was particularly conducive to the second of these, and creative individuals specialized in the generation of new technology. Intermediaries (that is, agents) also emerged during this period to facilitate this trade. However, by the early twentieth century, the capital requirements and cost of developing new technology made it increasingly prohibitive for creative individuals to pursue careers as independent inventors, and much of the development of new technology moved in-house to R&D labs.

The modern U.S. patent system was established in 1836. It had several desirable characteristics. First, the cost of obtaining a patent was relatively low. Second, patents could be awarded in the United States only to the first and true inventor anywhere in the world. Third, other inventors had free and open access to patent specifications, and the Patent Office published an annual list of inventions that had been awarded new patents. Originally, inventors received patents almost automatically by registering a new invention. However, by 1836 Congress "mandated that all inventions be scrutinized by professional examiners" to ensure that the new inventions did not infringe on prior patents. The enhanced property rights that followed the 1836 act resulted in a rapid rise in the number of patents and also in the number of patent assignments.

Business people seeking to invest in new technologies faced serious information problems if they themselves lacked technical expertise. As a result, in the late nineteenth century, a new group of professional patent agents and lawyers who had such technical expertise emerged in the country. These new professionals acted as brokers between business people seeking to invest in new inventions and the inventors themselves. These agents could also advise inventors on what types of technologies were most in demand. This new group was actively involved in the commercial exploitation of new technology.

Between 1871 and 1911 there was a notable rise in the proportion of new patents handled by registered agents. By 1911, registered agents were acting as correspondents for 55.7 percent of patents. Moreover, the use of registered agents increased the efficiency of the market for new technology. The evidence for this is that the percentage of patents that were assigned using registered agents was substantially higher than in the case when no registered agent was used.

Large firms with complex technologies faced several problems in the market for new technology. First, the firm could be shut out from new technology if rights to crucial patents were obtained by others. Second, these firms might find that patent holders who controlled the rights to different parts of their machinery could hold them up. One response by the turn of the century was to form industry-wide associations such as the Automobile Manufacturers' Association to cross-license to all members a patent obtained by any one of them.

These associations were only partially successful. The main response of these large corporations to extend their control over new technology was to increase the amount of R&D performed in-house. Individual inventors also faced a rising cost of developing new technology, particularly in terms of the investment in new capital equipment needed to pursue new inventions. The combination of an increased incentive for large firms to pursue in-house R&D and the increasing difficulty of independent inventors to finance their explorations for new technology shifted inventive activity away from independent inventors toward the large companies.

The first essay in this part, "Patents, Licensing, and Entrepreneurship: Effectuating Innovation in Multi-invention Contexts," by Deepak Somaya and David J. Teece, investigates the case of products that require the use of patents owned by several different entities. They argue that because of the increasing complexity of new technology, many new products brought to market are based on a set of new technologies that are often developed by different individuals or organizations. This development creates both new opportunities and new challenges for entrepreneurs. This paper is considerably more technical than the historical overview provided by Lamoreaux and Sokoloff.

The essay begins with a general discussion of intellectual property and the role of the entrepreneur: "An important function of the entrepreneur is to assemble assets and exploit complementarities among them." Competitive advantage is obtained when new assets are assembled and "yield joint returns that are more than the sum of the parts." The entrepreneurial firm is able to capture rents if the joint value of this new combination of assets is not fully realized in their supply prices. The authors then argue that the condition wherein factor owners and entrepreneurs have different beliefs about factor values is a normal condition in the real world. It also arises when entrepreneurs can perceive value when no one else can or are able to organize resources to achieve ends that others are unable to achieve: "Entrepreneurial opportunities thus depend on asymmetries of information, belief, and individual and organizational capability."

The chapter focuses on the particular opportunities and challenges afforded by multi-invention innovation, which requires entrepreneurial response. These opportunities and challenges are of two types. First, from the patent owners' perspective, a patent may have value in only a multi-invention context. Second, from the user perspective, "patents owned by others may appear to block the road ahead." The essay explores a variety of organizational responses to this situation, which may involve action in technology markets or in corporate control (such as mergers).

First a word about patent strategy. This involves three different elements: (1) the actual process of patenting, including renewals; (2) licensing, or the provision of both exclusive and nonexclusive rights to the invention; and (3) enforcement, which entails the use or threat of litigation to prevent infringement. Patent strategy can be thought of as a series of sequential choices, each of which has not only a set of associated benefits but also associated costs.

There are two general benefits of patenting. First, patents can protect new technologies from imitation by rivals (so-called "isolating mechanisms"). This strategy is appropriate when rents can be gained from own use of a patent. Second, patents can be used to capture revenue from other users through licensing. When patents are generic and provide utility to an entire industry, they may make ideal candidates for licensing.

In the multi-invention case, when several patents that are separately owned are needed to produce a new product, there are three general organizational strategies that can be followed. The first is the "component mode," which arises when one product requires at least two patents, at least one of the patents is embodied in a component, and the component is sold for inclusion in the final product. In this case, the sale of the component by one firm to another may be the appropriate solution. The second is the "licensing mode," when licensing or cross-licensing may provide the best solution. The third is the "integrated mode," when the merger of two (or more) firms that own the individual patents may be the optimal solution.

The most interesting case (from an analytical standpoint) is the licensing case. There are two major types of problems associated with the licensing mode. First, when many inventions must be licensed for the use in a multi-invention product, some transaction costs may be introduced by the diffuse nature of patent entitlements—in particular, when it is difficult to determine which technologies have a legitimate bearing on the product and who the relevant patent owners are. Second, there are often complex valuation problems when technical and commercial uncertainties exist. Besides technological uncertainty, the value contributed by an individual invention to a multi-invention product adds an additional element of uncertainty.

The authors then provide several interesting case studies of multi-invention products. The case studies include the formation of RCA, cross-licensing practices of AT&T, cross-licensing done by IBM, and licensing practices at Texas Instruments.

Chapter 9

Patents, Licensing, and Entrepreneurship: Effectuating Innovation in Multi-invention Contexts

DEEPAK SOMAYA AND DAVID J. TEECE

1. Introduction

In recent years, patents have become more significant as mechanisms to capture value from innovation. Simultaneously, the innovation context has become more complicated, not only because many patents are implicated in "multi-invention" or "systemic" innovation, but also because there is great dispersal in the ownership of patents. Accordingly, many new products require the use of patents owned by several different entities. This creates both challenges and opportunities for entrepreneurs. Sometimes these challenges are easily worked through; on other occasions it requires "new combinations" not just of patents, but of tangible assets, components, and technologies in order to enable innovations to proceed to market. This paper maps opportunities and challenges, identifies possible solutions, and discusses how (entrepreneurial) firms have responded to these opportunities and challenges.

2. Intellectual Property and Entrepreneurship

The patent system grants the inventor/patent owner time-bound exclusive rights to practice the technology that is covered by the patent. In exchange for this right, the inventor recognizes that the invention will be disclosed when the patent is published. Absent the patent system, inventions could be more readily imitated. It is frequently argued that patents are needed to help provide incentives not only for invention, but also for the commercial application of inventions (Kitch 1977). Small inventors and entrepreneurs are among the most enthusiastic supporters of the patent system. Their support stems in part from the perception that the system provides safeguards for the inventor, who might otherwise be subject to use of the invention without compensation. This is corroborated by a survey in the U.S. semiconductor industry (Hall and Ziedonis 2001), where small start-up firms were found to be champions of patents, who recognize that patents can assist them in acquiring investment funds from venture capitalists. And, it is in sharp contrast to the perception of some commentators that patents may be harmful to small firms and the entrepreneurship process.

In industries where innovation requires the combination of a very large number of inventions to create new products and services, what we term here the multi-invention or systemic innovation[1] context, additional opportunities and constraints arise from patenting. In these situations, patents may provide leverage to the entrepreneur or individual inventor, while at the same time requiring new entrants and incumbents alike to navigate patent thickets where the relevant patents required for a particular innovation have distributed ownership; that is, the patents needed to design and manufacture a product may be held by several unrelated entities. These environments may require the exercise of entrepreneurial skills as well as the establishment of potentially quite different organizational arrangements (modes) to enable an innovation to proceed to market.

According to Schumpeter (1934), the entrepreneur drives economic growth. The function of the entrepreneur is to innovate, to "carry out new combinations." In Schumpeter's treatment, the entrepreneur is not the inventor. Rather, the entrepreneur exploits the invention to effectuate innovation in the marketplace. Nor is the entrepreneur a risk bearer, as that function is performed by the capitalist (the venture capitalists in today's vernacular). The Schumpeterian entrepreneur has an organizing and decision-making role. Typically that role is exercised under considerable uncertainty, and usually with quite limited information.

An important function for the entrepreneur is to assemble assets and exploit complementarities among them. By exploring and exploiting co-specialization, rent streams can be generated (Teece 1986, 2003a). Competitive advantage is obtained when tangible and intangible assets are assembled that yield joint returns that are more than the sum of the parts (Lippman and Rumelt 2003).

Although possibly amplified in the context of untested patents,[2] the condition whereby factor/asset owners and entrepreneurs have different beliefs about the value of different factor/asset combinations is not uncommon in the economy. It is the role of the entrepreneur to perceive value that no one else can; or even if others perceive it, the entrepreneur is able to organize resources to achieve ends that other (nonentrepreneurial) individuals (or managers) are unable or unwilling to achieve. Entrepreneurial opportunities inherently depend upon asymmetries of information, belief, and individual and organizational capability.[3] As Baumol (1993) has explained, entrepreneurship is certainly not an optimization process by which people make mechanical calculations in response to a given set of alternatives imposed upon them. Clearly, entrepreneurship is a scarce resource. History is replete with examples where inventors and incumbents alike did not initially see commercial opportunities resulting from the invention of new technologies (Rosenberg 1994).

The particular opportunities and challenges afforded by multi-invention (systemic) innovation require particular entrepreneurial responses. These can be of two kinds. First, entrepreneurs must understand and address the challenges and opportunities of combining inventions from a variety of disparate sources in a multi-invention or systemic context. Organizational barriers and transaction costs can be a significant hurdle in unlocking the value hidden in a new invention or combination of inventions. Moreover, patents owned by others may appear to block the road ahead and amplify organizational challenges. Second, entrepreneurs must evaluate how best to appropriate value from the unique combinations that they create. There is no benefit to engaging in entrepreneurial efforts if another enterprise can simply appropriate all the returns. Entrepreneurs must therefore pay attention to how they will appropriate returns while at the same time creating the factor/asset combinations necessary to effectuate innovation.

In this essay we explain that workable solutions usually exist to both these challenges. A variety of organizational arrangements can help manage the challenges of combining inventions in multi-invention settings. Some solutions require action in technology and component markets, and some require actions in the market for corporate control (i.e., mergers). In other instances, the lowering of transaction costs in patent licenses may require certain bargaining and negotiating skills. Further, in each instance, there are implications for the role of patents in helping to appropriate returns for the entrepreneur. In other words, the organizational responses used to effectuate innovation in a multi invention or systemic context need to be supported by an appropriate patent strategy. To our knowledge, the literature has not explored these issues in any systematic way, and certainly not with attention to entrepreneurial solutions that are in our view central to the issues at hand.

3. The Multi-invention (Systemic Innovation) Context

In many high-tech sectors of the economy, multi-invention contexts are the norm; that is, very large numbers of inventions are combined to develop end products and services. In semiconductors, increasing miniaturization has made it feasible to manufacture large and complex electronics systems on a single chip (so-called systems-on-a-chip, or SOCs). This creates the need for large numbers of patented inventions to be combined in any single product (Teece 1998; Linden and Somaya 2003). In biotechnology, increasingly large portfolios of inventions in genomics, research tools, and other areas need to be assembled to bring new medical solutions to fruition. Similarly, hundreds or thousands of patentable software inventions may be combined in contemporary software programs, and this trend is intensifying with the increasing size and complexity of software products.

Innovation in these industries comes from multiple sources—from within large firms, from start-ups and specialized players, from firms outside the industry, and even from universities and other research establishments—creating phenomenal entrepreneurial opportunities to combine knowledge in innovative ways and create valuable new products. But these multiple sources of invention also imply a tangled web of patent rights, which must be navigated for commercial success. A central challenge for entrepreneurs in such multi-invention contexts is to determine how the production of end products from large numbers of potential inventions can be most effectively organized, and what role the entrepreneurial firm will play in this organizational structure.

Broadly, one can think of two types of organizational arrangements or modes (or business "models") by which inventions may be combined—integrated modes and nonintegrated modes. Integrated modes arise when firms innovate by using their own internal technologies and resources, without relying on external access. Nonintegrated modes can broadly be separated into licensing and component modes, where access to external technologies is obtained in abstract and product-embodied forms, respectively. Of course, these distinctions are somewhat stylized. In any given multi-invention context, entrepreneurs may choose to develop some technologies internally in an integrated fashion, and use market (nonintegrated) arrangements to access others. Furthermore, actual organizational arrangements (or business model choices) may exhibit hybrid integrated and nonintegrated characteristics—for example, interfirm alliances—or hybrid licensing and component characteristics—for example, transfer of highly flexible components (like a programmable chip) or highly codified product designs (which would enable component manufacture, but not transfer any know-how).

Which organizational mode should be chosen by the (entrepreneurial) firm for effectuating innovation depends on the associated organizational costs and benefits in each mode. Generally, integrated modes are considered to be advantageous for overcoming transaction costs of various kinds, whereas nonintegrated modes are considered advantageous in terms of incentives and access to best-of-class inventions or components.

When transaction costs in know-how, licensing, or component markets are low, it makes sense for entrepreneurs to innovate by transacting for complementary assets and inventions through these markets. Otherwise, the costs of developing the required technologies and capabilities in-house and the added cost of internal bureaucracy produce a significant drag on commercialization. However, when these transaction costs are high, it makes sense to seek more integrated solutions, either through internal development or through the market for corporate control (mergers and acquisitions).

The study of transaction costs has become a significant research enterprise (Williamson 1985, 1996; Shelanski and Klein 1995), to which we surely cannot do justice in the limited space available. However, we draw attention to some types of transaction costs that are particularly relevant in technology-related transactions. First, there are barriers that arise due to the *technological interconnectedness* (Linden and Somaya 2003) or *the systemic nature* (Teece 1996) of innovation in some multiproduct contexts. In essence, the difficulty of partitioning the problem domain in these contexts makes it very costly to transact because of the various technologies that must work together as a whole. Another source of transaction costs is the potential *leakage of know-how* through transactions in technology markets (Arrow 1971; Teece 1982). When (entrepreneurial) firms either buy or sell technologies and components, they may end up disclosing elements of inventions to their partners, which (despite the existence of nondisclosure agreements) subsequently undermines their own ability to appropriate returns. In addition, there are often disagreements between firms over the contribution to value that is created by each of their technologies when used together in a particular product. These *value allocation* problems can lead to significant delays in negotiating contractual arrangements, and are particularly exacerbated by the idiosyncratic nature of each invention (Merges and Nelson 1994; Somaya 2005), and by the fact that there may be uncertainty over patent validity and infringement.

The transaction cost issues surrounding valuation and know-how leakage tend to be somewhat greater with "know-how" and intellectual property markets compared to "product" or "component" markets. Components are tangible products with measurable performance characteristics. Components are often easier to value against competing alternatives; also, it is likely to be more difficult for the technologies embedded in a component to inadvertently leak out. In addition, component markets also have lower *monitoring and metering* costs than licensing markets because each use of the technology is limited to a single well-defined physical artifact. With know-how and intellectual property, it is often difficult to ascertain how, where, and how often a technology is being used by the licensee and whether patents are valid. Both questions can lead to uncertainties and disputes about value and royalty payments.

Ultimately, entrepreneurs must evaluate the potential costs and benefits arising from each organizational mode, and choose that which has the best performance characteristics. In other words, careful attention must be paid to the business model and the organizational challenges of innovation if entrepreneurship is to succeed in multi-invention contexts. In the case of Kentron, discussed below, the firm encountered high transaction costs in licensing and had to quickly modify its strategy to a component-focused one. Each organizational strategy in turn must be complemented by a suitable patent strategy so as to ensure that the firm is also able to appropriate returns from its innovation.

4. Understanding Patent Strategy

One can think of patent strategy as occurring in three related domains of activity—patenting, licensing, and enforcement. "Patenting" refers to the gamut of actions whereby patent rights are obtained, renewed, maintained, and protected, including through the purchase of others' patents in the secondary market. "Licensing" involves the provision of exclusive and nonexclusive rights to use the patent. Distinctions can be made between the instances in which patent rights are licensed along with know-how transfer, and those in which only patent rights are licensed. "Enforcement" entails the use or threatened use of litigation to persuade infringers to desist or pay royalties. Since no one would take a naked patent license absent fear of a court sanctions at some level, patent licensing (as distinct from pure know-how licensing) always takes place in the shadow of court-enforced sanctions against infringement.

Patent strategy ought to be formulated in the broader context of the business strategies required for establishing and maintaining competitive advantage at the enterprise level. While there are no doubt specific issues that arise in each domain of patent strategy—patenting, licensing, or enforcement—some important commonalities cut across all of them. Three generic patent strategies are presented below—namely, proprietary use, defensive use, and royalty generation.

4.1. *Proprietary Use (No Licensing)*

Patents and other forms of intellectual property have long been recognized as tools that can in some cases protect technologies from imitation by rivals. Put differently, patents are "isolating mechanisms" (Rumelt 1984) that can help protect "rent" streams. Indeed, in the popular literature, the role of patents in enabling firms to "stake out and defend a proprietary market advantage" has been characterized as "their most powerful benefit" (Rivette and Kline 2000, 4). The central insight here is that the ownership of IP conveys the right to *exclude* others from the use of patented invention. In most circumstances, of course, this does not convey the ability to exclude competitors from a market. Such power is only conveyed with very fundamental patents, which cannot be worked around for one reason or another. Even then, the period of exclusion is of course limited by the length of time the patent has to run. In the real world, situations where patents confer market power are quite rare. Furthermore, the use of patents to protect fundamental new areas of technology has been acknowledged as one of the critical functions of the patent system, without which firms might be reluctant to make additional investments to commercialize their inventions (Kitch 1977; Mazzoleni and Nelson 1998).

If a business enterprise has a fundamental interest in a particular opportunity, and seeks to control the technology, there are implications for how the enterprise will need to conduct its patent-related activities (Somaya 2003). One implication is that the firm would most likely need to invent follow on technologies and also patent these. Another implication, naturally, is that such patents will generally not be licensed. It is of course the patent owner's choice not to license. As discussed in Teece (1986), the strategy of eschewing licensing is likely to be preferred only if the enterprise's patent portfolio is strong, the enterprise does not need access to anyone else's patent, and the enterprise is well positioned in the complementary assets required to successfully commercialize the innovation. Furthermore, to sustain a proprietary strategy with respect to select patents, infringement of these patents by others would need to be prosecuted aggressively.

4.2. "Design Freedom" (Defensive) Patent Strategies

Defensive strategies relate to the actions of business enterprises to protect themselves against the use of patents by their rivals in the marketplace. In fast-paced high-technology industries, enterprises often desire the freedom to design, innovate, and manufacture without being too constrained by the patent rights, present and future, of other firms. In part, this desire for design and operating freedom may be motivated by irreversible investments that they have made or expect to make, including investments in highly capital intensive manufacturing facilities, as in the case of the semiconductor industry. These investments, and the firm's commercial interests in general, can potentially be put at risk by others' patents, including those that had not issued at the time investment or commercialization decisions are made. As a result, these patents pose a significant threat to the firm—entire lines of business may be put at risk and significant royalties may have to be paid to license necessary patents. These may reflect the firms' much higher ex post willingness to pay (Sherry and Teece 2003). Needless to say, these issues are more common in multi-invention contexts, where the likelihood of infringing one or more patents among hundreds or thousands is quite high.

In some cases, the enterprise's own patents can be used as bargaining chips. Attempts by rivals to assert their own patents can be countered with threats to enforce the firm's own patents against them. This situation of "mutual holdup" can facilitate the negotiation of reasonable terms between the parties, and the effective removal of patent barriers (Grindley and Teece 1997; Somaya 2003). Research in the semiconductor industry has demonstrated that firms often engage in reciprocal cross-licensing as part of their patent strategy. Such firms accumulate large portfolios of patents in part because they are desirous of achieving design and operating freedom (Hall and Ziedonis 2001). It is important to bear in mind, however, that defensive patenting may not be effective under all circumstances, especially because it assumes that the threat of reciprocal patent enforcement is effective. When this is not the case (for example, with individual inventors or universities who have few commercial interests that can be held up), this defensive strategy may not work and a license may need to be taken. This may be comparatively costly in many multi-invention contexts, particularly if the invention is important and good alternatives do not exist.

4.3. Royalty Generation Strategies

Licensing on an exclusive or nonexclusive basis is the other obvious strategy for capturing value from a patent. The licensing of technologies is a much-studied phenomenon in the management and economics literature (Teece 1986, 2000, 2003b; Arora 1995). Much of the literature has tended to assume that patents and know-how are always bundled together; however, patent-only licensing has grown considerably in recent years. Firms like IBM and Texas Instruments have earned very substantial licensing revenues from licensing patent rights (an average of $580 million a year over 1999–2001 for IBM alone).[4] While some know-how transfer may accompany patent-licensing deals, TI's and IBM's primary focus is the granting of rights to use patents to companies that are already using (i.e., infringing) the technology in question. When patents are strong and provide utility to an entire industry, they are natural candidates for licensing in this manner. If the incumbent firms are already infringing the patent(s) and have invested substantially in using patented technologies, they may have few practical alternatives to licensing the patent(s). Royalty generation in this manner is supported by the business enterprise's efforts to identify potential licensees, its negotiating and bargaining skills, and the implicit threat of sanctions obtained from a court (or the International Trade Commission if imported goods implicate the patent).

With respect to enforcement of property rights, there are significant differences between intangible and tangible goods. When the input is a tangible good, it is impossible for the manufacturer of the final product to produce it unless the physical input is delivered. Stolen goods are not acceptable. However, when the use of patented technology already known to the user is the input,[5] production can commence and sale of the final product can be completed without "delivery" of the IP rights. This is because the manufacturer can simply go ahead and infringe the patent. The only barrier is the prospect of a court-ordered injunction and the court's determination that damages should be paid. Therefore, legal enforcement of property rights (patents) plays a critical role with respect to intangible property, when compared with tangible property, for the collection of monies for the use of the input.

5. Entrepreneurship and Patent Strategy in Multi-invention Contexts

What, then, are the implications for entrepreneurship emerging from our understanding of multi-invention (or systemic) contexts and patent strategy? Interest in the role of patents in multi-invention settings goes at least as far back as Kitch (1977), who contended that patent rights should facilitate coordination between owners of related inventions. Subsequent research has focused considerable attention on a particular type of multi-invention context, namely sequential innovation (Merges and Nelson 1990, 1994; Scotchmer 1991, 1996; Chang 1995; Green and Scotchmer 1995). These studies have primarily addressed the desirable scope of patents, implicitly taking entrepreneurship as given (at what we think is a low level). More recent work has focused on the transactional challenges posed by patents in multi-invention contexts, leading—according to the authors—to the potential underutilization of innovative resources, a so-called "tragedy of the anticommons" (Heller and Eisenberg 1998). These transaction costs may arise from *diffuse ownership* and associated *royalty stacking* problems in patent licensing (Teece 2000, 208–9; Somaya 2005), or from *valuation disputes* that are due at least in part to the *fuzzy boundaries* of patents (Teece 2000, 149–50; Somaya 2005).

However, in our view, Eisenberg and Heller may have exaggerated the problems associated with the so-called "anticommons." They provide no compelling evidence of the scope of the "problem." It is well known that patents can also facilitate transactions in technology, for example by facilitating transactions in know-how without the fear of misappropriation (Teece 1982; Arora 1995; Oxley 1999). Ultimately, transaction costs, both in general and those induced (or remedied) by patent rights, speak to the need for entrepreneurship in multi-invention settings. Entrepreneurs play an important role in figuring out the right organizational arrangements (or business model) for innovation. In addition, entrepreneurs and managers must choose appropriate patent strategies to support their innovative efforts. These strategies are likely to depend in large part on the precise organizational arrangements chosen for commercialization. We assess the implications for both integrated and nonintegrated modes below, using mini case studies drawn from past multi-invention contexts.

5.1. Integrated Modes

Entrepreneurs and managers should choose an integrated mode to innovate when the transaction costs in licensing and component markets for complementary technologies are relatively high. Given this choice, the main challenge for the entrepreneur becomes how to assemble all the required assets and technologies within a single firm. Given the nature of innovation in multi-invention contexts, it would be highly unlikely that a single firm has invented and patented all the technologies necessary to commercialize the end product, and will continue to do so in the future. Integrated approaches therefore employ different ways of obtaining both the technologies and the patents rights needed for commercialization.

One alternative is to develop all the technologies needed in-house, but rely on patent licensing to obtain access to the patent rights *owned* by other enterprises. Access to patents could be obtained in a number of ways, including patent pools, cross-licenses, and other patent-sharing arrangements. Since this form of integrated innovation implicitly acknowledges the existence of patents that may be infringed by the enterprise, defensive patent strategies are especially important for ensuring freedom to design and innovate. In industries like semiconductors, electronics, and computers, these defensive strategies are often pursued through the building up of large patent portfolios, and the proactive development of cross-licensing relationships.

Beyond the firm's defensive needs, however, patents may also be used in this context to generate licensing revenues. Later entrants and noninnovators in such a market may have weaker patent portfolios, reflecting their limited contribution to technological advances in the industry. Firms with a more robust history of innovation and patenting need not license their own patents to these firms on a purely reciprocal basis. In other words, offsetting royalty payments can be negotiated to reflect the asymmetry among the patent portfolios. The case of AT&T, IBM, and Texas Instruments in electronics and semiconductors provides a graphic illustration of the entrepreneurial creation of patent exchange mechanisms to deal with defensive concerns, and the use of strong patent portfolios to generate royalty income.

CROSS-LICENSING IN ELECTRONICS AND SEMICONDUCTORS

In the electronics and semiconductor industries, the multi-invention context is frequently the norm. In many advanced products, the range of technology is simply too great for a single firm to develop its entire needs internally. The "state of the art" of the technology tends to be covered by a large number of different patents held by different firms. Companies may produce hundreds of products, which use literally thousands of patents, and many hundreds more may be added each year. One innovation builds on another. Overlapping developments and mutually blocking patents are inevitable. To solve these problems, the business practice of cross-licensing has emerged. Enterprises cross-license patents from others to ensure that they themselves have the freedom to innovate and manufacture without inadvertent infringement. Cross-licenses typically cover portfolios of all current and future patents in a field of use, without making specific reference to individual patents. It is simply too cumbersome and costly to license only specific patents needed for specific products. The portfolio approach reduces transactions costs and allows licensees freedom to design and manufacture without triggering infringement, inadvertent or otherwise.

Cross-licensing has developed in a quite sophisticated fashion (Grindley and Teece 1997).[6] An important feature is the calculation of balancing royalty payments, according to the relative value of the patent portfolios of each party. This calculation is made prospectively, based on a sample of each firm's leading patents. Weight is given to the quality and market coverage of the patents. The key to successful cross-licensing is a portfolio of quality patents that covers large portions of the licensing partner's product markets. A quality portfolio is a powerful lever in negotiating access to required technology and may lead to significant royalty generation or, at a minimum, to reduced payments to others. Obviously, a firm that is a large net user of other firms' patents, without contributing comparable IP in exchange, is likely to have to pay significant royalties. Significantly, for the balancing process, the firm should concentrate its patenting in those areas where it does best and has a comparative advantage to develop patents that its cross-licensing partners need. In this way, firms can develop complementary rather than duplicative technology, thereby also benefiting the public interest.

In patent cross-licenses, technology is not usually transferred, as the parties are often capable of using the technology in question without assistance. Rather, these licenses confer the right to use the intellectual property without being sued for infringement. The licensing agreements sometimes include transfer of trade secrets and know-how. However, these licenses are quite different, as they involve technology transfer, and may accompany a joint venture or strategic alliance.

AT&T'S CROSS-LICENSING PRACTICES

Cross-licensing is not a new phenomenon in electronics; it goes back almost to the beginning of the industry.[7] One of the most influential firms was AT&T, whose licensing and cross-licensing practices, especially from the 1940s until its breakup in 1984, were the initial templates for the development of similar programs by other firms. Over its long history, AT&T's licensing policy has had three phases, reflecting changes in its overall business strategy. First, from AT&T's establishment in 1885 until its first antitrust-related commitment in 1913, it used IP rights in a forthright exclusive fashion to establish itself in the service market.[8] In the second phase, from 1914 until 1984, AT&T was a regulated monopoly. The need for access to patents led to cross-license agreements between the major producers of telephone equipment, starting in the 1920s, which soon developed into a more widespread policy. In the last phase, dating from divestitures in 1984, AT&T was no longer bound by the consent decree, and its IP licensing has been increasingly aligned with its commercial needs (OTA 1985; Noll 1987, 161–78; Harris 1990, 105–24).

AT&T's policy was to openly license its IP to everyone for minimal fees. The 1956 consent decree required AT&T to license all patents at "reasonable royalties," provided that the licensee also grants licenses at reasonable royalties in return. AT&T was also required to provide technical information in exchange for the payment of reasonable fees, and licensees had the right to sublicense the technology to their associates.[9] The impact of AT&T's liberal licensing on the industry was considerable, especially when considered in parallel with that at IBM.

To a large extent, the licensing terms in AT&T's 1956 decree simply codified what was already AT&T policy. As an enterprise under rate-of-return regulation, it had little reason to maximize royalty income from its IP. It perhaps figured that its service customers would be better off if its technologies were widely diffused among suppliers, as this would lower the prices and increase the performance of procured components

(Levin 1982, 77). It appears to be the first company to have had "design freedom" as a core component of its patent strategy. However, it did not see licensing income as a source of funds for R&D, as Bell Laboratories' research was largely funded by the "license contract fee," assessed on the annual revenues of the Bell operating companies. By 1983, Bell Laboratories had received 20,000 patents, as compared to about 10,000 held by IBM in 1995 and 6,000 by Texas Instruments. AT&T's portfolio was fundamental, and included patents such as the transistor, basic semiconductor technology, and the laser, and indeed many other basic patents in telecommunications, computing, optoelectronics, and superconductivity.

Using its own portfolio as leverage, AT&T was able to obtain the (reciprocal) rights it needed to continue to innovate, unimpeded by the IP of others. An interesting aspect of AT&T's IP strategy was that technologies (though not R&D programs) were often selected for patent protection based on their potential value to other firms generating technology of interest to AT&T. Since the legal pressures by the regulators for open licensing did not extinguish all of AT&T's intellectual property rights, the company was able to gain access to the external technology that it needed (Kefauver 1993).

The terms of AT&T's licenses set a pattern that is still commonplace in the electronics industry through the "capture model," which was defined in the 1956 consent decree. Under this arrangement, the licensee is granted the right to use existing patents plus any obtained for inventions made during a fixed future capture period of no more than five years, followed by a survivorship period until the expiration of the patents. The licensing regimes this led to were persistent, since the long survivorship period on many of the basic patents provided only limited scope to introduce more stringent conditions for new patents.

The traditional cross-licensing policy of AT&T was greatly extended following the invention of the transistor in 1947. Widespread "field-of-use" licensing in the semiconductor industry is one of AT&T's legacies, as the industry was founded on the basic semiconductor technologies developed by the company. AT&T soon realized that other electronics companies were developing their own semiconductor technologies and obtaining patents, which led to its policy of cross-licensing by field of use.[10] These cross-licenses ensured that the company had reciprocal access to patents and was able to develop its own technology without risking patent infringement.

Not surprisingly, AT&T/Lucent Technologies has subsequently used its IP more strategically. No longer bound by the consent decree, with R&D facilities mainly in Lucent Technologies (which has legacy connections back to AT&T's manufacturing arm known as Western Electric), its IP policy has necessarily been linked more closely to particular business opportunities.

IBM'S CROSS-LICENSING PRACTICES

A second major influence on licensing practice across the electronics industry has been IBM. The company has long been involved in licensing and cross-licensing its technology, both as a means of accessing external technology and to gain profit (generate royalties). In many ways, it has been in a similar position to AT&T in that it has been a wellspring of new technology, and was subject to a 1956 consent decree that contained certain compulsory licensing terms. Under the consent decree, IBM was required to grant nonexclusive, nontransferable, worldwide licenses for all of its patents at reasonable royalties (royalty free for existing tabulating card/machinery patents)—provided the applicant also offered to cross-license its patents to IBM on similar terms.[11]

The importance IBM attaches to its patents for use in cross-licensing and negotiating access to outside technology is reflected in its public statements (Smith 1989, 817–23; Boyer 1990). The main object of its licensing policy has been "design freedom," and to ensure "the right to manufacture and market products" by obtaining rights to use technologies and patents owned by others. IBM acquires these rights primarily by trading access to its own patents, that is, through cross-licensing.[12] IBM has often had the reputation of being a "fast follower" in some areas of technology, and it has used the power of its patent portfolio to negotiate access. The company has noted that "You get value from patents in two ways; through fees, and through licensing negotiations that give IBM access to other patents. Access is far more valuable to IBM than the fees it receives from its 9,000 active (U.S.) patents. There is no direct calculation of this value, but it is many times larger than the fee income, perhaps an order of magnitude larger."[13]

IBM's cross-licensing activity continues today. But, the company has complemented this essentially defensive policy with a strategy to generate royalty income from its licenses. IBM initiated this more active approach to licensing in 1988, when it increased the royalty rates sought on its patents from 1 percent of sales revenue (on products using IBM patents) to a range of 1–5 percent.[14] The company has also adopted a proactive strategy for identifying potential patent infringement and negotiating royalty-yielding licenses with them. Cash revenues earned from IBM's patent and technology licensing agreements increased from $345 million in 1993 to $640 million in 1994, and were well over $1 billion per year by the end of the decade.[15] It is important to bear in mind that these revenues carry low incremental costs, and accrue in large measure to the company's bottom line. In terms of their profit impact, these licensing operations are equivalent to a multi-billion-dollar business for IBM. IBM is one of the world's leading innovators, with more U.S. patents granted to it than any other company in every year since 1993. The company's licensing strategy has enabled IBM to appropriate some of the returns to its inventions by essentially charging users for access to these technologies.

LICENSING PRACTICES AT TEXAS INSTRUMENTS

Like other parts of the electronics industry, the semiconductor industry is characterized by widespread use of cross-licensing.[16] The licensing procedures at Texas Instruments (TI) illustrate the ways in which cross-licensing is used in the modern electronics industry. TI has two main licensing objectives. The first and primary objective is to ensure freedom to operate in broad areas of technology, without running the risk of patent infringement litigation by other firms in given product markets. Thus the first strategic goal is fundamentally a defensive one. The second objective is to obtain value from the firm's IP, in the form of its patent portfolio, by generating royalty income. The purpose and result of royalty generation through cross-licensing agreements is "competitive re-balancing," which offsets the advantage for imitators who might otherwise free-ride on technology TI developed.

Establishing "freedom to operate" is vital in the semiconductor industry, with its rapid innovation, short product life cycles, and ubiquity of patents. At the start of an R&D program, possible patent infringements cannot be easily predicted, as firms are quite ignorant of the R&D and patenting plans of competitors. Yet when it invests in R&D and product development, TI needs to be confident that patents developed by others through independent R&D efforts will not hinder commercialization of its technology. This need is heightened by the significant investments TI makes in capital-intensive semiconductor manufacturing facilities. TI has responded to this challenge by building a robust portfolio of semiconductor patents, which it essentially uses to defend against other's patents and to negotiate preemptive cross-licenses. It has also divested from DRAM (**dynamic random access memory**) fabrication in part to minimize its potential infringement of others' patents, and to enhance the royalty generation capacities of its IP strategy.

There are two main models for cross-licensing agreements in the semiconductor industry: "capture" and "fixed period." In the "capture" model discussed earlier, the licensee retains "survivorship" rights to use the patents until they expire, sometimes up to 20 years later. In the "fixed period" model the licensee has similar rights to use patents existing or applied for during the license period, but with no survivorship rights once the license period has expired. Full renegotiation of the cross-license is required for succeeding periods. Texas Instruments (TI) has been a leader in the use of fixed period licensing, which has gained in popularity in the industry. The fixed period model allows more flexible commercialization of patent portfolios, since licensing terms can be periodically adjusted to account for changes over time. For example, it mitigates the possibility of being locked into a cross-license even though the licensing partner has stopped contributing new inventions to the focal field of use. Thus, fixed period licensing allows TI to carefully calibrate the "openness" of its cross-licensing policy to avoid potential abuse by noninventors. Like IBM, TI has also been successful in generating royalties for access to its pioneering patents through its licensing efforts and enforcement actions. In the latter half of the 1980s, when the company was facing stiff competition in the DRAM market, licensing royalties sometimes exceeded the net profits of the company. Absent these revenues, TI would not have been profitable.

Licensing arrangements, including the cross-licensing of patents, may not always be easy to achieve in multi-invention contexts. Reliance on such licensing assumes a willingness to license on the part of others, an assumption that will be strongly challenged if some patent owners have somewhat different strategic goals or a different appreciation of the value of their own technology. In these cases, entrepreneurs can sometimes overcome the barriers in the licensing market by using the markets for corporate control to acquire technologies and patents. Firms like Cisco Systems have championed this approach, typically acquiring smaller innovative firms with technologies (and patents) that the company needs. Similarly, in the agricultural biotechnology industry, a number of firms have consolidated to bring together germplasm, genomic, and plant variety patents relating to specific crops.

From the perspective of a small entrepreneurial firm, setting oneself up as an acquisition target would be an appropriate strategy when organizational costs dictate an integrated mode, but there are also significant barriers to developing complementary technologies in-house and to obtaining access to the necessary patents. A strong set of blocking patents, which has the potential for generating patent exclusivity for the merged firm, while simultaneously dissuading potential merger partners from a go-it-alone strategy, would increase the attractiveness of the entrepreneurial firm in the market for corporate control. Even among larger firms, entrepreneurial opportunities exist to agglomerate businesses across firms so as to pool technologies and patents, and overcome transaction costs in patent licensing. For example, in 1998, when a long-running patent dispute between Digital and Intel (relating to Digital's Alpha processor patents) had reached a stalemate, Intel was able to break the impasse by simply buying out Digital's semiconductor business. Perhaps one of the earliest examples of entrepreneurship to consolidate inventions into a single firm, in this case spurred by a major customer (the U.S. Navy), was the creation of RCA for the development of radio in the first quarter of the twentieth century.[17]

THE FORMATION OF RCA

Early developments in wireless radio epitomize the complexities surrounding intellectual property arrangements that may be encountered with systems innovation (or multi-invention) technologies. The commercialization of radio required a number of basic inventions. The scientific basis for wireless was developed by university scientists such as Maxwell, Hertz, and Lodge in the nineteenth century. Their discoveries were first applied to practical communication with the development of wireless telegraphy by Marconi in Britain in 1896. The first speech transmissions were made in the United States by Fessenden in 1900, using a high-frequency alternator. Further basic innovations were made over the next two decades.[18]

Many of these inventions were initially developed by individuals working independently of each other. Indeed, many carry the name of the inventor, such as Poulsen arc, the Fleming valve, and the de Forest triode.[19] As the potential for radio became apparent, and the need for large-scale R&D and investment grew, large corporations entered the field. The pace of development accelerated, and the number of patents multiplied. The companies involved included Marconi, General Electric (GE), Westinghouse, AT&T, Telefunken, and others. In addition to their considerable R&D effort, these corporations also acquired key patents (Archer 1938, 135; Maclaurin 1949, 106).[20] There was considerable competition, and with research teams in different companies working in parallel, patent interferences were common (Maclaurin 1949, 97).[21] By 1918, it was apparent that several technologies were needed to manufacture radio systems, and each of these technologies itself involved multiple patents from different firms. In the words of Armstrong, one of the pioneers of radio, "It was absolutely impossible to manufacture any kind of workable apparatus without using practically all of the inventions that were then known" (Federal Trade Commission 1923; Maclaurin 1949, 99).

The result was deadlock. A number of firms had important patent positions and could block each other's access to key components. They refused to cross-license. This held up the development of the industry (Archer 1938, 113–14; Douglas 1987, 8, 12; Maclaurin 1949, 77).[22] The situation arose in large part as a result of the way radio had developed.

Key patent portfolios had been developed by different individuals and corporations, who were often adamant about refusing to cross-license competitors. In addition, in a new industry in which large-scale patent overlaps were a novel problem, there was no well-developed means of coordinating licensing agreements between these groups.

The situation was resolved in the United States only when, under prompting by the U.S. Navy, the various pioneers formed the Radio Corporation of America (RCA) in 1919 (Archer 1938, 176–89; Maclaurin 1949, 105).[23] This broke a key source of the deadlock. RCA acquired the U.S. rights to the Marconi patents, and the other major U.S. patent holders became shareholders in RCA.[24] In this way, RCA acquired the U.S. rights to all the constituent radio patents under one roof—amounting to over 2,000 patents (Archer 1938, 195; Maclaurin 1949, 107).[25] It established RCA as the technical leader in radio, but also granted cross-licenses to the other firms to continue their own development of the technology for use in other fields or as suppliers to RCA.[26]

The RCA example highlights the perils to the economy when patent owners pursue exclusivity too vigorously in multi-invention contexts. Without the willingness to allow others access to one's own patents, there is virtually no prospect for reciprocal access. Because of the high transactions costs reflected in this reluctance to cross-license, technological progress and the further commercialization of radio was halted. In this case, the debacle was resolved only by the formation of RCA. However, it is now clear that the same ends—namely design freedom—may often be achieved more simply, without such fundamental reorganization, by cross-licensing alone. The wireless patent-licensing deadlock and the formation of RCA helped set the stage for further development of cross-licensing in electronics.

5.2. Nonintegrated Modes

Nonintegrated modes use licensing and component markets to supply intellectual property bundled-in with their technologies or component products. In this way, specialized firms can avoid the need to develop all the complementary technologies in-house. The use of such nonintegrated modes or "business models" usually occurs when the transaction costs in the associated (licensing or component) market are not especially high. One fundamental challenge for entrepreneurs is to recognize opportunities for commercializing inventions in this fashion, instead of resorting to integrated commercialization by default.

It is important to understand that when technologies are licensed or components are sold, there is definite risk that knowledge may leak out and the transaction partner may learn too much about the firm's technology. Attempts to barricade the company's know-how may fail because successful commercialization may require joint problem solving and the exchange of technical information. This is a very serious problem because uniqueness of the company's technology is often the primary business proposition of enterprises employing nonintegrated modes of innovation. Patents can play a vital role by limiting misappropriation of the firm's technology, and facilitating transactions between the entrepreneurial firm and its business partners. Naturally, enterprises relying on patent protection to sustain a licensing or component-product business model would take a more proprietary view in their IP strategy. We illustrate the type of entrepreneurship entailed in nonintegrated modes by reviewing two case studies, which highlight the differences in strategy not only between integrated and nonintegrated modes, but also among nonintegrated modes.

SYSTEM ON A CHIP (SOC) AND ARM, LTD.

In semiconductors, relentless miniaturization has made it possible to put entire electronic systems on a single semiconductor chip (Teece 1998; Linden and Somaya 2003). Market demand for the advantages in size, power consumption, and production cost that such systems-on-a-chip (SOCs) promise has also been growing rapidly. Previously, it was common for semiconductor technologies to be transferred between firms through the sale of various component integrated circuits (ICs), where the technology itself was transferred in "embodied" form. However, when entire electronic systems needed to be put on a single chip or IC, it became practically impossible to conduct transactions in technology by conducting transactions in components.

One solution to this problem in the component market was pioneered by new "chip-less" firms, who went about creating a licensing market for design modules that other firms can license and integrate into their own system-on-a-chip designs. ARM, Ltd., based in Cambridge in the United Kingdom, is one of the leading firms that adopted this approach. ARM's RISC (reduced instruction set computer) processor designs are used in literally tens of millions of cell phones and handheld devices sold around the world. ARM is a **spin-off** from the Power-PC consortium assembled by Apple Computer, IBM, and Motorola to design and manufacture microprocessors. The company resisted the temptation to be acquired by a large semiconductor firm, or to expand the scope of its own technological domain. Instead, it specialized in developing processor designs, which it then sought to license to other firms. As the SOC revolution took root, ARM's licensing-based strategy turned out be extremely successful.

ARM appears to have taken patent protection of its technologies very seriously and accumulated a portfolio of over 80 patents by 2000. When picoTurbo, a rival firm based in Milpitas, California, came up with a product that could essentially run any software written for ARM's processor, the company immediately filed suit.[27] PicoTurbo's technology threatened the exclusive position that ARM had built up in many ways. First and foremost, it threatened to invade the installed base of complementary ARM-related software and software programmers, and thus in effect invent around ARM's technology. Given the importance of an exclusive position for ARM's commercial success, it is no surprise that the company enforced its patents so aggressively. Eventually, the suit was settled with ARM simply acquiring picoTurbo with all its product designs and IP assets.

Dolby, which licenses its noise reduction designs for high-fidelity sound systems, and Rambus from the semiconductor industry are other prominent examples of firms that have pursued a licensing mode to commercialize their inventions. In both these cases, well-developed patent strategies are important to the viability of the licensing option, and indeed their business model more generally.

COMPONENTIZATION AT KENTRON TECHNOLOGIES

Sometimes licensing and component sales are transparent alternatives, in the sense that after pursing one strategy, the entrepreneur changes gears and adopts another. Kentron Technologies, a semiconductor firm, developed a technology to (effectively) double the bandwidth of DRAM modules by interleaving signals from two slower "single data rate" DRAMs, rather than using the patented "double data rate" technology developed by Rambus.[28] Kentron originally offered to license its technology for a 5 percent royalty, but did not get any takers. Kentron subsequently changed its patent strategy to offer "royalty free" licenses if DRAM users would buy special switches from Kentron that enable the interleaving to occur.[29]

Put differently, Kentron took the payment for the use of its technology and patents in the form of a premium price for the switches. Robert Goodman, Kentron's CEO, indicated that (1) the price of the special switch was set at a level that yielded Kentron the same revenue as a 5 percent royalty would have yielded, (2) users resisted taking a license from Kentron.[30] However, they were willing to pay Kentron for the use of its technology. Quite simply, the users may have perceived the transaction costs in the licensing market to be too high for Kentron's technology. The value of the technology may have seemed uncertain absent a physical component that could be evaluated, and potential licensees may have discounted its importance. There may have also been concerns about how well this technology would work with their own DRAM designs, in other words, about *technological interconnectedness*. Firms may also have wanted to avoid the monitoring and compliance costs associated with a license (tracking infringing sales, and calculating and paying royalties), and preferred to have the price of Kentron's technology built into the price of the physical switches instead. Because Kentron had a strong patent position built up around its pioneering technology, DRAM manufacturers could not simply appropriate its technology for internal use, nor could they effectively invent around Kentron's patent position.

The ARM and Kentron examples show how licensing a technology or selling components in which the technology is embedded are alternative strategies for commercialization. One of the functions of the entrepreneur is to recognize which organizational approach is most appropriate for generating value from an innovative idea, and to implement this organizational strategy. A second important function of the entrepreneur is to ensure that the firm captures value from its innovation, and does not simply dissipate it to other firms. In part, this implies designing the appropriate patent strategies for a given organizational mode.

6. Conclusion

In this chapter, we have described some of the challenges presented to entrepreneurs by multi-invention contexts, and analyzed implications for entrepreneurship and patent strategy in these contexts. Our analysis provides two main insights. First, to maximize chances of success, entrepreneurs must assess the relative organizational costs and benefits of different organizational modes or business "models," and commercialize inventions by using the most effective mode in a given multi-invention context. Second, patent strategies must be chosen to complement the choice of business model.

Entrepreneurship is critical for effectuating new combinations of assets, resources, and technologies in multi-invention contexts. Often incumbent firms face significant inertia to change their existing modes of behavior and organization. In many cases, they are unable to perceive the potential value that can be generated by developing a new invention or combining existing inventions in a new way. However, entrepreneurship is also likely to fail if the business models adopted are too cumbersome or flawed. In addition, it is not enough to unlock the potential value hidden in multi-invention or systemic contexts. It is equally important to devise strategies that appropriate some of this value to compensate for the entrepreneur's efforts. Appropriate patent strategy can play a useful role in capturing this value.

In response to transactional problems in multi-invention contexts, the instinctive public policy remedy sought by some is often a weakening of patent rights. While this solution may address certain transaction cost problems, it also means a weakening of incentives for innovation and the reinforcement of integrated modes of innovation and production. Licensing and component modes, on the other hand, benefit from patents because of stronger incentives, and in some cases, because of lower transaction costs. Evaluation of these alternative organizational forms and business models is essential in any attempt to address concerns about patents in multi-invention contexts. Often, astute management and entrepreneurial efforts are sufficient to allow technology and component markets to work effectively. Thus entrepreneurship and patent rights may have a symbiotic relationship that can be undermined by policy responses that do not account for all possible organizational arrangements through which innovation can take place.

Notes

1. For a discussion of systemic innovation, see Teece 2000.

2. By untested, we mean that the validity of the patent has not yet been tested in court.

3. The treatment of entrepreneurship here is sympathetic to the work of Hayek (1945), Casson (1982), Kirzner (1973), as well as Schumpeter himself.

4. IBM 2001 annual report.

5. This could be due to the user reading the patent, or it could be due to the user's independent invention of the patent, or hearing about it from some source.

6. Cross-licensing is not the same as "patent pooling," in which member firms contribute patents to a common pool and each member accesses them on the same terms and conditions. In cross-licensing, firms agree one-on-one to license their IP to each other and retain control over their proprietary technology, which is used for competitive advantage via product manufacturing and further licensing.

7. Note that the situation is different in other industries not characterized by cumulative systems technologies, such as chemicals and pharmaceuticals, where cross-licensing or, rather, reciprocal licensing, is typically aimed at exchanging technology rather than avoiding patent conflicts. In chemicals and pharmaceuticals, although patenting is extensive, individual technology development paths are less likely to overlap, and cross-licensing may be used to ensure broad product lines. For licensing strategy in the chemicals industry, see Grindley and Nickerson 1996, 97–120.

8. Historical perspective on competition in the telecommunications industry is given in Irwin 1977, 312–33; Brock 1981; OTA 1985; Noll and Owen 1989; and Rosston and Teece 1997.

9. The two substantive provisions of the 1956 consent decree were that (*a*) it confined AT&T to providing regulated telecommunications services, and its manufacturing subsidiary Western Electric to making equipment for those services (effectively prohibiting it from selling semiconductors in the commercial market), and (*b*) all patents controlled by the Bell System should be licensed to others on request. Licenses for the 8,600 patents included in existing cross-licensing agreements were royalty-free to new applicants, and licenses to all other existing or future patents were to be issued at a nondiscriminatory "reasonable royalty" (determined by the court if necessary). AT&T was also to provide technical information along with the patent licenses for reasonable fees. Licenses were unrestricted, other than being nontransferable (*USA v. Western Electric Co. Inc., and AT&T*, Civil Action, 17–49, Final Judgment, January 24, 1956; Brock 1981, 166, 191–94; Levin 1982, 9–101).

10. "We realized that if [the transistor] was as big as we thought, we couldn't keep it to ourselves and we couldn't make all the technical contributions. It was to our interest to spread it around" (AT&T executive, quoted in Levin 1982, 77, after Tilton 1971). The strategy appears to have been prescient. In the United States, during 1953–68, 5,128 semiconductor patents were awarded. Bell Laboratories was granted only 16 percent of these; the next five firms were RCA, General Electric, Westinghouse, IBM, and Texas Instruments, all AT&T cross-licensees (Tilton 1971).

11. The provision covered all existing patents at the time of the decree (i.e., as of 1956) plus any that were filed during the next five years. The rights lasted for the full term of the patents. If the parties could not agree on a reasonable royalty rate, the court could impose one. Patent rights could be very long lived, since, at that time, patent life was 17 years from the grant date, which might be some years after the filing date. The patent-licensing provisions ended in 1961. The decree also included other provisions related to the sale of IBM products and services (*USA v. International Business Machines Corporation*, CCH 1956 Trade Cases par. 68, 245, SDNY 1956).

12. Jim McGrody, IBM VP and director of research, in Boyer 1990, 10–11.

13. Roger Smith, IBM assistant general counsel, in Boyer 1990.

14. *Computerworld*, April 11, 1988, 105.

15. IBM Annual Report, 1993, 1994, 2000, 2001.

16. This section is based in part on discussion with Texas Instruments executives. However, the views expressed here are those of the authors, and should not be seen as reflecting those of Texas Instruments.

17. The early history of radio is described in Archer 1938; Jewkes, Sawers, and Stillerman 1969; Douglas 1987; and Merges and Nelson 1990, 891–96.

18. These included the high-frequency alternator, high-frequency transmission arc, magnetic amplifier, selective tuning, crystal detector, heterodyne signal detection, diode valve, triode valve, high vacuum tube, and directional aerials.

19. Not all early inventors were independent. E.F.W. Alexanderson—who improved the Fessenden alternator, invented a magnetic amplifier, electronic amplifier, and multiple tuned antenna, and co-invented the "Alexanderson-Beverage static eliminator"—was a General Electric employee.

20. AT&T acquired the de Forest triode and feedback patents in 1913–14 for $90,000, and his remaining feedback patents in 1917 for $250,000; Westinghouse cross-licensed the Fessenden heterodyne interests in 1920, and acquired the Armstrong super heterodyne patents in 1920 for $335,000 (Archer 1938, 135; Maclaurin 1949, 106).

21. The fact that GE and AT&T alone were each devoting major research attention to the vacuum tube led to no less than 20 important patent interferences in this area (Maclaurin 1949, 97).

22. To cite one important example, Marconi and de Forest both had critical valuable patents. Marconi's diode patent was held to dominate de Forest's triode patent. Both technologies were vital to radio, yet the interests refused to cross-license (Archer 1938, 113–14; Douglas 1987, 12). The application of the triode (audion) to feedback amplification was also the subject of a long-running patent priority dispute between de Forest and Armstrong (finally resolved in de Forest's favor by the Supreme Court in 1934). Its use in transmission oscillation was the subject of four-way patent interference between Langmuir, Meissner, Armstrong, and de Forest (Maclaurin 1949, 77). These problems held up the use of the triode—a crucial component of signal transmission. Detection and amplification, which has been called "the heart and soul of radio" (Douglas 1987, 8) and "so outstanding in its consequences it almost ranks with the greatest inventions of all time" (Nobel Prize physicist Rabi, quoted in Maclaurin 1949, 70).

23. RCA was formed by GE in 1919, and simultaneously acquired the American Marconi Corporation. Major shareholders included GE, AT&T (1920), and Westinghouse (1920) (Archer 1938, 176–89; Maclaurin 1949, 105). A major concern of the U.S. Navy was that international wireless communications were dominated by the British firm Marconi, and the patent impasse helped perpetuate this. The Navy favored the establishment of an "All American" company in international communications. A similar concern on the eve of U.S. entry into World War I prompted the U.S. government (the secretaries of war and the navy) to also intervene in the case of aircraft patents, and create a patent pooling arrangement in January 1917 (Bittlingmayer 1988).

24. As part of its role in the formation of RCA, the U.S. Navy also initiated cross-licensing to resolve the patent situation in radio manufacture. It wished to have clear rights to use the radio equipment it purchased, without risking litigation due to complex patent ownership—noting in 1919 that "there was not a single company among those making radio sets for the Navy which possessed basic patents sufficient to enable them to supply, without infringement, . . . a complete transmitter or receiver." A formal letter suggesting "some agreement between the several holders of permanent patents whereby the market can be freely supplied with [vacuum] tubes," sent from the navy to GE and AT&T in January 1920, may be seen as an initiating point for cross-licensing in the industry (Archer 1938, 180–86; Maclaurin 1949, 99–110).

25. RCA concluded cross-license agreements with firms including GE, Westinghouse, AT&T, United Fruit Company, Wireless Specialty Apparatus Company, Marconi (Britain), CCTF (France), and Telefunken (Germany) (Archer 1938, 195; Maclaurin 1949, 107).

26. A distinction was that the RCA cross-licenses typically granted (reciprocal) exclusive rights to use the patents in given territories or markets; compared with the nonexclusive cross-licenses that became the norm later. The cross-license with GE (and later Westinghouse) included provisions for the supply of components to RCA. The RCA cross-licenses were for very long terms—many for 25 years, from 1919 to 1945. They covered current and future patents. Other radio manufacturers took licenses with RCA, starting in the late 1920s. Some of RCA's cross-licensing policies were later questioned on antitrust grounds, and modified following a consent decree in 1932 (Archer 1938, 381–87; and Maclaurin 1949, 107–9, 132–52).

27. See online: http://www.reed-electronics.com/electronicnews/article/CA186719.html (accessed October 27, 2005).

28. One of the authors (Teece) is familiar with the Kentron example from his work as an expert in *In the Matter of Rambus, Inc.*, FTC Docket No. 9302. In this paper, we are relying only on the public testimony given by Mr. Robert Goodman, Kentron's CEO, and not on any information that is subject to the protective order in that case. See *In the Matter of Rambus, Inc.*, June 19, 2003, 6020–29, 6041, 6078–87.

29. As a news story indicates: "Kentron makes the special QBM module switches, which is [*sic*] used in its modules and those of licensees. Bob Goodman, Kentron's CEO, said the firm licenses its QBM technology on a royalty-free basis, and derives revenues from the sale of its QBM switches." See http://siliconstrategies.com/article/printableArticle.jhtmlarticle4ID=10806590 (accessed September 16, 2003).

30. At the public hearing *In the Matter of Rambus, Inc.*, FTC Docket No. 9302.

References

Archer, G. 1938. *History of Radio to 1926*. New York: American Historical Society.

Arora, A. 1995. "Licensing Tacit Knowledge: Intellectual Property Rights and the Market for Know-How." *Economics of Innovation and New Technology* 4: 41–59.

Arrow, K. J. 1971. *Essays in the Theory of Risk-Bearing*. Chicago: Markham.

Baumol, W. 1993. "Formal Entrepreneurship Theory in Economics: Existence and Bounds." *Journal of Business Venturing* 8: 197–210.

Bittlingmayer, G. 1988. "Property Rights, Progress, and the Aircraft Patent Agreement." *Journal of Law and Economics* 31 (1): 227–48.

Boyer, C. 1990. "The Power of the Patent Portfolio." *Think* 5: 10–11.

Brock, G. 1981. *The Telecommunications Industry: The Dynamics of Market Structure*. Cambridge: Harvard University Press.

Casson, M. 1982. *The Entrepreneur*. Totawa, N.J.: Barnes and Noble.

Chang, H. F. 1995. "Patent Scope, Antitrust Policy, and Cumulative Innovation." *Rand Journal of Economics* 26 (1): 34–57.

Douglas, G. 1987. *The Early Days of Radio Broadcasting*. Jefferson, N.C.: McFarland.

Federal Trade Commission. 1923. *The Radio Industry*. Washington, D.C.: Government Printing Office.

Green, J. R., and S. Scotchmer. 1995. "On the Division of Profit in Sequential Innovation." *Rand Journal of Economics* 26 (1): 20–33.

Grindley, P. C., and J. Nickerson. 1996. "Strategic Objectives Supported by Licensing." In *Technology Licensing: Corporate Strategies for Maximizing Value*, ed. R. L. Parr and P. H. Sullivan. New York: John Wiley and Sons.

Grindley, P. C., and D. J. Teece. 1997. "Managing Intellectual Capital: Licensing and Cross-Licensing in Semiconductors and Electronics." *California Management Review* 39 (2): 8–41.

Hall, B. H., and R. M. Ziedonis. 2001. "The Patent Paradox Revisited: An Empirical Study of Patenting in the Semiconductor Industry, 1979–1995." *Rand Journal of Economics* 32 (1): 101–28.

Harris, R. 1990. "Divestiture and Regulatory Policies." *Telecommunications Policy* 14: 105–24.

Hayek, F. A. 1945. "The Use of Knowledge in Society." *American Economic Review* 35 (4): 519–30.

Heller, M. A., and R. S. Eisenberg. 1998. "Can Patents Deter Innovation? The Anticommons in Biomedical Research." *Science* 280 (5364): 698–701.

Irwin, M. 1977. "The Telephone Industry." In *The Structure of American Industry*, ed. W. Adams. 5th ed. New York: Macmillan.

Jewkes, J., D. Sawers, and R. Stillerman. 1969. *The Sources of Innovation*. New York: Norton.

Kefauver, W. 1993. "Intellectual Property Rights and Competitive Strategy: An International Telecommunications Firm." In *Global Dimensions of Intellectual Property Rights in Science and Technology*, ed. M. Wallerstein, M. E. Mogee, and R. Schoen. Washington, D.C.: National Academy Press.

Kitch, E. W. 1977. "The Nature and Function of the Patent System." *Journal of Law and Economics* 20: 265–90.

Kirzner, I. 1973. *Competition and Entrepreneurship*. Chicago: University of Chicago Press.

Levin, R. 1982. "The Semiconductor Industry." In *Government and Technical Progress*, ed. R. Nelson. New York: Pergamon.

Linden, G., and D. Somaya. 2003. "System-on-a-Chip Integration in the Semiconductor Industry: Industry Structure and Firm Strategies." *Industrial and Corporate Change* 12 (3): 545–76.

Lippman, S. A., and R. P. Rumelt. 2003. "A Bargaining Perspective on Resource Advantage." *Strategic Management Journal* 24: 1069–86.

Maclaurin, W. 1949. *Invention and Innovation in the Radio Industry*. New York: Macmillan.

Mazzoleni, R., and R. R. Nelson. 1998. "The Benefits and Costs of Strong Patent Protection: A Contribution to the Current Debate." *Research Policy* 27 (3): 273–84.

Merges, R. P., and R. R. Nelson. 1990. "On the Complex Economics of Patent Scope." *Columbia Law Journal* 90 (4): 839–916.

———. 1994. "On Limiting or Encouraging Rivalry in Technical Progress: The Effect of Patent Scope Decisions." *Journal of Economic Behavior and Organization* 25 (1): 1–24.

Office of Technology Assessment (OTA). 1985. *Information Technology Research and Development: Critical Trends and Issues*. New York: Pergamon.

Oxley, J. E. 1999. "Institutional Environment and the Mechanisms of Governance: The Impact of Intellectual Property Protection on the Structure of Interfirm Alliances." *Journal of Economic Behavior and Organization* 38 (3): 283–309.

Noll, M. 1987. "Bell System R&D Activities: The Impact of Divestiture." *Telecommunications Policy* 11: 161–78.

Noll, R., and B. Owen. 1989. "The Anticompetitive Uses of Regulation: United States v. AT&T." In *The Antitrust Revolution*, ed. J. Kwoka and L. White. New York: Macmillan.

Rivette, K. G., and D. Kline. 2000. "Discovering New Value in Intellectual Property." *Harvard Business Review*, January–February, 2–12.

Rosenberg, N. 1994. *Exploring the Black Box*. Cambridge: Cambridge University Press.

Rosston, G. L., and D. J. Teece. 1997. "Competition and 'Local' Communications: Innovation, Entry, and Integration." In *Globalism and Localism* in Telecommunications, ed. E. M. Noam and A. J. Wolfson. North Holland: Elsevier.

Rumelt, R. P. 1984. "Towards a Strategic Theory of the Firm." In *Competitive Strategic Management*, ed. R. B. Lamb. Englewood Cliffs, N.J.: Prentice-Hall.

Schumpeter, J. 1934. *Capitalism, Socialism, and Democracy*. New York: Harper and Row.

Scotchmer, S. 1991. "Standing on the Shoulders of Giants: Cumulative Research and the Patent Law." *Journal of Economic Perspectives* 3: 29–41.

———. 1996. "Protecting Early Innovators: Should Second-Generation Products be Patentable?" *Rand Journal of Economics* 27 (2): 322–31.

Shelanski, H., and P. G. Klein. 1995. "Empirical Research in Transaction Cost Economics: A Review and Assessment." *Journal of Law, Economics, and Organization* 11 (2): 335–61.

Sherry, E., and D. J. Teece. 2003. "Standards Setting and Antitrust." *Minnesota Law Review* 87 (6): 1913–94.

Smith, R. 1989. "Management of a Corporate Intellectual Property Law Department." *AIPLA Bulletin*, April–June, 817–23.

Somaya, D. 2003. "Strategic Determinants of Decisions Not to Settle Patent Litigation." *Strategic Management Journal* 24: 17–38.

———. 2005. "Combining Inventions in Multi-invention Products: Patents, Organizational Alternatives, and Public Policy." Working paper, University of Maryland.

Teece, D. J. 1982. "Towards an Economic Theory of the Multiproduct Firm." *Journal of Economic Behavior and Organization* 3 (March): 39–64.

———. 1986. "Profiting from Technological Innovation: Implications for Integration, Collaboration, Licensing, and Public Policy." *Research Policy* 15 (6): 285–305.

———. 1996. "Firm Organization, Industrial Structure, and Technological Innovation." *Journal of Economic Behavior and Organization* 31 (2): 193–224.

———. 1998. "Capturing Value from Knowledge Assets: The New Economy, Markets for Know-how, and Intangible Assets." *California Management Review* 40 (3): 55–79.

———. 2000. *Managing Intellectual Capital.* New York: Oxford University Press.

———. 2003a. "Explicating Dynamic Capabilities: Asset Selection, Cospecialization, and Entrepreneurship in Strategic Management Theory." Working paper.

———. 2003b. *Essays in Technology Management and Policy.* Hackensack, N.J.: World Scientific Publishing.

Tilton, J. 1971. *International Diffusion of Technology: The Case of Semiconductors.* Washington, D.C.: Brookings Institution.

Williamson, O. E. 1985. *The Economic Institutions of Capitalism.* New York: Free Press.

———. 1996. *Mechanisms of Governance.* New York: Free Press.

Chapter 10

The Market for Technology and the Organization of Invention in U.S. History

NAOMI R. LAMOREAUX AND KENNETH L. SOKOLOFF

INVENTORS WHO ARE GIFTED at coming up with new technological ideas are frequently not as talented at developing them commercially. As a result, large benefits may be gained from a division of labor that allows creative people to specialize in what they do best. This division of labor can arise within economic units and be coordinated administratively (as, for example, when a firm sets up an in-house R&D laboratory). Or it can develop across economic units and be coordinated by the market.

Many scholars have argued for the general superiority of the within-firms division of labor on the grounds that problems of asymmetric information severely limit inventors' ability to sell new technological ideas at arm's length. Before they will invest in a technology, buyers need to be able to estimate its value—to assess, for example, the extent to which a new process will lower production costs, or whether a novel product is likely to appeal to consumers. According to these scholars, the protection offered by the patent system is too weak to assuage inventors' fears that buyers will steal their ideas, and so inventors typically are not willing to provide potential purchasers with enough information to effectuate sales (Arrow 1962; Mowery 1983, 1995; Teece 1986, 1988; Zeckhauser 1996).

Recently, however, another group of scholars has countered that the information problems associated with the market exchange of technological ideas have been greatly exaggerated (Arora 1995; Lamoreaux and Sokoloff 1996, 1999a, 1999b, 1999c, 2003; Arora, Fosfuri, and Gambardella 2001; Gans and Stern 2003). Although patent rights are not perfectly enforced, they provide substantial protection to inventors—certainly enough to enable them to engage in market exchange. Moreover, there are a number of ways to solve the information problems that still may inhibit trade. Firms seeking to purchase outside technologies can invest in developing a reputation for safeguarding inventors' interests; intermediaries can emerge who possess both the knowledge needed to facilitate this kind of trade and the trust of parties on both sides of the market; and talented inventors can establish track records that encourage buyers to seek them out. As this newer literature also shows, previous scholars did not adequately appreciate the magnitude of the problems of asymmetric information associated with in-house R&D. Firms have to worry about shirking by employees whose job it is to develop new technology. They also have be concerned that they learn about, and gain control of, the ideas their employees devise (Lamoreaux and Sokoloff 1999c).

Rather than one type of division of labor being generally superior to the other, it is likely that the relative incidence of these two alternatives will depend on such factors as the nature of the technology (for example, whether it is easy to patent), its complexity and cost (and hence the amount of human and physical capital required for effective invention), the state of development of financial institutions, the size distribution of firms, and the kinds of investments that economic actors have already made in resolving problems associated with the transfer of technological knowledge. As this chapter will demonstrate, the extent of the market for technology has waxed and waned over the course of U.S. history. During the second half of the nineteenth century, there was a great expansion of trade in new technological ideas. The first half of the twentieth century, however, witnessed the growth of in-house R&D and a corresponding decline in the extent of market exchange, as least as measured by the arm's-length sale of patented inventions. More recently, there appears to have been a shift back in the direction of the market as large firms have reduced the scope of their in-house R&D and devoted increasing resources to tracking and acquiring technologies developed outside their bounds.

The analytical framework that underpins our analysis is similar to that developed by Joshua S. Gans and Scott Stern (2003). We posit that, in the mid–nineteenth century, technologically creative people (we call them inventors) had two alternative ways of extracting the returns from their ideas: They could exploit them directly by starting their own businesses, or they could transfer the rights to others who would undertake the task of commercialization.[1] We argue that the U.S. patent system offered patentees a level of protection that was particularly conducive to the market exchange of technological ideas, and that talented inventors learned to exploit this market so that they could specialize in the generation of new technology. We also describe the emergence of intermediaries to facilitate this trade and show that firms invested both in building a reputation that would encourage inventors to bring them ideas and in tracking technological developments occurring elsewhere in the economy. Finally, we look at the circumstances that operated to reduce the scope of this market by the early twentieth century. We focus in particular on the growing complexity and capital intensity of technology, which raised the cost of effective invention and therefore made it more difficult for creative individuals to pursue careers as independent inventors.

The U.S. Patent System

The U.S. patent system as we know it was created in 1836. Its antecedents, however, go back much further—at least to the British Statute of Monopolies of 1624, which exempted patents for inventions from the act's general prohibition against grants of monopoly privileges and established a set of procedures for obtaining this form of property right (Dutton 1984; MacLeod 1988). The drafters of the U.S. Constitution believed that support for technological innovation was vital to the success of the new nation and wrote into the Constitution a clause authorizing Congress "to promote the progress of science and the useful arts by securing for limited times to authors and inventors the exclusive right to their respective writings and inventions."[2] Congress acted on this authorization almost immediately, passing legislation in 1790 and again in 1793 that provided inventors of novel and useful technologies monopoly property rights to their discoveries for a period of 14 years (U.S. Patent Office 1956).[3]

Even this early U.S. patent system represented a dramatic improvement on British practice. In the first place, the cost of obtaining a patent was much lower. In England, fees amounted to about four times annual per capita income as late as 1860—far higher if coverage was to be extended to Scotland and Ireland. Although the $30 fee for a U.S. patent was equivalent to several months wages for a laborer, the comparatively modest charge made patent protection affordable for a much broader spectrum of inventors, and patent rates per capita not surprisingly were significantly higher in the United States than in Britain (Khan and Sokoloff 1998). A second important difference was that patents could be awarded in the United States only to the first and true inventor anywhere in the world, whereas in Britain it was possible for noninventors to receive patents under certain circumstances.[4] Although there is ongoing debate over the benefits of first-to-invent versus first-to-patent rules (Scotchmer and Green 1990; Ordover 1991), this provision allowed inventors to reveal information about their devices to potential buyers before they received patent protection. Indeed, over the course of the nineteenth century, an increasing proportion of patents were assigned to arm's-length purchasers before they had even been granted (Lamoreaux and Sokoloff 1996, 1999b, 1999c). Third, unlike the British system, U.S. law furthered the dissemination of information about new technology. In Britain, it was cumbersome to study prior art because researchers had to pay a fee for each patent specification they wished to view. In the United States, by contrast, researchers not only benefited from free and open access to patent specifications stored in Washington, but the Patent Office published annual (by the 1870s, weekly) lists of inventions that had been awarded patents. It also encouraged private journals to improve on this service.[5] The most famous of these, *Scientific American*, which began publishing in 1845, printed lists of patents granted on a weekly basis, featured lengthy descriptions of the most important new technologies, and offered to send its readers copies of complete patent specifications for a small fee (Borut 1977; Lamoreaux and Sokoloff 1999b, 1999c).

A drawback of the early U.S. patent system was that it operated, like its British counterpart, on the registration principle.[6] Inventors received patents virtually automatically by filling out an application and filing a fee, and it was left to the federal courts to decide, in cases of infringement or other challenges to patent rights, whether the invention met the standards specified in the law ("Outline" 1936; U.S. Patent Office 1956). The courts generally were supportive of patent rights, and the number of cases actually litigated did not grow in proportion to the number of patents (Khan 1995). Nonetheless, opposition mounted against the "evils" that "must continue to . . . multiply daily" in a system that awards patent rights "without any examination into the merits and novelty of the invention." In the aftermath of a congressional inquiry headed by Senator John Ruggles of Maine, Congress passed a new statute in 1836 mandating that all inventions be scrutinized by professional examiners to insure that they met the law's criteria for novelty and usefulness before being awarded patent rights (Post 1976, 49–50).

One important consequence of the 1836 act was to increase the security of patent rights, because applications were now checked against the prior art before they were approved. Of course, patent rights could still be overturned by the courts, which retained final authority. But the stamp of approval of the Patent Office carried weight, and as B. Zorina Khan has shown, the probability that a patent would be upheld in court increased significantly after 1836 (Khan 1995). Some scholars have claimed that pressure from an increasingly powerful inventors' lobby induced patent examiners to approve most applications by the late 1850s, essentially returning the country to a registration system (Post 1976, 159–60). But though the strictness with which the Patent Office scrutinized applications undoubtedly varied over time, as did the percentage of applications approved, the high proportion of successful applications in the late nineteenth century did not represent a return to pre-1836 conditions. In the first place, there is abundant evidence that inventors took care to research prior art and prescreened their applications for novelty. In the second, applicants increasingly participated in an iterative process whereby they would submit an application, get a preliminary reading from examiners of whether the claims were likely to pass scrutiny, and then revise the claims accordingly, continuing the process until they were confident that their application would be approved.[7]

The enhanced security of property rights that followed from the 1836 act is evident in the rapid rise in the number of patents (see fig. 10.1) and, even more importantly, in the growing number of assignments (sales) of patents. In order to be legally binding, contracts for the sale of patent rights had to be recorded in the Patent Office within three months, so the number of these contracts can be counted. During the 1840s and 1850s, when high transportation costs made it feasible to sell geographically restricted rights in multiple markets, the number of assignments quickly soared to 5 to 10 times the number of patents. As transportation costs fell and buyers sought full national rights to patents, the ratio of the assignments to patents inevitably fell (its late-nineteenth-century peak was about 0.85),[8] but as we shall see, buyers were increasingly willing to pay high prices for patents that they thought represented important technological advances.

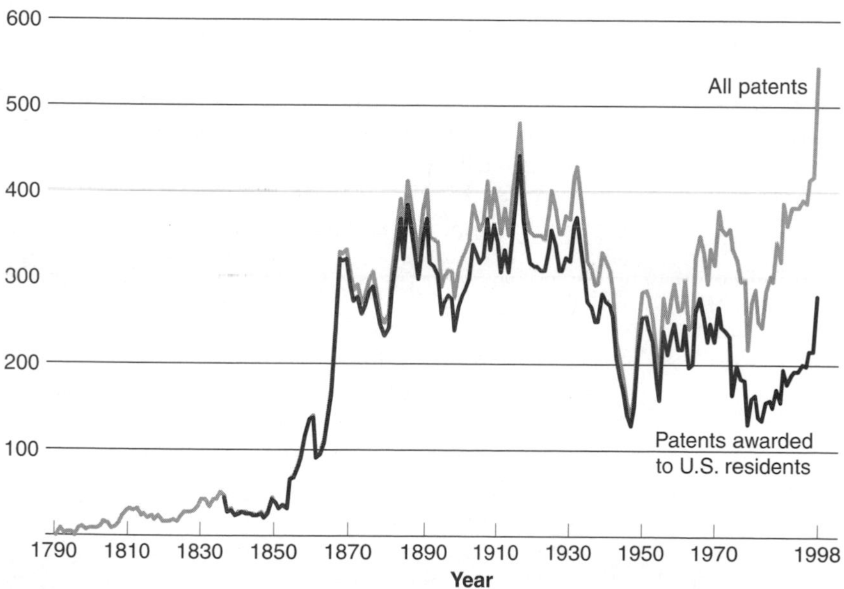

Figure 10.1. Rate of Patenting per Million Residents in the United States, 1790–1998

The Emergence of Specialized Inventors

As we have already suggested, inventions can be exploited directly by the individual (or firm, if the inventor is an employee) that develops them. Alternatively, the returns can be extracted by licensing or selling the technology in exchange for royalties or a lump-sum fee. Only the former option is possible under a property-rights regime that depends on trade secrets. Under a patent system, however, inventors (or firms) potentially can choose either strategy. Moreover, under some circumstances, they can pursue both alternatives at the same time. For example, the geographically segmented character of markets in the second quarter of the nineteenth century allowed Thomas Blanchard, inventor of the gunstocking lathe, to use his invention himself to manufacture gunstocks for the local Boston market and for export, and, at the same time, sell the right to use the invention to gun makers operating elsewhere. He also sold geographically restricted rights to producers of other types of goods that could be made with his lathe (for example, shoe lasts, tool handles, and wheel spokes) (Cooper 1991).

The emergence of a national product market with the expansion of the railroad network, and its completion in the years following the Civil War, made the purchase of geographically segmented patent rights less attractive, and not surprisingly this type of transaction declined in importance as buyers or licensors of patents increasingly sought full national rights to new technologies (Lamoreaux and Sokoloff 1999c). Some inventors continued to commercialize their inventions themselves, assigning only peripheral or foreign patent rights, if any.[9] But the most prolific inventors increasingly chose instead to sell off all rights to their inventions to others who were better situated to exploit them commercially. In that way they could devote more of their own time and resources to the generation of new technological ideas.

The new pattern is evident from tables 10.1 and 10.2, which examine the careers of a sample of the more than 500 patentees whose surnames began with the letter *B*.[10] The sample was generated, first, by drawing three random cross-sectional samples from the lists of patent grants reported in the *Annual Reports of the Commissioner of Patents* for the years 1870–71, 1890–91, and 1910–11; and then, for those patentees whose last names began with *B*, collecting data on all patents received during the 25 years before and after they appeared in our samples (including whether and to whom the patents were assigned at issue). In tables 10.1 and 10.2 we present the data in two different ways: by patentee (where each patentee appears in the calculations only once, based on the patent included in the original cross-sectional sample); and by patent (where each patentee appears as many times as he has patents).

Table 10.1 classifies the U.S. residents in our *B* sample into four categories: those who did not assign their patents at issue; those who made

TABLE 10.1
Descriptive Statistics on the Careers of Patentees in the "B" Sample

	1870–71	1890–91	1910–11	Total
	Means Computed over Patentees			
Not assigned at issue				
Average number of patents	7.9	10.7	6.9	8.2
Length of career (yrs.)	13.3	14.9	11.2	12.9
Career assignment rate (%)	8.6	12.2	9.7	10.1
Number of patentees	116	105	157	378
Share assignment				
Average number of patents	5.3	8.0	2.5	5.6
Length of career (yrs.)	10.5	12.9	6.9	10.4
Career assignment rate (%)	71.3	73.0	79.6	74.6
Number of patentees	12	17	13	42
Full assignment to individual				
Average number of patents	5.3	29.0	3.3	13.2
Length of career (yrs.)	12.0	18.3	5.3	12.7
Career assignment rate (%)	52.1	74.1	83.3	67.2
Number of patentees	7	6	4	17
Full assignment to company				
Average number of patents	22.0	28.3	34.4	30.6
Length of career (yrs.)	21.0	22.7	24.6	23.5
Career assignment rate (%)	47.0	70.7	78.6	73.1
Number of patentees	3	44	33	80
	Means Computed over Patents			
Not assigned at issue				
Average number of patents	19.5	41.2	41.1	35.1
Length of career (yrs.)	21.2	28.4	27.0	25.9
Career assignment rate (%)	14.7	24.3	22.8	21.1
Number of patents	851	1198	1008	3057
Share assignment				
Average number of patents	19.7	40.3	25.3	30.9
Length of career (yrs.)	20.9	27.3	25.8	25.3
Career assignment rate (%)	40.2	68.3	61.9	59.7
Number of patents	73	142	93	308
Full assignment to individual				
Average number of patents	27.0	76.4	36.1	58.4
Length of career (yrs.)	25.8	30.6	28.2	29.1
Career assignment rate (%)	41.1	77.1	67.9	67.7
Number of patents	80	223	68	371

(*Continued*)

TABLE 10.1
(*Continued*)

	1870–71	1890–91	1910–11	Total
	Means Computed over Patents			
Full assignment to company				
Average number of patents	35.1	62.8	141.2	103.6
Length of career (yrs.)	26.3	33.0	35.5	34.1
Career assignment rate (%)	52.2	77.8	84.8	80.6
Number of patents	75	884	1099	2058

Sources and notes: The table is based on a longitudinal data set constructed by selecting all of the inventors whose family names began with the letter B from three random cross-sectional samples drawn from the *Annual Reports of the Commissioner of Patents* for the years 1870–71, 1890–91, and 1910–11. We then collected from the *Annual Reports* information on all of the patents received by these inventors during the twenty-five years before and after they appeared in the samples. The estimates presented in the table include only those patentees who were resident in the U.S. The top panel treats each patentee as a single case, computing the averages on the basis of only one patent per inventor (the patent drawn in the original cross-section). The bottom panel analyzes all of the patents, providing averages that are effectively weighted according to the number of patents received by each inventor. The career assignment rate includes only those assignments that were recorded when the patent was issued.

only partial assignments of their patent rights at the time of issue, retaining shares in their patents for themselves; those who assigned away all their patent rights at issue to individuals; and those who assigned away all their rights at issue to companies. The table highlights the emergence by the late nineteenth century of two quite distinct classes of inventors. One group obtained relatively few patents but tended to retain at least some ownership rights to them; the other obtained many more patents but typically assigned away all their rights. For example, for the 1890–91 cohort, the means computed over patentees (patents) indicate that those who assigned away their patents at issue to companies received 28.3 (62.8) patents on average over their careers, and those who assigned full rights to individuals received an average of 29.0 (76.4) patents. By contrast, those who did not assign received only 10.7 (41.2) patents, and those who made partial assignments received 8.0 (40.3) patents. The contrasts between these two groups of patentees were evident as early as the 1870–71 but became starker over time, with those who assigned to companies becoming especially prominent in terms of the number of patents and length of their patenting careers by the 1910–11 cohort.

Those who received large numbers of patents over their careers not only tended to sell off their patents, but seem to have done so quite entrepreneurially, transferring their property rights to a diversity of individuals and firms. Table 10.2 breaks down the patentees in our sample by the number of different assignees with whom they dealt, as well as by their career totals of patents. Of the 545 patentees, 168 (30.8 percent) received 10 or more patents over the 50 years we followed them (accounting for 80.6 percent of the total 5,794 patents awarded to the 545 inventors), and 51 of these 168 (or just over 30 percent of the inventors with 10 or more career patents) sold their patent rights to four or more different assignees over their careers. These 51 patentees (9.4 percent of the total number of patentees) received 2,034 patents (or more than 35 percent of the total patents). These figures can be compared to

TABLE 10.2
Contractual Mobility and Career Productivity of Patentees: Distributions of Patents and Patentees

		Career Patent Total for Patentee				
Distributions of Patents		1–2 Patents	3–5 Patents	6–9 Patents	10+ Patents	*n*
No assignees	row%	23.8	25.3	15.2	35.8	875
	col%	76.8	52.1	30.9	6.7	15.1%
1 Assignee	row%	6.1	15.0	9.2	69.8	1042
	col%	23.3	36.8	22.3	15.6	18.0%
2–3 different	row%	-	2.4	8.1	89.6	1781
assignees	col%	-	9.9	33.5	34.2	15.8%
4+ different	row%	-	0.2	2.7	97.0	2096
assignees	col%	-	1.2	13.3	43.6	36.2%
n		271	424	430	4669	5794
		4.7%	7.3%	7.4%	80.6%	
Distributions of Patentees						
No assignees	row%	59.9	22.5	7.5	10.1	267
	col%	78.8	53.6	32.3	16.1	49.9%
1 assignee	row%	32.3	30.1	10.5	27.1	133
	col%	21.2	35.7	22.6	21.4	24.4%
2–3 different	row%	-	12.8	24.4	62.8	86
assignees	col%	-	9.8	33.9	32.1	15.8%
4+ different	row%	-	1.7	11.9	86.4	59
assignees	col%	-	0.9	11.3	30.4	10.8%
n		203	112	62	168	545
		37.3%	20.6%	11.4%	20.6%	

Source: See table 10.1.

the record of patentees with 10 or more career patents who sold their patents to only one assignee over their careers: 36 patentees (6.6 percent of all patentees) received 727 (12.5 percent of total patents). Because the possibility of having more assignees increased with the number of patents, this way of describing the patterns in the data slightly overstates the strength of the relationship we want to highlight, but the qualitative result is robust to other approaches. The most productive inventors, as gauged by their number of career patents, were highly entrepreneurial in the sense of exhibiting substantial contractual mobility.

The career of Elmer Sperry offers an excellent example.[11] Sperry, who was born into a upstate New York family of modest means, determined as a young man to pursue a career as an electrical inventor. Acting on the suggestion of one of the professors he sought out at nearby Cornell University, he designed a generator capable of supplying a constant current even though the load on its circuits varied, and then immediately scoured the local business community in search of financial backing. With support from the Cortland Wagon Company, whose executives included both inventors and investors interested in supporting new technological developments, he organized the Sperry Electric Light, Motor, and Car Brake Company in 1883. Although the company launched Sperry's career as an inventor, it was never a financial success. For Sperry, it proved to be a constant source of anxiety that absorbed all his attention and left him little time and energy for creative pursuits. Indeed, this period was the low point of his career in terms of generating new technological ideas. The 19 patents he applied for during his five years with the company amounted collectively to half his *annual* average over a career as an inventor that stretched from 1880 to 1930 (Hughes 1971, 44–45). Sperry emerged from this experience determined to devote his energies to research and development and never again become so deeply involved in the internal affairs of a company. But he was also determined to profit from his inventions. To this end, he sold off many of his patents to companies well placed to put the inventions to productive use. When well-heeled financial backers took the lead, he also participated in founding a number of new companies that bore his name, such as the Sperry Electric Mining Machine Company, the Sperry Streetcar Electric Railway Company, and the Sperry Gyroscope Company. But typically he limited his role in these companies to consultant, moving on quickly to other ventures. When the technical challenges and financial rewards were sufficiently alluring, he was also willing to work for stints as an employee or under contract for major companies such as American Can and National Battery. Never again, however, did he relinquish his independence or allow business responsibilities to impair his creativity.

Venture Capitalists and Intermediaries

One important reason why technologically creative people were able to pursue careers as independent inventors during the late nineteenth century was that many business people, functioning essentially as venture capitalists, were eager to buy national rights to promising new technologies. They were eager to make such purchases because it had become apparent that there was considerable money to be made by controlling important patents. Alexander Lyman Holley dramatically demonstrated this point by purchasing the U.S. rights to the Bessemer steel process in 1863. Holley had previously designed railroad locomotives and had written extensively on technical matters for a variety of publications ranging from the *American Railway Review* to the *New York Times.* During a trip to Britain to gather information on shipbuilding and armaments for the Union forces during the Civil War, he visited Henry Bessemer's plant in Sheffield and learned about his new process for making steel. Excited by what he saw, he returned to the United States, secured financial backing, purchased the U.S. patent rights, and then built a plant in Troy, New York, shrewdly adapting Bessemer's process to the demands of the American railroad market. He also negotiated an agreement with a group of entrepreneurs that controlled a potentially conflicting U.S. patent. The resulting Bessemer Association licensed a limited number of new steel plants, most of which Holley himself built, and profited handsomely as consumption of steel soared during the boom in railroad construction that followed the war (Temin 1964, 133–38; Misa 1995, 1–43).

Whether they were inspired by Holley's example, other similar success stories, or simply had sized up the opportunities on their own, business people displayed considerable eagerness to invest in patented technology during the late nineteenth and early twentieth centuries. Of course, like inventors, they too had to decide how to exploit the patents they obtained. Sometimes they bought patents with the idea of reselling them at a higher price or of profiting from the stream of licensing revenues. For example, Henry Tanner bought the rights to a patent for "double-acting" brakes and then resold it in 1855 to Thomas Sayles, who also secured rights to related patents with the idea of licensing this technology to the railroads (Usselman 2002, 108–11). Similarly, in 1905, a capitalist named Oliver offered an inventor $100,000 for the rights to a wireless radio receiver he intended to market to the U.S. government.[12] At other times, business people organized new companies to develop and commercialize the inventions they acquired. For example, the so-called Lynn syndicate, a group of Massachusetts shoe manufacturers seeking to profit from investments in new technology, provided the capital in 1883 for a company to exploit Elihu Thomson's inventions in electric lighting and power (Carlson 1991, 210–11). Still others kept their options open. For example, a group of Ohio capitalists contracted in 1890 with inventor Elmer Sperry to develop an electric streetcar, agreeing that if Sperry succeeded, they would either form a company to exploit his invention or handle the sale or licensing of the resulting patents (Hughes 1971, 70–73).

Regardless of the strategy they intended to pursue, business people seeking to invest in promising new technologies faced serious information problems if, unlike Holley, they lacked technical expertise. One solution was to back inventors such as Thomson and Sperry, who already had histories of significant technological achievement. Another, however, was to rely on experts to assess the merits of inventions being offered on the market. The patent examination system had fostered the rise of a new group of professional patent agents and lawyers, men who generally had as much or more technical training than they had legal expertise. Hence there was a large cadre of specialists to whom business people seeking such evaluations could easily turn.[13]

Because business people turned to these new professionals to assess the value of patents they thought they might buy, patent agents acquired firsthand information about who was interested in purchasing which types of inventions. At the same time, because inventors employed them to process their applications for patents, they were able to gain advance knowledge of technologies that would be coming on the market. They were thus in a unique position to match inventors who had patents to sell with business people likely to be interested in purchasing the rights and also to find investors for enterprises formed to commercialize promising inventions.[14] Indeed, from the very beginning they were involved in the commercial exploitation of new technology. Two of the nation's first patent agents, for example, helped to organize and promote the company formed to develop Samuel Morse's telegraph patents (Post 1976, 69–70).

By cultivating relations of trust with individuals on both sides of the market for technology, moreover, patent agents helped to resolve the information problems associated with this type of exchange. Inventors sometimes dealt repeatedly with the same patent agents, becoming comfortable enough to run ideas by them at an early stage to see whether they were likely to lead to anything valuable. Buyers also came to trust the judgment of agents they employed over and over and therefore required less information to be revealed than might otherwise have been the case. Of course, because patent agents stood to profit from the sale or licensing of patent rights, there was a risk that they would pursue their own interests at the expense of both patentees and assignees or licensees. For this reason, patent agents invested in building reputations for fair dealing, as well as for skill in assessing the value of patent rights. For example, Edward Van Winkle, a patent solicitor working in New York City in the early twentieth century, devoted a great part of each day to receiving visitors, calling on people, and meeting with inventors and businessmen over lunch or dinner, in this way cultivating personal relationships with people on both sides of the market for technology (Lamoreaux and Sokoloff 2003).[15]

In order to gain a quantitative sense of the role that patent agents and lawyers played in facilitating trade in patented technology, we collected information from the Patent Office's manuscript digests of assignments for all contracts filed during the first three months of 1871, 1891, and 1911 by patentees whose last names began with the letter *B*. We then classified each assignment contract (and the patents it included) by the identity of the person to whom all correspondence concerning the assignment was to be addressed. Working with lists of patent agents and lawyers from 1883 and 1905 (the only lists we have been able to locate), we distinguished correspondents who were formally registered with the Patent Office in at least one of these two years as a separate class of intermediaries. Correspondents who were principals to the contract were grouped together in a second category of intermediaries. A third category consisted of third parties who did not appear on either of the two lists of registered agents (some, of course, may have been agents registered in other years). A fourth category, "unknown," includes cases for which no correspondent was reported in the digest. Because some of the contracts in the sample covered more than one patent, we present the data with the unit of analysis defined in two different ways: the individual patent assigned and the complete assignment contract (with the descriptive statistics calculated on the basis of the first patent described in the contract).[16]

That the use of patent agents improved the functioning of the market for technology is suggested by table 10.3, which reports descriptive statistics (across both patents and contracts) for each of the correspondent classes for each year of the sample. The most striking trend in the table is the rising proportion of contracts handled by registered agents and the corresponding drop in the proportion handled by other third parties and especially by the principals themselves. By 1911, registered agents were acting as correspondents in 55.7 percent of the patents (58.1 percent of the contracts), third parties in 22.5 percent of the patents (19.2 percent of the contracts), and principals in only 11.2 percent of the patents (9.5 percent of the contracts). That the use of registered agents increased the efficiency of the market for technology is suggested by the disproportionate fraction of the assignments they handled that occurred before the patent was even issued. The gap was apparent as early as 1871, when 47 percent of patents

TABLE 10.3
Descriptive Statistics on Patent Assignments, by Correspondent Type, 1871–1911

		Registered Patent Agent	Patentee, Assignor, or Assignee	Unregistered Third Party	Unknown
1871					
% assigned before issue	patents	0.47	0.09	0.18	-
	contracts	0.61	0.08	0.23	-
% assigned to company	patents	0.28	0.24	0.20	0.66
	contracts	0.25	0.16	0.20	0.48
% secondary assignments	patents	0.35	0.33	0.32	0.85
	contracts	0.20	0.31	0.30	0.80
% national assignment	patents	0.89	0.53	0.71	-
	contracts	0.89	0.51	0.70	-
Number	patents	114	144	126	53
	contracts	85	98	82	21
Row percentage	patents	26.1	33.0	28.8	12.1
	contracts	29.7	33.9	29.4	7.0
1891					
% assigned before issue	patents	0.44	0.15	0.32	0.24
	contracts	0.52	0.18	0.40	0.37
% assigned to company	patents	0.39	0.28	0.48	0.68
	contracts	0.41	0.27	0.45	0.52
% secondary assignments	patents	0.20	0.31	0.37	0.81
	contracts	0.13	0.25	0.23	0.78
% national assignment	patents	0.91	0.78	0.86	-
	contracts	0.94	0.72	0.78	-
Number	patents	366	188	235	69
	contracts	219	89	88	27
Row percentage	patents	42.7	21.9	27.4	8.0
	contracts	51.8	21.0	20.8	6.4
1911					
% assigned before issue	patents	0.70	0.15	0.32	-
	contracts	0.72	0.18	0.41	-
% assigned to company	patents	0.61	0.55	0.46	-
	contracts	0.57	0.51	0.52	-
% secondary assignments	patents	0.15	0.28	0.31	-
	contracts	0.09	0.24	0.21	-
% national assignment	patents	0.97	0.69	0.89	-
	contracts	0.97	0.69	0.92	-
1911					
Number	patents	467	94	189	89
	contracts	337	55	112	77
Row percentage	patents	55.7	11.2	22.5	10.6
	contracts	58.1	9.5	19.2	13.2

(61 percent of contracts) assigned using registered agents occurred before issue, as opposed to 9 percent of patents (8 percent of contracts) of those where the correspondents were principals to the transaction. At that time, the average interval between application for and grant of a patent was very short—less than half a year. The high proportion of assignments handled by registered agents that nonetheless occurred before issue is consistent with the idea that these specialists were performing a matching function, bringing sellers and buyers of patents together before much public information about the inventions was available.

If these kinds of intermediaries did indeed offer advantages in trading patent rights, one would expect that the inventors who employed them would be those who were both more specialized at inventive activity and more inclined to extract the returns to their inventions by selling off their patent rights. In order to test this proposition, we retrieved, for each of the assigned patents in our sample, a five-year history of all patents obtained by the respective patentees (including information on whether the patent was assigned at issue), using the year the assigned patent was granted as the middle year. As table 10.4 shows, over time a clear difference emerged between patentees whose assignments were mediated by registered agents and those handled by other third parties or by the principals themselves. By 1911, the five-year patent totals for patentees who

---

Sources and notes: The data were collected from the Digests of Assignment Contracts, Record Group 241, Records of the Patent and Trademark Office, National Archives. Our data set includes information on all assignments made by patentees whose last name began with the letter *B* for the months of January through March, 1871, 1891, and 1911. Because some contracts involved the sale or transfer of more than one patent, and some encompassed multiple transfers of the same patent, we report one set of figures computed over all patents assigned and another set computed over all contracts. We categorized each patent and contract by the identity of the person to whom all correspondence about the assignments was to be addressed. Working with lists of patent agents and lawyers registered to practice before the Patent Office from 1883 and 1905, we distinguished correspondents who were formally registered in at least one of these two years as a separate class of intermediaries. Correspondents who were principals to the contract (either the patentee, the assignor, or the assignee of one of the patents involved) were grouped together in a second category of intermediaries. A third category consisted of third parties who did not appear on either of the two lists of registered agents that we relied upon and were not principles. It seems likely, however, that we would have been able to identify some of these correspondents as registered agents if we had rosters for additional years. Finally, we include an "unknown" category that is primarily comprised of cases where multiple patents were assigned together and where the details of the contract were summarized in the record of another patentee whose family name began with a letter other than B, and thus was in another Digest volume.

TABLE 10.4
Average Number of Patents and Assignments over Five-Year Period, by Correspondent Type, 1871–1911

		Registered Patent Agent	Patentee, Assignor, or Assignee	Unregistered Third Party	Unknown
1871					
Five-year total	patents	3.90	3.73	3.35	4.69
of patents	contracts	2.45	3.10	3.27	3.05
Number assigned	patents	1.47	0.88	0.80	0.88
at issue	contracts	1.08	0.64	0.88	0.70
1891					
Five-year total	patents	6.61	3.65	5.80	5.45
of patents	contracts	4.90	3.43	5.17	3.00
Number assigned	patents	4.29	1.10	3.50	3.65
at issue	contracts	3.39	1.27	3.43	1.74
1911					
Five-year total	patents	6.92	2.28	3.76	2.96
of patents	contracts	4.99	2.45	4.04	3.13
Number assigned	patents	5.97	0.69	2.66	2.49
at issue	contracts	4.21	0.84	3.11	2.64

Sources and notes: See table 10.3. For every patent in our sample of assignments, we compiled, using the *Annual Reports of the Commissioner of Patents*, a five-year record of all of the patents received by the inventor, using the year of the assigned patent as the central year. From this record, we computed the total number of patents the inventor received over the five years and the total number of these patents that he assigned at issue.

used registered agents averaged 6.92 weighted over patents (4.99 over contracts), compared to 3.76 (4.04) patents for those who used unregistered third parties, and 2.28 (2.45) for inventors whose assignments were handled by the principals themselves. Patentees who used registered agents also, on average, assigned higher proportions of their patents at issue: 86.3 (84.4) percent of the patents they received during the period, as opposed to 70.7 (77.0) percent for those who used unregistered third parties and 30.3 (34.3) for those who relied on principals. These results provide further confirmation that the development of a market for technology allowed creative individuals to shift to others the task of commercializing their inventions and to concentrate their energies and resources on coming up with new technological ideas.

Firms and the Market for Technology

Whether or not there was extensive trade in patented technology also depended on the behavior of firms—whether they acted in ways that encouraged inventors to submit ideas to them (Gans and Stern 2003). Anecdotal evidence suggests that inventors who revealed too much information to potential buyers sometimes did get burned. For example, Jacob D. Cox, founder of the Cleveland Twist Drill Company, traveled to Cincinnati in 1893 to examine a socket for twist drills invented and patented by a Mr. Andrew. Cox concluded that the invention had merit but that Andrew's $10,000 asking price was too steep. He then "devised a grip socket different from Andrew's, and in most respects superior to it" and applied for a patent himself (Cox 1951, 143–44).[17] This incident, however, did not prevent subsequent inventors from demonstrating their devices to Cox—sometimes to good effect. After a man named Morse demonstrated an optical pyrometer (a type of heat gauge) he had invented, Cox "saw at once what a tremendous help it could be to us in attaining uniform quality, and what an advantage we might gain over our competitors if we could acquire exclusive rights to his invention" and purchased the rights to the patent for the manufacture of twist drills (Cox 1951, 172–73).

Inventors certainly had to worry that the manufacturers to whom they demonstrated their devices might appropriate their ideas in some way, but some firms went to great lengths to cultivate a reputation for fair dealing.[18] For example, Robert Harris, chief operating officer of the Burlington and Quincy Railroad, sought to be known as a friend of inventors. Not only did he seriously investigate the merits of their devices for possible use by the Burlington and Quincy, but he helped inventors to publicize their inventions and advised them on how best to promote their ideas (Usselman 2002, 69, 107, 123–24). Similarly, executives at Western Union encouraged inventors to bring them their inventions, financing work on those they thought promising in exchange for assignments of the patents. After Elisha Gray (later one of the founders of what became Western Electric) demonstrated his invention of a self-adjusting telegraph relay before Western Union president Jeptha Wade and other company officers, Wade offered Gray work space and resources in one of the company's shops and access to its lines for testing purposes. When the company could not use an idea that otherwise had merit, Western Union executives sometimes tried to match the inventor with another firm that could. For example, in the early 1870s Western Union had no use for the typewriter invented by C. Latham Sholes and Carlos Glidden, but Vice President Anson Stager put the inventors in contact with Western Electric officers, who in turn arranged for the product to be manufactured by E. Remington & Sons, a manufacturer of rifles that then had considerable excess capacity (Adams and Butler 1999,

14–44). Similarly, it was Western Union executives who took the lead in putting together funding for Thomas Edison's experiments in incandescent lighting (the company had earlier financed exploitation of Edison's telegraph patents) and also the resulting Edison Electric Light Company in 1878 (Taylor 1978, 32–33; Lamoreaux and Sokoloff 2003, 245).

In the intensely competitive environment of the late nineteenth century, firms cultivated good relations with inventors because their survival depended on staying on the technological cutting edge (Baumol 2002). Firms could not afford to be foreclosed from promising new technologies by rivals' control of critical patents, so they were compelled to keep abreast of developments occurring elsewhere in the economy and purchase or license the rights to technologies that might prove important to their businesses. Of course, many firms that were formed to exploit promising new inventions often had technically trained people in ownership positions or on staff who continued to make (and patent) inventions and improvements. But even the largest enterprises of the time were reluctant to put too much weight on internal R&D (Lamoreaux and Sokoloff 1999c). Western Union, for example, sometimes financed the development of new technology in-house, but its managers seem not to have been convinced that this was the best strategy for staying on the cutting edge in a time of rapid technological change, and they frequently spun these enterprises off into separate companies.[19] Lest the reader think that Western Union was particularly backward in this respect and that this policy explains why AT&T succeeded at its expense, we hasten to note that AT&T's position at this time was even more extreme. As T. D. Lockwood, head of the company's patent department, explained: "I am fully convinced that it has never, is not now, and never will pay commercially, to keep an establishment of professional inventors, or of men whose chief business it is to invent."[20] Instead of in-house R&D, AT&T invested in building the capability to track and assess inventions generated in the external world. More generally, as David Mowery has argued, one of the most important functions of firms' early research facilities was to evaluate outside technologies (Mowery 1995).

The Decline of the Market for Technology

Although these kinds of investments in tracking capabilities facilitated trade in patents, the high stakes involved also stimulated investment in efforts to limit the market's scope. Firms operating in industries characterized by rapid technological change might benefit from securing property rights to promising new innovations, but they had to worry about being shut out from this technology if rights to crucial patents were obtained by others. Moreover, firms that operated costly complex equipment might find that patent holders who controlled the rights to different parts of their machinery could hold them up. The railroads, for example, faced these problems in installing self-acting brakes. The patent office had granted three different patents on these devices, and even when railroads purchased the rights to one or another of these patents they found themselves threatened with infringement suits unless they purchased licenses for the others as well.[21]

The railroads responded to these and other similar threats by banding together in associations that assumed responsibility for negotiating with individual patent holders on behalf of all the railroads, thus preventing the railroads from being played off against each other (Usselman 2002, 114–15, 171–75). Likewise, in the automobile industry during the early twentieth century, firms attempted to reduce the power of patent holders by organizing the Automobile Manufacturers' Association, which cross-licensed to all of its members patents obtained by any one of them (U.S. TNEC 1938, 134). Although similar organizations were formed in a few other industries, it is important not to overestimate their role in reducing the scope and importance of the market for technology. To the contrary, the record suggests that such agreements tended not to last very long. Certainly, the railroads' willingness to participate in patent associations declined precipitously after they won an important Supreme Court victory in the brake cases (Usselman 2002, 174–76). Similarly, the automobile pool atrophied as manufacturers gradually reduced the scope of their agreement so that the new technologies that they developed no longer came under its provisions (U.S. TNEC 1938, 134–35).

The main way in which firms extended their control over the process of technological change was to increase the amount of R&D they performed in-house (Baumol 2002). In this endeavor, however, they faced many difficulties. Talented inventors had a lot of clout in the market for technology; they might be hired, but they could not easily be controlled. George Westinghouse learned this lesson when he contracted with William Stanley to develop a transformer in-house. To Westinghouse's chagrin, Stanley claimed that a related discovery he made while working for the firm was his own property (Wise 1985, 70–71). Lesser inventors could be similarly unreliable. When they came up with a valuable idea, they often quit and attempted to exploit the invention on their own. For example, after two employees of the American Sheet and Tin Plate Company invented a catcher for tinning machines, building the device on company time with company resources and testing it in one of the company's plants, they resigned and contracted with a competitor to develop and commercialize the invention (Lamoreaux and Sokoloff 1999c).[22]

Nonetheless, by the early twentieth century inventors seem to have become increasingly willing to form long-term attachments with firms.

TABLE 10.5
Distribution of Patents by Assignee Type and Career Patents

	Categories of Patentees by Career Patents			
	1–2 Patents (Col. %)	3–5 Patents (Col. %)	6–9 Patents (Col. %)	10+ Patents (Col. %)
Not assigned				
1870–71 cohort	82.4	88.6	87.7	75.3
1890–91 cohort	72.9	70.5	60.6	45.6
1910–11 cohort	85.0	78.1	57.5	39.3
Assigned share to individual				
1870–71 cohort	10.3	3.6	4.1	5.5
1890–91 cohort	10.0	11.6	12.8	3.9
1910–11 cohort	7.5	6.5	5.8	2.8
Assigned in full to individual				
1870–71 cohort	2.9	5.0	2.5	8.8
1890–91 cohort	2.9	8.5	6.4	9.6
1910–11 cohort	1.5	3.2	1.7	3.2
Assigned to company with same name				
1870–71 cohort	0.0	0.0	0.0	1.7
1890-91 cohort	0.0	1.6	3.7	6.1
1910–11 cohort	0.0	0.0	5.8	24.6
Assigned to large integrated company				
1870–71 cohort	0.0	0.0	0.8	1.2
1890–91 cohort	1.4	0.0	0.5	9.9
1910–11 cohort	0.0	1.9	0.0	14.8
Assigned to other local company				
1870–71 cohort	1.5	0.7	2.5	4.5
1890–91 cohort	10.0	3.9	5.3	15.9
1910–11 cohort	1.5	3.9	15.8	8.4
Assigned to other company				
1870–71 cohort	2.9	2.1	2.5	2.9
1890–91 cohort	4.3	3.9	10.6	9.0
1910–11 cohort	3.9	6.5	13.3	7.0
Number of patents				
1870–71 cohort	*68*	*140*	*122*	*749*
1890–91 cohort	*80*	*129*	*188*	*2060*
1910–11 cohort	*133*	*155*	*120*	*1777*

TABLE 10.5
(*Continued*)

Sources and notes: See table 10.1 for a description of the *B* sample. These estimates were based on all patents obtained by patentees in the sample who were U.S. residents and who obtained 10 or more patents during their careers. Companies to whom the patentees assigned their inventions were classified as follows: We first checked to see whether the assignee was a company with the same name as the patentee. If not, we classified as "large integrated companies" all assignees for which financial information was reported in the *Commercial and Financial Chronicle* or in *Poor's* or *Moody's Manual of Industrial Securities* (indicating that the company was important enough to tap the national capital markets) or, alternatively, that were listed in an early-1920s National Research Council directory of companies with research laboratories. The remaining companies were divided into two groups: "other local companies," if the assignee was located in the same city as the patentee; and "other companies" for all the rest.

This change can be seen by looking more closely at the assignment behavior of patentees in the *B* sample. Table 10.5 divides the inventors into three different cohorts (according to the cross-sectional sample from which they were originally drawn) and also by the number of patents they obtained over their careers.[23] It then categorizes each of their patents according to whether or not it was assigned at issue, whether the assignment was in whole or part to an individual, or whether it was to a company. Assignments to companies were classified in the following way. We first checked to see whether the assignee was a company with the same name as the patentee (indicating that the inventor was likely a principal in the firm). If not, we classified as "large integrated companies" all assignees for which financial information was reported in the *Commercial and Financial Chronicle* or in *Poor's* or *Moody's Manual of Industrial Securities* (indicating that the company was important enough to tap the national capital markets) or, alternatively, that were listed in an early-1920s National Research Council directory of companies with research laboratories. The remaining companies were divided into two groups: "other local companies," if the firm was located in the same city as the patentee; and "other companies" for all the rest.

As table 10.5 indicates, by the third cohort, inventors with 10 or more career patents assigned at issue more than 60 percent of all the patents they were awarded, up from only 25 percent for the first cohort. Of the patents assigned by these productive patentees, nearly two-thirds went either to enterprises that bore their names or to large integrated firms, about 25 percent to other companies, and less than 10 percent to individuals. In stark contrast, between the second and third cohorts, assignment rates actually fell for the least productive categories of patentees. Inventors in the third cohort who had only 1 or 2 career patents, for example, assigned at issue only 15 percent of their patents, with nearly two-thirds of those going to individuals and none to firms in the first two categories. This differentiation in experience across classes of inventors developed over time, but the most dramatic changes occurred between the 1890–91 and 1910–11 cohorts. It was during this interval, moreover, that large integrated companies and companies named after inventors became dominant in the market for patented inventions: more than 32 percent of all of the patents ever awarded to the inventors in the 1910–11 cohort were assigned at issue to firms in these two categories.

One possible source of this change was the growing capital intensity of technology, which, by raising the amount of investment required to engage in inventive activity, may have made it more difficult for inventors to pursue independent careers. In order to explore the possibility that inventors increasingly associated themselves with firms because they found it difficult otherwise to keep inventing, we examine the assignment behavior of the most productive of the *B* patentees at different points in their careers. For each cohort, we present in table 10.6 the distribution of patents awarded to inventors with 10 or more career patents by the stage of the inventor's career (indicated by years since his first patent) and the type of assignment. For all three cohorts, there is evidence that patentees on average were better able to transfer their property rights later in their careers than early on. The proportion of their patents that were not assigned at issue fell with the passage of years, as did the proportion of those assigned in which they maintained an interest. What is most striking about the evidence in the table, however, is the disproportionate extent to which assignments to companies bearing the inventor's name occurred during the later phases of patentees' careers. For the last cohort, only 1.3 percent of the patents obtained by inventors in the first five years of their careers went to companies that bore the patentee's name. During the next 10 years of their careers the figure increased to 17.1 percent and, after 15 years had elapsed, to 35.4 percent. There was a similar, though less pronounced, pattern in assignments to large integrated companies. Productivity at patenting, moreover, was becoming increasingly skewed toward the later stages of inventors' careers. For the first cohort, numbers of patents obtained were on average distributed fairly evenly over the three stages of the patentees' careers. By the third cohort, however, inventors received on average only 17 percent of their patents during the first five years of their careers and only 27 over the next 10 years.

In combination, these patterns suggest that, by the early twentieth century, technologically creative people had to prove themselves by obtaining a noteworthy patent before they could really establish themselves as inventors worthy of substantial financial support. Even then, however, it was increasingly difficult to pursue an independent career. A good example is Charles J. Van Depoele, who developed an electrical motive system

TABLE 10.6
Distribution of Patents by Assignee Type and Stage of Career

	Stage of Career		
	≤5 Years since First Patent (Col. %)	>5 Years and ≤15 Years since First Patent (Col. %)	>15 Years since First Patent (Col. %)
Not assigned			
1870-71 cohort	81.9	75.3	68.9
1890-91 cohort	62.0	52.7	36.6
1910-11 cohort	45.6	50.3	32.1
Assigned share to individual			
1870-71 cohort	6.2	6.7	3.6
1890-91 cohort	4.0	5.4	3.0
1910-11 cohort	6.9	4.0	0.9
Assigned in full to individual			
1870-71 cohort	4.1	11.4	10.8
1890-91 cohort	12.1	11.1	8.0
1910-11 cohort	7.2	3.1	1.9
Assigned to company with same name			
1870-71 cohort	0.4	0.0	4.8
1890-91 cohort	2.2	4.2	8.4
1910-11 cohort	1.3	17.1	35.4
Assigned to large integrated company			
1870-71 cohort	0.0	0.0	0.0
1890-91 cohort	7.1	6.3	12.9
1910-11 cohort	12.1	7.3	19.2
Assigned to other Local company			
1870-71 cohort	6.6	3.1	7.6
1890-91 cohort	8.4	15.1	18.6
1910-11 cohort	17.1	11.7	4.1
Assigned to other company			
1870-71 cohort	0.8	3.5	4.4
1890-91 cohort	4.3	5.4	12.6
1910-11 cohort	9.8	6.5	6.3
Number of patents			
1870-71 cohort	*243*	*255*	*251*
1890-91 cohort	*323*	*651*	*1086*
1910-11 cohort	*305*	*479*	*993*

Sources and notes: See tables 10.1 and 10.5.

for trolleys. After nearly a decade of striving unsuccessfully to raise the capital he needed to exploit his discovery and continue his inventive work, he gave up trying and in 1888 took a position with the Thomson-Houston Electric Company, the predecessor of General Electric. In exchange for assignments of all of his past and future patents, he obtained an annual salary of $5,000, plus a royalty of $5 for each car on which the company used his patents.[24] Others were more successful in securing financial backing to form their own firms, often with the assistance of patent agents and the venture capitalists who were associated with them. For example, New York solicitor Edward Van Winkle promoted two such companies in 1905, the Simplex Machine Company and the Automatic Security Signal Company, to exploit devices patented by inventor William M. Murphy (Lamoreaux and Sokoloff 2003). Sometimes, however, inventors first had to work for a stint in a large firm in order to build the reputation they needed to attract financial backers. Before forming his own steel company, Samuel Wellman established himself as a leader in open-hearth technology through his position as chief engineer for Otis Steel (Sicilia 1989). The Brush Electric Company spawned a whole series of spin-offs, each organized around an inventor who had gotten his start, and established his prowess at invention, in the company's shops (Lamoreaux, Levenstein, and Sokoloff 2006).[25]

Implications

The movement of inventive activity inside firms coincided with the end of the long, nineteenth-century rise in patenting rates per capita and the beginning of a downward trend that would persist for most of the twentieth century (see fig. 10.1). Of course, the drop in patenting rates does not necessarily imply a slowdown in the pace of technological change. It is possible that large firms may have directed the intellectual resources under their control toward systematically working out technological details in ways that were not patentable but that substantially improved productivity. Certainly, the rise of in-house R&D was associated in time with substantial rates of growth in total factor productivity (Kendrick 1961).[26] It is also possible that firms that developed new technology in-house chose to rely less on patenting and more on trade secrets to protect their intellectual property.[27]

The most we can say, therefore, is that the decline in patenting rates demarcated a significant transformation in the way technological change was organized in the U.S. economy—from a division of labor between invention and commercialization that operated primarily across firms to a division of labor that occurred to a much greater degree within firms.

To the extent, however, that this change resulted in less reliance by firms on patents as way of protecting their intellectual property, it is likely that it had important implications for the transmission of technological knowledge. Obviously, the whole point of relying on a strategy of trade secrets is to block the flow of information beyond the firm. Technology that is patented, by contrast, is at least in formal terms public knowledge. Moreover, to the extent that transactions such as licensing play an ongoing role in the transfer of technological knowledge (Baumol 2002), the magnitude and importance of the effect is dependent on the base of inventions that are patented and therefore licensable.

In recent years there has been a revival of patenting rates and also of trade in patented technology. It is beyond the scope of this chapter to analyze the causes of this reversal, but the change appears to have had some relation to the emergence of venture capital institutions capable of tapping novel sources of finance in support of small innovative companies. In addition, it seems to have been associated with a shift in strategy on the part of large firms, which have curtailed their investments in in-house R&D in favor of devoting greater resources to tracking, and acquiring the rights to, technologies developed outside their bounds (Kortum and Lerner 2000; Arora, Fosfuri, and Gambardella 2001). In other words, in recent years the organization of invention has shifted back toward its nineteenth-century form. Intriguingly, there is growing consensus that the result has been a palpable increase in the technological dynamism of the American economy, so that in this way too, present-day performance is more like that of the "golden era of the independent inventor."[28]

Notes

1. Although the division of labor we posit between invention and commercialization is in some ways similar to Joseph Schumpeter's distinction between invention and innovation, we reject his denigration of the role of the inventor (Schumpeter 1934). We find that inventors could be as entrepreneurial—as intent on the pursuit of wealth—as those who commercialized their inventions. Our view is similar to that of Jacob Schmookler, who argued that "invention is largely an economic activity which, like other economic activities, is pursued for gain" (1966, 206).

2. This clause seems to have been noncontroversial. The subject was not discussed during the convention, and the issue was not raised during the debates in the states over ratification ("Outline" 1936, 55–58).

3. The term was increased to 17 years in 1861.

4. Noninventors could receive patents in Britain if they were the first to introduce a technology to the country. There is also evidence that employers were able to patent devices invented by employees (MacLeod 1999). In the United States, by contrast, the first-to-invent rule was so rigorously enforced by the courts that

even slave owners were prevented from patenting their slaves' inventions (Khan and Sokoloff 2004).

5. During the 1850s, for example, the Patent Office helped to support *Scientific American* and several other publications by publishing petitions for the extension of patent rights on the advertising pages of these journals (Borut 1977, 143).

6. The first (1790) patent act set up an examination system under which inventors submitted applications to a commission, consisting of the U.S. secretaries of state and war and the attorney general, who would award patents to inventions that were "sufficiently useful and important" and that otherwise conformed to the law. The members of the commission did not have adequate time to devote to scrutinizing patent applications, however, and the resulting delays led Congress to institute a registration system in 1793 ("Outline" 1936).

7. According to Borut (1977), the high proportion of applications rejected during the late 1840s and early 1850s was a result of novice inventors attempting to file applications on their own. Once inventors started filing through patent agents, who specialized in researching prior art and interviewing examiners, the rejection rate fell dramatically.

8. Unfortunately, it is not possible to calculate the proportion of patents that were ever assigned because it would be prohibitively expensive to track assignments subsequent to issue through the "liber" volumes of recorded assignment contracts stored at the National Archives, Record Group 241 (Records of the Patent and Trademark Office). On the ratio of patents to assignments and the relative decline in geographically specific sales of patent rights, see Lamoreaux and Sokoloff 1999c and Khan and Sokoloff 2004.

9. Of course, patentees could still follow a dual strategy at least to some extent. For example, they could exploit their technology domestically and license foreign rights to other producers. Or, if their invention had value in several different industries, they could exploit their invention themselves in one industry and license the rights to producers in the other industries.

10. For further discussion and analysis of these samples, see Lamoreaux and Sokoloff 1999a, 1999b, and 2003.

11. The following discussion is based on Hughes 1971.

12. Diary entry, May 20, 1905, Edward Van Winkle Papers, Ac. 669, Rutgers University Libraries Special Collections. For more on this transaction and others involving Oliver, see Lamoreaux and Sokoloff 2003.

13. The following discussion of patent agents as intermediaries draws on Lamoreaux and Sokoloff 1999a and 2003. Although there was some differentiation of function between agents and lawyers, the two types of professionals are difficult to distinguish in this era when barriers to entry into the legal profession were low, and so we use terms interchangeably. The first patent agents established their offices in Washington, where they could have frequent contact with examiners in the Patent Office. Very quickly, however, they spread throughout the country, locating especially in areas like southeastern New England where there were already significant numbers of inventors.

14. Many agents developed correspondent relationships with patent solicitors located in Washington and in other major cities. Relationships with agents in Washington allowed those far away to have a representative on the spot who

could check records in the Patent Office for relevant prior art and also get first-hand advice from examiners about the sustainability of patent claims. Relationships with agents in other cities gave them access to information about both the supply of, and demand for, inventions in different parts of the country (Lamoreaux and Sokoloff 2003).

15. For a more formal analysis of an analogous type of intermediary, see Wolinsky 1993. The important role that intermediaries can play in facilitating the market for technology is discussed in Gans and Stern 2003.

16. For further description and analysis of the data, see Lamoreaux and Sokoloff 2003. The following discussion is drawn from that article.

17. The story has an interesting twist because Andrew learned about Cox's invention before the patent was awarded and himself applied for a new patent on the same device, "claiming priority of invention." The result was a long legal battle that Cox ultimately won (Cox 1951, 143–44).

18. Moreover, producers of machine tools had, from early in the century, developed a code of honor that enabled them to share technological knowledge and benefit from each other's expertise without fear that their ideas would be stolen (Wallace 1972, 211–39).

19. For example, Western Union financed the consolidation of the innovative partnership of Gray and Barton with its own machine shop, but the resulting enterprise, Western Electric, operated as an independent firm. When Elisha Gray began work on his harmonic telegraph (essentially the telephone), he resigned his position as superintendent of Western Electric but continued to work in its facilities as an independent inventor (Adams and Butler 1999, 29–38).

20. Lockwood did hire inventors from time to time but successfully opposed any sustained investment in in-house R&D. Not until Theodore N. Vail became president of the company in 1907 was this policy reversed. See Lloyd Espenschied, "Early Company Inventing—a Revealing Letter," Western Electric Collection, location 91 05 140, folder 6; "Memorandum of Messrs. Root, Ballantine, Harlan, Bushby & Palmer," November 22, 1949, pp. 30, 68, Divestiture Collection, location 451 01 01, folder 17; and T. D. Lockwood, "Duties of Patent Department," November 23, 1885, AT&T Collection, box 1302, AT&T Corporate Archives. See also Galambos 1992.

21. These suits led to a complicated and expensive litigation that dragged on for years and resulted in important changes in the extent to which businesses like the railroads were exposed to infringement proceedings (Usselman 2002, 108–13, 168–71).

22. At that time, the courts generally refused to give firms more than shop rights to technology developed by their employees in the absence of express agreements assigning the resulting patents to the company. Employees were reluctant to sign such agreements, which did not become standard until at least the 1920s. See Lamoreaux and Sokoloff 1999c; and Fisk 1998.

23. For a more complete analysis of this and the following table, see Lamoreaux and Sokoloff 2005.

24. See the folder labeled "Business Papers—Agreements, etc. 1877–89," Charles J. Van Depoele, 1877–92, MSS 867, Unbound Papers, Baker Library, Harvard Business School. See also Carlson 1991, 216.

25. This pattern of spin-offs may explain why, by the third cohort, productive inventors assigned so many patents to large companies during the early years of their careers (see table 10.6). In many of these startups, the inventor was given the title of vice president and allowed to continue to focus his energies on developing his inventions and generating new technology. The facilities in which these inventors worked often grew into R&D labs (Lamoreaux, Levenstein, and Sokoloff 2006).

26. It is doubtful that the drop in patenting rates resulted to any great extent from a decline in the propensity to patent low-quality inventions. In the first place, the drop was associated with an increase in the proportion of inventions obtained by patentees with relatively few career patents—that is, by a relative shift toward those less likely to produce high-value inventions. Second, there is evidence that the movement of inventive activity inside firms may actually have increased the tendency to patent low-quality inventions, as firms attempted to solve the agency problems they now faced by patenting all of their employees' ideas and by offering bonuses and promotions as rewards for patents (Lamoreaux and Sokoloff 1999c).

27. Developments in both the case law and in statutory law made trade secrets an increasingly viable form of protection by the early twentieth century (Fisk 2001).

28. The phrase is from Hughes 1989, 15.

References

Adams, Stephen B., and Orville B. Butler. 1999. *Manufacturing the Future: A History of Western Electric*. New York: Cambridge University Press.

Arora, Ashish. 1995. "Licensing Tacit Knowledge: Intellectual Property Rights and the Market for Know-How." *Economics of Innovation and New Technology* 4 (1): 41–59.

Arora, Ashish, Andrea Fosfuri, and Alfonso Gambardella. 2001. *Markets for Technology: The Economics of Innovation and Corporate Strategy*. Cambridge: MIT Press.

Arrow, Kenneth J. 1962. "Economic Welfare and the Allocation of Resources for Invention." In Universities–National Bureau Committee for Economic Research and the Committee on Economic Growth of the Social Science Research Council, *The Rate and Direction of Inventive Activity: Economic and Social Factors*. Princeton: Princeton University Press.

Baumol, William J. 2002. *The Free-Market Innovation Machine: Analyzing the Growth Miracle of Capitalism*. Princeton: Princeton University Press.

Borut, Michael. 1977. "The *Scientific American* in Nineteenth Century America." Ph.D. diss., New York University.

Carlson, W. Bernard. 1991. *Innovation as a Social Process: Elihu Thomson and the Rise of General Electric, 1870–1900*. New York: Cambridge University Press.

Cooper, Carolyn C. 1991. *Shaping Invention: Thomas Blanchard's Machinery and Patent Management in Nineteenth-Century America*. New York: Columbia University Press.

Cox, Jacob Dolson, Sr. 1951. *Building an American Industry: The Story of the Cleveland Twist Drill Company and Its Founder*. Cleveland: Cleveland Twist Drill Co.

Dutton, H. I. 1984. *The Patent System and Inventive Activity during the Industrial Revolution, 1750–1852*. Dover, N.H.: Manchester University Press.

Fisk, Catherine L. 1998. "Removing the 'Fuel of Interest' from the 'Fire of Genius': Law and the Employee-Inventor, 1830–1930." *University of Chicago Law Review* 65 (Fall): 1127–98.

———. 2001. "Working Knowledge: Trade Secrets, Restrictive Covenants in Employment, and the Rise of Corporate Intellectual Property, 1800–1920." *Hastings Law Journal* 52 (January): 441–535.

Galambos, Louis. 1992. "Theodore N. Vail and the Role of Innovation in the Modern Bell System." *Business History Review* 66 (Spring): 95–126.

Gans, Joshua, and Scott Stern. 2003. "The Product Market and the Market for 'Ideas': Commercialization Strategies for Technology Entrepreneurs." *Research Policy* 32 (February): 333–50.

Hughes, Thomas Parke. 1971. *Elmer Sperry: Inventor and Engineer*. Baltimore: Johns Hopkins Press.

———. 1989. *American Genesis: A Century of Invention and Technological Enthusiasm*. New York: Viking.

Kendrick, John W. 1961. *Productivity Trends in the United States*. Princeton: Princeton University Press.

Khan, B. Zorina. 1995. "Property Rights and Patent Litigation in Early Nineteenth-Century America." *Journal of Economic History* 55 (March): 58–97.

Khan, B. Zorina, and Kenneth L. Sokoloff. 1998. "Patent Institutions, Industrial Organization, and Early Technological Change: Britain and the United States, 1790–1850." In *Technological Revolutions in Europe: Historical Perspectives*, ed. Maxine Berg and Kristine Bruland. Cheltenham: Edward Elgar.

———. 2004. "Institutions and Democratic Invention in Nineteenth-Century America." *American Economic Review Papers and Proceedings* 94:395–401.

Kortum, Samuel, and Josh Lerner. 2000. "Assessing the Contribution of Venture Capital to Innovation." *Rand Journal of Economics* 31 (Winter): 674–92.

Lamoreaux, Naomi R., Margaret Levenstein, and Kenneth L. Sokoloff. 2006. "Financing Invention during the Second Industrial Revolution: Cleveland, 1890–1920." In Naomi Lamoreaux and Kenneth L. Sokoloff, eds. *Financing Innovation in the United States, 1870 to the Present*. Cambridge, MA: MIT Press, forthcoming.

Lamoreaux, Naomi R., and Kenneth L. Sokoloff. 1996. "Long-Term Change in the Organization of Inventive Activity." *Proceedings of the National Academy of Sciences* 93 (November): 12686–92.

———. 1999a. "The Geography of the Market for Technology in the Late-Nineteenth- and Early-Twentieth Century United States." In *Advances in the Study of Entrepreneurship, Innovation, and Economic Growth*, vol. 11, ed. Gary D. Libecap. Greenwich, Conn.: JAI Press.

———. 1999b. "Inventive Activity and the Market for Technology in the United States, 1840–1920." NBER Working Paper No. 7107.

———. 1999c. "Inventors, Firms, and the Market for Technology in the Late Nineteenth and Early Twentieth Centuries." In *Learning by Doing in Markets, Firms, and Countries*, ed. Naomi R. Lamoreaux, Daniel M. G. Raff, and Peter Temin. Chicago: University of Chicago Press.

———. 2003. "Intermediaries in the U.S. Market for Technology, 1870–1920." In *Finance, Intermediaries, and Economic Development*, ed. Stanley L. Engerman et al. New York: Cambridge University Press.

———. 2005. "The Decline of the Independent Inventor: A Schumpeterian Story?" NBER Working Paper No. W1654. Cambridge, MA: National Bureau of Economic Research, September.

MacLeod, Christine. 1988. *Inventing the Industrial Revolution: The English Patent System, 1660–1800*. Cambridge: Cambridge University Press.

———. 1999. "Negotiating the Rewards of Invention: The Shop-Floor Inventor in Victorian Britain." *Business History* 41 (April): 17–36.

Misa, Thomas J. 1995. *A Nation of Steel: The Making of Modern America, 1865–1925*. Baltimore: Johns Hopkins University Press.

Mowery, David C. 1983. "The Relationship between Intrafirm and Contractual Forms of Industrial Research in American Manufacturing, 1900–1940." *Explorations in Economic History* 20 (October): 351–74.

———. 1995. "The Boundaries of the U.S. Firm in R&D." In *Coordination and Information: Historical Perspectives on the Organization of Enterprise*, ed. Naomi R. Lamoreaux and Daniel M. G. Raff. Chicago: University of Chicago Press.

Ordover, Janusz A. 1991. "A Patent System for Both Exclusion and Diffusion." *Journal of Economic Perspectives* 5 (Winter): 43–60.

"Outline of the History of the United States Patent Office." 1936. *Journal of the Patent Office Society* 18 (July).

Post, Robert C. 1976. *Physics, Patents, and Politics: A Biography of Charles Grafton Page*. New York: Science History Publications.

Schmookler, Jacob. 1966. *Invention and Economic Growth*. Cambridge: Harvard University Press.

Schumpeter, Joseph A. 1934. *The Theory of Economic Development: An Inquiry into Profits, Capital, Credit, Interest, and the Business Cycle*. Trans. Redvers Opie. Cambridge: Harvard University Press.

Scotchmer, Suzanne, and Jerry Green. 1990. "Novelty and Disclosure in Patent Law." *Rand Journal of Economics* 21 (Spring): 131–46.

Sicilia, David B. 1989. "Samuel Thomas Wellman." In *Iron and Steel in the Nineteenth Century*, ed. Paul F. Paskoff. New York: Facts on File.

Taylor, Jocelyn Pierson. 1978. *Mr. Edison's Lawyer: Launching the Electric Light*. New York: Topp-Litho.

Teece, David J. 1986. "Profiting from Technological Innovation: Implications for Integration, Collaboration, Licensing, and Public Policy." *Research Policy* 15 (December): 285–305.

———. 1988. "Technological Change and the Nature of the Firm." In *Technical Change and Economic Theory*, ed. Giovanni Dosi et al. London: Pinter.

Temin, Peter. 1964. *Iron and Steel in Nineteenth-Century America: An Economic Inquiry*. Cambridge: MIT Press.

U.S. Patent Office. 1956. *The Story of the United States Patent Office, 1790–1856*. 3rd ed. Washington, D.C.: Government Printing Office.

U.S. Temporary National Economic Committee (TNEC). 1938. *Verbatim Record of the Proceedings of the Temporary National Economic Committee*. Vol. 1, no. 1. Washington, D.C.: Government Printing Office.

Usselman, Steven W. 2002. *Regulating Railroad Innovation: Business, Technology, and Politics in America, 1840–1920*. New York: Cambridge University Press.

Wallace, Anthony F. C. 1972. *Rockdale: The Growth of an American Village in the Early Industrial Revolution*. New York: Knopf.

Wise, George. 1985. *Willis R. Whitney, General Electric, and the Origins of U.S. Industrial Research*. New York: Columbia University Press.

Wolinsky, Asher. 1993. "Competition in a Market for Informed Experts' Services." *Rand Journal of Economics* 24 (Autumn): 380–98.

Zeckhauser, Richard. 1996. "The Challenge of Contracting for Technological Information." *Proceedings of the National Academy of Sciences* 93 (November): 12743–48.

Part VI

INNOVATION AND TRADE

Introduction and Comments

YOCHANAN SHACHMUROVE

In this short introduction, I would like to concentrate on a few issues that, as a direct consequence of reading William Baumol's *The Free-Market Innovation Machine: Analyzing the Growth Miracle of Capitalism* (2002a), motivate my research.

According to Baumol, a major source of the growth miracle of the past two centuries is the surge of innovation that probably first reached a substantial pace in the first third of the nineteenth century. Baumol contends that without innovation, the economic growth process would have been insignificant. He recognizes that innovation and not invention alone explains the free market's unmatched growth performance. In this introduction, I explore Baumol's ideas by examining the activity and performance of venture capital in and outside the United States. I then use the Index of Economic Freedom (IEF) to ascertain the relationship between that index, economic growth, and innovations. I apply the IEF not only to developed countries but also to the troubled region of the Middle East and northern Africa. I also investigate trends in patent approvals and GDP. I conclude with a few thoughts on the impacts of trade barriers on productivity, innovation, and research activities.

In the modern economy, many rival oligopolistic firms utilize innovation in order to both surmount and protect themselves from competitors. Each firm is driven to conclude that at least matching their competitors' spending on innovation is crucial in remaining competitive. Since in such an economy firms do not dare relax their innovation activities for fear of being beaten out of the market, a constant stream of innovation can be expected (see Baumol 2002a; 2002b, 5).

One way to test this hypothesis is to explore the venture capital literature in order to show that venture-backed initial public offerings (IPOs) continue to be traded despite not having done as well as some in the literature claim. I have done this in multiple articles. The first, published in the *Journal of Entrepreneurial Finance* (Shachmurove 2001), examines the performance of 3,063 IPOs of companies that were backed by venture capital between 1968 and 1998 across various stages of financing. Table A demonstrates the low returns that such IPOs gain across the board. The

TABLE A
Annualized Returns by Stages of Financing, All Firms

	Unknown Stage	Acquisition for Expansion	Acquisition	Bridge	Early Stage	Expansion	First Stage	LBO	Open Market Purchase
Mean	−83.16	−33.92	−18.18	−57.54	−41.19	−29.27	−47.3	−46.429	−54.29
Median	−100	−62.05	2.3	−100	−48.65	−50.9	−49.5	−77.65	−100
S D	59.97	82.58	61.93	61.62	74.48	193.70	60.27	57.75	57.87
Skewness[a]	8.20	1.87	−0.38	1.23	3.19	13.96	1.70	0.43	0.81
Kurtosis	98.14	6.09	−1.37	0.65	20.54	234.27	6.26	−1.20	−0.29
Minimum	−100	−100	−100	−100	−100	−100	−100	−100	−100
Maximum	718.1	303.9	67.7	135.4	563.5	3296.1	297.7	104.2	147.8
T:Mean = 0[b]	−25.19	−2.53	−1.06	−7.17	−8.85	−2.93	−10.08	−9.85	−11.49
Pr>|T|[(c)]	0.0001	0.016	0.31	0.0001	0.0001	0.0036	0.0001	0.0001	0.0001

	Other Acquisition	Other Early	Other Expansion	R&D	Second Stage	Seed	Special Situation	Start-up	Third Stage	Turnaround
Mean	−44.9	−48.85	−100	−72.4	−21.306	−32.96	−52.54	−41.071	−39.16	−41.93
Median	−44.9	−58.2	−100	−100	−46.4	−25.55	−100	−43.3	−39.2	−29.3
S D	77.92	54.91	0	47.16	177.47	59.48	54.88	68.84	58.85	55.02
Skewness[a]		0.58		1.23	7.83	1.83	0.35	2.39	0.59	0.01
Kurtosis		−0.46		−0.81	77.16	10.36	−1.88	14.38	−0.10	−1.94
Minimum	−100	−100	−100	−100	−100	−100	−100	−100	−100	−100
Maximum	10.2	185.7	−100	−0.9	1813.3	373.2	35.3	550	157.9	36.9
T:Mean = 0[b]	−0.81	−18.08		−4.06	−1.48	−8.58	−4.28	−11.89	−7.14	−2.64
Pr>|T|[(c)]	0.56	0.0001		0.007	0.142	0.0001	0.0004	0.0001	0.0001	0.023

[a] Pearson coefficient of skewness.
[b] *t*-statistic testing the mean equal to zero.
[c] *p* value of the *t*-statistic.

data is divided into the following stages of financing: unknown stage, acquisition for expansion, general acquisition, bridge, early-stage expansion, first stage, leveraged buy-out (LBO), open-market purchase, other acquisition, other early stage, other expansion, research and development financing, second stage, seed, special situation, start-up, third stage, and financing for turnaround purposes.

The most striking element of table A lies in the mean of annualized returns, which is in the red for all stages of financing. Except for second-stage financing and acquisition (both general and otherwise), each mean is significantly different from zero; moreover, the bottom three quartiles show negative returns for a number of financing stages—including bridge, first stage, other expansion, R&D, and special situation—and of the remaining stages, all but the unknown stage, acquisition, and other acquisition show negative returns for the bottom two quartiles.

Despite these discouraging numbers, the media often reports the astronomical capital gains of IPO share prices, such as eBay (1,240 percent increase in three months) or Inktomi (618.8 percent increase in five months). It would therefore seem that some firms have been able to produce astonishing returns on their innovation. Yet table A again demonstrates the rarity of such a case; the return at the ninetieth percentile tops out at less than 20 percent at most stages of financing: 19 percent during bridge financing, 18.4 percent during first-stage financing, and only 13.6 percent for open-market purchases. Only at the top decile do the annualized returns appear impressive: 53.3 percent or higher at the acquisition stage, 36.9 percent or more during third-stage financing, and 32.5 percent and above during acquisition for expansion. While the rates of return for these venture-backed IPOs may vary across assorted stages of financing, as table A thus reveals, most produce returns conspicuously close to zero. This is a direct implication of Baumol's observation that one should not expect higher than normal returns for these IPOs since the reason they are backed by venture capitalists is for their survival rather than for above-normal profits.

In a follow-up to Y. Shachmurove 2001, A. Shachmurove and Y. Shachmurove (2004) and E. Shachmurove and Y. Shachmurove (2004) examine the performance of 2,895 IPOs of companies that were backed by venture capital between 1968 and 1998 across various types of industries. Table B demonstrates the low returns that such IPOs gain across 11 sectors of the economy. These sectors are biotechnology, communication, computer hardware, computer software and services, consumer related, industrial/energy, Internet specific, medical–health, other health products, semiconductors and other electronics, and unknown.

The annualized means presented in table B appear significant; the mean annual return for each of the 11 sectors remains negative and statistically

TABLE B

Annualized Returns by Industry, All Firms and 11 Sectors

	All Sectors	Biotech-nology	Commu-nication	Computer Hardware	Computer Software & Services	Cons-umer Related	Industrial/ Energy	Internet Specific	Medical Health	Other Products	Semicon-ductors/ Other Electric	Un-known
N	2895	237	331	317	381	306	199	152	408	303	258	3
Mean	−45.34	−36.55	−50.18	−61.7	−38.97	−50.74	−51.66	−25.93	−48.79	−45.29	−30.61	−100
Median	−100	−25.6	−100	−100	−63.3	−100	−100	−100	−47.8	−100	−14.1	−100
SD	99.57736	50.9929	126.9502	57.69082	88.73	57.49	52.46	298.55	52.85	59.28	69.47	0
Skewness[a]	16.34027	0.09873	10.62067	1.930253	3.32	0.76	0.4	9.45	0.497821	0.440546	2.654701	
Kurtosis	483.99	−0.9	145.78	6.48	18.75	−0.22	−1.33	102.96	−0.75	−1.11	19.1	
Minimum	−100	−100	−100	−100	−100	−100	−100	−100	−100	−100	−100	−100
Maximum	3296.1	105.2	1813.3	312.5	718.1	178.1	104.2	3296.1	149.7	135.4	550	−100
T:Mean = 0[b]	−24.498	−11.036	−7.191	−19.041	−8.574	−15.441	−13.889	−1.071	−18.648	−13.299	−7.078	
Pr > |T|[c]	0.0001	0.0001	0.0001	0.0001	0.0001	0.0001	0.0001	0.2859	0.0001	0.0001	0.0001	
75% Q3[d]	0.2	2.5	−10.7	−13.3	3.9	−0.9	0.2	−58.4	−1.7	7.6	5.5	−100
25% Q1[e]	−100	−100	−100	−100	−100	−100	−100	−100	−100	−100	−100	−100
99%[f]	173.8	83	219.3	157.9	367.2	88.3	64.6	614.1	82	82.4	190.6	−100
95%[g]	42.2	41.5	28.1	26.8	69.8	35.2	25.3	250	31.6	40.2	40.6	−100
90%[h]	21.9	19.8	11.9	10.3	42.2	22.6	15.4	103.2	19	24.6	24.9	−100

[a] Pearson coefficient of skewness.

[b] *t*-statistic testing the mean equal to zero.

[c] *p* value of the *t*-statistic.

[d] Third quartile point.

[e] First quartile point.

[f] Ninety-ninth percentile point.

[g] Ninety-fifth percentile point.

[h] Ninetieth percentile point.

different from zero with the exception of the Internet-specific sector. For this sector, the mean is still negative but not statistically different from zero. Furthermore, the median annualized return for all sectors remains negative. Many sectors, such as communication, computer hardware, consumer related, Internet specific, and medical-health, even show negative annual returns at the third quartile. On a brighter note, it should be observed that, with the exception of the "unknown" category, all sectors show positive returns at the ninetieth percentile, with some sectors doing quite well. Among active software and services firms, for example, we see an annualized return of 64.5 percent at the ninetieth percentile, while the Internet-specific sector demonstrates an astonishing 125.3 percent. Even the lowest of these sectors, medical health, exhibits a 19 percent return at the ninetieth percentile.

Despite these more encouraging data on venture-backed IPO returns when stratified by sector, the low annual returns for the median—and in many cases, for the third quartile—illustrate the difficulty of sustaining a high level of return. The reality remains dispiriting. Most IPOs continue to produce returns markedly close to zero, and all but a few achieve far less than the staggering levels celebrated in the media.

Additional factors greatly affect the incentives to invest in innovation. Although it would seem that the high risk associated with innovation—an expensive and demanding process—necessitates high economic profit, empirical evidence suggests the opposite. Despite the fact that returns on venture-backed IPOs fall close to zero in most cases, firms have to continue financing innovation in order to compete and avoid losing market shares. This striking reality illustrates the importance of innovation in oligopolistic competition, and it also provides an explanation for the high levels of innovation responsible for the economic growth miracle. This crucial feature of oligopolistic competition is made possible by free competition, by which is meant competition independent of any severe government restrictions or tightly enforced rules. In such an environment, firms, especially oligopolies, are motivated to compete in the market, forcing them to—as discussed above—consistently develop innovations in order to combat their respective rivals (see Baumol 2002a, 2002b).

Logically, it follows that countries with a greater degree of free competition will produce firms with more motivation to invest in innovation, resulting in productivity growth and subsequent economic growth.

To test this hypothesis, I have used a catalog of economic freedom scores and the corresponding rankings of 25 countries from the *Index of Economic Freedom* (Miles et al. 2004). Since 1995, the index has served as a means by which diverse economies can be compared on a standard scale; the index defines economic freedom as "the absence of government coercion or constraint on the production, distribution, or consumption of goods and services beyond the extent necessary for citizens to protect and maintain liberty itself." The results are summarized in table C. Figures A and B demonstrate the relationship between innovation and economic freedom by plotting the correlation between patents issued in a given country during the 14-year period 1988–2001 and that country's economic freedom rank. The two figures display an inverse correlation between frequency of patents and economic freedom (note: a lower number on the economic freedom rank denotes a higher level of freedom). For figure A, which includes Japan, the correlation between the two variables does remain low ($r = -0.086$), while in figure B, once Japan is excluded, the correlation increases ($r = -0.264$). In either case,

TABLE C
Patents Produced between 1988 and 2001 and Economic Freedom Score and Rank, 25 Countries

Country	1988–2001 Patents	EF Score	EF Rank
Argentina	479	3.48	116
Australia	8,925	1.88	11
Austria	5,854	2.08	20
Belgium	7,084	2.19	22
Brazil	980	1.98	80
Canada	38,092	1.98	16
Denmark	5,040	1.8	8
Finland	6,231	1.95	14
France	47,764	2.63	44
Germany	117,269	2.03	18
India	799	3.53	121
Ireland	1,127	1.74	5
Israel	7,329	2.36	29
Italy	21,240	2.26	26
Japan	354,898	2.53	38
Luxembourg	554	1.71	4
Mexico	815	2.9	63
Netherlands	15,456	2.04	19
New Zealand	1,247	1.7	3
Norway	2,365	2.35	28
South Africa	1,672	2.79	53
South Korea	22,520	2.69	46
Spain	2,897	2.31	27
United Kingdom	44,051	1.79	7
Venezuela	389	4.18	147

Note: The Index of Economic Freedom lists the scoring categories as follows: Free: 1–1.99, Mostly Free: 2–2.99, Mostly Unfree: 3–3.99, Repressed: 4–5.

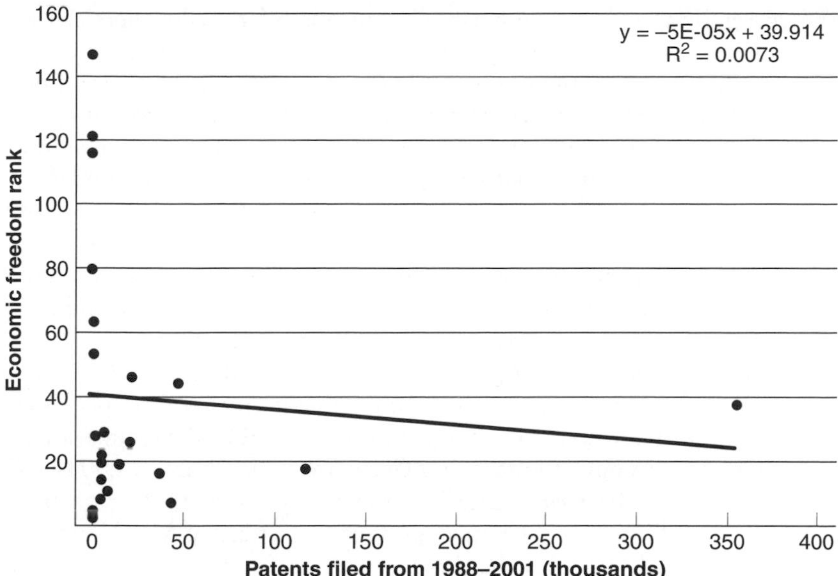

Figure A. Correlation between Number of Patents Issued 1988–2001 and Economic Freedom Rank, 25 Countries ($r = -0.086$)

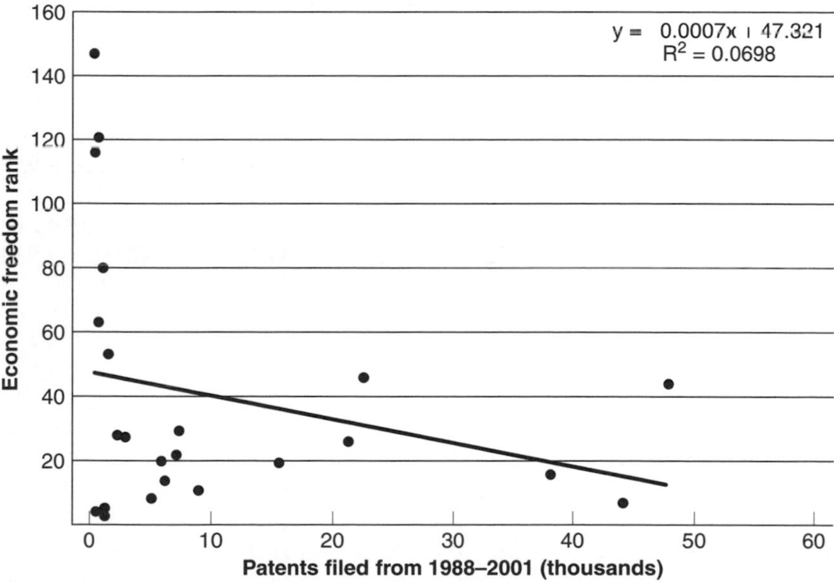

Figure B. Correlation between Number of Patents Issued 1988–2001 and Economic Freedom Rank, 24 Countries (excluding Japan; $r = -0.264$)

the correlation is shown to exist. The inverse relationship between the two suggests that, in a country which allowed greater economic freedom and thus higher up on the *Index of Economic Freedom*, competition produces greater innovation, as indicated by a higher level of patenting.

The link between economic freedom and growth can be discerned more clearly through countries that have *failed* to produce such a climate and must consequently endure poor economies. In the Middle East and North Africa (MENA), the governments of such countries as Algeria, Yemen, and Saudi Arabia continue to exercise extensive control over their respective economies. As a result, these countries suffer from levels of GDP and gross national income (GNI) per capita that pale in comparison to less interventionist economies. Table D demonstrates this disparity. Restrictive countries such as Syria and Iran were only able to muster GNI per capita levels of $1,130 and $1,710 respectively, as opposed to the comparatively astronomical earnings of France and Germany, which boast a 2003 GNP per capita of $22,010 and $22,670, respectively. In part, the reason for this inequality lies in the restrictive economic practices of MENA governments. Figure C compares the 2004 economic freedom ratings for the

TABLE D
Gross National Income (GNI) Characteristics for 20 Countries

Country	GNI Per Capita ($U.S.)	Informal Economy (% GNI)	Population
Algeria	1,720	34.1	30,835,000
Egypt	1,470	35.1	65,176,940
Iran	1,710	18.9	64,528,160
Israel	16,510	21.9	6,326,950
Jordan	1,760	19.4	5,030,800
Kuwait			2,044,270
Lebanon	3,990	34.1	4,384,680
Morocco	1,190	36.4	29,170,000
Oman	7,720		2,478,000
Saudi Arabia	7,065	18.4	21,408,470
Syria	1,130	19.3	16,593,210
Tunisia	2,000	38.4	9,673,600
Turkey	2,500	32.1	68,529,000
United Arab Emirates	20,217	26.4	2,976,290
Yemen	490	27.4	18,045,750
France	22,010	15.3	59,190,600
Germany	22,670	16.3	82,333,000
Japan	33,550	11.3	127,034,880
United Kingdom	25,250	12.6	58,800,000
United States	35,060	8.8	285,318,016

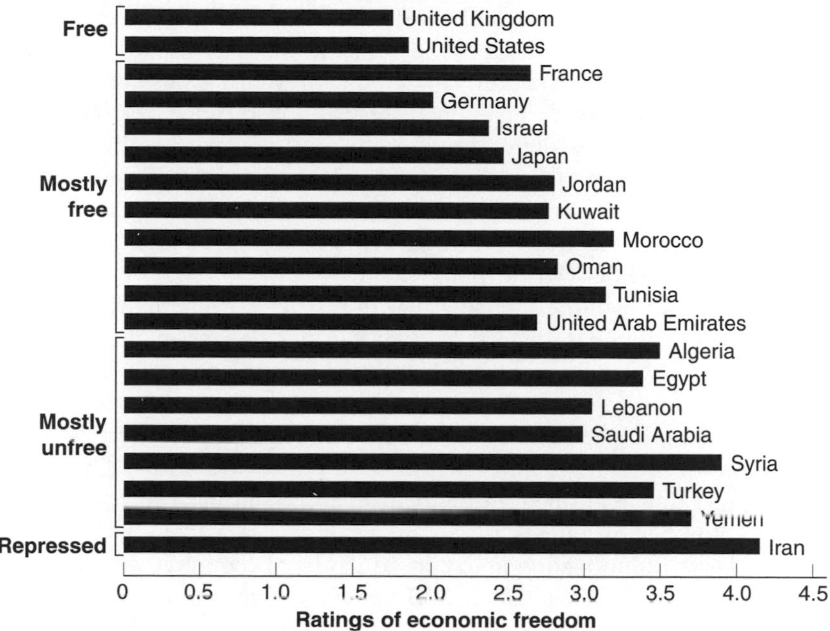

Figure C. Economic Freedom Ratings for 20 Countries, 2004

same 20 countries. Most noticeably, none of the MENA countries can be characterized as being "free," and only six have been rated "mostly free." By contrast, all of the capitalist economies are rated "mostly free" or "free," and all appear above their MENA counterparts. While only one MENA country, Iran, was rated "repressed," seven of the 15 MENA countries were labeled "mostly repressive."

According to the World Bank, five factors affect an entrepreneur's investment decision—the costs of starting a business, hiring and firing workers, enforcing contracts, getting credit, and closing a business. The economic restrictions in MENA countries severely limit the freedom of the entrepreneur with respect to all five. First, the tedious and corrupt process necessary to start a business legally in MENA countries, which includes obtaining the necessary permits and licenses and completing all of the required inscriptions, verifications, and notifications that enable the company to start its operation, limits the number of entrepreneurs willing to start a business. Second, the strict regulations on hiring and firing workers and dictating conditions of employment in MENA countries have adverse effects on unemployment, labor force participation, and the transparency of economic activity (i.e., its remaining official). Third, inefficiencies in court enforcement of contracts induce informal relationships based on family ties or previous transactions and limit investment, trade, and, ultimately, economic growth. Fourth, the inefficiency of credit markets limits the dissemination of credit, preventing business growth. Finally, inefficient bankruptcy processes and insolvency resolutions in MENA countries allow inept businesses to exist, despite misallocation of assets and human capital. In addition, inefficient judicial processes can act against the interest of creditors in instituting a formal insolvency resolution and can lead creditors to abstain from using the formal bankruptcy procedures altogether (World Bank Group 2003).

Clearly, these countries possess highly restrictive, interventionist economies, and the consequences of such policies appear in their modest GNI statistics. As long as the MENA economies are controlled by interventionist governments and lack efficient regulatory institutions, such dismal economic performance is going to be the rule rather than the exception (Shachmurove 2004).

The preceding assessment of innovation and economic growth assumes that the number of patents issued by a country is a likely indicator of the regularity of innovation and, consequently, of economic growth. This assumption should be justified and tested. Patents grant the right to exclude others from the production or use of a specific new device, apparatus, or process for a stated number of years. The grant is issued to the inventor after an examination that focuses on both the novelty of the item and its potential utility. The right embedded in the patent can be assigned by the inventor, usually to an employer, that is, a corporation, or sold to or licensed for use by somebody else. This right can be enforced only by a lawsuit in the courts for infringement damages. The stated purpose of the patent system is to encourage invention and technical progress both by providing a temporary monopoly for the inventor and by forcing the early disclosure of the information necessary for the production of this item or the operation of the new process. As Baumol observes, a patent plays "a crucial role in encouraging the dissemination of technology. Rather than always serving to deny use of technology to others, its primary role is often to ensure that the inventor can obtain satisfactory compensation for its use by others. In this way, patents serve in helping to internalize the externalities of innovation, simultaneously encouraging investment in innovative activity *and rapid dissemination of the novel products of that activity*" (see Baumol 2002a; 2003, 438).

The patent system relies on the power of the rule of law, which enforces the validity of patents in event of a breach. Had such a system not developed, the absence of incentive for firms to become active participants in the market for technology would have stifled innovation and technological growth. Thus, without the rule of law, the growth miracle of capitalism may have been impossible (Baumol 2002b, 10). In countries in which the rule of law has allowed for the establishment of a proper patent system, it would seem that a greater frequency of patent distribution indicates, a higher level of innovation and dissemination of invented technology, culminating in higher economic growth rates.

One way to test this hypothesis is to find the correlation of patents to gross domestic produce (GDP) for a given country. I have produced this data for 25 countries by correlating the number of patents issued in each country with that country's GDP between the years 1989 and 2001. The findings are summarized in table E. As can be seen in the table, the results vary, but overall, patent frequency and GDP seem to be highly correlated. Of the 25 countries, 11 exhibit a correlation of 90 percent or above, with a few—such as Canada, Belgium, and Denmark—revealing correlations close to 100 percent (0.97, 0.95, and 0.95 respectively). Of the remaining 14 countries, eight show correlations above 75 percent. Only six countries—Luxemburg, South Africa, Venezuela, Germany, Austria, and

TABLE E
Correlation between Number of Patents and GDP for the Period 1988–2001 in 25 Countries

Country	Mean GDP	Patents 1988–2001	Correlation
Argentina	34.21	479	0.82
Australia	637.5	8,925	0.88
Austria	418.14	5,854	0.68
Belgium	506	7,084	0.95
Brazil	70	980	0.90
Canada	2,720.86	38,092	0.97
Denmark	360	5,040	0.95
Finland	445.07	6,231	0.90
France	3,411.71	47,764	0.89
Germany	8,376.36	117,269	0.65
India	57.07	799	0.92
Ireland	80.5	1,127	0.91
Israel	523.5	7,329	0.91
Italy	1,517.14	21,240	0.82
Japan	25,349.86	354,898	0.83
Luxembourg	39.57	554	0.53
Mexico	58.21	815	0.92
Netherlands	1,104	15,456	0.71
New Zealand	89.07	1,247	0.85
Norway	168.93	2,365	0.85
South Africa	119.43	1,672	0.57
South Korea	1,608.57	22,520	0.91
Spain	206.93	2,897	0.94
United Kingdom	3,146.5	44,051	0.78
Venezuela	27.79	389	0.60

the Netherlands—do not have correlations above this point. Therefore, while innovation cannot account for all of GDP growth, the high correlation between patents and GDP in many highly innovative countries seems to indicate a general trend. The issue of patents, which have been explicitly designed to encourage both invention and dissemination, seems to indicate general economic growth, thus supporting the hypothesis that patents stimulate the economy through greater innovation.

In summary, Baumol has observed the fundamental importance of innovation in a free-market economy, and has identified it as a crucial element of the miraculous growth rate of capitalist economies. Indeed, preliminary studies do link these two phenomena by establishing the persistence of IPOs despite poor performances, demonstrating the necessity of innovation for competitive firms. Furthermore, correlation studies between economic freedom and patent frequency capture the association between highly competitive free markets and high levels of innovation. The importance of economic freedom is further demonstrated when comparing capitalist economies with poor, restrictive economies in the Middle East and Africa. Finally, the high correlation between patent frequency and GDP in numerous countries illustrates the important role that innovation plays in boosting GDP, serving to emphasize the magnitude of consistent innovation in producing the astronomical growth of the modern, capitalist economy.

I conclude with a humbling reminder of the extent of supplementary research eclipsing my own. Ralph Gomory and William Baumol, in chapter 11, and Jonathan Eaton and Samuel Kortum, in chapter 12, present work exploring the varying effects of innovation. Both essays deserve a brief introduction.

Gomory and Baumol tackle issues of innovation in international trade. Technical change has transformed world trade; geographic distance and natural advantage have been all but erased by the ease of modern transportation and the nature of technologically advanced goods: "Semiconductor plants or athletic shoe assembly plants can be located almost anywhere, independent of climate." The reality of technologically advanced international trade has caused disputes as to whether the development of new productive capabilities throughout the globe is in the interest of traditional productive giants, particularly the United States. The controversy over outsourcing, for example, is a product of these innovative changes in world trade. Thus, Gomory and Baumol have attempted to pinpoint the true beneficiaries of such developments by comparing equilibrium outcomes before and after improvements in productivity abroad, based on the standard linear Ricardo model of international trade. Their conclusion varies with the specifics of each country included in the model, but most often, "A country is better off with a less developed trading partner." The modern ability of smaller economies to acquire advantages in "swing industries" (industries where no maximal productivity advantages exist) presents a financial threat to countries such as the United States that lose utility through the sacrifice of elements of their share in world production. This conclusion refutes the traditional economic faith in comparative advantage and could lead to questioning the logic of outsourcing and similar developments in modern international trade.

Eaton and Kortum's essay, entitled "Innovation, Diffusion, and Trade," examines research specialization to determine the effects of technology dissemination on innovation and trade. Eaton and Kortum devise a two-region model of innovation and diffusion in order to explore the incentives to innovate within each region under various assumptions concerning the speed of diffusion and the size of impediments to trade. The model distinguishes between cases in which one country uses only those technologies that are exclusive to it, both countries use common technologies but one exports the resulting goods to the other, and both countries use common technology but no such exporting takes place.

Eaton and Kortum find that without diffusion, the level of research remains equal in both countries, despite size disparities, with the more productive country producing higher returns. In the case of instantaneous diffusion, the allocation of research activity depends on the existence of trade barriers; a distinct comparative advantage leads to specialization in research activity; while higher trade barriers produce results similar to the case of no diffusion. Thus, a lowering of trade barriers, Eaton and Kortum conclude, can lead to greater research specialization. Finally, while higher levels of trade and diffusion may shift research activity across countries, Eaton and Kortum find that the level of overall research will not necessarily increase, as globalization exposes researchers to higher levels of competition in addition to larger markets. With this, they conclude that since intermediate levels of diffusion can produce differing levels of research specialization, the relative size of a country is significant in determining the degree of specialization but ambiguous in direction. As a result, both large and small countries are among the most active in research. Nevertheless, Eaton and Kortum hold the most important determinant in research specialization to lie in the overall productivity of research in a given country.

References

Baumol, William J. 2002a. *The Free-Market Innovation Machine: Analyzing the Growth Miracle of Capitalism*. Princeton: Princeton University Press.

———. 2002b. "Towards Microeconomics of Innovation: Growth Engine Hallmark of Market Economic." *Atlantic Economic Journal* 30 (1): 1–12.

———. 2003. "Innovations and Growth: Two Common Misapprehensions." *Journal of Policy Modeling* 25: 435–44.

Hall, Bronwyn H., Adam B. Jaffe, and Manuel Trajtenberg. 2000. "Market Value and Patent Citations: A First Look." National Bureau of Economic Research Working Paper No. 7741, June. http://emlab.berkeley.edu/users/bhhall/index.html#teach0203.

Miles, M., E. Feulner, M. O'Grady, A. Eiras, and A. Schavey. 2004. *Index of Economic Freedom*. Washington, D.C.: Heritage Foundation and Dow Jones. Available at www.heritage.org/index.

Shachmurove, Yochanan. 2001. "Annualized Returns of Venture-Backed Public Companies Categorized by Stage of Financing: An Empirical Investigation of IPOs in the Last Three Decades." *Journal of Entrepreneurial Finance* 6 (1): 44–58.

———. 2004. "An Introduction to the Special Issues on Financial Markets of the Middle East." *International Journal of Business* Volume 9 Issue Number (3): 211–36.

Shachmurove, Amir and Shachmurove Yochanan, 2004. "Annualized and Cumulative Returns on Venture-Backed Public Companies Categorized by Industry." *The Journal of Entrepreneurial Finance and Business Ventures* 9 (3): 41–60.

Shachmurove, Emanuel, and Shachmurove Yochanan, 2004. "Annualized Returns of Ventured-Backed Public Companies Stratified by Decades and by Stage of Financing." *The Journal of Entrepreneurial Finance and Business Ventures* Volume 9(2): 109–23.

World Bank Group. 2003. *Doing Business*. rru.worldbank.org/doingbusiness/default.aspx.

Chapter 11

Innovation and Its Effects on International Trade

RALPH E. GOMORY AND WILLIAM J. BAUMOL

The Effect of Innovation on the Setting of World Trade

Technical change has completely transformed the setting of world trade. It has lowered, and in some cases almost erased, the effects of geographic distance. This effect was felt in manufacturing with the arrival of cheap seaborne goods transport in the form of container ships. Today, the effect of fiber optic cables is to make the sending of bits around the world almost instantaneous and remarkably cheap. This has opened up totally new possibilities in competition for services such as call centers.

Innovation has also changed the nature of the goods traded. The proliferation in the goods made and consumed in the modern world, many of which do not depend on natural advantage, is reflected in the volume and variety of international trade. This, coupled with the technological changes mentioned above, allows manufacture of this vast array of goods, or provision of many services, to occur wherever on the globe labor, capital, and know-how can be brought together.

Rapid transportation of people, goods, and bits has also made the spread of know-how easier. Companies have become international, and within a single company we now have plants sharing knowledge around the world. Developing countries are starting to provide well-educated cohorts within their labor forces. Tariff barriers have been lowered by conscious and organized global efforts.

This new situation contrasts profoundly with the world in which David Ricardo discussed international trade. In that world, production capabilities were likely to be determined by natural advantages: England was relatively good at wool, Portugal was relatively good at wine. In Ricardo's world it was far more likely that England would produce wool and Portugal wine than the other way around. But today comparative advantage is more likely to be acquired than to be due to natural endowments. Semiconductor plants or assembly plants for athletic shoes can be located almost anywhere, independent of climate. Consequently the outcomes of free trade are not predetermined, but rather depend on which possible capabilities an area actually develops. Many free-trade outcomes become possible.

All these factors have given rise to the development of new productive capabilities abroad. This in turn leads to disputes as to whether these developments are in the interest of the United States. Usually these disputes pit those who have lost jobs as a result of foreign competition against those who say that the improvement in goods and services provided to the United States more than makes up for the local pain of those who are directly negatively affected. Economists, citing comparative advantage, are usually to be found in this second camp.

Our Approach to the Effect of International Trade in Its New Setting

When many outcomes are possible, we need to be able to compare them. We need to be able to say which are good for one country, which are good for its trading partner, which are good for both.

Our approach, which is based in new analytic methods, is to compare the equilibrium outcomes before and after improvements in productivity abroad. In fact we will provide a general model that considers *all possible productivities* and their corresponding equilibrium outcomes for the countries involved. Our model is based directly on the standard linear Ricardo model of international trade.

What we will find is that improvements in productivity abroad are sometimes helpful and sometimes harmful to the home country. These variations in outcome are not random but rather follow a definite pattern. We will describe that pattern and the circumstances under which a country is likely to gain or lose from developments abroad. The same analysis will also show that: *Often, though not always, a country is better off with a less developed trading partner.*

We will use, throughout, the standard Ricardo model of international trade. We will discuss the case of two countries trading with each other in n industries. The size of the labor force in Country 1 is quantity $L1$ and that of Country 2 is $L2$. The country spending preferences are Cobb-Douglas in form, so the spending on good i by Country j is a fixed fraction $d_{i,j}$ of its national income. On the production side, we will consider two forms of the model, the first with the usual linear production functions in which the quantity produced $q(I, j)$ is related to the labor input by $q(i, j) = e(i, j)L1$, and a second with increasing returns to scale in production.

We will use a standard set of equilibrium equations described in the appendix.

In our linear model, the quantities $q_{i,j}$ produced of each good i in Country j are determined by linear production functions $e_{i,j}l_{i,j}$.

If we fix the labor forces and demand parameters of the two countries, an equilibrium is then completely specified by the vector of productivity coefficients $\epsilon = \{e_{i,j}\}$. However, instead of dealing with just one equilibrium, we will discuss the equilibrium outcomes of the *family of models* obtained by considering *all productivity coefficients* ϵ *subject only to a maximal productivity condition* $e_{i,j} \leq e^{\max}{}_{i,j}$ and holding everything else constant. This will enable us to analyze the effect of different possible productivity levels on the welfare of the two countries.

The Basic Graph

For any given vector of productivity parameters $\epsilon = \{e_{i,j}\}$, there is a stable equilibrium giving a national income Y_j and a utility U_j for each country. From the Y_j we can compute *relative* national income $Z_j = Y_j / (Y_1 + Y_2)$. We can then plot this equilibrium as a pair of points in a diagram that displays Z_1 horizontally and the utilities of the two countries, U_1 and U_2,on the vertical axes.

In figure 11.1 we show such an equilibrium. The equilibrium is represented by a pair of points. The black point represents Country 1's utility in Country 1 autarky units, measured against the right vertical axis, and the gray point represents Country 2's utility in Country 2 autarky units measured against the left vertical axis.

Now that we have this way of representing equilibria, we can represent many different equilibria in a single graph. In figure 11.2 we show

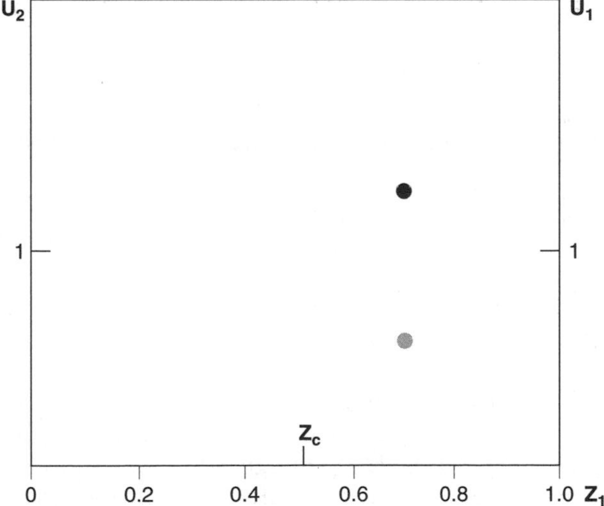

Figure 11.1. One Equilibrium

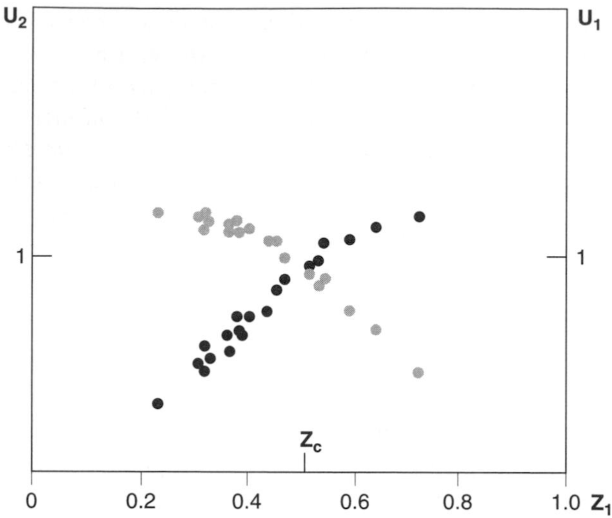

Figure 11.2. Eighteen Equilibria

18 equilibria obtained by changing some of the productivities of an 11-good model.

In the (randomly chosen) example in figure 11.2, we see that the equilibria that yield the most utility for Country 1 tend to yield a low utility for Country 2 and vice versa. We also see that utility seems to increase with country share. Are these general phenomena, or are they the result of the way the 18 equilibria were chosen?

All Possible Equilibria

We next turn to an analysis that enables us to deal with *all possible equilibria*, not just a chosen subset.

In each industry the limits of what is currently known impose an upper bound on productivity. We can be constrained by either a technological limit due to the current state of the art, or a limit due to inherent natural resource or climate limitations. For each industry in each country there is therefore a *productivity limit* peculiar to that industry and that country. We denote this quantity by $e^{\max}{}_{i,j}$. In our analysis we will now consider *all possible productivities*, that is all productivities $e_{i,j}$ with $e_{i,j} \leq e^{\max}{}_{i,j}$. We have developed mathematical methods that enable us to carry out this analysis.

The result of doing that is shown in figure 11.3. It contains all possible equilibria for an 11-industry model with two equal-sized countries and a set of maximal productivities. The black line marks the upper boundary

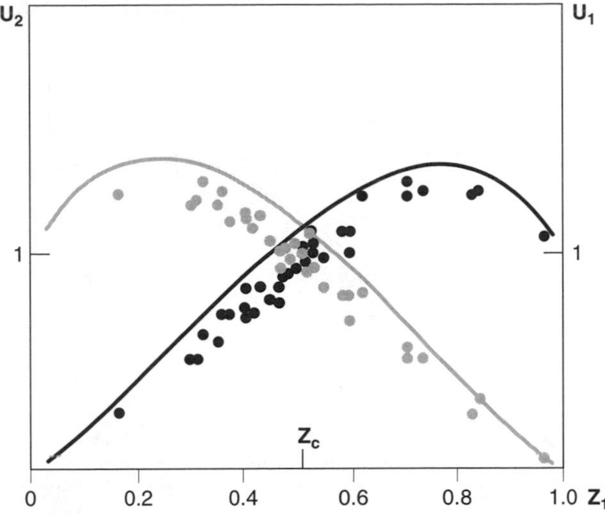

Figure 11.3. All Possible Equilibria

of a region that is in fact filled solidly with black dots. A few black dots are shown as examples. Each black dot, whether shown individually or not, has its counterpart gray dot from the same equilibrium. The gray line marks the upper boundary of a region filled with these gray dots. Again only a few are shown individually, the counterparts of the visible black dots; however the region on or below the gray line is solidly filled with gray dots, each one the counterpart of a black dot. The possible equilibrium pairs always have their Country 1 utility value on or below the black line, and their Country 2 equilibrium value on or below the gray line.

In figure 11.4, which is the same 11-industry example, we have marked the best possible equilibrium for Country 1 with a large black dot at the peak of the black boundary curve. The corresponding utility for Country 2 is the large gray dot directly below. Similarly, the best possible equilibrium for Country 2 is the large gray dot at the top of the peak of the gray boundary curve. The corresponding utility value for Country 1 is the large black dot directly below. Note that in both cases the best equilibrium for one country is a poor one for the other.

The result we show in figure 11.4 holds generally. For problems of reasonable size (eight or more industries), the exact regional boundary for Country 1 can be very well approximated by a smooth curve that has height 0 at $Z_1 = 0$, then rises to a single peak, and then descends to the utility level that Country 1 has in autarky. The boundary for Country 2 similarly starts at 0 at $Z_1 = 1$, rises to a single peak to the left of the Country 1 peak as Z_1, decreases, and then descends to the Country 2

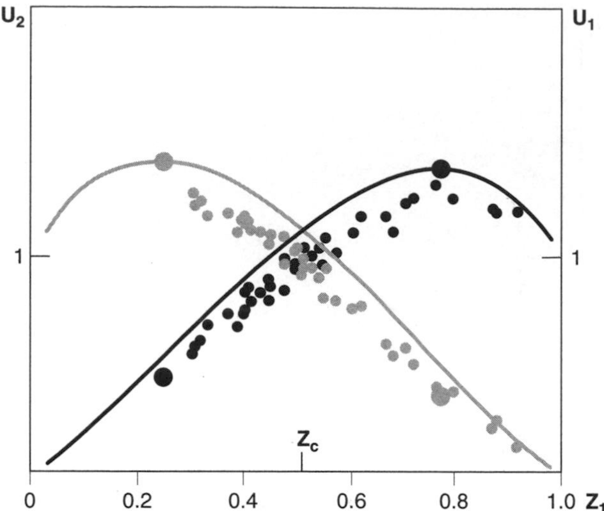

Figure 11.4. The Best Equilibrium for Country 1 and the Best Equilibrium for Country 2

autarky value. For all these models, it is true that the best outcome for one county is a poor one for the other.

We will discuss the exact shape of the boundary below, taking into account models with very few industries as well as those with many industries.

However, at this point, to complete our picture of how the outcomes vary with changing productivities, we introduce the *regions of maximal productivity*.

Regions of Maximal Productivity

We will say that an equilibrium is a *maximal productivity equilibrium* if for each industry, one of the producers is producing at maximal productivity. These are the equilibria that produce the greatest utility, and we would expect that over time one producer would attain state-of-the-art capability. Indeed, that level of performance may well define the practical state of the art.

Our methods allow us to single out the maximal productivity equilibria and calculate the boundaries of the region in which they lie. In figure 11.5 we show the regions of maximal productivity for the 11-industry model. Note that all maximal productivity equilibria lie in the region of maximal productivity, but not all equilibria in that region are maximal productivity equilibria.

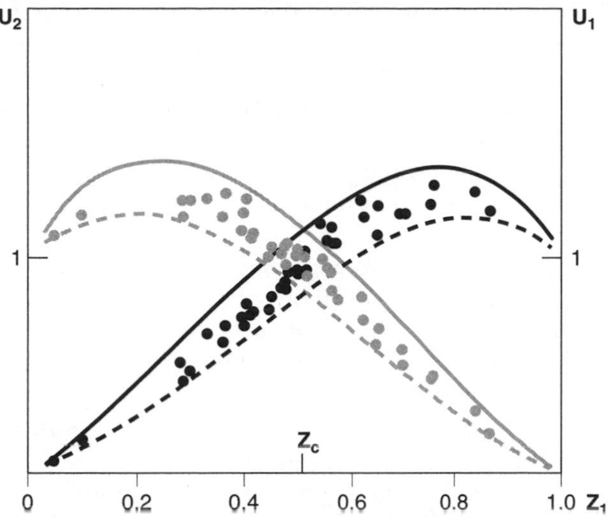

Figure 11.5. Regions of Maximal Productivity

In figure 11.6 we divide the regions of figure 11.5 into *regions of conflict* and *regions of mutual gains*. In the leftmost region of mutual gains, an increase in share by Country 1 will usually increase utility for both countries. In the next region, the region of conflict, increase in Country 1's

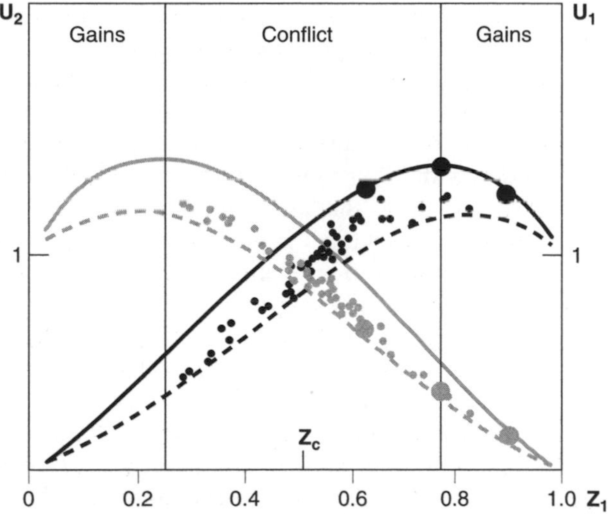

Figure 11.6. The Region of Conflict and the Regions of Mutual Gains

share still increases Country 1's utility but usually decreases that of Country 2. In the third region, further increases in Country 1's share decrease the utility of both countries. In this second region of mutual gains, it is losses in Country 1's share and increases in Country 2's share that produce mutual gains.

Where do these regions and their boundaries come from? They come from solving a maximization problem. We obtain the height of Country 1's regional boundary (the black boundary in the figures) by that assignment of production to the two countries which meets the conditions of equilibrium, does not use productivities beyond the maximal productivities, *and maximizes utility for Country 1.*

There is a similar maximization that finds the regional boundary for Country 2. Remarkably enough, these maximization problems turn out to be reasonably simple ones. There is considerable work in getting to this simplicity, but in the end it is there.

The result is the *exact boundary theorem*: The utility of each point of the boundary curve $C_1(Z_1)$ for $Z_1 \leq Z_C$ is obtained by solving the maximization problem in integer x:

$$C_1(Z_1) - Max_x\, u(x,Z_1,\epsilon^{max}) = Max_x\, Lu(x,Z_1,\epsilon^{max})$$

$$\Sigma_i x_{i,1}(d_{i,1}Z_1 + d_{i,2}Z_2) < Z_1, \qquad x_{i,1} + x_{i,2} = 1$$

The Linear Programming Approximation

Often linear programming provides a good approximation to an integer programming problem. This is the case here for problems with a large number of industries. The linear programming approximation smoothes out the jagged ins and outs of the exact boundary and is easier to analyze theoretically. Its connection with the exact regional boundary is usually very close for models with 10 or more industries (we will see examples of this below), and we can prove that as the number of industries increases, the difference between the exact and approximate boundaries approaches zero. It is for the linear programming approximation that we can prove this result on the general regional shape.

Denote by the classical share, Z_c the share Country 1 has when both countries are fully developed ($e_{i,j} = e^{max}{}_{i,j}$ all i, j). Then for the linear programming approximation we can state:

The approximate regional boundary for Country 1 always starts with height 0 at $Z_1 = 0$, rises monotonically to a single peak to the right of the classical share, and then descends to the autarky value at $Z_1 = 1$. There is a similar statement for the boundary of Country 2, whose peak occurs to the left of the classical share. In all the figures the classical share is marked by the short vertical line labeled Z_c.

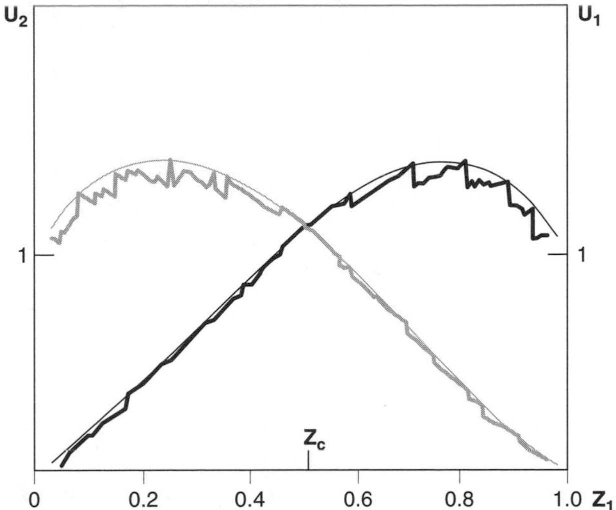

Figure 11.7. Exact and Approximate Boundaries, 10 Industries Example

In figure 11.7 we use thick lines to show the exact boundary for a 10-industry model, and we show the linear programming approximate boundary with the thinner lines.

In figures 11.8, 11.9, 11.10, 11.11, and 11.12, we show examples with eight, six, four, three, and finally two industries.

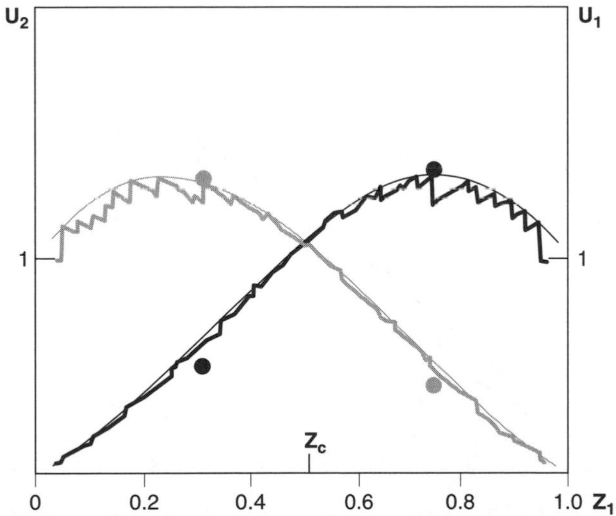

Figure 11.8. Exact and Approximate Boundaries, 8 Industries Example

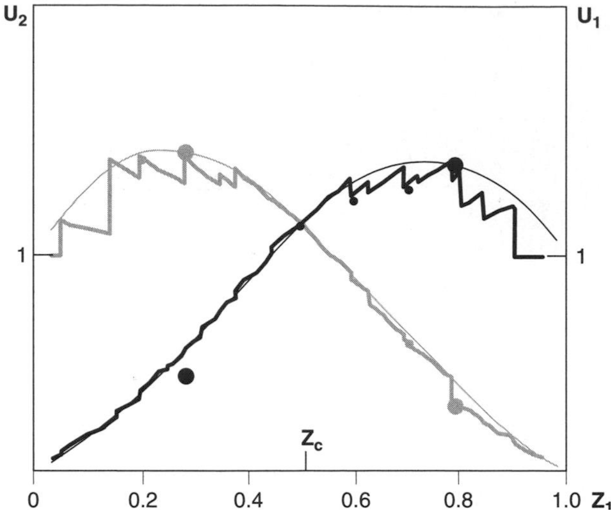

Figure 11.9. Exact and Approximate Boundaries, 6 Industries Example

Although the more jagged exact boundary and the smooth approximating boundary diverge more and more as the number of industries decreases, the exact boundary retains its two-peak shape until the final

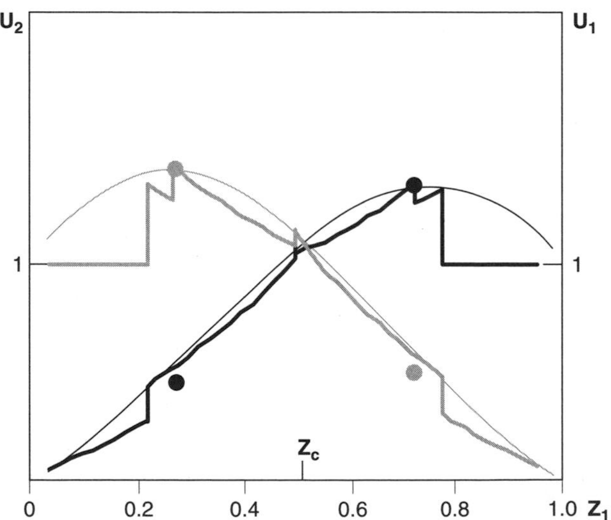

Figure 11.10. Exact and Approximate Boundaries, 4 Industries Example

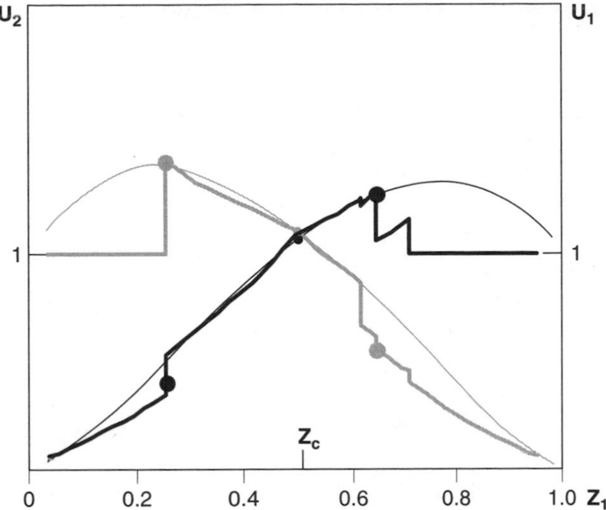

Figure 11.11. Exact and Approximate Boundaries, 3 Industries Example

example with two industries. This, the two-industry model common in the literature, is a version of the classical English wool, Portuguese wine model, and in this case there is a single equilibrium at the classical share that is the best equilibrium outcome for both countries.

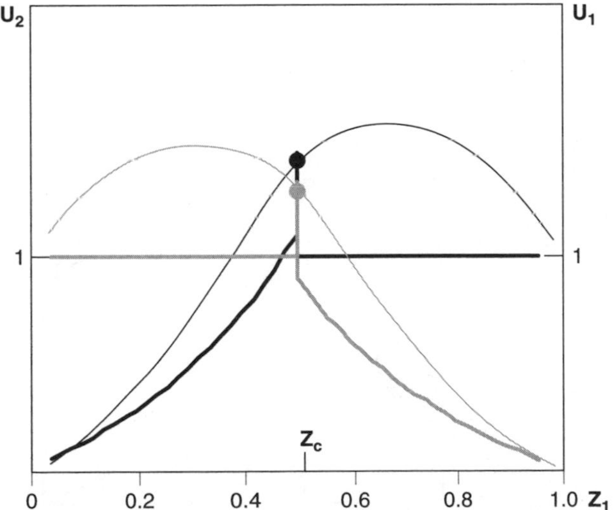

Figure 11.12. Exact and Approximate Boundaries, 2 Industries Example

What Makes the Large Examples Different from the Small Ones?

We have already presented a discussion in terms of the linear programming approximation versus the exact boundary. We will now discuss this difference in more economic terms.

While large problems can have groups of industries where one country or the other has an overwhelming productivity advantage, large problems will also tend to have some industries where there is no overwhelming maximal productivity advantage of one country over the other. We call these *swing industries*. Most instances of acquired advantage, such as in the assembly of athletic shoes or of printers or in the fabrication of semiconductors, have this intermediate characteristic. If one country or the other acquires these swing industries, its share of world production goes up, while the total world production does not change very much because the change does not result in much greater output. Therefore, the acquiring country gains share, the losing country loses share, and the total they are dividing does not change very much. These outcomes lead to regions of conflict.

In two-industry examples, there is no room for a swing industry. However, with a three-industry model, if, for example, we add an intermediate leather industry to wool and wine with the comparative advantage of England less in the intermediate good, it is easy to construct

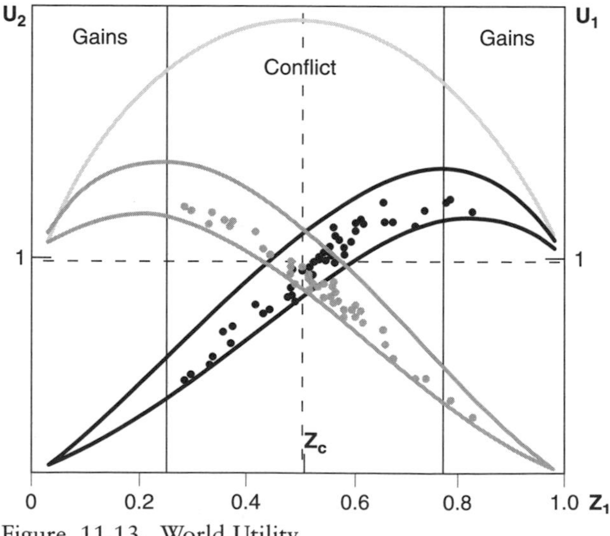

Figure 11.13. World Utility

examples that have two peaks and where England's utility decreases when Portugal becomes more productive in leather.

While we have concentrated on the boundaries of the two trading partners, we can also look at the utility of the total world output. This is especially meaningful when the two countries have similar demand structures, but we can get a measure of world utility in any case by measuring the total world output with the utility function of one or the other country.

In figure 11.13 we show a world utility boundary as well as the boundaries for countries 1 and 2. World utility tends to peak near the classical share. This is the pie that the shares of the other countries divide. World utility is relatively flat near its peak, so in that area the countries are dividing a relatively unchanging total and their interests tend to be in conflict.

Summary

Often, though not always, a country is better off with a *less* developed trading partner. Our diagrams describe the circumstances under which a country is likely to gain or lose from developments abroad.

A larger utility is often achieved by obtaining or retaining a larger share of world production. That is easier to do with a less developed trading partner.

Clearly, countries as a whole have a stake in the fate of their home industries.

Appendix

Stable Equilibria

From the national incomes Y_j of each of two countries we can compute *relative* national income $Z_j = Y_j / (Y_1 + Y_2)$. We also normalize all our pecuniary expressions, so p_i, the price of good i, and w_j, the wage in Country j, are also divided by total income $Y_1. + Y_2$. Country j's *consumption* of good i is denoted by $y_{i,j}$ and its *production* of good i by $q_{i,j}$. Country j's *production share* or *market share* of world output of good i is represented by $x_{i,j} = q_{i,j} / (q_{i,i} + q_{i,2})$, so that the vector $x = \{x_{i,j}\}$ describes the pattern of production.

We can now describe our equilibrium conditions, noting that the equilibria we describe will be *stable* equilibria. First, (relative) national income of Country j must equal the total revenue from domestic and foreign sales of that country's products. Since with a Cobb-Douglas utility function, Country i's expenditure on good i will be $d_{i,j}Z_j$, this condition is

$$\Sigma_i x_{i,j}(d_{i,1}Z_1 + d_{i,2}Z_2) = Z_j$$

for each country. However, only one of the two equations is needed.[1] Second, we have a zero-profit condition. World expenditure on Country j's output of good i all goes into the wages of the labor $l_{i,j}$ employed in that industry, so

$$w_j l_{i,j} = x_{i,j}(d_{i,1}Z_1 + d_{i,2}Z_2)$$

Third is the full-employment requirement for each country. This is expressed as the condition that the wage rate times the country's total labor force equals national income:

$$w_j L_j = Z_j$$

Fourth, we have the requirement that, for each good, quantity supplied equals quantity demanded, or equivalently, that the value of the output of good i at the equilibrium price equals the amount consumers are willing to spend on it,

$$p_i(q_{i,1} + q_{i,2}) = d_{i,1}Z_1 + d_{i,2}Z_2 \quad or \quad p_i q_{i,j} = w_j\, l_{i,j}$$

where the second form of this condition follows directly from the first by multiplying through by $x_{i,j}$ and using the zero-profit condition. Finally we have the stability conditions that make entry by nonproducers unprofitable. These require producers not to have higher unit costs than nonproducers. For example, if Country 1 is the producer in industry i and Country 2 is a nonproducer, we must have $e_{i,1} / w_1 \geq e_{i,2} / w_2$. More generally:

$$\begin{array}{llll} if\ x_{i,1} > 0 & and \quad x_{i,2} = 0 & then & e_{i,1}/w_1 \geq e_{i,2}/w_2 \\ if\ x_{i,2} > 0 & and \quad x_{i,1} = 0 & then & e_{i,1}/w_1 \leq e_{i,2}/w_2 \\ if\ x_{i,2} > 0 & and \quad x_{i,1} > 0 & then & e_{i,1}/w_1 = e_{i,2}/w_2 \end{array}$$

These conditions are, of course, a form of the familiar comparative-advantage criterion.

In our model then, equilibrium is determined by the relative national income relation, supply-demand equality for each good, zero profit in each industry, full employment in each country, and the stability conditions.

Note

1. Since $Z_1 + Z_2 = 1$ and $x_{i,1} + x_{i,2} = 1$, the two equations are dependent.

Reference

Gomory, Ralph E., and William J. Baumol. 2000. *Global Trade and Conflicting National Interests*. Cambridge: MIT Press.

Chapter 12

Innovation, Diffusion, and Trade

JONATHAN EATON AND SAMUEL S. KORTUM

1. Introduction

Research indicators reveal strong and consistent patterns of specialization in innovation. Table 12.1 reports the number of business sector research scientists per thousand workers in industry among OECD and selected non-OECD members, in descending order of research intensity. By virtue of their size and high research intensity, most research is done in the United States and Japan. Research-intensive countries tend to be wealthy, but some wealthy countries, such as Australia and Italy, don't do much private sector research. Moreover, with the exception of the recent emergence of Finland as a research center, patterns of research specialization have remained very stable over time. The countries contributing the most to innovation now are mostly the same ones as half a century ago.[1]

What characteristics of a country determine specialization in research, and how does openness affect the incentive to innovate? This question has been posed in a number of contexts in which openness has meant different things. It could refer to the absence of trade barriers, but also to the absence of barriers to the diffusion of ideas themselves. While trade allows consumers in another country to benefit from an innovation by importing a good that embodies the idea, technology diffusion allows them to benefit through local production making use of that idea. Expanding one conduit or the other may have very different implications for the incentive to innovate in either location. A related question is the role of country characteristics in determining international patterns of specialization in innovative activity. Do large countries, for example, naturally do more research because their inventors have quicker access to a large internal market?

The literature on international technology diffusion is large. Keller (2004) provides a comprehensive survey. A number of papers have looked at the effect of one type of openness taking the degree of openness of the other type as given. Examples are Helpman (1993), Eaton, Gutierrez, and Kortum (1998), Eaton and Kortum (henceforth EK) (1999), and EK (2001b).

TABLE 12.1
Business Sector Research Scientists (per 1000 Industrial Workers)

COUNTRY	Scientists	Income	Population
Finland	12.2	69	5176
United States	10.2	100	275423
Japan	9.8	73	126919
Sweden	7.7	69	8871
Luxembourg	6.8	138	441
Russia	6.6	28	145555
Belgium	6.2	70	10254
Norway	6.0	90	4491
Canada	5.9	81	30750
Germany	5.5	67	82168
Singapore	5.3	80	4018
France	5.1	66	60431
Denmark	4.5	80	5338
Ireland	4.4	76	3787
Korea	4.2	42	47275
United Kingdom	4.2	68	59756
Taiwan	4.2	55	21777
Austria	3.9	70	8110
Netherlands	3.6	72	15920
Australia	2.4	76	19157
Slovenia	2.0	48	1988
Spain	1.8	53	39927
New Zealand	1.7	56	3831
Italy	1.6	64	57728
Slovak Republic	1.6	35	5401
Czech Republic	1.4	42	10272
Hungary	1.4	31	10024
Romania	1.4	14	22435
Poland	0.8	27	38646
Portugal	0.7	48	10005
China	0.7	11	1258821
Greece	0.5	44	10558
Turkey	0.2	21	66835
Mexico	0.1	27	97221

Data are for 2000 or the previous available year.
Income is relative to the United States (100).
Population is in 1000's.
Sources: OECD (2004) and Heston, Summers, and Aten (2002).

Helpman (1993), for example, finds that, with no trade costs, faster diffusion to an imitating country can spur innovation by reducing the wage, and hence the cost of innovation, in the innovating country. In a model with no diffusion, EK (2001b), find that the degree of openness to trade has no effect on innovative activity: While exporting increases the size of the market that a successful innovator can capture, it also means that an innovator faces a higher hurdle in terms of competition from abroad through imports. The two forces exactly offset each other. In their model, unlike Helpman's, all countries engage in innovative activity.

To explore these issues further we develop a two-region model, like Helpman's, of innovation and diffusion. In contrast to much of the literature, innovation can in principle take place in either region, although research productivities may differ. Ideas can diffuse between locations, but with a lag. We allow for an arbitrary level of trade barriers, with costless trade a special case. We then explore the incentives to innovate under different assumptions about the speed of diffusion and about the magnitude of trade barriers.

While our model could be extended to analyze the implications of imperfect protection of intellectual property, that is not our purpose here. To isolate the effects of geographical barriers to the movement of goods and ideas, we make the simplest assumption for our purposes, that innovators can appropriate the entire returns to their innovation at home and abroad.[2]

We proceed as follows. Section 2 develops a static two-country model of technology, production, and trade along the lines of the Ricardian model developed in EK (2002). In their many-country model, the distribution of technologies is treated as independent from country to country. Such an outcome is consistent, for example, with a world in which each country relies on its own innovations for production, or one in which an innovation applying to a particular good in one country applies to some different good where it diffuses. Here we consider the more natural, but much more complicated, case in which an innovation, when it diffuses, applies to the same good. This extension forces us to distinguish between innovations that are in the exclusive domain of the innovating country, and those that have diffused to a common pool that both countries can access. Because of the many different situations that can arise, we limit ourselves to a two-country case. Even here we need to distinguish among situations in which: (i) one country uses only those technologies that are exclusive to it, leaving the common technologies to the other country, (ii) both countries use common technologies, with one country exporting goods produced using these technologies to the other country, and (iii) both countries use common technologies, with no trade in goods produced using them. The first case replicates the situation in EK (2002), since the technologies that each country actually uses are drawn from independent distributions. Diffusion has no impact on the extent of trade. In the second two cases, diffusion substitutes for trade, as at least a range of the goods produced with the common technology are nontraded. Nontradedness arises not because transport costs for these goods are higher, but because similarities in efficiency between countries have eliminated any scope for exploiting comparative advantage.

Section 3 introduces simple dynamics into the analysis. Each country innovates at an exogenous rate, and ideas diffuse from one to another at exogenous rates. The processes of innovation and diffusion generate a world steady-state growth rate in which the two countries, depending on their abilities to innovate and to absorb ideas from abroad, have (except by coincidence) different relative income levels. The framework can deliver "product cycles," as in Krugman (1979), in which the innovator initially exports the good using the technology it has developed, but later imports it once the technology has diffused abroad. In our model other outcomes are also possible. If the innovation is sufficiently small, before diffusion, the other country may continue to produce the good on its own using inferior technology rather than import the good from the innovator. In fact, its own technology could even be superior, so that the innovation is never useful outside the country of innovation.

Section 4 endogenizes inventive activity. It first calculates the value of ideas in each country, which determine the returns to innovation. The trade-off between the returns to innovation and to production governs the extent of inventive activity in each country. We consider the role of openness in the form of (i) lower trade barriers and (ii) faster diffusion on inventive activity in each country. A special case is no diffusion, returning us to EK (2001b): Each country allocates the same share of resources to invention regardless of its size or research productivity. Turning to the other extreme of immediate diffusion, we find that the same result emerges if the trade barrier exceeds the ratio of research productivities. But if the trade barrier is lower than the ratio of research productivities, the more efficient researcher specializes in innovation along Ricardian lines.

Section 5 offers some concluding remarks.

2. A Model of Technology, Production, and Trade

Our production structure is Ricardian. Following Dornbusch, Fischer, and Samuelson (1977, henceforth DFS), we consider a world with a unit continuum of goods, which we label by $j \in [0, 1]$. There are two countries, which we label N (for North) and S (for South). Each country has a set of available technologies for making each of the goods on the continuum. Some technologies, denoted N, are available only to the North while another set, S, are available exclusively to the South. A third set C are commonly available. A technology is the ability to produce $z_i(j)$ units of good j with one worker, where, depending on which type of technology we are talking about, $i = N, S, C$. (It is convenient for us to use i to index both the three types of technologies $i = N, S, C$ and the two countries $i = N, S$ that have exclusive knowledge of technologies $i = N, S$ respectively.)

We treat the $z_i(j)$'s as realizations of random variables Z_i drawn independently for each j from the Fréchet distributions:

$$F_i(z) = \Pr[Z_i \leq z] = \exp[-T_i z^{-\theta}] \tag{1}$$

which are independent across $i = N, S, C$. In this static context the T_i's reflect the average efficiencies across the three sets of technologies. (We consider how these distributions arise from a dynamic process of innovation and diffusion in sections 3 and 4.)

The best technologies available in country i are realizations of:

$$Z_i^* = \max[Z_i, Z_C] \; i = N, S.$$

Thus the random variable Z_i^* has distribution:

$$F_i^*(z) = \Pr[Z_i^* \leq z] = \exp[-T_i^* z^{-\theta}]$$

where $T_i^* = T_i + T_C$. The T_i^* reflect the average efficiencies across the set of technologies available to country $i = N, S$.

EK (2002) consider a case in which there is no common technology, so that $T_C = 0$. An implication is that the distributions of efficiencies available to each country are independent. Here there is independence across the exclusive technologies, but the common technologies induce a positive correlation between Z_N^* and Z_S^*. Because of this correlation we will find it easier to work with the three independent technology distributions of Z_N, Z_S, and Z_C.

As is standard in a Ricardian setting, workers are identical and mobile across activities within a country, but cannot change countries. The wage is w_N in the North and w_S in the South. We take the wage in the South to be the numeraire, although we leave w_S in formulas for clarity. Labor market clearing conditions, introduced below, establish the relative wage. Without loss of generality we will impose restrictions on exogenous variables so that in equilibrium $w_N \geq w_S$.[3]

As in DFS, demand is Cobb-Douglas, which we further simplify by assuming that expenditure shares are the same across goods. Hence expenditure in country i on good j is:

$$X_i(j) = X_i,$$

where X_i is total expenditure.[4]

Also as in DFS, goods can be transported between the countries, but in order to deliver one unit to the destination $d \geq 1$ units need to be shipped from the source (the standard "iceberg" assumption). Unfortunately, even in low-dimensional Ricardian problems, taxonomies are inevitable. There are three cases to consider: (1) If $w_N > w_S d$ then the commonly available technologies are used only in the South; the North uses only those technologies unique to it. (2) If $w_N = w_S d$ then the commonly available technologies may be used in both countries, but goods produced using these technologies are exported only by the South. (3) If $w_N < w_S d$ then each country will use the commonly available technologies. Goods produced using these technologies aren't traded since it is more expensive to import the good than to make it oneself.

2.1. Cost Distributions

To mitigate the proliferation of special cases, we introduce the term w_{ni} to indicate the effective wage, inclusive of transport cost, for goods sold in country n produced using technology i. Here $n = N, S$ and $i = N, S, C$. Taking the case of the Northern market, $w_{NN} = w_N$ and $w_{NS} = w_S d$, while $w_{NC} = \min\{w_S d, w_N\}$ is the wage paid to labor producing goods using the common technologies and sold in the North (including transport cost should the South be the sole user). Hence $w_{NC}/z_C(j)$ is the cost of selling good j in the North if it is produced using a common technology. In the first case above $w_{NC} = w_S d < w_N$; in the second $w_{NC} = w_N = w_S d$, and in the third, $w_{NC} = w_N < w_S d$. For the Southern market $w_{SS} = w_{SC} = w_S$ and $w_{SN} = dw_N$.

The lowest cost for good j in the North is thus:

$$\begin{aligned} c_N(j) &= \min\{w_N/z_N(j), w_{NC}/z_C(j), w_S d/z_S(j)\} \\ &= \min_{i=N,S,C}\{w_{Ni}/z_i(j)\} \end{aligned}$$

while in the South it is

$$\begin{aligned} c_S(j) &= \min\{w_N d/z_N(j), w_S/z_C(j), w_S/z_S(j)\} \\ &= \min_{i=N,S,C}\{w_{Si}/z_i(j)\}. \end{aligned}$$

Note that, for all j, $d \geq c_S(j)/c_N(j) \geq 1/d$, with equality on the left if N exports j to S and equality on the right if S exports j to N.

For $i = N, S$, the lowest cost $c_i(j)$ is the realization of a random variable C_i whose distribution derives from the distribution of the underlying technologies Z_i. We denote the cost distribution in i by $H_i(c) = \Pr[C_i \leq c]$. The cost distribution in the North is:

$$\begin{aligned} H_N(c) &= 1 - \Pr[Z_N \leq w_N/c]\Pr[Z_S \leq w_S d/c]\Pr[Z_C \leq w_{NC}/c] \\ &= 1 - F_N(w_N/c)F_S(w_S d/c)F_C(w_{NC}/c) \\ &= 1 - \exp\left[-\Phi_N c^{\theta}\right] \end{aligned}$$

where

$$\begin{aligned} \Phi_N &= T_N w_N^{-\theta} + T_S(w_S d)^{-\theta} + T_C w_{NC}^{-\theta} \\ &= \sum_{i=N,S,C} T_i w_{Ni}^{-\theta}. \end{aligned}$$

Similarly, for the South:

$$H_S(c) = 1 - \exp\left[-\Phi_S c^{\theta}\right]$$

where

$$\begin{aligned} \Phi_S &= T_N(w_N d)^{-\theta} + T_S w_S^{-\theta} + T_C w_S^{-\theta} \\ &= \sum_{i=N,S,C} T_i w_{Si}^{-\theta}. \end{aligned}$$

As in EK (2002), the probability that country n will find technology of type i the lowest cost source for some good is:

$$\pi_{ni} = \frac{T_i w_{ni}^{-\theta}}{\Phi_n} \tag{2}$$

where $N = N, S$ and $i = N, S, C$. The difference from EK (2002) is that the sources are not necessarily countries, but rather sets of technologies.

2.2. *Trade Patterns and Wages*

We now complete the description of the static equilibrium by describing how labor market clearing determines wages in each country, and characterize patterns of trade. We posit that each country i has L_i^P production workers $i = N, S$. To keep things simple, here we assume perfect competition, introducing Bertrand competition in section 4 where we endogenize innovation.

Under many standard assumptions about market structure (including perfect competition or Bertrand competition), π_{ni} defined in (2) is the fraction of country n's expenditure devoted to goods produced with technology of type i. If X_n is total spending by country n, spending on labor producing goods using exclusively Northern technologies is:

$$w_N L_N^E = \pi_{NN} X_N + \pi_{SN} X_S. \tag{3}$$

Here L_N^E is the measure of Northern workers using exclusively Northern technologies.

We now need to distinguish among the three kinds of equilibria.

2.2.1. CASE 1: THE NORTH USES ONLY ITS EXCLUSIVE TECHNOLOGIES

In this case, $L_N^E = L_N^P$, where L_N^P are all Northern workers engaged in production. Since only the South uses commonly available technologies, $w_{NC} = w_S d$. The solution needs to satisfy $w_N > dw_S$ in order for the North not to use them.

Under perfect competition, all L_i^P workers in each country are engaged in production and labor is the only source of income, so that $X_i = w_i L_i^P$. In this case expression (3) above, combined with expression (2) for the trade share π_{ni} becomes:

$$\frac{w_N}{w_S} = \left[\left(\frac{T_N/L_N^P}{T_S^*/L_S^P} \right) \frac{T_N w_N^{-\theta} + T_S^*(w_S d)^{-\theta}}{T_N(w_N d)^{-\theta} + T_S^* w_S^{-\theta}} \right]^{1/(1+\theta)} \tag{4}$$

where, as defined above, $T_S^* = T_S + T_C$. While the equation does not admit an analytic solution, it is easy to solve numerically.

Since the North does not use the common technologies, all goods produced are equally tradeable regardless of which type of technology they employ. The fact that the North has access to common technologies is irrelevant since it does not use them. The outcome is isomorphic to one in which the North knows only the technologies that are exclusive to it, while the common technologies are exclusive to the South, as in EK (2002).

2.2.2. CASE 2: THE NORTH AND THE SOUTH BOTH USE COMMON TECHNOLOGIES, WITH TRADE IN SOME GOODS PRODUCED USING THEM

In this case $w_{NC} = w_N = w_S d$. Hence the relative wage is pinned down by the transport cost, since $w_N/w_S = d$. The demand for workers using exclusively Northern technologies is:

$$\frac{L_N^E}{L_N^P} = \frac{T_N}{T_W} + \frac{T_N d^{-2\theta}}{T_N d^{-2\theta} + T_S^*} \frac{L_S^P}{dL_N^P} \tag{5}$$

where $T_W = T_N + T_C + T_S$, a measure of world technology. For this case to emerge parameter values must be such that L_N^E/L_N^P not exceed one. Otherwise we are in Case 1 above. We also need the demand for workers using the South's exclusive technologies L_S^E not to exceed the supply of Southern workers. This condition requires that the ratio

$$\frac{L_S^E}{L_S^P} = \frac{T_S}{T_W} \frac{dL_N^P}{L_S^P} + \frac{T_S}{T_N d^{-2\theta} + T_S^*}$$

not exceed one. Otherwise we are in Case 3 below.

In Case 2 the range of goods produced using common technologies in the North are not traded. Hence, unlike case 1, technology diffusion results in less trade than otherwise. Diffusion substitutes for trade.

2.2.3. CASE 3: GOODS PRODUCED WITH COMMON TECHNOLOGIES ARE NOT TRADED

In this case $w_{NC} = w_N < w_S d$. Labor market equilibrium requires a wage w_N that solves:

$$w_N L_N^P = (\pi_{NN} + \pi_{NC})X_N + \pi_{SN} X_S,$$

which, using (2), becomes:

$$\frac{w_N}{w_S} = \left[\left(\frac{T_N/L_N^P}{T_S/L_S^P} \right) \frac{T_N^* w_N^{-\theta} + T_S(w_S d)^{-\theta}}{T_N(w_N d)^{-\theta} + T_S^* w_S^{-\theta}} \right]^{1/(1+\theta)}$$

where, as defined above, $T_N^* = T_N + T_C$ and $T_S^* = T_S + T_C$ Again, there is no analytic solution, but solving for the wage numerically is straightforward.

Here all goods produced with common technologies are not traded. Technology diffusion reduces the scope for trade even further.

2.3. *Trade and Prices*

What is the relationship between technology, wages, and prices in each of these cases? In Cases 1 and 2 the wage in the North is higher than that in the South by a factor of at least d while the prices of goods produced using common technologies are higher by a factor of exactly d. Hence the real wage in the North is higher.

In Cases 2 and 3, some or all goods made with the common technologies are produced in both countries. Since the wage is higher in the North these goods are more expensive there, delivering the (Balassa-Samuelson) implication that the relative price of untraded goods is lower in the South.

3. Simple Technology Dynamics

We have so far considered the static equilibrium in which parameters of the technology distribution are given. Over time, however, we can envisage processes of innovation and diffusion governing the evolution of the T_{it}'s (introducing a time subscript). We first follow the specification in Krugman (1979), for example, which allows us to stick with perfect competition: Each country innovates at an exogenous rate that is proportional to its current knowledge, and ideas flow from the exclusive to the common pool at rates that are proportional to the stocks of exclusive ideas. We introduce four parameters, ι_N, the rate at which the North innovates, ι_S, the rate at which the South innovates, ϵ_N, the rate at which the South learns about exclusively Northern ideas, and ϵ_S, the rate at which the North learns about exclusively Southern ideas: Thus T_{Nt}, T_{St}, and T_{Ct} evolve according to:

$$\dot{T}_{Nt} = (\iota_N - \epsilon_N)T_{Nt} + \iota_N T_{Ct} = \iota_N T^*_{Nt} - \epsilon_N T_{Nt}$$

$$\dot{T}_{St} = (\iota_S - \epsilon_S)T_{St} + \iota_S T_{Ct} = \iota_S T^*_{St} - \epsilon_S T_{St}$$

$$\dot{T}_{Ct} = \epsilon_N T_{Nt} + \epsilon_S T_{St}.$$

While the analytic solution to this dynamic system is complex, it is straightforward to show that as long as the innovation and diffusion parameters are strictly positive and the initial value of at least one T_i is positive, the system evolves to a steady state in which all three types of knowledge grow at the same rate.

In general, the resulting growth rate of technology is the solution to an unpleasant cubic equation. It can be shown, however, that the steady-state growth rate is increasing in both the innovation and diffusion parameters (see, e.g., EK, 1999). In the special case of symmetry, $\iota_N = \iota_S = \iota$, and $\epsilon_N = \epsilon_S = \epsilon$, the steady-state growth rate is merely quadratic:

$$g_T = \frac{\iota - \epsilon + \sqrt{(\iota - \epsilon)^2 + 8\iota\epsilon}}{2},$$

strictly increasing in ι and ϵ. A world with more innovation but also more diffusion grows faster. Krugman (1979) considers a special case in which only the North innovates, so that $i_S = 0$ and the growth rate is just ι_N while $T_S = 0$.

4. Endogenizing Innovation

We now extend the model to endogenize innovation. We continue to assume that exclusive ideas flow into common knowledge at a common exogenous rate ϵ.

As in Kortum (1997), we model innovation as the production of ideas. An idea is a way to produce a good j with output per worker q. We assume that an idea is equally likely to apply to any good in the unit interval, and that q is the realization of a random variable Q drawn from the Pareto distribution:

$$F(q) = \Pr[Q \leq q] = 1 - q^{-\theta} \qquad q \geq 1. \tag{6}$$

Only an idea that lowers the cost of serving a market will be used.

Initially, ideas from country n are usable only for production there. Hence, for an idea from country n to lower the cost of producing good j for the home market, q must satisfy:

$$w_n/q \leq c_n(j) = \min_{i=N,S,C} [w_{ni}/z_i(j)]$$

where $z_N(j)$, $z_S(j)$, and $z_C(j)$ represent the states of the art in the exclusively Northern, exclusively Southern, and commonly available technologies, respectively. (Recall that w_{ni} is the transport cost-inclusive wage applying to technology i in market n.) To lower the cost of of producing good j for the foreign market $m \neq n$ it must satisfy:

$$w_n d/q \leq c_m(j) = \min_{i=N,S,C} [w_{mi}/z_i(j)].$$

Given the current local cost $c_n(j)$ of good j, the probability that a local innovation will lower cost is:

$$\Pr[w_n/Q \leqslant c_n(j)] = \Pr[Q \geqslant w_n/c_n(j)] = [w_n/c_n(j)]^{-\theta}$$

while given the cost in the foreign market m, $c_m(j)$, the probability that it lowers cost abroad is:

$$\Pr[w_n d/Q \leqslant c_m(j)] = \Pr[Q \geqslant w_n d/c_m(j)] = [w_n d/c_m(j)]^{-\theta}.$$

Since, with the possibility of trade, the cost of a good can never differ between countries by a factor greater than d, and can differ by less, the criterion for exporting is tougher. Small innovations may be used to produce only for the home market, while larger ones will be used for export as well.

We need to introduce an incentive for innovation. We follow the quality-ladders framework (Grossman and Helpman, 1991, Aghion and Howitt, 1992) and posit that the owner of an innovation has the ability to use it to produce and sell a product at the highest price that keeps the competition at bay. Thus an inventor who can produce good j at unit cost $c^{(1)}(j)$ can set a price $c^{(2)}(j)$, the unit cost of the second-lowest-cost producer.

4.1. *The Distribution of the Markup*

Consider the markup $M_{nit} = C_{nt}/(w_{ni}/Q)$ (where capital letters denote random variables) of a good produced with an idea in technology class $i = N, S, C$ in market $n = N, S$. The efficiency Q is drawn from the distribution (6) while the alternative cost C_{nt} is drawn independently from the relevant cost distribution:

$$H_{nt}(c) = 1 - \exp\left[\Phi_{nt}c^{\theta}\right].$$

If the realization of M_{nit} is less than one, of course, the idea is not used in market n at all. If it exceeds one it will be sold at price C_{nt}. The probability that the markup exceeds some value m is:

$$\begin{aligned} b_{nit}(m) &= \Pr[M_{nit} \geq m] = \Pr[C_{nt} \geq w_{nt}m/Q] \\ &= \int_{1}^{\infty} \Pr[C_{nt} \geq mw_{ni}/Q|Q = q]\theta q^{-\theta-1}dq \\ &= \int_{1}^{\infty} \exp[-\Phi_{nt}(mw_{ni})^{\theta}q^{-\theta}]\theta q^{-\theta-1}dq \\ &\approx \frac{m^{-\theta}}{\Phi_{nt}w_{ni}^{\theta}}, \end{aligned}$$

where the last approximation becomes exact as Φ_{nt} gets large. (Since we consider a steady state in which w_{nt} is constant, we do not index it by t.)

For the good to be sold, of course, requires $M \geq 1$, which occurs with probability:

$$b_{nit}(1) = \frac{1}{\Phi_{nt} w_{ni}^{\theta}}$$

which, using (2), we can rewrite:

$$b_{nit}(1) = \frac{\pi_{ni}}{T_{it}}.$$

An idea will be used if and only if $m \geq 1$. The distribution of the markup conditional on $m \geq 1$ is just:

$$G(m) = \frac{b_{nit}(1) - b_{nit}(m)}{b_{nit}(1)} = 1 - m^{-\theta} \quad n = N, S; \; i = N, S, C,$$

the Pareto distribution with parameter θ.

Integrating across the markup distribution $G(m)$, the expected flow of profit from an idea conditional on selling in country n is:

$$X_{nt} \int_{1}^{\infty} (1 - m^{-1}) dG(m) = \frac{X_{nt}}{1 + \theta}; \quad n = N, S$$

which is also the total profit generated in country n. The fraction of total profit earned by using technology of type $i = N, S, C$ in market n is π_{ni}. Taking into account the probability that an idea will be useful in that country, the expected profit in market n of an idea from technology i at time t is:

$$\Pi_{nit} = \frac{1}{1 + \theta} \frac{\pi_{ni} X_{nt}}{T_{it}}.$$

As time passes, X_{nt} and T_{it} both grow. The first causes expected profit from an idea to rise over time as the size of the market grows. The second causes expected profit from the idea to fall over time through the hazard of losing the market to a cheaper source of production. Conditional on still being of value, one idea is just like any other in terms of the distribution of its quality Q, regardless of when it was invented.

With these expressions in hand we are now armed to calculate the value of ideas.

4.2. The Value of Ideas

Taking into account possible diffusion, as well as changes in the price level, the expected real value of an idea developed in country i over its lifetime is:

$$V_{it} = \frac{P_{it}}{1+\theta}\int_t^{\infty} \frac{e^{-\rho(s-t)}}{P_{is}}\left[e^{-\epsilon(s-t)}\left(\frac{\pi_{Ni}X_{Ns} + \pi_{Si}X_{Ss}}{T_{is}}\right)\right.$$

$$\left. + \left[1 - e^{-\epsilon(s-t)}\right]\left(\frac{\pi_{NC}X_{Ns} + \pi_{SC}X_{Ss}}{T_{Cs}}\right)\right]ds.$$

where ρ is the discount rate. The expression $\pi_{Ni}X_{Nt} + \pi_{Si}X_{St}$ is total spending on goods made with technologies of type i. Here P_{it} is the price level in country i at time t With Cobb-Douglas preferences and Bertrand competition, the price of a good j is the second lowest cost of producing it $c^{(2)}(j)$. This cost has distribution:

$$II_{it}^{(2)}(c) = 1 - \left(1 + \Phi_{it}c^{\theta}\right)\exp(-\Phi_{it}c^{\theta}).$$

(See equation (8) of Bernard, Eaton Jensen, and Kortum, 2003, setting $c_1 = c_2$). With Cobb-Douglas preferences:

$$P_{it} = \exp\{E[\ln C^{(2)}]\} = \exp\left(\frac{1-\gamma}{\theta}\right)\Phi_{nt}^{-1/\theta}$$

where γ is Euler's constant (.5772 . . .).

We assume that both labor forces grow at rate g_L, with $L_N = \lambda L_S$. We require that $g_L/\theta < \rho$. In steady state, wages and the π_{ni} are constant, while the T's grow at rate g_T, so that prices fall at rate g_T/θ. Profit is a constant share of income, which also grows at rate g_L.

Because of royalty payments on technologies used for domestic production that were invented abroad, we need to distinguish country i's income X_{it}, which includes net royalty income from abroad, from its output, which we denote Y_{it}. We can write the income of country i, X_{it}, in terms of outputs Y_{it} and Y_{nt}, $n \neq i$, as:

$$X_{it} = \left(1 - \frac{\omega_{in}}{1+\theta}\right)Y_{it} + \frac{\omega_{ni}}{1+\theta}Y_{nt}$$

where ω_{ni} is the share of the technology used in country n owned by inventors from country i. Since labor income from production in country i is $w_i L^P_{it}$, where L^P_{it} denotes production workers, we can relate output to labor income as follows:

$$Y_{it} = w_i L^P_{it} + \frac{Y_{it}}{1 + \theta} = \frac{1 + \theta}{\theta} w_i L^P_{it}.$$

Hence:

$$X_{it} = \frac{1}{\theta}[(1 + \theta - \omega_{in})w_i L^P_{it} + \omega_{ni} w_n L^P_{nt}]. \tag{8}$$

We use these expressions for income in deriving the value of ideas in the various cases we consider below.

4.3. *The Rate of Innovation*

As is common in the endogenous growth literature, we introduce a production function for innovation, with country i having research productivity α_i, $i = N, S$. The rate at which ideas in technology i are created is thus $\alpha_i r_{it} L_{it}$, $i = N, S$, where r_i is the share of country i's labor force doing research and L_i is its total labor force. We assume that an idea transits from either exclusive technology into the common technology with a common hazard ϵ.

We define the ratio of technology exclusive to country i to country i workers at time i as $t_{it} = T_{it}/L_{it}$. It evolves according to:

$$\begin{aligned} \frac{\dot{t}_{it}}{t_{it}} &= \frac{\dot{T}_{it}}{T_{it}} - \frac{L_{it}}{L_{it}} \\ &= \frac{\alpha_i r_{it} L_{it}}{T_{it}} - (g_L + \epsilon). \end{aligned}$$

In steady state both r_i and t_i are constant, so that $t_i = \alpha_i T_i/(g_L + \epsilon)$ and $g_T = g_L$. Finally, defining $t_{Ct} = T_{Ct}/(T_{Nt} + T_{St})$, the ratio of common to exclusive technologies, t_C evolves according to:

$$\dot{t}_{Ct} = \epsilon - t_{Ct} \frac{\dot{T}_{Nt} + \dot{T}_{St}}{T_{Nt} + T_{St}}.$$

Thus in steady state t_C is constant and equals ϵ/g_L.

Since in steady state $g_T = g_L$, our expression for the value of ideas (7) becomes:

$$V_{it} = \frac{1}{\rho + \epsilon - g_L/\theta} \frac{\pi_{Ni}X_{Nt} + \pi_{Si}X_{St}}{(1 + \theta)T_{it}} + \left(\frac{1}{\rho - g_L/\theta} - \frac{1}{\rho + \epsilon - g_L/\theta}\right) \frac{\pi_{NC}X_{Nt} + \pi_{SC}X_{St}}{(1 + \theta)T_{Ct}} \quad (9)$$

where the X_{it} are given by (8) above, where $i, n = N, S, i \neq n$.

In an equilibrium in which workers in a country engage simultaneously in production and in innovation, the return to each activity should be equal. More generally, the conditions for labor market equilibrium are that:

$$\begin{aligned} \alpha_i V_{it} &= w_{it} \quad r_{it} \in [0, 1] \\ \alpha_i V_{it} &\leq w_{it} \quad r_{it} = 0 \\ \alpha_i V_{it} &\geq w_{it} \quad r_{it} = 1 \end{aligned} \quad (10)$$

for $i = N, S$.

A steady-state equilibrium is a solution for r_N, r_S, and w_N/w_S consistent with (10) and product market clearing as derived in section 2.

4.4. *Steady State Research and Growth*

Because of the taxonomy of situations that can arise, we avoid trying to provide a general analytic solution. But under each of four particular assumptions about diffusion and trade barriers the model yields insight into the effects of globalization on research: (i) no diffusion ($\epsilon = 0$), (ii) instantaneous diffusion ($\epsilon \to \infty$), (iii) no trade ($d \to \infty$), and (iv) costless trade ($d = 1$). As these four cases circumnavigate the full range of possibilities, they provide insight into the general solution:

4.4.1. NO DIFFUSION

Setting $\epsilon = 0$ gives us EK (2001b). Each country has to use its own ideas for production. Hence, spending on goods produced with ideas exclusive to country i corresponds with the total production of country i, $Y_{it} = \pi_{Ni}X_{Nt} + \pi_{Si}X_{St}$. Substituting this expression into value of ideas above and solving for labor market equilibrium in each country gives:

$$r = \frac{g_L}{\rho\theta}.$$

In steady state all countries do the same amount of research relative to their labor forces regardless of their size or their research productivity. Since there are no common technologies, we are in Case 1 above.

We now explore how much international technology diffusion upsets this stark result.

4.4.2. INSTANTANEOUS DIFFUSION

Consider the opposite case in which diffusion is instantaneous ($\epsilon \to \infty$) Now all ideas are common, so that $\pi_{nC} = 1, n = N, S$. Since all ideas diffuse immediately they have the same value regardless of their origin. We can write the value of an idea from either country as:

$$V = \frac{1}{\rho\theta - g_L} \frac{w_N L_N(1 - r_N) + w_S L_S(1 - r_S)}{T_C}.$$

Define $\tilde{t} = T_C/L_N$. Differentiating with respect to time reveals that in steady state:

$$\tilde{t} = \frac{\alpha_N r_N \lambda + \alpha_S r_S}{g_L \lambda}$$

where, as defined above, $\lambda = L_N/L_S$. Since the South can use all the same technologies as the North, for the North to engage in production requires that $w_N \leq w_S d$. (Remember that $w_N \geq w_S$ throughout our analysis.)

What happens depends on the relative size of α_N/α_S and d:

1. Say that $\alpha_N/\alpha_S \geq d$. Then, as long as the North continues to produce, $w_N = w_S d$ and we are in Case 2 above. The North does all the research ($r_S = 0$) The share of workers in the North doing research is:

$$r_N = \frac{g_L}{\rho\theta}(1 + 1/d\lambda) \tag{11}$$

(which cannot exceed one). Note that, compared with the case of no diffusion, the amount of research is higher in the North in proportion to the relative size of the South ($1/\lambda$) discounted by the trade barrier ($1/d$). Because of this discounting, the number of people engaged in research in the world is smaller than with no diffusion. But since $\alpha_N/\alpha_S \geq d$, effective research is higher since Northern research workers are more productive. This condition is what ensures that if the North is both producing and doing research then the South does not find research worthwhile. In this equilibrium the South runs a trade surplus with the North to pay for the ideas it uses in production. The location of production of any particular good is indeterminate.[5]

2. Say instead that $\alpha_N/\alpha_S \leq d$. We are in Case 3 above. Both countries will do research, and the relative wage will reflect research productivity, i.e., $w_N/w_S = \alpha_N/\alpha_S \leq d$. Since the trade barrier exceeds the wage difference, each country will produce its own goods. Since there is no goods trade, royalty payments must balance, which requires that $r = r_N = r_S$. For each country to find research worthwhile requires that:

$$r = \frac{g_L}{\rho\theta} \tag{12}$$

as in the case of no diffusion.

Hence our Ricardian assumptions yield starkly Ricardian results. If research productivity differences exceed trade barriers, countries specialize in research according to comparative advantage. But if differences in research productivity fall short of trade barriers, countries do their own research, while making use of each other's ideas. Knowledge flows rather than goods flows are how countries benefit from each other's innovation.

What about the more realistic scenario in which ideas cross borders, but only with delay? Special situations without trade and with costless trade deliver insight, although the results are not as clean, demanding numerical simulation.

4.4.3. NO TRADE

Say that trade barriers are so high that there is no trade ($d \to \infty$). This assumption was implicit in the model used to estimate innovation and diffusion among the top five research economies in EK (1999).[6]

Without trade in goods, royalty payments need to balance, so that $X_n = Y_n$, $n = N, S$. We can also set: $\pi_{nn} = T_n/(T_n + T_C)$, $\pi_{ni} = 0$, $n \neq i$, and $T_{nC} = T_C/(T_n + T_C)$, $i, n = N, S$. The value of ideas (9) then becomes:

$$V_i = \frac{1}{\rho\theta - g_L}\frac{w_i L_i(1 - r_i)}{T_i + T_C} + \left(\frac{1}{\rho^\theta - g_L} - \frac{1}{(\rho + \epsilon)\theta - g_L}\right)\frac{w_n L_n(1 - r_n)}{T_n + T_C} \tag{13}$$

for $i, n = N,S$; $i \neq n$. The first term on the right-hand side represents the value of the idea at home and the second its value abroad. Since goods are not traded, diffusion into the common pool has no implication for the value at home, while any return from abroad must await diffusion.

In steady state, balanced trade in royalties implies that:

$$\frac{T_N}{T_N + T_S}\frac{T_C}{T_S + T_C} w_S L_S(1 - r_S)$$

$$= \frac{T_S}{T_N + T_S}\frac{T_C}{T_N + T_C} w_N L_N(1 - r_N). \qquad (14)$$

Substituting expression (14) into (13) and solving for steady-state values of T_N,T_S, and T_C gives conditions for research intensity in each country:

$$\Lambda = \frac{r_N}{1 - r_N}\frac{Ar_N + Br_S}{DAr_N + \epsilon\theta r_S}$$

$$\Lambda = \frac{r_S}{1 - r_S}\frac{r_S + BAr_N}{Dr_S + \epsilon\theta Ar_N}$$

where:

$$\Lambda = \frac{g_L}{(\rho\theta - g_L)D}$$

$$A = \frac{\alpha_N\lambda}{\alpha_S}$$

$$B = \frac{\epsilon}{g_L + \epsilon}$$

$$D = (\rho + \epsilon)\theta - g_L.$$

There is no analytic solution for the general case, although with $\epsilon = 0$ or $\epsilon \to \infty$ we of course get back to $r_N = r_S = g_L/\rho\theta$. Imposing symmetry ($A = 1$) we get the following expression for the ratio of research workers to nonresearch workers:

$$\frac{r}{1 - r} = \frac{g_L}{\rho\theta - g_L} G$$

where:

$$G = \frac{(\rho + 2\epsilon)\theta - g_L}{(\rho + \epsilon)\theta - g_L}\frac{g_L + \epsilon}{g_L + 2\epsilon}.$$

Note that G is the product of two fractions, the first exceeding one and the second less than one. If $G = 1$ we are back to $r = g_L/\rho\theta$. The first fraction reflects the added opportunities for earning royalties abroad that diffusion allows, which increases the incentive to do research. The second reflects the fact, with diffusion, foreign ideas compete with domestic ones at home, reducing research incentives. Which effect dominates depends on particular parameter values. More diffusion means more research if $g_L/\rho\theta$ exceeds $1/(1 + \theta)$ and vice versa. Simulations suggest that deviations from $r = g_L/\rho\theta$ are small regardless.

What about the role of country size, as measured by A? Researchers in a larger country face less competition from foreign ideas, but have a smaller foreign market in which to earn royalties. In fact, our simulations reveal that the direction of the effect of country size on research intensity depends on parameter values.

We solve numerically for research intensity for the parameter values:

g_L	.01
ρ	.02
θ	8
ϵ	.02
$\alpha_N\lambda/\alpha_S$	1

In the symmetric case research intensity in each country is .057 (compared with .063 with no diffusion). We find that increasing the relative size of the North by a factor of 10 leads research activity there to increase to a labor share of .062 while the share in the South falls to .051. Raising g_L to .02, however, reverses the effect of size on research activity (although deviations from symmetry are slight).

4.4.4. COSTLESS TRADE

Say that trade is frictionless, meaning that $d = 1$. Case 3, with each country producing its own goods with the common technology, is, except by coincidence, eliminated as a possibility. If parameter values leave us in Case 2 above, then the wage in the two economies is identical, as is the value of an idea. If research productivity in the South is lower, only the North will undertake research. If the return is the same the location of research is indeterminate. In either case the world share of world labor engaged in research is the same as the closed economy value of $g_L/\rho\theta$.[7]

More interesting is a set of parameter values that leave us in Case 1 above, with the Northern wage above the South's. In this case the North uses only its own exclusive technologies, but earns royalties from technologies that have diffused into the common technology and are used in the South. The expression for the value of ideas, (9) above, simplifies by recognizing that spending on goods produced using Northern technologies is the same as spending on goods produced by Northern workers. Hence:

$$\pi_{NN}X_{Nt} + \pi_{SN}X_{St} = Y_{Nt} = \frac{1+\theta}{\theta}w_N L_{Nt}(1 - r_N).$$

Only the South uses commonly available technologies, while it also uses its own exclusive technologies. Total demand for Southern labor is thus:

$$(\pi_{NC} + \pi_{NS})X_{Nt} + (\pi_{SC} + \pi_{SS})X_{St} = Y_{St} = \frac{1+\theta}{\theta}w_S L_{St}(1 - r_S)$$

Substituting these expressions into the value of ideas (9), and solving for the steady-state levels of r_N and r_S gives:

$$r_N = \frac{g_L + \epsilon}{\rho\theta + \epsilon\{1 + \theta[1 - (\alpha_N/\alpha_S)(w_S/w_N)]\}} \tag{15}$$

$$r_S = \frac{g_L}{\rho\theta} - \frac{\epsilon}{g_L + \epsilon}(\alpha_N\lambda/\alpha_S)r_N\left(1 - \frac{g_L}{\rho\theta}\right).$$

To solve for the relative wage we need to refer back to our solution (4) for the static case above, setting $d = 1$ and replacing L_i^P with $L_i(1 - r_i)$. Solving out for r_S we are left with:

$$\frac{w_N}{w_S} = \left[\frac{r_N}{1 - r_N}\frac{\alpha_N}{\alpha_S}\frac{\rho\theta - g_L}{g_L + \epsilon}\right]^{1/(1+\theta)}. \tag{16}$$

Case 1 requires, of course, that $w_N/w_S > 1$. This solution also requires that r_S exceed zero. For many parameter values, the South will end up doing no research at all. We do not explore this situation further, focusing on outcomes in which both countries continue to do research.

Note that r_N and the wage ratio w_N/w_S can be solved in terms of each other, with r_S determined as a function of r_N. Of course with no diffusion we are back to $r_N = r_S = g_L/\rho\theta$. With diffusion, more Northern research lowers how much goes on in the South below this level. At the same time, a graphical analysis of the system establishes that, for reasonable parameter values, an increase in diffusion from 0 raises research effort in the North. Hence introducing diffusion shifts research activity from the South to the North, in line with comparative advantage.

Solving the model numerically, an interesting base case emerges with the values:

g_L	.01
ρ	.02
θ	8
α_N/α_S	5
λ	.1

With no diffusion ($\epsilon = 0$) a fraction .0625 of workers in each country pursue research, and the relative wage is 1.20 times higher in the North. Raising diffusion so that $\epsilon = .005$ raises the share of researchers in the North to .254 and lowers it in the South to .023. The Northern wage advantage rises to a factor of 1.37. Taking into account the higher productivity of researchers in the North, along with the smaller number of workers there, the effective level of research in the world rises by 60 percent.

5. Conclusion

What does our analysis suggest about the implications of globalization, either in the form of greater diffusion of ideas or of lower trade barriers, for research incentives? And what role does country size play? In our base case with no diffusion, countries engage in the same amount of research regardless of their relative size and research productivity. Openness to trade does not alter research specialization. More research productive countries are richer, since the same research effort yields more new technology.

Jumping to a world with instantaneous diffusion can have a major effect on the allocation of research activity, or none at all, depending on the importance of trade barriers relative to differences in research productivity. When comparative advantage in research is more pronounced, instantaneous diffusion leads to Ricardian specialization in research activity. But if trade barriers are more significant, countries continue to do the same amount of research as with no diffusion. Given the amount of diffusion, a lowering of trade barriers can lead to more specialization in research.

Intermediate levels of diffusion deliver less stark results. Under plausible parameter values we find a tendency for greater diffusion to shift research toward countries with greater research productivity.

While more trade and diffusion may cause research activity to shift across countries, our analysis provides little to suggest that greater openness of either form will increase research effort overall. Globalization, either in the form of lower trade barriers or more rapid diffusion, provides researchers larger markets, but also exposes them to more competition.

Even in our relatively simple model, intermediate levels of diffusion imply complex patterns of specialization in research. Size can matter, but the direction of the effect is ambiguous. It is not surprising, then, that we see some of the largest and smallest nations among the most active researchers. At the same time, there is reason to think that countries that do more research do so because they are better at it.

Notes

We thank the National Science Foundation for support under grant number SES-0339085.

1. Eaton, Gutierrez, and Kortum (1998) and, Eaton and Kortum (1999, 2001a), provide further analysis of research indicators across countries and over time.

2. The role of intellectual property protection was a main concern of Helpman (1993). The issue has been revisited recently by Gancia (2003) and by Dinopoulos and Segerstrom (2005).

3. Below, we consider the case in which technologies and the labor forces evolve over time. Since in this section we solve the static equilibrium given these magnitudes, we omit time subscripts for now.

4. A generalization to CES preferences is straightforward. See, for example, Bernard et al. 2003.

5. If the South is very large compared to the North (λ near 0), then the value of r_N in expression (11) can exceed one. In this case the North will specialize completely in research ($r_N = 1$) and w_N can exceed $w_s d$. Depending on parameter values, the South might find research worthwhile as well. We leave this case as an exercise.

6. The model in EK (1999) differs in several respects. For one thing, ideas in that paper are about inputs, which are not traded. But costless trade in final output allows for unbalanced royalty payments. For another, that paper allows for diminishing returns to research activity at the national level. Diminishing returns are needed to reconcile observations on the small share of workers doing research and their apparently large contribution to productivity growth. Since our purpose here is a better understanding of the properties of the basic model rather than a realistic application to data, we do not introduce this complication here. Finally, that model allows for imperfect protection of innovations, both at home and abroad.

7. This outcome requires that the share of the world labor force in the North exceed $g_L/\rho\theta$. Otherwise the North will specialize completely in research, and its wage can be higher. Again, we leave this case as an exercise.

References

Aghion, Philippe, and Peter Howitt. 1992. "A Model of Growth through Creative Destruction." *Econometrica* 60: 323–51.

Bernard, Andrew B., Jonathan Eaton, J. Bradford Jensen, and Samuel Kortum. 2003. "Plants and Productivity in International Trade." *American Economic Review* 93: 1268–90.

Dinopoulos, Elias, and Paul S. Segerstrom. 2005. "A Theory of North-South Trade and Globalization." http://web.hhs.se/personal/Segerstrom/Global.pdf.

Dornbusch, Rudiger, Stanley Fischer, and Paul A. Samuelson, 1977. "Comparative Advantage, Trade, and Payments in a Ricardian Model with a Continuum of Goods." *American Economic Review* 67: 823–39.

Eaton, Jonathan, Eva Gutierrez, and Samuel Kortum, 1988. "European Technology Policy." *Economic Policy* 27: 405–38.

Eaton, Jonathan, and Samuel Kortum, 1999. "International Technology Diffusion: Theory and Measurement." *International Economic Review* 40: 537–70.

———. 2001a. "Trade in Capital Goods." *European Economic Review* 45: 1195–1235.

———. 2001b. "Technology, Trade, and Growth." *European Economic Review* 45: 742–55.

———. 2002. "Technology, Geography, and Trade." *Econometrica* 70: 1741–80.

Eaton, Jonathan, Samuel Kortum, and Josh Lerner. 2004. "International Patenting and the European Patent Office: A Quantitative Assessment." In Organization for Economic Cooperation and Development, *Patents, Innovation and Economic Performance*. Paris: OECD.

Gancia, Gino. 2003. "Globalization, Divergence, and Stagnation." Institute for International Economic Studies Working Paper No.720, Stockholm.

Grossman, Gene M., and Elhanan Helpman. 1991. *Innovation and Growth in the Global Economy*. Cambridge: MIT Press.

Heston, Alan, Robert Summers, and Bettina Aten, 2002. *Penn World Table 6.1*. Center for International Comparisons at the University of Pennsylvania (CICUP) (October). http://datacentre2.chass.utoronto.ca/pwt/.

Helpman, Elhanan, 1993. "Innovation, Imitation, and Intellectual Property Rights." *Econometrica* 60: 1247–80.

Keller, Wolfgang. 2004. "International Technology Diffusion." *Journal of Economic Literature* 42: 752–92.

Kortum, Samuel. 1977. "Research, Patenting, and Technological Change." *Econometrica* 65: 1389–1419.

Krugman, Paul R. 1979. "A Model of Innovation, Technology Transfer, and the World Distribution of Income." *Journal of Political Economy* 87: 253–66.

Organization for Economic Cooperation and Development, 2004. *Main Science and Technology Indicators*. http://www.sourceoecd.org.

Part VII

FINANCE AND INNOVATION IN THE FREE-MARKET ECONOMY

Introduction and Comments

ALAN S. BLINDER

When people think of the free market's "innovation machine," they normally think of physical goods that embody some sort of improvable technology—such as automobiles, aircraft, computers, VCRs, DVDs, and the like. Building better mousetraps, if you will. But some of the most impressive, and terrifically interesting, achievements of the innovation machine have come in what might be called the "soft" sector—including software itself, retailing (think of Wal-Mart), and, most germane to this session, the financial service industries.

The two fascinating chapters that comprise this part of the volume deal with two very different aspects of financial innovation: Burton Malkiel explores the role of venture capital in promoting innovation (generally in nonfinancial businesses), and Robert Shiller explains some of his "radical" (his term) ideas for major financial innovations for the future. But it is worth pointing out in this introduction that, after being a productivity laggard for a long while (and thus a prime case-in-point for the Solow paradox), the financial sector in the United States has lately become a significant contributor to what has been a national productivity miracle since about 2000. Over the past few years, the major financial service industries as a whole have roughly matched the stellar productivity performance of the overall private sector in the United States. Yes, all those computers—plus a goodly amount of brainpower—have finally paid dividends in the financial services, or so it would appear.

But the story told in Malkiel's essay, the second of the two in this part of the volume, is not about productivity gains in the financial sector. Instead, it is about the pivotal role of one tiny sliver of the financial sector—venture capital—in promoting innovation in information technology, in biotechnology, and elsewhere in the economy. William Baumol has pointed out with characteristic insight that much innovation is now routinized in large corporations, where it has become one of the prime avenues of industrial competition—perhaps even more important than price competition. But there is another major source of innovation from small companies, especially the small, start-up companies that often fail but sometimes grow up to be Cisco or Starbucks or Microsoft. Unlike the big, established companies, these fledgling enterprises are typically starved for capital. And the uses to which they propose to put the capital are often quite risky. This is where the venture capitalists come in, mediating between those with ideas and those with capital.

As you look around the world, the United States seems to be far better than other countries at providing new, entrepreneurial firms with the seed money necessary to launch new enterprises. And, if these young firms appear to have promising futures, they are able to access the capital markets in more substantial and durable ways. In Malkiel's view, it is the venture capital (VC) industry that plays the crucial role in this particular form of financial intermediation, making the United States "unique in providing fuel for the free-market innovation machine."

According to Malkiel, VC firms assist the innovation machine in several important ways. They screen prospective projects and firms, separating the "wheat" from the "chaff." They serve as mentors to budding (often young) capitalists who may know more about, say, computers than they do about running a business. They play a gatekeeper role, regulating access to the capital markets—typically through initial public offerings (IPOs). In terms of sheer volume, venture capital firms have traditionally financed only a small fraction of business investment, even in the United States. But, as Malkiel shows, that fraction rose dramatically during the great boom (or was it the great bubble?) of 1998–2000, when VC financing soared.

Yet, as he frankly points out, there is also a "dark side" to all this entrepreneurial zest—a dark side that was amply displayed, for example, by the great Internet boom and bust. As he notes, "each boom in [venture] financings seems to have been overdone," leading to "considerable wasted investment" and "some instability" in the general economy. Put slightly differently, VC financing (and other types of high-octane entrepreneurial activity) tend to go to extremes, producing booms followed by busts—speculative bubbles, if you will.

One crucial question for students of capitalism is whether these periods of—why not say it?—craziness are an inherent part of the creative destruction that is at the heart of capitalism. Or are bubbles unnecessary detours that could and should be avoided? Malkiel clearly leans toward the first interpretation, as do I. Overdoing it now and then may be part of the price we pay to maintain the vibrant, innovative capitalism extolled so eloquently by Baumol. Could it be that the innovation machine must be fueled by a dose of excessive optimism—at least from the entrepreneurial minority of the population? If so, it seems to me, and to Malkiel, that the price is well worth paying.

Robert Shiller's fascinating contribution to this book is in what might be called the Bobby Kennedy tradition: Shiller looks at financial markets that never were and asks, Why not? He asserts that "massive gains in human welfare" could be achieved by using a variety of new financial instruments that he believes should be invented—or, indeed, that he and his collaborators are in the process of inventing and marketing. It is a theme that will be familiar to readers of Shiller's two remarkable books on the subject, *Macro Markets* (1993) and *The New Financial Order* (2003). But those who have not read these works are in for a treat.

Shiller imagines new financial markets in which people can insure away some of the huge pecuniary risks inherent in their choice of occupation. He imagines, and has even helped to create, home equity insurance policies that reduce the financial risk of a decline in the price of one's home—which is the largest asset by far in most people's portfolio. He imagines "macro markets" where people and countries could trade financial instruments whose payouts are linked to, say, the GDP of a particular nation.

As Shiller notes, no one should expect innovation to be easy: "the history of invention shows that formidable obstacles stand in the way of implementing simple ideas." And he explores a few of these obstacles in this essay: the force of simple inertia, the difficulty of measuring certain risks and attaching probability distributions to them, the difficult psychology of "framing" unfamiliar things, and what appears (to behavioral economists) to be risk-loving behavior when it comes to losses. Each of these is a clear impediment to the sale of the new risk management tools that Shiller envisions.

But, in the end, he is optimistic about innovation—just as Baumol is. Shiller observes, for example, that "radical" innovations such as life insurance and fire insurance seemed strange and unfamiliar at the time they were being invented and first marketed. Yet they eventually caught on and are now so common that the very ideas seem prosaic. He also notes that technology should help. Large new databases and the ability to manipulate them electronically have made it possible to write contracts that were simply not possible years ago—such as contracts that settle on indexes of home prices rather than on the actual price of a particular home (where moral hazard may be an overwhelming problem).

Viewed as a pair, these two chapters extend the analysis of Baumol's innovation machine in creative new directions that are both qualitatively and quantitatively important. And they are written by two talented authors in a lively, provocative style. Enjoy!

Chapter 13

Radical Financial Innovation

ROBERT J. SHILLER

THE BASIC PRINCIPLES OF RISK management—pooling, diversification, and hedging—inherently suggest much more dramatic and effective reduction of risks than we now observe offered by our institutions of insurance, securities and banking, or by any other institutions. To achieve such risk reduction, some radical financial innovation will be required.

By radical financial innovation I mean innovation that permits risk management to be extended far beyond its former realm, covering important new *classes* of risks. This is innovation that changes the assumptions about what can be insured, hedged, or diversified, and that has major impact on human welfare. It involves the "routine innovation" that, Baumol argues in his book (2002), oligopolistic firms see as part of their regular survival strategy, but it goes further. It is a form of innovation that requires changes in society that reach far beyond one firm, and most likely require changes in an array of institutions, and depends for its success on substantial public education as well.

Radical innovation requires serious experimentation, serious effort to find the precise form of financial or insurance structure that will perform well, serious effort to educate the potential clients about the new risk management tool, a commitment by the innovators to make it work, and an involvement with other institutions and thought leaders to make the variety of changes possible to make the innovation succeed. After the utility of a radical financial innovation is demonstrated, the innovation tends to be copied all around the world, just as are engineering innovations such as automobiles or airplanes after they are invented.

I wish to argue here that there has been radical financial innovation in the past and that, continuing what we have seen in the past, there will be radical financial innovation in the future. This will be a continuation of a long trend towards greater application of the principles of risk management.

To continue this trend over coming decades, applications of the newly appearing information technology will play a major role, as will also the improved understanding of behavioral finance that has been arising in response to developments in psychology applied to finance.

In this essay, I will review some of the main areas where risk management can advance, and I will compare past advances with future advances, looking at the nature of innovation that produced past success and the possibilities for major future innovation, in each of these areas.

Incompleteness of Existing Risk Management

According to the intertemporal capital asset model as developed by Robert Merton (1973) and as developed further by Douglas Breeden (1979), complete risk sharing in a stochastic endowment economy with nonstochastic preferences would imply that real consumption fluctuations are perfectly correlated across all individuals in the world. This result follows since with complete risk management any fluctuations in individual endowments are completely pooled, and only world risk remains. But, in fact, real consumption changes are not very correlated across individuals. As Backus, Kehoe, and Kydland (1992) have documented, the correlation of consumption changes across countries is far from perfect. In fact, the correlation of consumption changes across countries is even lower than the correlation of income changes across countries; the presence of any effective risk sharing, let alone complete risk sharing, would at least suggest the reverse.

Individuals do not succeed in insuring their individual income risks (Cochrane 1991). Moreover, individual consumption over the life cycle tends to track individual income over the life cycle (Carroll and Summers 1991), even though different people may have very different life-cycle income patterns that have little or nothing to do with aggregate risk. Risk management advice given to individuals tends to be focused on the short term, and to neglect such longer-run considerations as risk in future reinvestment rates (Merton 2003).

Another way of observing that risk management has a long way to go is to note that the institutions we have tend to be directed towards managing some relatively small risks, or risks with relatively small probabilities. An extreme case is flight insurance, which insures a passenger against the risk of an airplane crash (Eisner and Strotz 1961). Other risk management institutions have an inordinate importance today compared to when they were first invented. Life insurance was very important in past centuries when life expectancies were in the forties and when parents with young children frequently died; today the deaths of young parents against which life insurance insures is relatively rare. Fire insurance was very important in past centuries before the advent of modern fire departments, when candles and fireplaces were the norm around houses; now too the risk of loss of a house by fire is relatively small.

We have well-developed institutions for risks that were important long ago, and not for the significant risks of today. This gap reflects the slowness of invention to adapt to the changing structure of economic risks.

According to a theoretical model developed by Stefano Athanasoulis and myself (Athanasoulis and Shiller 2000, 2001; analogous models in Athanasoulis 1995 and Demange and Laroque 1995), the most important risks to be hedged first can be defined in terms of the eigenvectors of the variance matrix of deviations of individual incomes from world income, that is, of the matrix whose *ij*th element is the covariance of individual *I*'s income change deviation from per capita world income change with individual *j*'s income change deviation from per capita world income change. Moreover, the eigenvalue corresponding to each eigenvector provides a measure of the welfare gain that can be obtained by creating the corresponding risk management vehicle. So a market designer of a limited number *N* of new risk management instruments would pick the eigenvectors corresponding to the highest *N* eigenvalues.

Using a calibrated-estimated variance matrix for the period since World War II, and some conventional assumptions about individual utilities, we found that institutions that swap risks between major groupings of people would have enormous welfare gains. Even one or two well-chosen swaps just among the people in the G-7 countries would improve their welfare by several percentage points. That there could be myriads of contracts that provide risk management going beyond the G-7 countries, where risks appear to be larger, or extending down to the individual level, would suggest the possibility of massive gains in human welfare. And yet little such risk management is in evidence today.

Obstacles to Be Overcome by Financial Innovation

The ideal of risk sharing developed by Kenneth Arrow, in which there is a market for every risk and a price for every state of nature, is an abstract ideal that cannot be approached to any significant extent without an apparatus, a financial and information and marketing structure. The design of any such apparatus is far from obvious. There are unique challenges that designers of risk management devices face, challenges that have different origins from those faced by engineers who must design bridges or airplanes.

Risks can be very difficult to measure, the probabilities can be hard to determine, and the outcomes may be hard to verify. Asymmetric information problems, the associated selection bias, and moral hazard created by the risk management may create costs that make the risk management impossible to achieve in practice.

Major economic risks evolve amid a continually changing economic structure, whose parameters can never be known with the kind of precision envisioned by those actuarial scientists who conceived of life insurance.

Beyond all these purely economic problems, there are also problems of human behavior: a human difficulty appreciating risks and a weakness of will to take measures against them. The "risks as feelings" theory (Loewenstein et al. 2001) draws on neurological theory to describe the human weaknesses as regards risks. Human ability to take action requires emotional pathways in the brain that must be triggered if action is to follow. Mechanisms that drive people to take action against immediate risks, for example, the risk of falling from a high place, are well designed through repeated experience over the course of human evolution. But the human brain does not have the same kind of reaction to risks that are revealed only by abstract calculation or that unfold gradually over many years. These generate intellectual, but not strongly emotional, concerns, and there may be little impetus to take action against these risks. Risk management devices need to be designed so that people will use them.

Human behavior is also vulnerable to inconsistencies when confronted with making decisions involving choices among risks. Kahneman and Tversky (2000) have shown in a number of experiments that people's decisions in choices among risks can be easily influenced by changes in framing, by changes in the context, presentation, or environment that accompanies the decision problem. Risk management devices have to be designed so that people will tend to use them properly.

Financial innovators have had to overcome the obstacles to all of these problems. The institutions of risk management today, of insurance, securities, and banking, represent centuries of experience with these obstacles, and a significant body of knowledge about them. The successes of risk management to date have depended on knowledge of the nature of the underlying institutions and patterns of human behavior.

Managing Livelihood Risks

Initial efforts to manage risks to livelihoods were confined to the kinds of risks that could readily be verified as not due to moral hazard with the information technology of the day: life insurance and disability insurance. Deaths and disabilities are objective events. Suicides or self-mutilation to collect on policies are relatively unlikely. That is why initial efforts at insurance to manage the livelihoods of families covered these risks and not the more difficult-to-measure risks to the economic value of one's labor income.

But, as I argued in *The New Financial Order* (2003), it is incumbent upon us to use our better understanding of risk management and our better understanding of psychological barriers to risks to develop much more comprehensive policies against livelihood risks.

The life insurance industry first came into its own in the seventeenth century when the first elements of probability theory were understood. It was in that century that the first life tables were developed, reflecting a conceptualization that made possible the first understanding of actuarial science.

However, the application of the principle of insurance was slow to get started. Initially, only certain very narrow risks were insured, such as the risks of early death, ships sinking, or homes burning down. Gradually, the list of insurable risks has expanded. Life insurance was extended with disability insurance, and fire insurance was extended to cover other risks associated with ownership of property, such as floods or accidents. Still, some of the most critical risks are not insured even today. The risk that is covered by life insurance—essentially that a parent with young children dies—is not so great, compared to the risk that the parent suffers economic misfortune such as a loss of career opportunities.

Even when these limitations were accepted, life insurance and disability insurance were hard sells, and until the middle of the nineteenth century, very few such policies were sold. Studies of the marketing of insurance in the nineteenth century outline a number of limiting factors that were eventually overcome by better marketing and design of life insurance policies (see Stalson 1969; Zelizer 1983).

One problem is just a basic reluctance to pay to prevent a loss when one has the probability of getting by without any loss. According to the prospect theory of psychologists Kahneman and Tversky, people are "risk lovers" when it comes to losses. Kahneman and Tversky mean by this that people have an impulse, when facing a situation involving possible losses, to try to get away scot-free, without any loss at all. People are tempted to accept large potential losses in exchange for the possibility, the hope, of having little or no losses.

One of Kahneman and Tversky's experiments will illustrate this risk-loving behavior. They asked their subjects to consider a choice between two bad situations. They were asked to assume that they have no way of avoiding both situations; they have only the possibility of choosing which they dislike less. The first situation was an 80 percent chance of losing $4,000, and a 20 percent of losing nothing. The second situation was a 100 percent chance of losing $3,000. Their subjects showed a strong preference for the first situation: 92 percent of their subjects made this choice. By conventional canons of rational behavior, this is the wrong choice. People should prefer the sure loss of $3,000, since it is less than the expected loss of \$3,200 (=\$4,000 × 0.8) in the other situation, and is less uncertain. By conventional theory of rational behavior, people should view the larger potential loss of \$4,000 as particularly serious to them, since it reduces their income to the point where the value of a dollar to them is much higher, and they should therefore, in making their choice, give high weight to the possibility of such a bad outcome. But, instead, people seemed to want to be affected by the 20 percent chance of losing nothing.

This behavior creates problems for marketers of any kind of insurance. Paying an insurance premium is a sure loss. Not buying the insurance offers the possibility of getting away scot-free, with no loss at all. Prospect theory therefore offers a psychological explanation for people's tendency to underinsure.

Of course, people do buy some insurance even if they do not insure enough and do not insure against all risks. Moreover, note that 8 percent of the Kahneman and Tversky subjects made the "right" choice, which would suggest that there is a market for insurance among at least that fraction of the population. But if we are to secure a substantial fraction of the population in risk sharing, we must try to deal with the psychological obstacles in the design of the risk management device.

The risk-loving behavior described by prospect theory is not a sure thing, and indeed all of the implications of the theory are only tendencies in behavior, not entirely predictable behavior. One explanation of the varied outcomes across subjects can be had in terms of uncertainties of framing.

Framing in psychology refers to the point of view from which an individual assesses a situation. In the case of the experiment described above, the question suggested that the point of view from which to judge the situations was one's current income. The quantities were identified as "losses." But, some people might choose a different framing. Some might view the situation from the standpoint of the \$4,000 maximal loss. Then, the first situation is a 20 percent chance of getting \$4,000, an 80 percent of getting nothing. The second situation is a sure gain of \$1,000. When viewed from this standpoint, the normal risk-averse behavior for gains would, according to their theory, make the second choice much more attractive.

Since different people, or people in different circumstances, out of habit or suggestion, choose different framing, we get different choices. The Kahneman–Tversky framing interpretation for the variation in answers suggests that those people who make the "rational" choice, the choice that is less risky, do so because of chance suggestions or associations, not any careful thought or intelligible reasons. The Kahneman–Tversky interpretation suggests that promoters of risk management devices might encourage the use of these devices by structuring the description or appearance of the product, and managing a publicity campaign, so as to suggest a loss point of reference, rather than the status quo frame of reference.

An important milestone in the development of life insurance occurred in the 1880s when Henry Hyde of the Equitable Life Assurance Society conceived of the idea of creating long-term life insurance policies with substantial cash values, and of marketing them as investments rather than as pure insurance. The concept was one of bundling, of bundling the life insurance policy together with an investment, so that no loss was immediately apparent if there was no death. This innovation was a powerful impetus to the public's acceptance of life insurance. It changed the framing from one of losses to one of gains. Hyde's invention was copied all around the world.

It might also be noted that an educational campaign made by the life insurance industry has also enhanced public understanding of the concept of life insurance. Indeed, people can sometimes be educated out of some of the judgmental errors that Kahneman and Tversky have documented. There is some evidence that people may tend to give answers that are more in accord with standard notions of rational behavior if they have had the experience of someone's thinking through with them the issues. The psychologist Gigerenzer (1991) repeated some of Kahneman and Tversky's experiments after carefully reasoning with subjects about their choice and making sure that they understood all of its consequences. The reasoning with these subjects was done so as to be something other than a mere suggestion of a new point of reference. Gigerenzer found that people made, much more often, the rational choice. The Gigerenzer interpretation of the risk-loving impulse suggests that promoters of risk management devices might encourage the use of these devices by working to educate people about the true consequences of their actions. But doing this inevitably requires the involvement of others: opinion leaders, professional or labor organizations, and schools. Thus, radical financial innovation cannot be pursued by individual firms alone. These examples of the design of life insurance institutions, and of the proper marketing of them, need to be carried forward if we are to carry livelihood risk management into a more comprehensive insurance on livelihoods, and to form a pervasive element of our lives. In my book (2003) I discussed some important new forms that livelihood insurance can take in the twenty-first century, to manage risks that will be more important than death or disability in coming years. But, making such risk management happen will require the same kind of pervasive innovation that we saw with life insurance.

Managing Risks to Homes

Risks to homes are of extreme importance, since the home comprises the most significant component of wealth for most people, and loss of the home, or loss of value of the home, can be devastating. People rely on their homes for more than just housing services. Houses are also a store of value that may play a significant role in their risk management, and sold and consumed either in a bad economic draw or, after retirement, to make up for lost income. Thus, a decline in home value can represent a significant welfare loss.

With the information technology of the 1600s, when insurance on homes was first conceptualized and pursued on a systematic basis, the insurable risks were necessarily limited to risks whose outcomes could reasonably be confirmed and moral hazard limited with the information technology of that day. The risk of fire was the predominant risk that could be insured at that time. As the centuries progressed, the information technology and the associated legal system improved, so that more kinds of home risks could be insured. By the twentieth century, fire insurance was renamed homeowners insurance to reflect the wider class of risks that it covered.

Still, the major cause of risk to home value, the risk of change in the price of a home, has never been an important insurance institution. Today, when we can confirm with our repeat sales price indexes using electronic databases of home prices and associated characteristics that whole cities can decline in value by 30 percent in a matter of a few years, we are much more concretely aware of such risks, and in a position to extend homeowners insurance to cover such risks.

The first home equity assurance program was launched in the Village of Oak Park, Illinois, in 1977. The plan was created by the village and subsidized by the taxpayers in the village. To enroll for the program, an Oak Park homeowner needed only pay for an appraisal of the value of the home, after which the home was covered for 80 percent of any loss on later sale as measured by the selling price or a second appraisal. The original spur for this innovation was something rather different from pure risk calculations, and this motivation was to help prevent the decline of home prices at a time of racial change. Oak Park residents, who saw an influx of minority home buyers, worried that there could be a speculative price collapse in the city as a sort of self-fulfilling prophecy, as people sold merely because they thought that home prices would drop at a time of racial change. Oak Park today is a successfully racially integrated community and it has not seen village-wide home price declines.

The designers of the Oak Park program were in entirely new territory—there being no examples of home equity assurance programs in the past. They were confronted by design decisions that they resolved as best they could with their limited resources.

They were well aware that they needed to deal with various forms of moral hazard, and they attempted to do so by a number of terms in the insurance contract. The village reserved first refusal to buy the house, in order to prevent non-arm's-length sales being contracted at below-market prices. There were provisions about time on the market, a demand that the home be listed with the Oak Park River Forest Board of Realtors Multiple Listing Service, and a provision that a certified appraiser was to be called in at sale to estimate how much value was lost due to failure to maintain the property. These provisions complicated the process and imposed costs on both homeowners and on the insurance plan. The village was running risks with this pioneering program, including that the village itself would have to buy a substantial number of its homes. It was the high idealism of Oak Park to welcome minorities into a stable town that stimulated them to take these risks.

With the original Oak Park program, since the program was designed to prevent loss of home value due to racial change, the program was designed so that it was narrower than a program representing the risk of price declines of homes. The ordinance that created the program said that "The purpose of this program is not to protect against a regional or national decline in the single-family housing market. Therefore, in the event of a general decline in the value of single-family homes in the Chicago—Cook County—Metropolitan Area single-family home market, the President and Board of Trustees of the City of Oak Park reserve the right to review, revise and suspend payments under the Equity Assurance Program."[1]

The designers of the Oak Park program were trying to limit the risk to the town of Oak Park, so as to keep the cost of managing the risk low. Unfortunately, they did not have a rigorous way to do this, since in 1977 there were no reliable home price indexes for the city, county, or metropolitan area. A weakness of this program as it was initiated then was that it was vaguely defined, depending on some unspecified judgment in the future. This was a weakness of the information technology of the day, for there was nothing better that the designers could do to prevent these problems when there were no good indexes.

Making the policy suspendable at the discretion of the village also limited its success, since the eagerness of home buyers to purchase the insurance was reduced. According to experiments of Kahneman and Tversky, people are relatively less interested in risk-management products that afford only partial protection against loss; they view partial insurance, or probabilistic insurance as Kahneman and Tversky define it, with relative indifference. Kahneman and Tversky demonstrate this human tendency by tabulating responses to the following question:

> Suppose you consider the possibility of insuring some property against damage, e.g., fire or theft. After examining the risks and the premium you find that you have no clear preference between the options of purchasing the insurance or leaving the property uninsured.
>
> It is then called to your attention that the insurance company offers a new program called probabilistic insurance. In this program you pay half of the regular premium. In case of damage, there is a 50 percent chance that you pay the other half of the premium and the insurance company covers all the losses; and there is a 50 percent chance that you get back your insurance payment and suffer all the losses. For example, if an accident occurs on an odd day of the month, you pay the other half of the regular premium and your losses are covered; but if the accident occurs on an even day of the month, your insurance payment is refunded and your losses are not covered.
>
> Recall that the premium for full coverage is such that you find this insurance worth its cost.
>
> Under these circumstances, would you purchase probabilistic insurance? (1979, 169–70).

When presented with this question describing a quite unusual form of insurance, 80 percent of their respondents said no, only 20 percent yes. People behave as if they view the prospect of cutting the probability of loss in half as of less value than the prospect of cutting it in half again, to zero.

The aversion to probabilistic insurance is, as Kahneman and Tversky noted, troubling because really all insurance is probabilistic; there is no way to avoid all risks. The difference apparently has to do with framing. If we are thinking of a single risk, without considering others, we will be attracted much more to a policy that eliminates this risk completely. But if we are considering this risk among others, so that buying this same policy does not eliminate the combined risks altogether, then the policy will appear less attractive. The design of new risk management vehicles can be more successful if a single product protects against a set of risks that appears to the client to be comprehensive.[2]

Another problem with home equity insurance has to do with money illusion, the tendency to confuse nominal price changes with real price changes (Fisher 1928; Shafir, Diamond, and Tversky 1997). At the time of the insurance created in Oak Park in 1977, inflation in the United States was running at double-digit ranges. At this rate, the price level would double in less than ten years. The real concern of homeowners was that their home price would not keep up with inflation. And yet the Oak Park program only protected the nominal value of homes, not the real value. One of the most pervasive problems facing financial innovators is overcoming the public misunderstanding of inflation, and the public's general failure to demand indexation (Shiller 1997). The problem can best be solved if we adopt, and promote widely through society, a new system of economic measurements, that is, indexed units of account representing important economic concepts, so that we can break the habit of public thinking in nominal terms (Shiller 2003). But such a new system of measurements is another invention that must overcome the same sort of obstacles to purely financial invention.

Programs along the lines of the Oak Park program were created in southwest Chicago; northwest Chicago; Aurora, Illinois; Patterson Park/Baltimore; Ferguson, Missouri; Flourissant, Missouri; and Pittsburgh. As is the case with successful inventions, there was copying of the original invention in other places, and, as with other inventions, there tends to be a geographic spread of the concept. The home equity insurance concept spread from its origin in Oak Park to other towns in Illinois, and then to further cities and towns in the eastern half of the United States. Still today, as far as I have been able to determine, such policies have not spread beyond the United States.

The spread has been slow, and none of the original home equity insurance plans wrote a lot of policies within their communities. The Oak Park and the other policies persuaded no more than a few percent of homeowners to sign up for the insurance. When I spoke to an administrator of the Oak Park program about why it did not capture a larger share of homeowners, she offered that it did not have a substantial marketing budget and that homeowners may have had unfounded fears that submitting the results of a new appraisal to the village might result in their property taxes being raised. She also thought that homeowners merely were inertial, postponing indefinitely the steps needed to enroll in the program.

Another problem that has inhibited the spread of home equity insurance programs is the moral hazard problem that was not fully addressed by Oak Park. The risk is that people will neglect to maintain their house, or will alter it in such a way that its market value declines. The concept of relying on an appraiser to estimate the amount of neglect at the time of the home sale is fraught with difficulties, since ways of reducing home value are multifaceted and hard to quantify or observe well. As Allan Weiss and I argued (2000), this moral hazard can be dealt with by making the policies settle on indexes of home prices, rather than on the actual home price itself. Since the homeowner can have virtually no influence on a city or neighborhood index, there is little moral hazard.

The first home equity insurance policies that were created to be settled on an index were a part of a joint project between Yale University, the City of Syracuse, New York, and the nonprofit Neighborhood Reinvestment Corporation, with a subsidy from the U.S. government. Starting in 2002, homeowners in Syracuse could buy the insurance policy with a one-time-only payment of 1.5 percent of the value of the home, and then they would be insured for a period of 30 years against any decline of home value, at time of sale, as measured by the citywide price index.

The Syracuse home equity insurance program is an important example that may one day be copied by private insurance companies. And yet, still, there are obstacles that limit its spread. After a year of offering such policies in Syracuse, less than 100 homeowners had signed up for policies. Some design elements still remain to be worked out in the framing or marketing dimensions to encourage people to enroll.

Managing Country Risks

The risks that individual countries face, particularly developing countries, have repeatedly dominated international news. Debt crises in less developed countries are regular events, and they are unquestionably connected to changes in the economic fortunes of the countries.

There do not seem to be any well-developed institutions whereby a less developed country can buy insurance against its macroeconomic risks. Each country is expected to bear its own risks alone. The consequence of this lack of risk sharing is tragic: countries that start from a low living standard cannot afford economic failure. The existing institution of international lending provides some element of risk management for a country in the sense that, should the country find itself in great economic difficulty, it may expect to see the debt rescheduled or eliminated altogether. And yet this is a very disorderly system. Defaulting on national debt is not something that is achieved smoothly or reliably, and the default on the debt can disrupt the economy for many years.

One idea, applicable to small countries whose economies are dominated by certain commodities, is, at the date of the initial issuance of the debt, to tie their national debt to the prices of these commodities. Such debt arrangements, with what are called "value recovery rights," were actually made by Mexico, Venezuela, Nigeria, and Uruguay in the 1990s, though, surprisingly, the practice has not spread widely. Mexico has issued bonds tied to the price of the oil that it exports. Caballero (2002) has argued that Chile, a major copper exporter whose GDP has shown a substantial correlation with world copper prices, should index its debt to copper prices. But still Chile is not issuing such bonds.

Indexation of debt or other securities to macroeconomic variables has been mentioned at various times in the past. Brainard and Dolbear (1971) spoke of creating risk management contracts related to occupational incomes. Merton (1983) described consumption-linked national debt as a part of an improved pension plan system. In a *Business Week* article, Norman Bailey (1983) advocated converting defaulted debt into a share of exports. Krugman (1987) and Froot, Scharfstein, and Stein (1990) considered whether a defaulting country should index its debt to commodity prices or, alternatively, to its GDP, and worried about the moral hazard problems associated with the latter. Barro (1995) described bonds indexed to aggregate consumption as a vehicle for his scheme for optimal intertemporal national debt management. More recently, Borensztein and Mauro (2002, 2003) at the International Monetary Fund have advocated that less developed countries' sovereign debt be tied to the country's own nominal GDP.

In my book *Macro Markets* (1993) I argued that, just as the stock exchange is a market for long-term claims on corporations' incomes, there should be a market for long-term claims on all major aggregate income flows: gross domestic products, occupational incomes, and service flows from commercial and residential real estate. The creation of a market for a wide array of income flows would provide a major step forward in terms of opportunities for comprehensive risk management, as well as provide price discovery for major risks that are invisible today.

Issuance of instruments whose payouts are linked to the GDP of a country, or to other indicators of that GDP, whether these instruments are called securities or shares or bonds, could do a great deal to reduce country risk and promote welfare. But it has been difficult to get such markets started.

There are a few examples. With the help of Citibank, Bulgaria issued sovereign debt in 1994 whose repayment to international investors was tied to its own GDP. This has helped Bulgaria manage with rather disappointing economic growth overall since then. The idea of GDP-linked debt was copied by Bosnia and Herzegovinia and Costa Rica, but despite some advocacy (Dreze 2000), it has not spread further. Proposals have recently been aired that Argentina create GDP linked debt (Varsavski and Braun 2002) and Argentina actually issued GDP warrants in 2005.

Another indicator of macroeconomic risks is real estate risks. When, starting in 1990, Karl Case, Allan Weiss, and I tried to persuade futures exchanges to create new contracts for single-family home prices (Case et al. 1993), our efforts yielded only very limited immediate success. We did manage to persuade the Chicago Board of Trade to issue a press release in 1993 announcing tentative plans to create indexed-based futures markets for single-family homes, but they never carried out these plans. However, 13 years later, in May 2006, we launched both futures and options markets for ten U.S. metropolitan areas and for a composite U.S. index with the Chicago Mercantile Exchange and Standard & Poor's.

Recently, markets for macroeconomic aggregates were created, as part of the efforts of a New York company, Longitude, LLC, created by Jeffrey Lange and Andrew Lawrence from a theory developed by Lange and Economides (2001). Their trading system has been implemented by Deutsche Bank and Goldman Sachs in their new Economic Derivatives Market. They began trading U.S. nonfarm payroll, a monthly economic indicator in October 2002. But at the present time their market is very short term and does not provide price discovery for the price today of a long-term claim on a macroeconomic aggregate.

Allan Weiss and I secured a patent (1999) for a security, which we called macro securities, that might provide a way for a broad investing public to take positions on long-term claims on indexes, such as home prices by city or gross domestic product by country. Our invention was to set up a framework whereby an exchange stands ready automatically to issue or redeem pairs of shares, a long and a short share, that together bear no risk, but that can be sold separately, the separate components entailing risk. The exchange invests the proceeds of its sale in safe investments such as the money market. The exchange sets up a cash account for both members of the pair, and keeps the balance in the long security's account proportional to the index by shifting funds between the long and short accounts. The exchange pays both the long and short interest on their respective cash account balances.

Thus, the exchange has created a security whose dividends rise and fall with the index, and a security whose dividends move opposite the index. The design is more user-friendly to investors than current futures markets are, and the form of these securities is familiar: it would appear like an ordinary stock. A person wishing to hedge an economic risk that is measured by an index can take either a short or long security to offset this risk, and doing so does not require any more attention or expertise than buying a stock today.

With the help of Sam Masucci and a number of people at the American Stock Exchange, we (at our firm MacroMarkets LLC) have been working to develop macro securities. At this point we have completed the legal work to make these securities salable to accredited investors, and there is a good prospect of creating securities that can be marketed to general retail investors, eventually to be listed on the American Stock Exchange.

Still, the envisioned initial applications for these securities are to more familiar risks, such as stock prices or commodities, because of the formidable marketing problems in getting consumers interested in hedging the more important risks to livelihoods and homes. The trouble has been that our efforts to innovate to allow management of unconventional and important risks winds up, at least at first, applied to conventional risks.

Conclusion

The history of invention shows that formidable obstacles stand in the way of implementing simple ideas, but that innovations in design can eventually make them possible. I have stressed here that some of the most important obstacles are psychological, and that proper innovation can achieve better psychological framing of the innovations. Achieving this involves both design and marketing progress.

Achieving radical financial innovation is never easy. Doing so requires careful attention to design, experimentation to find the right design, and extensive marketing, and it requires cooperation from more of our society than just the isolated innovating firms that Baumol has stressed.

Historic changes in our risk management institutions are less frequent than historical innovations in science or engineering. But once such workable innovations are found, they eventually will be just as significant.

Notes

1. "Ordinance Providing for an Equity Assurance Plan for Single Family Residences in the Village of Oak Park," 1977, p. 1, http://www.newfinancialorder.com/ordinance.pdf.

2. For example, Bodie (2003) proposes bundling together retirement annuities and long-term care insurance, so that people approaching retirement can perceive a single product as covering their most important risks.

References

Allen, Franklin, and Douglas Gale. 1994. *Financial Innovation and Risk Sharing.* Cambridge: MIT Press.

———. 2000. *Comparing Financial Systems.* Cambridge: MIT Press.

Arrow, Kenneth J. 1974. *Essays in the Theory of Risk-Bearing.* Amsterdam: North Holland.

Athanasoulis, Stefano. 1995. "Essays in Risk Sharing, Derivatives Design, and Macroeconomic Policy." Ph.D. diss., Yale University.

Athanasoulis, Stefano, and Robert J. Shiller. 2000. "The Significance of the Market Portfolio." *Review of Financial Studies* 13 (2): 301–29.

———. 2001. "World Income Components: Measuring and Exploiting Risk-Sharing Opportunities." *American Economic Review* 91 (4): 1031–54.

Athanasoulis, Stefano, Robert J. Shiller, and Eric van Wincoop. 1999. "Macro Markets and Financial Security." *Federal Reserve Bank of New York Economic Policy Review* 5 (1): 21–39.

Athanasoulis, Stefano, and Eric van Wincoop. 2000. "Growth, Uncertainty, and Risksharing." *Journal of Monetary Economics* 45 (3): 477–505.

Backus, David K., Patrick J. Kehoe, and Finn E. Kydland. 1992. "International Real Business Cycles." *Journal of Political Economy* 100 (4): 745–75.

Bailey, Norman. 1983. "A Safety Net for Foreign Lending." *Business Week,* January 10.

Barro, Robert J. 1995. "Optimal Debt Management." NBER Working Paper No. 5327.

Baumol, William. 2002. *The Free-Market Innovation Machine: Analyzing the Growth Miracle of Capitalism.* Princeton: Princeton University Press.

Baxter, Marianne, and Urban Jermann. 1997. "The International Diversification Puzzle Is Worse Than You Think." *American Economic Review* 87: 170–80.

Baxter, Marianne, Urban Jermann, and Robert G. King. 1998. "Synthetic Returns on NIPA Assets: An International Comparison." *European Economic Review* 42: 1141–72.

Bodie, Zvi. 2003. "Thoughts on the Future: Life-Cycle Investing in Theory and Practice." *Financial Analysts Journal* 59 (1): 24–29.

Bodie, Zvi, and Dwight B. Crane. 1999. "The Design and Production of New Retirement Savings Products." *Journal of Portfolio Management* 25 (2): 77–82.

Borensztein, Eduardo, and Paolo Mauro. 2002. "Reviving the Case for GDP-Indexed Bonds." IMF Policy Discussion Paper PDP/02/10, International Monetary Fund, Washington, D.C., September.

———. 2003. "Innovation in Sovereign Securities." Unpublished paper, International Monetary Fund.

Brainard, William C., and F. Trenery Dolbear. 1971. "Social Risks in Financial Markets." *American Economic Review* 61: 360–70.

Breeden, Douglas T. 1979. "An Intertemporal Asset Pricing Model with Stochastic Consumption and Investment Opportunities." *Journal of Financial Economics* 7: 265–96.

Caballero, Ricardo. 2002. "Coping with Chile's External Debt Vulnerability: A Financial Problem." In *Economic Growth: Sources Trends and Cycles,* ed. Norman Loayza and Raimundo Soto. Santiago: Central Bank of Chile.

Carroll, Christopher, and Lawrence H. Summers. 1991. "Consumption Growth Parallels Income Growth: Some New Evidence." In *National Saving and Economic Performance,* ed. B. Douglas Bernheim and John Shoven. Chicago: University of Chicago Press.

Case, Karl E., Robert J. Shiller, and Alan N. Weiss. 1993. "Index-Based Futures and Options Trading in Real Estate." *Journal of Portfolio Management*, Winter, 83–92.

Cochrane, John H. 1991. "A Simple Test of Consumption Insurance." *Journal of Political Economy* 99: 957–76.

———. 1995. "Time Consistent Health Insurance." *Journal of Political Economy* 103 (3): 445–73.

DeMange, Gabrielle, and Guy Laroque. 1995. "Optimality of Incomplete Markets." *Journal of Economic Theory* 65: 218–32.

Dreze, Jacques H. 2000. "Globalization and Securitization of Risk Sharing." CORE Université Catholique de Louvain, Belgium. http://www.core.ucl.ac.be/staff/dreze.html.

Eisner, Robert, and Robert H. Strotz. 1961. "Flight Insurance and the Theory of Choice." *Journal of Political Economy* 69: 355–68.

Fisher, Irving. 1928. *The Money Illusion*. New York: Adelphi.

Froot, Kenneth A., David S. Scharfstein, and Jeremy C. Stein. 1990. "LDC Debt Forgiveness, Indexation and Investment Incentives." NBER Working Paper No. W2541.

Gigerenzer, G. 1991. "How to Make Cognitive Illusion Disappear: Beyond Heuristics and Biases." *European Review of Social Psychology* 2: 83–115.

Kahneman, Daniel, and Amos Tversky. 1979. "Prospect Theory: An Analysis of Decision under Risk." *Econometrica* 47 (2): 263–91.

———. 2000. *Choices, Values and Frames*. Cambridge: Cambridge University Press.

Krugman, Paul. 1987. "Bootstrap Debt Relief." Unpublished paper, Massachusetts Institute of Technology.

Lange, Jeffrey, and Nick Economides. 2001. "A Parimutuel Market Microstructure for Contingent Claims Trading." Unpublished paper, Longitude, Inc., New York.

Loewenstein, George F., Christopher K. Hsee, Elke U. Weber, and Ned Welch. 2001. "Risk as Feelings." *Psychological Bulletin* 127 (2): 267–86.

Merton, Robert C. 1973. "An Intertemporal Capital Asset Pricing Model." *Econometrica* 41 (5): 867–78.

———. 1983. "On Consumption-Indexed Public Pension Plans." In *Financial Aspects of the United States Pension System*, ed. Zvi Bodie and John Shoven. Chicago: National Bureau of Economic Research and University of Chicago Press.

———. 2003. "Thoughts on the Future: Theory and Practice in Investment Management." *Financial Analysts Journal* 59 (1): 17–23.

Obstfeld, Maurice, and Giovanni Peri. 1998. "Regional Nonadjustment and Fiscal Policy." In "EMU: Prospects for the Euro," ed. David Begg, Jürgen von Hagen, Charles Wyplosz, and Klaus F. Zimmerman. Special issue of *Economic Policy*.

Shafir, Eldar, Peter Diamond, and Amos Tversky. 1997. "Money Illusion." *Quarterly Journal of Economics* 112 (2): 341–74.

Shiller, Robert J. 1993. *Macro Markets: Creating Institutions for Managing Society's Largest Economic Risks*. Oxford: Oxford University Press.

———. 1997. "Public Resistance to Indexation: A Puzzle." *Brookings Papers on Economic Activity* 1: 159–211.

———. 2003. *The New Financial Order: Risk in the 21st Century*. Princeton: Princeton University Press.

Shiller, Robert J., and Allan N. Weiss. 2000. "Moral Hazard and Home Equity Conversion." *Real Estate Economics* 28: 1–10.

Stalson, Owen J. 1969. *Marketing Life Insurance: Its History in America*. Homewood, Ill.: Richard B. Irwin.

Varsavsky, Martín, and Miguel Braun. 2002. "¿Cuánto interés tienen que pagar los bonos Argentinos?" *La Nación*, February 4. http://www.lanacion.com.ar/02/02/04/de_371608.asp.

Weiss, Allan N., and Robert J. Shiller. 1999. *Proxy Asset Data Processor*. U.S. Patent No. 5,987,435.

Zelizer, Viviana A. Rotman. 1983. *Morals and Markets: The Development of Life Insurance in the United States*. New York: Transaction.

Chapter 14

Finance and Innovation

BURTON G. MALKIEL

THE IMPORTANT PARTNERSHIP between individual entrepreneurs and high-tech corporations that exploit their innovations comprises what William J. Baumol has called "The Free-Market Innovation Machine." This innovation machine is largely responsible for the remarkable growth in free-market economies and for the productivity improvements that have been an integral and essential condition for this growth. This essay will focus on the role of finance in encouraging innovative breakthroughs and in making it possible for many entrepreneurs, and especially many new companies, to obtain the capital necessary to bring such innovations to the market.

Entrepreneurs cannot create value if they are unable to attract the resources necessary to exploit their innovations. I will argue that the remarkable flexibility and responsiveness of the capital-raising system, particularly in the United States, has played an essential role in providing the fuel for the free-market innovation machine. I will discuss the critical importance of both the venture capital industry in providing *seed capital* and *managerial support* for new ventures and the investment-banking community in providing *follow-on* capital as a mechanism for liquefying the investments of the venture capitalists and thereby helping to encourage new rounds of initial-stage financing.

As illustrations of the crucial role of those financial institutions in encouraging innovation, I will present data on two industries that, over the past two decades, have been enabled to flourish by the availability of risk capital. The first is the biotech industry, which experienced rapid growth, beginning in the 1980s, both in the number of start-up companies and in the development of new products. The second is the information technology (IT) industry (including the Internet companies of the 1990s), comprising not only software and service companies but also the hardware necessary to make the Internet run.

While these two examples illustrate the beneficial role of our flexible financial system in encouraging innovation, they also illustrate the darker side of the process. There is no doubt that the discipline provided by the capital-financing process has left much to be desired. In both the biotech and IT industries capital was, if anything, too readily available, and many dubious projects and companies were financed. I suspect that such a side effect may be an inevitable consequence of the flexibility of the capital-raising process, but it is important to recognize that the same process that encourages innovation can, in certain circumstances, lead to considerable overinvestment. And, not infrequently, unrestrained optimism generated by the discovery of new technology or the creation of a new industry can generate financial market bubbles that threaten serious consequences.

Venture Capital Firms

Venture capital has been an increasingly important facilitator of entrepreneurial effort. Venture capital organizations raise money from wealthy individuals and from institutional investors to make investments in early-stage businesses that offer high potential rewards (often from the exploitation of new technology) as well as high risk. While the industry plays only a small role in financing the hundreds of thousands of new business corporations in the United States, and while the amount of venture capital investment is only a small fraction of total business fixed investment and of total corporate R&D expenditures each year, the importance of the industry should not be underestimated. Virtually all of the major growth companies of the past 25 years have been provided with seed capital by the venture capital industry. These companies include Amazon, Amgen, Apple Computer, Cisco Systems, Intel, Federal Express, Juniper Networks, Microsoft, Genentech, Starbucks, eBay, Yahoo, and Google. The VC industry has played a major role in commercializing leading-edge scientific breakthroughs and in the creation of entirely new industries such as those associated with the Internet.

Venture capital firms perform an important screening function in selecting new projects and new firms with the greatest opportunities for innovation. Indeed, Qian and Xu (1998) find that bureaucratic governments and large companies are far less successful in selecting high-potential projects. Moreover, Hellmann and Puri (2000) report that VC firms are more likely to fund innovators rather than imitators and that VC financing is responsible for a significant reduction in the time it takes for innovators to bring a product to market.

Lerner and Kortum (2000) have estimated that while the ratio of venture capital funding to total research and development spending in the United States averaged less than 3 percent during the 1983–92 period, VC funding was probably responsible for 8 percent of industrial innovation during the period as measured by patented innovations. VC-backed firms not only produced more patents, but the patents produced were also more valuable.[1] According to Gompers and Lerner (2001), by the turn of the twenty-first century, VC-backed firms accounted for almost 20 percent of innovative activity.[2] Finally, venture capitalists often provide an important mentoring (management consulting) and monitoring role. They typically hold a majority of seats on the boards of directors of companies they have financed and are usually helpful in assuring that the entrepreneur has established a business management team that can push the enterprise forward (see, e.g., Sahlman 1990). Moreover, by their active participation in the new enterprises, they can ameliorate the inevitable agency problems that bedevil new technology start-up companies.

A noteworthy feature of VC financing is described by Gilson (2003), who reports that it is common for VC investors to have the right to name a majority of the portfolio company's directors even though they may own less than a majority of the firm's voting stock. In effect, this provision turns the famous Berle and Means dilemma of the separation of ownership from control on its head. Rather than having owner investors at a disadvantage relative to the managers, the venture capitalists have disproportionately more control (including the ability to replace management) than their ownership interest would imply.[3]

In effect, venture capital investing helps bring about an alignment of interests and a structure of corporate governance that minimizes agency problems. Specialized investors are skilled at serving as board members and mentors to entrepreneurs and managers. Managers and entrepreneurs expect that their returns will come from a growth in value of their substantial equity stakes rather than from current compensation. A November 2004 interview with Thomas Brands, a principal of the venture capital company Accel-KKR, provides a good illustration of the way the professional firm works with the management of a start-up company.

"Before we make an investment, we sit down with the management team and lay out the plan to add value and get on the right track in the first 100 days. We want to make sure before we wire money that we have buy-in from the management team to a shared plan as to how value can be created going forward. Sometimes we find out we're not on the same page as management and we decline to make the investment. Many times, it's a great cathartic process for the management team to help lay out how they plan to build value and work with us. We lay out what needs to be done, when it needs to be done and who's going to do it and we measure against those metrics for the first 100 days. We think it helps improve the operations of our companies and the financial performance and ultimately the returns we can get for our investors on those investments."[4]

Two additional factors characterizing the U.S. venture capital industry are important in understanding the success of VC companies in encouraging innovation and in providing appropriate incentives for new entrepreneurs. The initial round of financing for the new venture is typically far smaller than will ultimately be necessary to exploit the new idea, invention, or technology. The VC investors, in effect, make the decision whether to continue to support the company with follow-on financing. This gives the VC investor a valuable option: the right to abandon the project unless certain milestones are attained. Such a threat creates powerful performance incentives for the entrepreneur. And by agreeing to such milestones in advance, the entrepreneur is provided an incentive to avoid exaggeration of either the new company's prospects for success or the time period over which such success can be achieved. If the milestones are passed, the supporting VC firm provides the future funding required for the entrepreneur to achieve scale sufficient to permit an initial public offering.

An important risk-limiting feature of venture capital funds is that they are typically organized to have limited lives. Thus, while venture capital investors accept the illiquidity entailed in their inability to withdraw their funds, the limited life of the fund provides a later exit opportunity. Moreover, if some companies in the VC portfolio have matured sufficiently so as to qualify for an initial public offering of equity securities, those proceeds, whether in cash or stock, must be distributed to the investors in the VC fund. Such mandatory distributions, as well as fixed limits for the life of the fund, ensure that profits must be returned to investors. If the venture capitalists wish to make new investments, they will typically create a new fund, which will be facilitated if earlier funds have been successful. Gilson (2003) argues that the venture capitalist's eventual exit gives the entrepreneur an important performance incentive: essentially a call option on regaining control of a successful enterprise. Moreover, Gompers and Lerner (2001) show that VC-backed firms tend to go public earlier than non-VC-backed firms and that even after they go public, VC-backed firms outperform their competitors in the same industries.

The Volume of Venture Capital Financing

Evaluation of the economic contribution of VC activity is facilitated by data on its magnitude. Figure 14.1 presents data on the volume of venture capital financing and the number of companies financed from the 1980s.

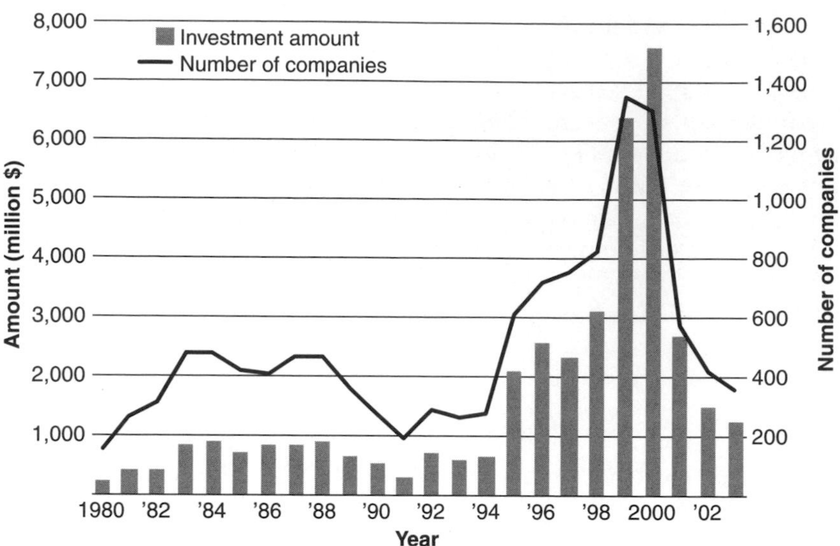

Figure 14.1. Venture Capital Funding: Seed/Start-up Investment in U.S. Companies, All Industries

The data include only seed moneys invested in start-up companies. Moneys invested by VC firms in leveraged buyouts and other corporate restructurings are not included. The figure shows that seed financing peaked during the late 1990s and early 2000s.

Figures 14.2 and 14.3 present data on the volume of seed financings and the number of companies financed for two of the industries at the forefront of innovation: biotechnology and information technology, including those start-ups associated with the Internet. The figures show that the volume of biotechnology start-up financings began to rise during the late 1980s and peaked in the middle to late 1990s. Financing of companies associated with the Internet showed a dramatic increase during the late 1990s and then fell off sharply in 2001, 2002, and 2003 after the collapse of what I will describe below as the Internet bubble. What is clear, however, is that the VC industry has been remarkably responsive in financing those industries at the cutting edge of technological change. When entrepreneurs saw promising opportunities to form companies for the exploitation of technological change, the venture capital industry showed remarkable responsiveness in providing the required risk capital.[5]

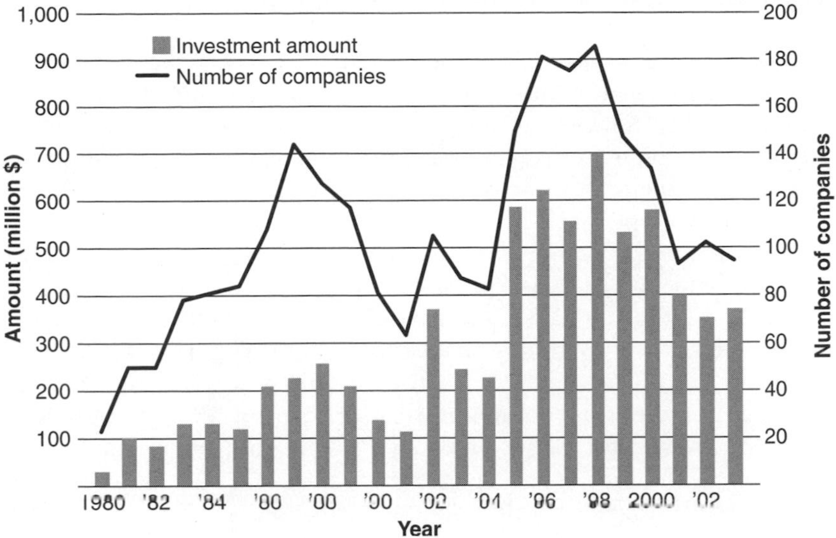

Figure 14.2. Venture Capital Funding: Seed/Start-up Investment in U.S. Companies, Biotechnology

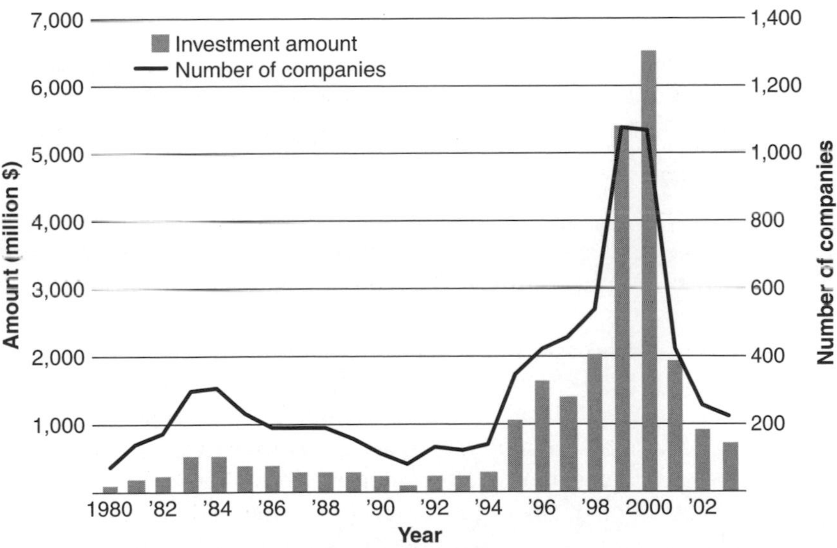

Figure 14.3. Venture Capital Funding: Seed/Start-up Investment in U.S. Companies, Information Technology

The United States versus the Rest of the World

The venture capital industry in the United States is unique in providing fuel for the free-market innovation machine. Despite the efforts of some European governments to subsidize a venture capital industry, the European VC market remains a small fraction of that in the United States. Controlling for the size of the United States and European economies, Gompers and Lerner (2001) find that in 1995 venture capital financing in the United States was eight times that of Europe. Gilson (2003) provides an excellent discussion of the failure of the German government to jump-start a VC industry during the 1970s.[6] According to Gilson, Germany's program provided no incentives (profits were limited and managers of the fund were neither rewarded nor penalized for performance), there was no monitoring or control of the companies financed (investments were completely passive), and the political representation in the fund management (involving stakeholders from many different constituencies) all combined to produce dismal negative returns.

Governments have had somewhat more success in getting the incentives right in programs in Israel and Chile, and some Asian countries have had recent success in the funding of entrepreneurial activity. Venture capital financing has grown rapidly in China and will no doubt continue to reach new highs each year for the foreseeable future. But most of the financing was raised from foreign sources. Only a minority of the financial resources were provided by local investors. The extraordinary success of the U.S. venture capital industry in encouraging innovation in small new firms has not generally been repeated around the world.

The Market for Initial Public Offerings

Central to the success of the venture capital industry in spurring innovations is the success of the investment-banking industry in providing an effective initial public offering (IPO) market for small innovative companies. It is the IPO market that offers an important exit strategy to the venture capitalists, enabling them to liquefy their successful investments, thereby providing the capital for follow-on early stage VC funds. Figure 14.4 shows the total amount of money raised in IPOs as well as the number of issues from 1980 through 2003. Figures 14.5 and 14.6 show similar data for the biotechnology and information technology industries. Comparing these exhibits with the earlier data on VC financing, one can observe that the more ebullient

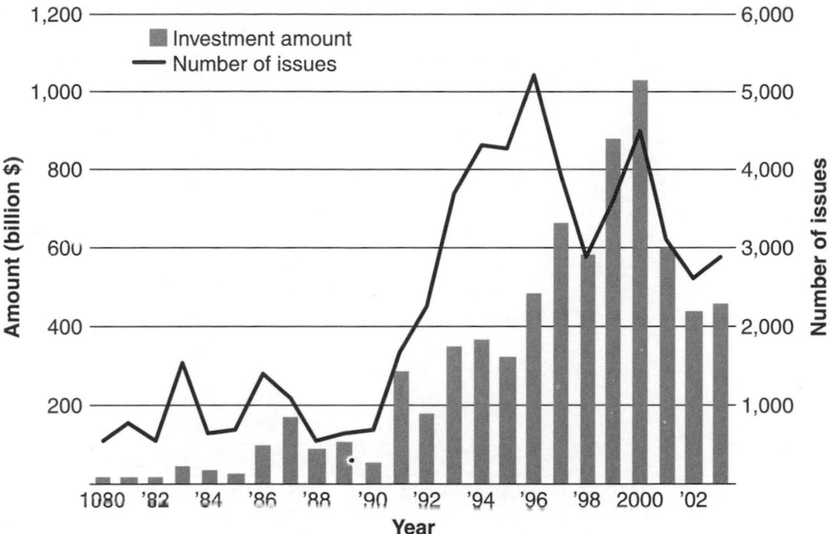

Figure 14.4. Initial Public Offerings: Principal Amount Raised in Global Markets, All Industries

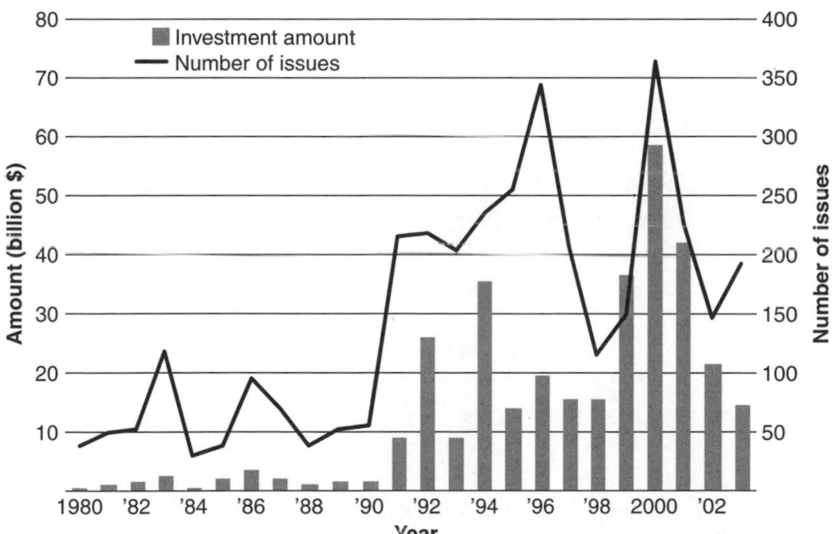

Figure 14.5. Initial Public Offerings: Principal Amount Raised in Global Markets, Biotechnology

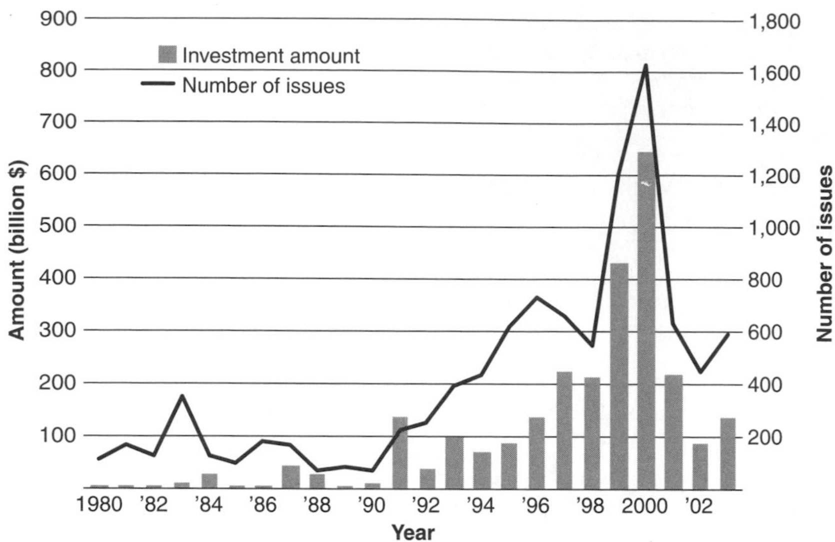

Figure 14.6. Initial Public Offerings: Principal Amount Raised in Global Markets, Information Technology

the public market, and the more IPO activity there is, the greater is the amount of VC activity.

In the decades up to the 1960s, investment banking was a very stable and noncompetitive industry. Certain top-tier firms (sometimes called "bulge-bracket firms") dominated the industry. Lower-tier firms typically did not compete aggressively for new business out of fear that the top-tier firms could retaliate by cutting them out of lucrative future syndicates. The IPOs that were completed usually represented quite mature companies that had achieved several years of profitability.

Starting in the 1960s, however, as trading volume began to grow and new industries such as electronics began to flourish, the volume of financing opportunities also began to grow. The expanding pie tempted lower-tier firms as well as new entrants to compete aggressively. Moreover, progressive weakening of the Glass-Steagall Act of 1933 allowed natural competitors such as commercial banks to enter the market. By the 1980s and especially the 1990s, underwriting standards were progressively loosened. The old view that required a firm to have (at least) a five-year history of profitability gave way to a new view that any promising company, whether profitable or not, could be brought to the public market. A large number of promising but unprofitable biotechnology companies were brought to market during the early 1990s and a wave of Internet-related companies, with neither earnings nor significant sales, were successfully floated during the late 1990s. All this availability of capital encouraged a large increase in entrepreneurial activity.

Gompers and Lerner (2001) estimate that by 2000, VC-backed companies that went public made up about one-third of the market value of the total stock market. VC-backed companies represented more than three-quarters of the total market capitalization of information technology companies (see Gompers and Lerner 2001, 67, 70).

The Darker Side of the Responsiveness of Financial Markets

There can be little doubt that the remarkable flexibility of financial markets (especially in the United States) has been a major support of the free-market innovation machine. But a fair assessment of the role of finance in innovation must recognize the darker side of the process. The preceding figures show that both private VC and public IPO financing have boom-and-bust characteristics. The ebb and flow of fund-raising and investing displays considerable herding characteristics, as has been emphasized by behavioral financial economists (see, e.g., Shiller 2000). Each boom in financings seems to have been overdone, leading to an overshooting of real business investment. In the end, considerable wasted investment occurred and some instability was injected into the general economy in the early 2000s as business fixed investment dropped dramatically.

What I would describe as a mini-bubble occurred in the biotechnology industry during the late 1980s and early 1990s. When Genentech came to market in 1980, the stock almost tripled in value during the first 20 minutes of trading. Over-optimistic investors foresaw an explosion of earnings for the industry, and stock valuations of biotech companies reached unprecedented levels. As may be expected, such enthusiasm in the public markets led to large increases in both VC and IPO financings later in the decade. Potential problems such as delayed approvals from the U.S. Food and Drug Administration, patent clashes, profits siphoned off to the marketing partner (usually a major drug company), and overestimated sales forecasts were all ignored. Many investors suffered staggering losses.

By far the biggest bubble occurred during the late 1990s and involved Internet-related companies. Most bubbles in history have been associated with some new technology or some new business opportunity. The Internet entailed both. The promise of the Internet spawned the largest creation and largest destruction of wealth of all time. When the bubble burst during the early 2000s, over seven trillion dollars of market value evaporated.

During the first quarter of 2000, 916 venture capital firms invested over $5 billion in start-up Internet companies. During the previous quarter, 159 IPOs had been successfully completed (see Malkiel 2004). It seemed that any even possibly plausible business idea could get VC financing and then quickly be sold to the public via an IPO. After the IPO was completed, shares would typically rise by over 70 percent during the first day of trading, thus encouraging even more new offerings in the future. VA Linux, one of the IPOs of the period, rose 730 percent in the first day of market trading. It appeared that any company that could claim some connection to the Internet could be financed in the public market. Stocks continued to rise as enthusiasm for "new economy" stocks appeared to be boundless.

The overinvestment in computer equipment and related accessories was staggering. Enough long-distance fiber optic cable was laid to circle the globe 1,500 times. The bubble was also associated with a host of fraudulent practices in both the business and the financial communities. The resulting overinvestment and waste of resources had significant deleterious effects on domestic economies around the world during the early 2000s.

Concluding Comments

I have chronicled the important role of finance in providing fuel for the free-market innovation machine. There is no doubt that the flexibility and responsiveness of the financial system (especially the VC and investment-banking industries in the United States) have played a crucial role in facilitating innovation and productivity growth over the past decades. We have seen that the VC industry in particular has played a critical role not only in providing the risk capital required to fund entrepreneurial start-up companies, but also to provide the management support so necessary for the start-ups to exploit the innovations they have developed. The noteworthy growth record of the United States in the 1990s, relative to other countries, is arguably ascribable in substantial part to the superiority of American financial institutions that focus on entrepreneurial activity.

To be sure, this financing mechanism was subject to excesses, and the discipline provided by financial markets has often been less than desired. But I suggest that this is an inevitable side effect of the free-market financing system. And as many mistakes as the free market has made, it is still undoubtedly a better allocator of capital than the government. Indeed, as we have seen, we have compelling evidence that government attempts to provide equivalent pools of risk capital have not proved successful.

Notes

I am grateful to William Baumol, Alan Blinder, and John Quigley for extremely helpful comments and to Derek Jun for excellent research assistance.

1. Because of the inverse relationship found by Kortum and Lerner (2000) between innovation and firm size, R&D expenditures by large firms are an imperfect substitute for venture capital financing of entrepreneurial small early-stage companies. See Bankman and Gilson 1999 for a fuller discussion of the advantages of the start-up firm in fostering innovation.

2. Gompers and Lerner also suggest that VC-backed firms' patents were more likely to be cited by other patent applications and to be involved in patent-infringement litigation, suggesting that they are of high quality.

3. See Gilson 2003. Gilson also reports a study by Hellmann and Puri (2000) finding that more than half of founding Silicon Valley entrepreneurs were replaced by professional managers at the behest of the VC-investing firms.

4. "Meet the Manager," PrivateEquityCentral.net, November 19, 2004.

5. There obviously have been earlier historical periods where innovation has flourished without the help of venture capitalists. But such innovation has not occurred without the availability of financing. The initial financing in early periods of history was more likely to come from individual financial entrepreneurs such as the Rothschilds, Andrew Carnegie, and John D. Rockefeller.

6. Gilson's analysis draws from Becker and Hellmann 2005.

References

Bankman, Joseph, and Ronald J. Gilson. 1999. "Why Startups?" *Stanford Law Review* 51: 289–308.

Becker, Ralf, and Thomas Hellmann. 2005. "The Genesis of Venture Capital: Lessons from the German Experience." In *Venture Capital, Entrepreneurship, and Public Policy*, ed. C. Keuschnigg and V. Kanniainen. Cambridge: MIT Press.

Gilson, Ronald J. 2003. "Engineering a Venture Capital Market: Lessons from the American Experience." *Stanford Law Review* 55: 1067–1104.

Gompers, Paul A., and Josh Lerner. 2001. *The Money of Invention*. Boston: Harvard Business School Press.

———. 2000. *The Venture Capital Cycle*. Cambridge: MIT Press.

Hellmann, Thomas, and Manju Puri. 2000. "The Interaction between Product Market and Financing Strategy: The Role of Venture Capital." *Review of Financial Studies* 13 (4): 959–84.

Kortum, Samuel, and Josh Lerner. 2000. "Assessing the Contribution of Venture Capital to Innovation." *Rand Journal of Economics* 31 (4): 67–92.

Malkiel, Burton G. 2004. *A Random Walk Down Wall Street.* 8th ed. New York: Norton.

Qian, Yingyi, and Chenggang Xu. 1998. "Innovation and Bureaucracy under Soft and Hard Budget Constraints." *Review of Economic Studies* 65 (1): 151–64.

Sahlman, William A. 1990. "The Structure and Governance of Venture-Capital Organizations." *Journal of Financial Economics* 27 (2): 473–521.

Shiller, Robert. 2000. *Irrational Exuberance.* Princeton: Princeton University Press.

Part VIII

TOWARD SOME LESSONS

Introduction and Comments

ROBERT J. STROM

The central feature of William Baumol's "free-market innovation machine" is the unlikely alliance—the "David and Goliath partnership"—between small, independent entrepreneurs and large, high-technology corporations. While the entrepreneurs serve as the source for innovative breakthroughs in this alliance, the large corporations are responsible for continually fine-tuning the entrepreneurs' novel products and processes. Together, the entrepreneurs and the corporations create an "innovation machine" that, according to Baumol, has been responsible for the unprecedented growth of free-market economies during the past two centuries.

Much of the previous discussion in this volume centers on the free-market innovation machine's role in the growth miracle that has occurred in the U.S. economy. The two fascinating chapters that make up this final part of the volume, however, extend the concept of the innovation machine to the critical issues of the economic welfare of developing economies and the performance of the continental western European economies.

As a pair, these essays by Edmund Phelps and by Eytan Sheshinski demonstrate the richness of the free-market innovation machine as an analytical tool in two very different applications. As each of these authors applies the principles of the free-market innovation machine to a specific problem, each concludes that the machine needs to be fueled and maintained if it is to produce economic growth, prosperity, and welfare gains. Proper fuel and maintenance, they agree, are necessary to ensure that the gears of this machine are unrestrained and that they work to produce a growing economy.

In this part's first provocative essay, Edmund Phelps applies the idea of the free-market innovation machine to continental western European economies. Phelps argues that one can view the selection of economic institutions as a key factor in economic policymaking that provides the equivalent of both the fuel and maintenance that Baumol's machine needs to produce growth and prosperity. Contending that there is an important linkage between the degree of dynamism in a nation's economy, the development of key economic institutions, and the nation's subsequent prosperity, he points to the failure of the continental western European countries to provide the fuel and maintenance that the free-market innovation machine needs. In his critique of these countries' policies that resulted in low employment and slow growth, Phelps argues that too much emphasis has been given to neoclassical policy instruments (e.g., tax rates, social contributions, and public expenditures) at the expense of more innovative thinking about policies that will support a well-performing economy. Corporatism specifically, he contends, has been harmful for both productivity and prosperity.

Indeed, corporatism can be seen to be in direct conflict with the underlying assumption of Baumol's machine—the idea that innovation will come from independent entrepreneurs. If corporatism restricts the actions of the independent entrepreneur in favor of a broader social framework for economic and business decisions, the free-market innovation machine effectively is robbed of the fuel it requires from those entrepreneurs to produce its growth miracle.

In the second essay, Sheshinski reaches his conclusions through an exploration of the potential welfare dilemma inherent in the idea of exempting developing countries from pharmaceutical patents. Applying Baumol's concept to a global context, Sheshinski's compelling essay asks if pharmaceutical patenting in these countries robs the free-market machine of fuel and maintenance, thereby inhibiting its ability to enhance economic welfare in these countries by slowing the spread of disease. Sheshinski analyzes the impact of both competitive and monopolistic pricing strategies on global welfare, the economic welfare of the developing country, and the incentives for the firm and the industry to engage in research and development expenditures. He finds that a variety of competing patent laws across countries—both product and process patents—further complicate this already difficult problem.

In this context, perhaps welfare gains can be found through the substantial impact of innovation's spillover benefits, articulated insightfully by Baumol in chapter 8 of *The Free-Market Innovation Machine*. An exploration of the extent to which these positive externalities can be directed to the areas of the developing world identified in Sheshinski's paper may offer another lens through which to view the complex question Sheshinski's poses here.

Sheshinski's and Phelps's applications of the lessons of the free-market innovation machine in a global context offer us much to consider. Sheshinski sheds light on the welfare loss in the developing world, and Phelps brings new ideas to the table in his discussion of the corporatist practices of the western European economies. Both authors, in fact, demonstrate the qualities of Baumol's independent entrepreneur in the innovative thinking and analysis they bring to broad economic issues. In the spirit of Baumol's free-market innovation machine, it is this sort of thinking and analysis that can lead to policies and practices that further support growth and prosperity.

Chapter 15

The Economic Performance of Nations: Prosperity Depends on Dynamism, Dynamism on Institutions

EDMUND S. PHELPS

SELECTING ECONOMIC INSTITUTIONS, I will argue, may very well be, in most if not all countries, the most critical area of economic policymaking, and yet it has been decades since it held center stage. A surface cause is that our understanding of institutions is relatively meager. A deeper reason is that it has been hard even to get started: We cannot have a reasoned discussion of the performance of institutions and the selection among them—which institutions are working well, which must be altered, and which new ones brought in—until we are willing and able to specify (for the sake of argument, at any rate) the kind of economy we desire to have. Here I want to propose a conception of the kind of economy that economic policymaking would do well to aim for—a notion of the desirable economy.[1] Such a conception can serve as the moral criterion for choosing among alternative structures of economic institutions. It also serves to put the whole discussion of economic policy in a somewhat new perspective.

The criterion most often used, implicitly or explicitly, in policy discussion is the static efficiency criterion applied in neoclassical economics and utilized in neoliberal/supply-side analyses of economic policy. In this doctrine, the focus is on incentives to work, to save, and to invest; and economic policies are judged by their disincentive effects on these decisions. We have all assimilated this neoclassical message, of course, the radical postwar Keynesianism being a thing of the past. We understand that countries *can* cause considerable mischief through misjudged settings of various policy parameters—excessive marginal tax rates, prohibitive replacement ratios, and so forth. The neoclassical/neoliberal/supply-side critique of the continental western European economies, however, goes farther, much farther: It states that, in fact, these *mistunings* of policy parameters *are* causing—indeed they are the *main* cause of—the low employment and growth slowdown there (see Layard, Nickell, and Jackman 1991).[2]

I do not want to insinuate that this neoclassical analysis is without merit or that it makes no contribution at all to accounting for the relative stagnation still present on the Continent and in Japan. My own work, for that matter, has taken account of the effects of tax rates on labor income, especially the short-run effects (Phelps 1994).[3] It has also placed much emphasis, perhaps more than is warranted, on employment and unemployment effects of a bloated level of welfare-state entitlements (Phelps and Zoega 1997). By now, a wide range of policy influences on economic activity and on growth have been indicted (see Heckman 2004).[4] So, while insisting that any assessment is subject to uncertainty, I agree that *some* appreciable part of the sag in activity and the slowdown in productivity in western continental Europe from the early 1980s onward, and in Japan from the early 1990s, results from these and other mistunings. The open question is the *degree* of importance of these neoclassical policy shocks. It could be that the estimated part played by escalating welfare entitlements and successive tax hikes in statistical explanations of the rise of unemployment on the Continent in the 1980s and 1990s relative to the United States is *largely* the result of a spurious correlation of those forces with the slowdown of technical progress, unfavorable demographic developments looming in the future, and other influences—not all of which are easy to implement in statistical analyses. If we look at the cross-section of nations belonging to the OECD, we do not find that intercountry differences in unemployment and labor-force participation rates are appreciably explained by differences in the tax rate on labor, the replacement ratio, and the size of the public sector.[5]

My complaint is that economic policymaking has gone from seeing neoclassical analysis as having a necessary place to regarding it as sufficient. Efficiency has gone from being an element of the good economy to being the sole criterion. The preponderance of actual and proposed reforms in Europe in the past few years have seldom looked beyond readjustments in the fine-tuning of the neoclassical instruments: tax rates, social contributions, and public expenditures. Believing the inflated welfare state to be the main problem, some countries are planning to retract it a notch, starting with expansions of the contribution time—in Italy, from 35 years to 40. Seeing high income tax rates as a big problem, some countries plan cuts—in Germany, by 10 percentage points, in France by 9 points. Believing that the replacement ratio in unemployment benefits to be crucial, some countries plan to scale it back—in France, to shorten the duration.[6] Believing that a shortage of infrastructure is also at fault for Europe's ills, the European Commission plans a program of increased bridges and tunnels—two billion euro's worth within 10 years. It is almost laughable that policy planners would suppose these modest, incremental policy reforms could be sufficient to make a noticeable difference in employment or in productivity growth. The deeper point, however, is that these responses show no deep or original thought about what constitutes a well-performing economy. So let me give my view on that matter and go on to discuss some preliminary, but suggestive, findings.

The Desirable Economy: High Performance as Productivity and Prosperity

What is wanted in policy discussion is an explicit conception of economic performance—of what a desirable business life is. Clearly, working-age people want a wide range of careers open to them. That in turn requires that wage rates be high in a wide range of jobs, hence a high-productivity economy. (Establishing a generous level of entitlements, such as the demogrants and tuition-free education for all, would permit people to choose the work they like regardless of how low the relative pay is; the difficulty would be that the high-productivity work needed to generate the tax revenues to pay for such entitlements would not generally be chosen.) Another point here is that active-age people need conditions in which they can function: to be able to think, to work and rest, and so forth. These conditions in turn require that people be able to afford adequate space around them, protection from severe cold and severe heat at home and at work; and affording these things requires high productivity. Nevertheless, high productivity is just one element of good economic performance.

For an economy to be said to be performing well, its participants also need to be prospering. Prosperity means the available jobs are engaging and rewarding in more than pecuniary ways. It means the availability of work enlisting the minds of the jobholders, offering challenges in problem solving, leading them to discover some of their talents and causing them to expand their abilities. The personal growth that comes from the discovery and development of talents is basic to what is often called job satisfaction. Clearly this prosperity is an end in itself, not merely an instrument to a high level of economic activity. Yet job satisfaction has knock-on effects such as promoting high participation in the labor force; also, a high level of employee morale, or loyalty, serves to lower unemployment and thus adds to the availability of such good jobs. So the degree of prosperity may be rather well *proxied* by some relatively well-measured things like the level of business activity—the participation rate (L/P), the unemployment rate ((L − N)/L) and the activity rate (N/P).

If that is our conception of a good business life—problem solving and discovery of talents, which in turn rest on the economy's dynamism, it is hard to see why the neoclassical preoccupations with disincentives should be accorded center stage. Correcting the calibrations of tax rates, social contributions, and public expenditures will not make resources more productive. And it will not make jobs more engaging and more rewarding. That is basically why the plan to add to the stock of bridges and tunnels strikes us as a sort of joke, even if we cannot put our finger right away on why it is funny. It seems unlikely that more bridges and tunnels on the Continent will contribute measurably to the sense of prosperity that those countries are so acutely and visibly missing.

Is it the generally accepted conception of high performance, though? In Europe? Or anywhere? The notion of high economic performance, of the desirable economy, that I have just outlined is commonly said to be peculiar to the United States.[7] Probably many readers will feel that this notion of performance—more broadly, the elevation of work and business—does resonate in varying degrees and respects with some memorable American writers, among them Franklin, Emerson, Lincoln, William James, John Dewey, John Rawls, Richard Rorty, and Derek Curtis Bok.[8] Nevertheless, the commonly held impression that this conception of high performance is foreign to European values is unfounded. Quite the contrary.

The humanist thesis that discovery, independence, enterprise, and participation are the route to personal development and achievement was, after all, first articulated and developed by Europeans. This humanism grew out of ancient Greece, the Renaissance, and the Enlightenment. Aristotle, in the *Nicomachean Ethics*, starts from the premise that "all men desire knowledge" and goes on to discuss the relations among work, learning, development, enjoyment, and happiness. Cellini in his *Autobiography* is the prototype of the liberated individualist bent on accomplishment and success. Smith propounds the social value of self-help and competition, and he champions broad participation in such a business life. J.-B. Say extols entrepreneurs as constantly reinventing the economy in their quest for higher yields, and Condorcet elevates the productivity of these economic entrepreneurs over the zero-sum results of political entrepreneurs vying for political favor.[9] Evidently American values derive from this European thought. And this line of thought goes on beyond the eighteenth century. In later centuries, Henri Bergson sees the potential for change as the *élan vital*, and the good life as one of constant "becoming" rather than mere "being." Marshall dwells on the workplace as the source of most of people's mental activity, and Myrdal views jobs as soon to be a richer source of most people's satisfaction than their consumption.

There is evidence, direct and indirect, that elements in Europe revolted from some of these core Western values. Nineteenth-century Europe saw strains of social thought directed against individualism, commercialism, and materialism. Such a revolt might be inferred from the fact that, in the early decades of the twentieth century, much of the Continent turned away from the vibrant capitalism of 1913: eastern Europe chose communism, later market socialism, while two western European nations, Italy and Spain, developed and installed the system called corporatism. Yet the matter is not so simple. A majority of the proponents of each of these countermovements supported it on the argument that this system was *superior* to capitalism in its ability to generate investment and harness science for progress, thus economic growth, and superior also in the offering jobs that engaged the mind and enlarged the responsibilities of the worker. The suggestion that the humanist tradition is now utterly foreign to European values and unique to American ones is therefore not historical and much exaggerated.

What is sometimes suggested, however, is that there has been a considerable erosion in the influence of these values on the behavior of typical Europeans. In Europe, the observation goes, people work to live and in America people live to work. It is suggested that more than a century of anti-business sentiment, some of it the result of Christian teaching, some of it an exasperation with fluctuations and inequality, has weakened the force of the old Western values.[10] It is thought by some that these new values lie behind a slow decline of the Continent's economic vitality. That hypothesis raises questions. What is the main source of prosperity? Is it economic institutions—the presence of some and the avoidance of others? Or is it culture? Or what? Or is it a vast panorama of things? But before we can even touch on that subject, we need to take some further steps.

Prosperity Depends on an Economy's Dynamism, Maybe Productivity Too

What must be present for an economy to offer this prosperity, which is so important an element of high performance? At one level, I would say the answer is that there must be *productive change*, which I call "dynamism." First, for the employed to be prospering, there must be the stimulus and challenge of change going on in the workplace—hence new problems to be solved, new tasks to be mastered, new abilities to strive for. Second, and less obviously, a country does not want misguided or pointless change; it wants investments that appear to the financial sector to have good prospects of creating productive change, that is, gains in productivity.

Is there any empirical support for that thesis? In the late 1990s, I realized there was circumstantial evidence unfolding that some countries had lower levels of dynamism than others and that the countries inferred to have low dynamism showed signs of poor economic performance—low prosperity, in particular, whether or not also low productivity. When the Internet and communications revolution broke out, some nations went into an investment boom while others were barely responsive. Of the 12 large OECD economies, three looked to be low in dynamism: Germany and Italy missed the investment boom, and France was very late to it. I realized that these same three economies had also been showing signs of poor rewards in the workplace and thus poor morale as a result (relative to the other nine economies): these signs included low labor-force participation and high unemployment.

Does productivity, the other element of performance, also depend on dynamism? Here the evidence is mixed, to say the least. The fact that the UK economy shows significant responsiveness at least occasionally to market opportunities, which is a sign of some dynamism, and yet appears to have relatively low productivity next to the levels in France and Germany, which show relatively little sign of dynamism, may be an indication that relatively high dynamism is not sufficient for relatively high productivity. (Another possibility, of course, is that the data of the late 1990s have misled me into grouping the UK among the economies with relatively high dynamism. Gordon Brown, chancellor of the exchequer in Britain, remarked that Britain did not have a boom in the late 1990s, contrary to my calculation. Yet another possibility is that France's measured productivity is flattered by its effective exclusion of its "unqualified.")

The fact that both France and Germany have relatively high productivity in the set of 12 large OECD countries I have twice referred to may indicate that relatively high responsiveness, thus relatively high dynamism, is not *necessary* for relatively high productivity. A familiar characterization of Europe, after all, is that it owes its high productivity to its clever imitation of what is proven to work in the United States after the heavy costs of innovation and the frequent experience of failure have been borne overseas. Yet, to elaborate on a parenthetical remark above, when some rough allowance is made for the rather poor rates of inclusion of various disadvantaged workers from jobs in the French economy, it is not at all clear that France does rank relatively high in productivity. In any case, this whole matter has to be left to future research.

An Economy's Dynamism Depends on Its Economic Institutions

How is a country to generate this dynamism on which prosperity depends? My thesis in this connection is that the degree of dynamism in a nation's economy hinges on its development of some key economic institutions—company law and corporate governance, the population's preparation for business life, the development of financial instruments such as the stock market, and so forth. Such general institutions as the rule of law and provision of enough personal and national security to safeguard earning, saving, and investing are needed for any market economy, even market socialism; they are insufficient for dynamism. To say that is in no way to depreciate the pioneering work of Douglass North bringing out the paralysis of an economy not supported by property rights; neither is it to depreciate the ambitious research by Andrei Shleifer confirming the large explanatory power enjoyed by some of the property rights he studies. It is only to say that there is more to dynamism than what North introduced and Shleifer tested and reinforced. The North-Shleifer thesis is based on classical considerations, and my additions are modernist, resting on actors' imperfect knowledge. The contrast between ballet traditions drawn by Twyla Tharp applies here: "Modern is classical plus more."

Evidence exists for this thesis on sources of dynamism too. We could have predicted very well (even as early as 1990) the ranking of the 12 large countries by the strength of their booms, if any—thus how they were going to rank over the late 1990s in terms of the dynamism they are inferred to have—simply from knowing how they ranked (in 1988 or 1990, say) by the percentage of the population with a university degree, the OECD index of licenses required for opening new businesses, and the breadth of the stock exchange as proxied by the market value of the shares outstanding (relative to GDP).

The two pieces of evidence I have brought up, the first linking circumstantial evidence of prosperity to the quality I have called dynamism and the second piece positively linking dynamism in turn to some institutions, for example, a broad stock market, and negatively linking dynamism to some other institutions, for example, licensing requirements on new firms, is, I think, a modest but significant advance. I would stress two tentative conclusions from this kind of analysis. First, there is considerably more to dynamism, it appears, than private property rights. Second, unemployment is not entirely or mainly the effect of misguided labor-market legislation. However, needless to say, this fragmentary evidence cannot speak to the whole wide range of issues over reform now facing Europe.

Is there evidence *directly* associating high performance—that is, prosperity and its visible sign, high employment, and high productivity—with the presence of institutions believed helpful to dynamism and the absence of those believed harmful? Such evidence emerges even with the small sample of just 12 large OECD economies.

An informal cross-country analysis of those economies that I have conducted with Gylfi Zoega examined three measures of economic performance: the employment rate (relative to the working-age population), the unemployment rate (relative to labor force), and labor productivity—the first two of these measures being observable proxies for job satisfaction, personal development for work, and so on. Taking one institution at a time, we found that university education improves all three measures of economic performance: employment, unemployment, and productivity too. Another institution, the "red tape" impeding innovators, as measured by the OECD index of barriers to entrepreneurs, is bad for all three elements of performance. Finally, legislation providing a high level of job protection is bad for productivity, but does not have a clear effect on either employment rate or unemployment rate.[11]

Searching for Effects of European Corporatism

As everyone knows, a system often called "corporatism" took shape in the interwar period, specifically from 1925 to 1940, in parts of continental Europe, South America, and east Asia. The fundamental corporatist idea was to retain the private income, private wealth, and private ownership of firms that was so central to capitalism (and found in avant-garde examples of market socialism too) but to remove the brain of capitalism—to curtail and to modify the mechanism of experiments and discoveries undertaken by unorganized entrepreneurs and financiers on which capitalism relied upon for its direction(s)—and to replace it with a selection mechanism governing investment and innovation that would require a consensus of key social groups. The main allocative decisions, such as the start-up of a firm or its close, are to have the approval of the designated groups constituting the society. Corporatism sought to interpose the interests of the whole society in a range of decisions affecting the directions taken in the business sector. The visible structure of this economic system, whatever the main uses to which it was actually put in this or that country, had several prominent features—nearly comprehensive labor unions, employer confederations, and big banks. In the postwar period, workers councils became another distinctive feature of the continental system.[12] And a new rhetoric grew up around these continental systems that introduced such terms as "social partners," indicative planning, "co-determination" and *concertazione*.

As was previously mentioned in passing, proponents and designers of the new system generally claimed it was inherently superior, at least in the sense of potentially preferable, to the capitalist systems then operating because it made possible a more rational resource allocation through the opportunities it offered for coordination in wage setting, investment decisions, and so forth. Corporatist theoreticians no less than socialist theoreticians saw it as an ex ante advantage of their system that it would or could be an instrument for scientific management of the economy. The contrary view that began to arise in the 1980s held that corporatism, in setting up machinery to facilitate direct interventions over a wide swath of economic decision-making, ended up giving one or more interest groups a power to veto every proposal for progress unless and until a satisfactory bribe was paid.[13] These powerful groups were not the Rawlsian least-advantaged and seldom if ever were represented by far-seeing and selfless statesmen.

I have inclined to the hypothesis that corporatist systems are harmful on balance for both productivity and prosperity—all things considered.[14] As I and some others see it, the peculiar corporatist institutions, to the extent they are still present in some continental economies, do not necessarily block *imitation* of known and uncontroversial advances in other economies—witness the continental "catch up" in the postwar decades. But, it appears to me, the corporatist institutions and the corporatist mind-set that motivated their establishment do operate to inhibit indigenous *innovation*. In this hypothesis, to the extent that a continental nation retains vestiges of corporatist institutions and thinking, these causal influences may appreciably account—more than the nation's welfare state—for the alienation from business, the dearth of innovations, and therefore the apparently low levels of job satisfaction, the low participation, and the generally high unemployment rates that have become familiar on the Continent.

Of course, what was left of the corporatist structure in this or that continental economy may in many cases have experienced further changes over the second half of the century. So not only is there the difficult task of weighing the ill effects of corporatism against the possible good effect. The question also is the extent to which the avowedly corporatist countries of decades past have moved away—for good or ill—from their corporatist mode of operation and corporatist mode of thinking.

Some tentative findings from elementary statistical analyses of the data on the 12 large OECD countries are interesting, I think. Gylfi Zoega and I found that, among these nations, a high degree of corporatism—as commonly measured by the degree of "coordination" among labor unions and among employers—is loosely associated with low employment and low productivity. This much is rather widely granted, with Sweden being something of an exception, or "outlier." That finding is just a simple correlation analysis of the 12 data points.[15] When we allow one or two other institutions to enter simultaneously into the analysis—a multiple regression analysis—the picture changes. The OECD index of red tape obstructing entrepreneurs explains the poorer performance of some of the countries. And employment protection legislation is another institution helping to explain differences between the good performers and the poor performers. But these two institutions, red tape and job protection, are themselves rather strongly correlated with corporatism as measured by the coordination variable. As a result, when these two institutions, which can be viewed as primary effects of corporatism, are included in the analysis, there are no remaining differences for the coordination variable to explain. The coordination of labor unions and employers does not directly exert a negative effect on economic performance. The harms from corporatism apparently come more from the ancillary institutions that corporatist thinking inspires than from coordination per se. It is even possible that, with further analysis, the degree of union and employer coordination will be found to be a small "plus," *given* the other institutions, some of which may have a strong corporatist flavor.

It is possible, therefore, that the early theoreticians of corporatism were not wrong in claiming a slender potential benefit in the brave new system. However, it is beginning to appear quite likely that the overall impact of the corporatist system and corporatist mind-set have done great harm to Europe's dynamism and, in turn, to its economic performance.

Does Culture Play a Part in Economic Performance?

With continental Europe still languishing more than two decades after the onslaught of shocks felt in the 1970s and early 1980s and with India, China, and parts of Southeast Asia showing enormous energy and initiative, whatever the support and the impediments their economic institutions are bringing, it is not unreasonable that economists and noneconomists should begin to speculate that some as yet undetermined *part* of the conspicuous intercountry differences in current-day participation, investment, and so forth may stem from a causal influence *other than* the neoclassical policy differences and the economic institutions just discussed: Perhaps differences in culture are an important influence on economic performance.

Recently I wondered aloud whether the Continent's culture must share the blame with some of its economic institutions for its economic problem—its dearth of prosperity and its less than first-place level of productivity.[16] Several points sprang to mind. In some European nations there is an expressed uneasiness about making money. As Hans Werner Sinn said to me, a German would rather say that he inherited his wealth than to say that he had made his fortune. Some Belgian businessmen told me they thought Europeans were more risk-averse than Americans. There is also the practice of shielding teenagers from any sort of job experience or earning any money, so that the business world must seem rather foreign to them as they are growing up. It has been suggested that European schooling drains children of some of their playfulness and creativity. There is the point that the protection of European culture effectively means protecting the older and more established people, which may cause young people to believe it is wrong to compete and risk upsetting the established order. I might add that I did not suggest that Europeans are deficient in some sort of genetic material. (After all, the Americans are largely of European stock.)

These speculations are interesting to me and apparently to nearly everyone. The question "Is it economic institutions or culture?"—would make for an almost irresistible debate. Yet speculations such as these are met with some ambivalence by those economists who think, very plausibly, that economists should specialize in finding causes in the areas in which they have expertise, not in areas already heavily populated by psychologists and sociologists. And Europeans themselves are rather sensitive to suggestions that their culture, which is one of the things of which they are most proud, might play a part in their relatively poor economic performance.

My research strategy continues to be one focusing not on culture but on economic institutions, such as those I have mentioned above and some others. This is presumably the strategy in which economists have a comparative advantage. We will see to what extent we can explain in the statistical sense the differences in (proxies for) economic performance among European countries and between the Continent on the one hand and, on the other, the United States and other salient comparators. Perhaps this venture will fail for the very reason that culture is the greater determinant of the degree of dynamism and thus economic performance. Or, almost as bad, we may find that institutional choices by countries appear to be the cause of differences in economic performance, but these institutional differences across countries are mere reflections of differences in culture whose primary influence is direct, not through institutions.

But this seems to me to be assuming what is to be proved. Maybe culture has no independent influence that will defeat or invalidate such an analysis. It could be that when the institutions are right, jobs are engaging, business is exciting, and the culture evolves to recognize and reinforce the gratifications of a healthy business life. Where the economic institutions are receptive and conducive, the "entrepreneurial spirit" comes to life.

The challenge presented by a rival cause, culture, is not the only challenge that this institutional research faces. It has been suggested that institutions lack the sort of exogeneity that would qualify them to be causal forces in the etiology of healthy and sick economies. My reply is that countries have little idea of what is the best set of economic institutions for them. Rats, psychologists say, look around to see how other rats do after eating suspicious foods. No doubt, countries also try to engage in such "social learning," sometimes adopting an institution because it is presumed to be good choice in view of the satisfactory performance obtained in some other countries that adopted the same institution.

But, obviously, when institutions are manifold and connected in networks, such inferences are highly uncertain. To me, there seems to be an enormous amount of arbitrariness in each country's network of institutions. (Of course, if all continental economies simply copy one another's institutions, statistical analysis cannot proceed, even if the chosen set of institutions is exogenous to the whole sample of countries. However, that is a different proposition.)

Another objection, which is best faced right now, starts from the contrary premise that institutions do *not* change from one decade or even milieu to the next and yet, very typically, a country has a golden age at one time and tough sledding in another. (Maybe a country's set of institutions has evolved in such a way as to be good on the average, so it looks good in one era and looks bad in another.) This objection observes that the Continent's rapid growth and high employment were the envy of the world in the postwar decades—only a few decades ago, when the Continent had much the same economic institutions as now. It is a mistake, therefore, to infer that continental institutions are at fault now for the difficulties in which most of the large continental economies have found themselves in the past 20 years.

But, obviously or not, this argument must first establish that the institutions on the Continent during the "glorious years" from the mid-1950s to the mid-1970s were indeed good. And that is not established. To rush to the inference that the Continent's institutions were good in those years would be to overlook the unusual market forces operating in that period. After the rubble of the war-torn countries was finally cleared away and the bricks and tracks all put back together, the Continent found itself with a onetime opportunity to catch up with the technical progress that had taken place in the American economy during the 1930s and 1940s (and in a sector of the Japanese economy later on). The fact that the Continent's set of economic institutions was not obstructive enough to block the extensive—though part-way—catch-up in that extraordinary situation, with its low-hanging fruit ready to be plucked at low cost, does not disprove that some of the Continent's economic institutions are unfavorable to dynamism, as hypothesized here. Institutions that are good enough for imitation and part-way catch-up (starting from a yawning gap) may not be good enough to generate a creative business sector of considerable and well-chosen indigenous innovation. The logical slip in the objection is that it mistakes the rapid growth rate and ensuing rise of employment to record levels in the glorious years with an economy *structured* for high economic performance in *normal* as well as unusually opportune times. (Of course, such a structure does not deliver unfluctuating growth and employment.)

A similar rebuttal applies to a mistaken analysis of China. The fact that China's present set of economic institutions is not so obstructive as to block the extensive—though part-way—catch-up with the West now seemingly under way does not suggest that those institutions could even begin to support an economy of dynamism in China were the low-hanging fruit of technology transfer and partnerships with foreign corporations not present. To say this, though, is not to deny that China has in fact fashioned some new institutions peculiar to China to facilitate catch-up with the West. It has invented new ways of achieving entrepreneurialism. So the Chinese institutions are a hugely interesting case to study.

In sum, I see no compelling reason to be so pessimistic as not to try to understand the influence on various economies of their prevailing economic institutions. Possibly we do well to take as largely or appreciably exogenous each country's set of economic institutions—many of which are historical accidents and in no way optimal even if deliberately chosen. And possibly we do well not to be deterred by leaps of inference about sui generis episodes that may be total misreadings. It could be that we are quite right to hypothesize that the stock of institutions is the primary cause—or at any rate a primary cause—of the degree of dynamism and consequent economic performance of nations.

NOTES

I gratefully acknowledge some recent collaborations with Gylfi Zoega in this research area.

1. This abstracts from matters of economic justice. A desirable economic system might be run justly or unjustly from some standpoint but might be more preferable to other systems in either case.

2. I suggested that market forces were at least as important if not more so, such as the extraordinary elevation of real interest rates in the 1980s (Phelps 1992) and the slowdown, apparent by the late 1970s, of productivity in Europe and, to a much lesser extent, the United States (Hoon and Phelps 1997).

3. Holding constant the other tax rates, such as the rate on nonlabor incomes.

4. In part, Heckman's scrutiny extends to some of the economic institutions that I have been writing about recently (Phelps 2003a, 2003c) and will be here.

5. Perhaps a multiple regression analysis would enable us to tease out some satisfactory results.

6. These points were made in a column by me (Phelps 2003b) and independently by another observer (Raphael 2004).

7. This was remarked (in passing) in a comment by Ralph Gomory at the conference where this essay was first presented. At the time I did not disagree, if I remember correctly. But I am begging to differ somewhat now.

8. During his American years (at Harvard, where he is again), Amartya Sen distilled much of this literature, making "doing things" and "capabilities" central to freedom and justice.

9. See Rothschild 2001, 33, a book in which Condorcet is prominent.

10. Americans were not as exposed to an antimaterialist strain in some Christian teaching, were not racked by wars to the degree the Europeans were, and were less inclined to see inequality as disqualifying when economic growth appeared to promise so much. I don't know whether these stabs at an explanation are convincing. (Europe was similarly cut off from America's pragmatist school of philosophy, which flourished in its first phase from 1880 to 1930, and remains influential today.)

11. Some of these results are displayed in scatter plots in a commentary (Comment II) appearing in Phelps 2003a.

12. A striking fact uncovered by Rajan and Zingales (2003) is that, in most countries of continental Europe, stock market capitalization as a ratio to GDP had by 1980 still not recovered to the zenith reached in 1913.

13. Two of the pioneers were Herbert Giersch and the late Ezio Tarantelli. The former wrote as if the medieval guilds were still operative in West Germany (Giersch 1993). The latter, on the other hand, saw a more complex picture in which union "coordination" was beneficial (Tarantelli 1986a, 1986b).

14. My first efforts were in a book (Phelps 2002a) with a focus on Italy; my latest effort is a lecture given at Chatham House (Phelps 2003c).

15. Some scatter plots illustrating some of these propositions are shown in Phelps 2003a.

16. See the brief digression in my lecture in Munich (Phelps 2002b) and a paragraph in a newspaper column on Europe's economic performance and economic institutions (Phelps 2002c).

References

Bergson, Henri. 1911. *Creative Evolution*. Trans. Arthur Mitchell. New York: Macmillan.

Giersch, Herbert. 1993. *Openness for Prosperity*. Cambridge: MIT Press.

Heckman, James J. 2004. "Flexibility, Job Creation and Economic Performance." *CESifo Forum,* 4, Summer: 29–32.

Hoon, Hian Teck, and Edmund Phelps. 1997. "Growth, Wealth and the Natural Rate: Is Europe's Jobs Crisis a Growth Crisis?" *European Economic Review* 41 (April): 549–57.

Layard, Richard, Steven Nickell, and Richard Jackman. 1991. *Unemployment: Macroeconomic Performance and the Labour Market*. Oxford: Oxford University Press.

Phelps, Edmund. 1992. "A Review of *Unemployment* by Layard, Nickell and Jackman." *Journal of Economic Literature* 30 (September): 1476–90; reprinted *Journal of Economic Studies* 20 (1–2): 7–26.

———. 1994. *Structural Slumps*. Cambridge: Harvard University Press.

———. 2002a. *Enterprise and Inclusion in Italy*. Boston: Kluwer Academic Publishers.

———. 2002b. "The Continent's High Unemployment: Possible Institutional Causes and Some Evidence." Keynote Address, Conference on Unemployment in Europe, CES/ifo, Munich, December 6–7.

———. 2002c. "European Myths, European Realities." Syndicated column, Project Syndicate, December–January.

———. 2003a. "Reflections on Parts III and IV." In *Knowledge, Information, and Expectations in Modern Macroeconomics: In Honor of Edmund Phelps*, ed. P. Aghion, R. Frydman, J. E. Stiglitz and M. Woodford. Princeton: Princeton University Press.

———. 2003b. "The Dynamism of Nations." Syndicated column, Project Syndicate, January–February.

———. 2003c. "Economic Underperformance in Continental Europe." Lecture, Chatham House, London, March.

Phelps, Edmund, and Gylfi Zoega. 1997. "The Rise and Downward Trend of the Natural Rate." *American Economic Review Papers and Proceedings* 87 (May): 283–89.

Raphael, Thérèse. 2004. "Europe's Great Reform Wimp-Out." *Wall Street Journal*, January 26.

Rajan, Raghuram, and Luigi Zingales. 2003. "The Great Reversals: The Politics of Financial Development in the 20th Century." *Journal of Financial Economics* 69: 5–50.

Rothschild, Emma. 2001. *Economic Sentiments: Adam Smith, Condorcet, and the Enlightenment*. Cambridge: Harvard University Press.

Tarantelli, Ezio. 1986a. "The Regulation of Inflation and Unemployment." *Industrial Relations* 25 (1): 1–15.

———. 1986b. *Economia Politica del Lavoro*. Turin: UTET.

Chapter 16

Pharmaceutical Patenting in Developing Countries and R&D

EYTAN SHESHINSKI

> India, a major source of inexpensive AIDS drugs, passed a new patent law that groups providing drugs to the world's poorest patients fear will choke off their supply of new treatments. . . . [While] all Western countries grant "product patents," India has granted "process patents," which allow another inventor to patent the same product as long as it was created by a novel process . . . [thereby] creating competition that drives down prices. . . . In Africa [it] helped drive the annual price of antiretroviral treatment down from $15,000 per patient a decade ago to about $200 now.
>
> —*New York Times*, March 23, 2005

1. Introduction

There is an ongoing controversy on the question of whether developing countries, particularly in Africa, should be exempt from pharmaceutical product patents.[1] It is argued that in a world of AIDS, tuberculosis, and other diseases that overwhelmingly afflict developing countries, economic welfare will be enhanced by allowing these countries to free-ride on pharmaceutical innovations made and patented in the first world, compared to charging them monopolistic prices.

The counterargument is that if drugs are supplied to developing countries at competitive prices, this will lead to an increase in prices in the developed countries and, most importantly, will lead to a decrease in research and development (R&D) expenditures of the pharmaceutical industry with detrimental long-term effects on global welfare. The objective of this essay is to provide some insight into this issue.[2]

Based on a standard multiproduct monopoly model, I demonstrate that the effects of exempting developing countries from pharmaceutical patent rights, while always increasing drug sales and welfare in these countries at prevailing R&D levels, may also lead to *increased* sales of drugs in developed countries and to an *increase* in R&D expenditures by the pharmaceutical industry.

Total sales of Western pharmaceutical firms may increase because firms may find it advantageous to sell in developing countries even at competitive prices. A larger output sold in developing countries will in turn induce, due to economies of scope, larger sales in developed countries and, consequently, to an increase in R&D expenditures, provided these reduce marginal common production costs.

I present a model of a firm, representing the Western pharmaceutical industry, which produces and sells a product (drug) in two markets; one represents the developed countries, the other the developing countries.

Costs of production display economies of scope, and have a joint costs component as well as separable costs. Joint costs depend positively on total output and negatively on R&D expenditures. Presumably, with low or no R&D expenditures, costs are prohibitively large, decreasing as R&D expenditures increase.

Initially, the firm has a monopoly over both markets. The monopoly is based on patent rights. This equilibrium is compared to one where patent rights are enforced only in the first market (developed countries), while in the second market (developing countries) the drug is supplied at a fixed price that is lower than the monopoly price. This price, termed the *competitive price*, represents a potential infinitely elastic supply by firms that are not bound by patent laws, such as in India, where patents are granted to specific processes, not to products, and consequently a huge reverse-engineering industry flourishes.

The firm faces a dilemma: Either it undercuts the potential supply in market 2 by charging a price slightly lower than the competitive price, or it abandons the competitive market and remains only in the monopolized market. In view of the assumption about the costs structure, namely the existence of economies of scope, it is never optimal for the firm to share any market with competitors. Hence the stark alternatives.

It is of interest to develop necessary and sufficient conditions for the firm deciding on one or the other solutions. These are discussed in section 5.

The focus of my analysis is on the effect of eliminating patent rights in market 2 on the output (equal to sales) in market 1 and on the level of R&D expenditures. Clearly, in market 2 output increases and welfare is enhanced. It is shown that the effect on the level of sales in market 1 and on R&D expenditures is indeterminate. I state conditions on the costs function that will sign the outcome.

2. Monopoly and R&D

I treat all pharmaceutical firms in developed countries as one firm that has, because of patent rights, monopoly power over a product, X. The firm is selling this product in two markets, numbered 1 and 2. Market 1 represents the developed countries, lumped together, and market 2 represents the developing countries, also lumped together. The firms' outputs (and sales) in markets 1 and 2 are denoted by x_1 and x_2, and the prices it charges are p_1 and p_2, respectively.

Demands for the product in the two markets are assumed to be independent.[3] The levels of these demands depend implicitly on income, population size, and other characteristics of these countries and, more importantly, on the incidence of the disease(s) for which this product provides treatment. All these factors are taken as given and hence are not brought up explicitly.

Revenue in market 1 as a function of output is denoted $R_1(x_1)$ and for market 2, $R_2(x_2)$. Thus, prices p_i, are $p_i = \frac{R_i(x_i)}{x_i}$, $i = 1{,}2$.

There are common ("set-up") production costs, denoted C, which depend on total output, $x_1 + x_2$, and on research and development expenditures, K: $C = C(x_1 + x_2, K)$. These costs are assumed to display decreasing average costs (economies of scope) and decreasing or constant marginal costs: $C(x_1 + x_2, K)/(x_1 + x_2)$ decreases with $x_1 + x_2$, $C_1(x_1 + x_2, K)$ $\left(= \frac{\partial C}{\partial(x_1 + x_2)}\right) > 0$ and $C_{11}(x_1 + x_2, K) \left(= \frac{\partial^2 C}{\partial(x_1 + x_2)^2}\right) \leq 0$.

Expenditures on R&D decrease costs: $C_2(x_1 + x_2, K) \left(= \frac{\partial C}{\partial K}\right) < 0$ at a nonincreasing rate, $C_{22}(x_1 + x_2, K) \geqq 0$. It is, presumably, impossible to produce the drug without some positive K ($\lim_{K \to 0} C(x_1 + x_2, K) = \infty$ will ensure a positive K), and as R&D expenditures increase, effectiveness of the product is enhanced, reflected in a decrease in costs.[4] Unit costs of R&D are assumed to be constant, q. There are also separable costs in each market (marketing, etc.) assumed to display constant marginal and average costs. Denoting these unit costs by c_i, $i = 1, 2$, total costs are given by

$$C(x_1 + x_2, K) + c_1 x_1 + c_2 x_2 + qK. \tag{1}$$

Total profits, Π, are

$$\Pi(x_1, x_2, K) = R_1(x_1) + R_2(x_2) - C(x_1 + x_2, K) - c_1 x_1 - c_2 x_2 - qK. \tag{2}$$

The firm is a natural multiproduct, patent-based monopoly. Maximum-profits conditions are

$$\frac{\partial \Pi}{\partial x_i} = R_i'(x_i) - C_1(x_1 + x_2, K) - c_i = 0 \qquad i = 1,2 \qquad (3)$$

$$\frac{\partial \Pi}{\partial K} = -C_2(x_1 + x_2, K) - q = 0. \qquad (4)$$

Equations (3)–(4) are three equations in three unknowns, x_1, x_2, and K. These are the standard conditions equating marginal revenue to marginal costs. Equation (4) equates the marginal benefit of R&D expenditures to marginal costs. In appendix A, I state sufficient second-order conditions for the solution, denoted $(\hat{x}_1, \hat{x}_2, \hat{K})$, to be unique. Corresponding to the quantities $(\hat{x}_1, \hat{x}_2)$, the market-clearing prices established by the monopoly are $\hat{p}_1 = \frac{R_1(\hat{x}_1)}{\hat{x}_1}$ and $\hat{p}_2 = \frac{R_2(\hat{x}_2)}{\hat{x}_2}$, respectively.

It will be useful to display these conditions in two diagrams. Figure 16.1 displays conditions (3) for a given $K = \hat{K}$.

The shape of the two curves and their relative position at E are justified by second-order conditions.

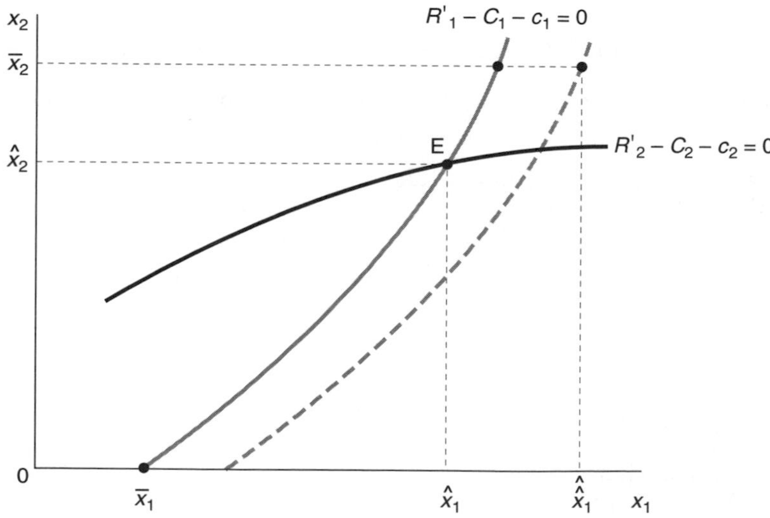

Figure 16.1. Conditions (3), given $\hat{K}$

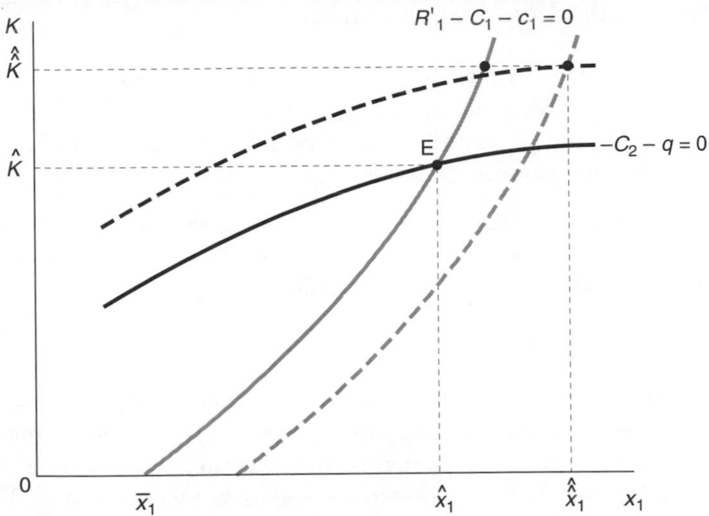

Figure 16.2. Conditions (3) and (4)

Figure 16.2 displays condition (3) with respect to market 1 and condition (4) in the (x_1, K) plane. These curves are drawn for a given $x_2 = \hat{x}_2$. The curves are drawn for the case $C_{12} < 0$. The shape of these curves at the equilibrium point, E, is determined by second-order conditions.

Now, suppose that patent protection is not provided in market 2. It is assumed that there are firms that offer the drug at a fixed price, $\overline{p}_2$. We disregard the dynamics of the process, namely, how long it will take for these firms to develop and bring to market a generic drug identical (or close) to the one offered by the patent holder. We focus on the effect of the opening of the market on long-term equilibrium.

Henceforth, market 1 is termed the *monopoly market* and market 2 the *competitive market*. In the competitive market, the price $\overline{p}_2$ may be equal to the variable costs c_2 of the monopoly firm, but this is not necessary. What is assumed, to make this an effective change, is that the competitive price is below the monopoly price, $\overline{p}_2 < \hat{p}_2$.

Demand for the product in the competitive market at price $\overline{p}_2$, $\overline{x}_2$, is larger than the quantity sold by the monopoly when protected by its patent: $\overline{x}_2 > \hat{x}_2$, where $\overline{x}_2$ is the defined by $\overline{p}_2 = \dfrac{R_2(\overline{x}_2)}{\overline{x}_2}$. Since average and marginal joint costs are, by assumption, nonincreasing, the monopoly firm will choose one of two possibilities: charge a price just below $\overline{p}_2$ and continue to satisfy the entire demand (rather than share it with other firms) or abandon market 2 and concentrate on the monopoly market.

3. Staying in the Competitive Market

Suppose first that the firm stays in both markets. Then the conditions that determine the new levels of x_1 and K, denoted by $(\hat{\hat{x}}_1', \hat{K}')$, are (3), pertaining to $i = 1$, and (4), with $x_2 = \bar{x}_2$ in both conditions. It can be shown that the following proposition holds:

Proposition 1. If market 2 becomes competitive and the firm stays in the competitive market, then the level of x_1 increases and the level of K increases (decreases) if and only if C_{12} is negative (positive).

Proof. See appendix B.

As stated above, figures 16.1 and 16.2 describe the case $C_{12} < 0$. In figure 16.1, as x_2 increases from $\hat{x}_2$ to $\bar{x}_2$, then, for a given $\hat{K}$, the optimal quantity of x_1 increases along the original curve. In figure 16.2, the two original curves shift (the dotted curves) as x_2 increases to $\bar{x}_2$. Hence $\hat{\hat{x}}_2 > \hat{x}_1$ and $\hat{\hat{K}} > \hat{K}$. In figure 16.1, in turn, the shift to the dotted curve takes into account the increase in K, further increasing x_1 to the new equilibrium level $\hat{\hat{x}}_1$.

Here, as in subsequent analysis, the sign of C_{12} turns out to be important. This is the effect of an increase in R&D expenditures on common marginal production costs. There are no compelling reasons to assume a particular sign. Two examples: (a) $C(x_1 + x_2), K = f(x_1 + x_2)h(K)$ (where, by our assumptions, $f > 0$, $f' > 0$, $f'' \leq 0$, $h > 0$, $h' < 0$, $h'' \geq 0$). In this case, $C_{12} < 0$; (b) $C(x_1 + x_2, K) = f\left(\dfrac{x_1 + x_2}{h(K)}\right)$ (where $f > 0$, $f' > 0$, $f'' \leq 0$ $h > 0$, $h' > 0$ and, as a sufficient condition, $h'' < 0$). Here, $C_{12} \gtreqless 0$ as $\dfrac{f''(z)z}{f'(z)} + 1 \lesseqgtr 0$. The first functional form may be called the case when R&D is *cost augmenting*, the second *output augmenting*.

4. Abandoning the Competitive Market

Suppose that the firm, facing competition in market 2, decides to abandon this market, focusing on market 1. The profit-maximizing conditions are again (3) (for $i = 1$) and (4), with $x_2 = 0$ in both conditions. Denote this solution by $(\tilde{x}_1, \tilde{K})$. This is called in the literature the *stand-alone* solution. An argument similar to the previous analysis leads directly to the following result:

Proposition 2. If competition in market 2 leads the firm to abandon the competitive market, focusing on the monopoly market, then the optimal level of x_1

decreases while the optimal level of K decreases (increases) if C_{12} is negative (positive).

The results in propositions 1 and 2 suggest a potential welfare dilemma. The elimination of patent rights in market 2 (developing countries) unambiguously increases sales in this market, either by the competitive "fringe" (generics) or by the previous patent holder, due to the threat of entry. The effect on sales in market 1 and on the level of research and development expenditures is indeterminate. If both increase, then the overall welfare effect is clearly positive. If, however, the levels of x_1 and K decrease, this may entail a decrease in overall welfare if the welfare loss in market 1 exceeds the welfare gain in market 2.

It is of interest to consider what conditions will lead the firm to choose one or the other strategy.

5. Undercut Price or Abandon the Competitive Market?

Profits of the firm, Π, are

$$\Pi(x_1, x_2, K) = R_1(x_1) + R_2(x_2) - C(x_1 + x_2, K) - c_1x_1 - c_2x_2 - qK. \quad (5)$$

The maximum of (5) is attained at $(\hat{x}_1, \hat{x}_2, \hat{K})$. If market 2 becomes competitive, then the firm either undercuts the price $\bar{p}_2$ and continues to clear demand, or it abandons the competitive market, focusing on the monopoly market.

The firm will stay in market 2 if the following condition holds:

$$\Pi(\hat{x}'_1, \bar{x}_2, \hat{K}') \geq \Pi(\tilde{x}_1, 0, \tilde{K}), \quad (6)$$

where $(\hat{x}'_1, \hat{K}')$ is the *best response* of the output in market 1 and the level of K when the output in market 2 is $\bar{x}_2$ and the firm stays in market 1, while $(\tilde{x}_1, \tilde{K})$ are the optimal corresponding levels when the firm abandons market 2 (termed the *stand-alone* solution). When the inequality opposite to (6) holds, then the firm will leave market 2.

In order to derive necessary and sufficient conditions for these cases, define the concept of *incremental costs*. The incremental costs of x_2, denoted $IC_2(x_1, x_2, K)$, are the difference between the costs of production of x_2, given x_1 and K, compared to no production, $x_2 = 0$:

$$IC_2(x_1, x_2, K) = C(x_1 + x_2, K) + c_1x_1 + c_2x_2 - C(x_1, K) - c_1x_1. \quad (7)$$

Notice that the incremental costs of x_2 depend on the levels of x_1 and K. A *sufficient condition* for (7) is that

$$\Pi(\widetilde{x}, \overline{x}_2, \widetilde{K}) \geq \Pi(\widetilde{x}_1, 0, \widetilde{K}). \quad (8)$$

This is a sufficient condition because the best-response, $(\hat{x}_1', \hat{K}')$ maximizes profits when $x_2 = \overline{x}_2$.

Rearranging terms, applying definition (7), this is seen to be equivalent to

$$R_2(\overline{x}_2) - IC_2(\widetilde{x}_1, \overline{x}_2, \widetilde{K}) \geq 0. \quad (9)$$

Revenue exceeds incremental costs in market 2 when $x_2 = \overline{x}_2$ and x_1 and K are at the stand-alone levels.

A *necessary condition* for (7) is that

$$\Pi(\hat{x}_1', \overline{x}_2, \hat{K}') \geq \Pi(\hat{x}_1', 0, \hat{K}'). \quad (10)$$

since the stand-alone solution, $(\widetilde{x}_1, \widetilde{K})$, maximizes profits when the firm abandons market 2. This condition, applying (7), can be seen to be equivalent to

$$R_2(\overline{x}_2) - IC_2(\hat{x}_1', 0, \widetilde{K}') \geq 0. \quad (11)$$

That is, revenue exceeds incremental costs in market 2 when $x_2 = \overline{x}_2$ and (x_1, K) are at the *best response* levels.

Appendix A

The matrix

$$\begin{bmatrix} R'' - c_{11} & -c_{11} & -c_{12} \\ -c_{11} & R'' - c_{11} & -c_{12} \\ -c_{12} & -c_{12} & -c_{22} \end{bmatrix}$$

has to be negative definite. The necessary conditions are $R_i'' - C_{11} < 0$, $i = 1, 2,$ $C_{22} > 0,$ $R_1''R_2'' - C_{11}(R_1'' + R_2'') > 0,$ and $R_1''R_2''(C_{11}C_{22} - C_{12}^2) - R_1''R_2''C_{22} < 0$

Convexity of C ensures that the last condition is satisfied. We shall assume that all these conditions are satisfied at the monopoly profit-maximizing point $(\hat{x}_1, \hat{x}_2, K)$. This, in turn, ensures that the solution to (3) – (4) in the text is unique.

Appendix B

The first-order condition for the optimal x_1 and K are

$$\begin{aligned} R_1'(x_1) - C_1(x_1 + x_2) - c_1 &= 0 \\ -C_2(x_1 + x_2) - q &= 0 \end{aligned} \tag{B.1}$$

At the initial equilibrium, $x_2 = \hat{x}_2$ (and, accordingly, $x_1 = \hat{x}_1$ and $K = \hat{K}$). Now $x_2 = \overline{x}_2 > \hat{x}_2$. Treating the increase in x_2 as exogenous,

$$\frac{d\hat{x}_1}{dx_2} = \frac{-1}{\Delta'}(C_{11}C_{22} - C_{12}^2)$$

and (B.2)

$$\frac{d\hat{K}_1}{dx_2} = \frac{R_1''}{\Delta'}C_{12},$$

where $\Delta' = (C_{11}C_{22} - C_{12}^2) - R_1''C_{22} > 0$.

Hence $\dfrac{d\hat{x}_1}{dx_2} > 0$ and $Sgn\dfrac{d\hat{K}}{dx_2} = -SgnC_{12}$.

Notes

1. The Uruguay TRIPS rounds and then the Doha WTO conference required that patents be granted, but delayed enforcement until 2016.
2. A definitive survey of the issues and empirics is Kremer 2002. An interesting discussion on the effects of patent restrictions on the level of R&D is Scherer 2004.
3. Interdependence of demands may arise, for example, due to the possibility of *reimportation*. This is an interesting issue in itself, but it will carry us beyond the objective of this essay to analyze it in detail here.
4. Alternatively, the level of K can be assumed to affect demands positively.

References

Kremer, M. 2002, "Pharmaceuticals and the Developing World," *Journal of Economic Perspectives* 4: 67–91.

Scherer, F. M. 2004, "A Note on Global Welfare in Pharmaceutical Patenting." *World Economy*, July, 1127–42.

Contributors

Kenneth J. Arrow is Professor Emeritus at Stanford University. He was awarded the Nobel Prize in Economics in 1972.

William J. Baumol is Harold Price Professor of Entrepreneurship, and Academic Director, Berkley Center for Entrepreneurial Studies, Leonard N. Stern School of Business, at New York University, and Professor Emeritus and Senior Economist at Princeton University.

Alan S. Blinder is Gordon S. Rentschler Professor of Economics at Princeton University.

Jonathan Eaton is Professor of Economics at New York University.

Ralph E. Gomory is President of the Alfred P. Sloan Foundation.

Boyan Jovanovic is Professor of Economics at New York University and Research Associate of the National Bureau of Economic Research.

Samuel S. Kortum is Professor of Economics at the University of Minnesota.

Naomi R. Lamoreaux is Professor of History and Economics at UCLA and Research Associate of the National Bureau of Economic Research.

Ying Lowrey is Senior Economist, Office of Advocacy, U.S. Small Business Administration.

Burton G. Malkiel is Chemical Bank Chairman's Professor of Economics at Princeton University.

Sylvia Nasar is John S. and James L. Knight Professor of Business Journalism at Columbia University.

Douglass C. North is Spencer T. Olin Professor in Arts and Sciences at Washington University in St. Louis. He was awarded the Nobel Prize in Economics in 1972.

Corey Phelps is Assistant Professor of Management and Organization at the University of Washington.

Edmund S. Phelps is McVickar Professor of Political Economy, Columbia University. He was awarded the Nobel Prize in Economics in 2006.

Nathan Rosenberg is Professor of Economics (Emeritus) in the Department of Economics at Stanford University and Senior Fellow at the Stanford Institute for Economic Policy Research.

Peter L. Rousseau is Associate Professor of Economics at Vanderbilt University and Research Associate of the National Bureau of Economic Research.

Melissa A. Schilling is Associate Professor of Management at the Stern School of Business, New York University.

Yochanan Shachmurove is Professor of Economics at City College of New York.

Eytan Sheshinski is Sir Isaac Wolfson Professor of Public Finance at the Hebrew University of Jerusalem.

Robert J. Shiller is Stanley B. Resor Professor of Economics, Department of Economics and Cowles Foundation for Research in Economics, Yale University, and Fellow at the International Center for Finance, Yale School of Management.

Kenneth L. Sokoloff is Professor of Economics at UCLA and Research Associate of the National Bureau of Economic Research.

Robert M. Solow is Institute Professor Emeritus in the Department of Economics at MIT. He was awarded the Nobel Prize in Economics in 1987.

Deepak Somaya is Assistant Professor in the Robert H. Smith School of Business, University of Maryland.

Robert J. Strom is Director of Research and Policy at the Ewing Marion Kauffman Foundation in Kansas City.

David J. Teece is Director of the Institute of Management, Innovation and Organization, Haas School of Business, University of California, Berkeley.

Barry R. Weingast is Senior Fellow, Hoover Institution, and Ward C. Krebs Family Professor, Department of Political Science, Stanford University.

Michael M. Weinstein is Chief Program Officer for the Robin Hood Foundation and Manager of Institutes for Journalists for The New York Times Company Foundation.

Edward N. Wolff is Professor of Economics, New York University.

Index